THE DEAF SCHOOLCHILD

The Deaf Schoolchild

LANGUAGE AND COGNITIVE FUNCTION

R. Conrad Medical Research Council,
Applied Psychology Unit

Harper & Row

First published 1979
Harper & Row Ltd
28 Tavistock Street
London WC2E 7PN

ISBN 0 06 318085 5

Designed by Richard Dewing 'Millions'
London
Typeset by Input Typesetting Ltd
Printed and bound by Butler and Tanner Ltd

Into those hands ... This too.

Contents

Introduction

The education of children born deaf is essentially a war against cognitive poverty. In Britain, as in most countries, educators have committed themselves to the exclusive deployment of spoken language to wage this war. Our study here surveys the scene ten years later, when for most deaf children formal education is ending. We have provided a quantitative account of progress in communication in spoken and written language. If this phase of the war has not been lost, it demonstrably has not been won. Most deaf children leave school massively disabled with respect to their ability to understand speech, to be understood when they speak, or to comprehend meaning in written language.

We believe it is important for teachers to have access to the wider view so easily obscured by the pervasive detail of day-to-day classroom practice. We believe too that parents of deaf children need to be able to evaluate the probable outcome of the education of their children so that they can, with greater realism, perceive the social role and status likely to be achieved, and be relieved of some of their lonely guilt. We believe that those who make policy for the education of deaf children require a surer foundation of factual evidence than has hitherto reliably been available.

We do not presume to offer definitive solutions for the manifest problems. We have observed a disturbing scene which, were all said and done, might yield to no all-embracing pedagogic formulation. But all has not been said or done. The debate on means – the classic oral-manual controversy – has been conducted largely in polemic terms. In emphasizing fundamental aspects of deaf children's cognitive development which have had too little consideration, we hope to contribute towards the establishment of a more rewarding empirical base for that still necessary debate.

So we enquire into the development of thinking as well; deaf children's ability to internalize the language they have to be taught, and their ability to manipulate its symbols with profit. We see this as crucial to the fabric of cognitive function, inextricably interwoven with fragile neurological processes, and see its flowering as a touchstone for the validity of the educational process. If this development fails, the war is lost.

We also address ourselves therefore to psychologists. Not only to those professionally concerned with the welfare and rehabilitation of deaf children, but also to those engaged in the exploration of mind. In recent years advances in the study of dyslexia have led to significant understanding of the underlying operations in reading; studies of amnesic patients into hitherto inaccessible problems of memory; studies of aphasia into the innermost cognitive structure of language. Disproportionately, the theoretical potential of congenital deafness has been neglected. In presenting our data within a framework of cognitive function, we hope at least to suggest that the framework is appropriate, and that the normal child who has never normally heard language may also prove to be a fruitful source of wider insight.

PREFACE

So many people to thank – and with more than just a conventional glance. Sir Harold Himsworth, at one time Secretary to the Medical Research Council, and Dr. D. E. Broadbent, formerly Director of the Council's Applied Psychology Unit; both for encouraging and supporting my inconvenient incursion into deafness research. Mr. J. A. M. Martin, Director of the Nuffield Hearing and Speech Centre, who for a time provided an office and permitted me to observe at his clinical sessions. Later Dr. L. Weiskrantz, Professor of Experimental Psychology at the University of Oxford, joined the growing list of my benefactors by welcoming me as a (rather permanent as it turned out) visitor to his department. It was there, still financed by the Medical Research Council, that the study reported here was conceived and based.

I was immensely lucky to be joined by Miss Anne Morris and Miss Morag McKenzie, dedicated teachers who became dedicated research assistants. Mrs. Barbara Weiskrantz continued her part-time collaboration, joining in testing and all the other chores of research. I feel especially fortunate to have had Dr. J. G. Kyle as a member of the team, advising, analysing, and arguing. Closely associated though he has been with the study, the defects are mine – often in spite of his counsel. My warm thanks also to Mrs. Doreen Attwood who typed ... and typed ... and typed; and much else. And how, adequately, to thank Miss Mary Plackett, Librarian of the Royal National Institute for the Deaf? I do not know how this book could have been put together without her knowledge and patience.

Finally, my gratitude and greetings to those 600 children who will never read these pages, but who contributed so very much to them ... and to their teachers who made it all possible and easy.

Oxford 1978

1

A Language for Thought: I

When a coach full of deaf children was involved in a multiple motorway collision ... fifteen of the children ... were hurt.

The coach ... was carrying about fifty children aged between five and 16, who had been collected in London after spending the weekend with their families.

Doctors at the ... hospital ..., had difficulty in identifying and treating the children because of their disabilities. Some doctors, not realizing at first that they were deaf, thought they were silent through shock. Police found members of a local church for the deaf at evening service, and took them to the hospital to communicate with the children ...(*The Times*, 9 February, 1976)

There seems to be no room for doubt that a pattern of growth which involves capacity to understand ordinary spoken language, to read it, to use it in thinking and, as far as possible, to speak and write, is the only one which can be considered satisfactory for any deaf child. (Ewing, 1960, pp. 2–3)

Sir Alexander Ewing has been perhaps the most influential figure in the modern history of education of deaf children both in Britain and far afield wherever British institutions served as models. When he wrote the words we have quoted, few of the people who understood the savagely difficult educational and social problems of deaf children would have disagreed. Few would disagree today. Yet, when those deaf children were hurt, other deaf people had to be found because the children were unable to communicate with hospital staff. By chance, shortly before the coach crash, we had given tests of educational attainment to the fifteen-year-old children attending that school. Whatever else, there was nothing unusual about their level of intelligence; it was very close to the average of the nation's deaf children. Why then so great a gap between Ewing's ideal and the sordid reality of those injured, frightened, and helpless children returning from a weekend at home?

All education is debate and none more so than that of deaf children. Yet the goals have wavered little. The choice is stark. A child who, through deafness, hears little speech will, unaided, be capable of little speech, and will be unable to receive speech either by ear or by eye, through "reading" speech on the lips of others. Is the attempt to teach these skills worth while? There is an alternative. Most deaf communities have a deeply rooted vernacular sign language. It is a language involving fingers, hands, arms, facial gesture – all visible. It is as easy for a deaf child to acquire sign language naturally in a signing home as it is for a hearing child to acquire spoken language (Siple, 1978). But where speech is the language of millions, sign is the language of no more than thousands. Faced with the choice of what seems like deaf ghetto or deaf integration, no modern society has hesitated. The logical conclusion is irrefutable; the goal crystal clear. Only the way has proved elusive.

As with all education, fashions have come and gone. But more so perhaps with deafness because technological advances have both shifted the threshold at which special intervention is required, and at the same time broadened the scope for novelty and change in teaching procedures. The transistorized hearing aid allied to advances in psycho-acoustics and techniques of audiological investigation have all served to provide some children whose hearing would otherwise have been only partial with what can be virtually normal hearing. We do not know where the limits of this advance will be. But in the foreseeable future neither physical nor biological science will offer amelioration of substance to that significant proportion of children who are born profoundly deaf, often due to a genetic condition amenable only to eugenic intervention. At the same time, technology has advanced intensively into the classroom. Systems of group amplification, radio aids, appropriate acoustic treatment of whole environments, devices for presenting speech in visible or tactile form have all provoked the imaginative teacher into developing new "treatments"; new programmes for moving a child towards that provocative goal – the deaf but oral child. Yet the children in that fated bus could communicate ... only with the deaf.

In succeeding chapters the difficulties and achievements will be reviewed and analysed. But the quintessential nature of the experience of congenital profound deafness will be untouched. How can we, the hearing, begin to conceive of existence within this silent world? It is a world of no more than the tantalizing faintest whisper of sounds of speech; a world thereby impoverished of all auditory imagery. In a letter to the magazine *TALK* (Autumn, 1977), Mr. A. F. Dimmock writes:

Being deaf and dumb, I never had the chance to know how words were sounded. In my mind words are "seen" just as they are printed or finger-spelt, never as sounded. I am sometimes able to visualise whole sentences mentally and know the meaning instantly. When undergoing light reading as in novels or newspapers, pictures are the predominate aspects that appear in my mind.

The early years

When a hearing child enters school, perhaps at the age of five, he has already behind him a long history of spoken language acquisition and language usage. Even by the age of six months Weir (1966) has reported that the babbled utterances have taken on the tonal quality of the surrounding language; Chinese babies make detectably different sounds from American babies. The immensely enriching reinforcement which comes, intrinsically through auditory feedback and extrinsically through the rewards afforded by parents and others in the various expressions of their evident pleasure, stimulates and encourages. At about this same age the natural babbling which is a normal stage in a deaf child's development begins to peter out; the child is already becoming "dumb". Mavilya (1971), in a study of the babbling behaviour of hearing-impaired infants, has even reported that at about six months there was an abrupt decline.

Meanwhile, the hearing child's speech develops with great rapidity. Babble has become utterance; utterances become words which appear by eighteen months. Lenneberg (1967, p. 130) reports that by twenty-four months the child may have a vocabulary of fifty words: "Some children seem to be able to name everything in (the) environment." Then two-word phrases begin to occur. By the age of three years Lenneberg indicates a vocabulary of 1000 words and, "grammatical complexity of utterances is roughly that of colloquial adult language".

And the deaf child? The deaf child is now silent. His hearing impairment has probably not yet been diagnosed. Rawlings (1971) presents data on some 22,000 children in the USA known to have been born deaf. Fewer than half of them had been diagnosed as deaf before they were three years old. At an age when hearing children are speaking grammatically like adults and using 1000 words to do so, more than half of the deaf children in one of the world's medically most sophisticated societies were not yet known to be deaf. Some of this may have been neglect on the part of parents or social services; some would have arisen from the reluctance of parents to face the fact of a strange and irreversibly handicapping condition; some would be due to the technical difficulties of diagnosis of deafness in babies.

These children then reach school age with little concept of the existence of verbal language and effectively no experience of it. They may not even know that the facial gestures centred on the mouth that they see around them are accompanied by sounds and are used to effect communication – to express feelings, desires, frustrations, pleasures. They will not know that objects have names; that they can be referred to when they are not immediately present. They will not know how to bring the past into the present or project the present into the future. Most of these children will be without sign language, and therefore without any language.

From their 1000-word vocabulary at the age of three years, hearing children at five now reach out to grasp the greatest gift that language can bestow – the gift of thinking in words. This gift comes slowly, not contemporary with the main growth of speech or of spoken language, but developing in sequence (Flavell, Beach, and Chinsky, 1966; Conrad, 1971a). The child's speech now becomes a cognitive tool directing actions. It is no longer con-strained to communications with other people. They can now talk to themselves – and purposively. At first the need to vocalize prevails. The child can think, but only aloud. Soon comes the completion and fulfilment. The development which begins with the first awareness of sound passes with dramatic swiftness – within the span of a small fraction of a lifetime – to the capability of silent verbal thought, which knows no limits and to which no door is closed. This is the point at which the child born deaf begins the infinitely arduous climb towards the very first handholds of language. Were it simply that deaf children begin this climb three–four years after their hearing peers, and reach the summit three–four years late, there would be little need to write this book.

The development of speech and language and thinking does not occur independently of all other growth. The opposite is true. We see a pattern of growth of the most complex interdependences but based firmly upon a neurological substrate still far from fully understood. This physical maturation will at times itself require concomitant language development for successful advance. But each of the threads will have its own identity. At some points, growth will be halted until another thread has reached a predetermined state – and only then perhaps continue. But it also seems certain that in some cases, if the neurological tryst is not met, there may be no reprieve. The laggard thread, without the missed support, may strive in vain. This we may see in a child's subsequent attainment. In Chapter 9 we shall discuss more formally what may be happening. But we may be sure that a child entering school with no external language because of deafness will have no internal language either.

Hearing children enter school poised for education, vibrant with the means to gather in and grow on the inundation of symbolic knowledge that school displays before them. They cannot read; but all of the processes without which they could not read are present. They cannot reason; but the processes without which they could not reason are present. Their minds are open and knowledge pours in. School does not need to teach them to speak, nor to teach them the rules of the grammar of spoken language; they are already efficient learning organisms.

When a deaf child enters regular school, it is rare that they are ready for the kind of education normal for hearing children. Generally they are without a mother-tongue. The principal initial goal must be to achieve a means of communication. The school is in the unique position of having to choose a mother-tongue and to create the conditions for its acquisition; and only then can the stuff of conventional education be essayed. But the chosen mother-tongue must not merely be convenient for static classroom interchange like ship-to-ship signalling. This is to be the language in which children will think – the tongue they will need to use to communicate with themselves, the language which will subsume the cognitive processes without which they will remain intellectually inert. If at this point the child is failed – and for most deaf children only the school is technically equipped for success – the failure will probably be for ever. A poor education can delay the full flowering of the developed mind of a bright hearing child. A poor education for a deaf child which fails to provide a language for thought, a language upon which the development of cognitive process can advance, will not merely delay; it could destroy. If school for a deaf child can do no more than inform, it will have totally failed.

Speech in thinking

The education of deaf children has to be judged – and in this context the word judged has the appropriate gravity – by its success in providing a child with a language for thought. For Britain at least, the challenging goal so succinctly expressed by Ewing must be evaluated in this way – and Ewing saw it so. For him, the appropriate language was speech. At the time he wrote the passage we quoted, this philosophy was well established. It formed the basis of teacher training and the guidelines, with varying degree of flexibility, for school curricula. In spite of decades of debate only in the most recent years has a tremor of dissent found expression in classroom practice. For the most part there can be little dispute that an evaluation of the education of deaf children in Britain is inevitably an evaluation of "oralism" which depends on the use of spoken language, not only for reading and writing, but crucially for thinking. In evaluating oral education we may look at the surface outcomes with conventional measuring instruments. But we also have a duty to try to determine whether the spoken language that a deaf child might acquire extends below the surface skin of the exchange of facts and into the texture of thought.

The early history of the analysis of the role of speech in the developing intellect of hearing children has been amply documented; it is a history dominated by the towering figures of Jean Piaget and Lev Semenovich Vygotsky. Their brilliant observations provided the insights upon which, in the past two or three decades, experimental studies have rested, clarifying and amplifying. It is because of this history that we come to recognize the overwhelming significance of the role of speech in the development of cognitive processes.

Because the exact nature of this role remains in doubt it is not always certain whether authors are discussing the same or different phenomena when they use the same terms, and in some cases translation into English from other languages may well lose specificity of definition. But apart from that technical source of ambiguity, there remain genuine problems of definition. For example, Vygotsky (1962) in English translation from the original 1934 publication uses the phrase "inner speech" to describe the relationship between speech and thinking. Inner speech is not a stream of words like vocal speech, but it is "thought connected with words" (p. 149). But in the formulation of the words, "there is no direct correspondence between inner speech and the subject's tongue or larynx movements" (p. 48). Sokolov (1972), on the other hand, whose concepts derive directly from his fellow Russian, clearly uses "inner speech" quite differently, devoting a substantial portion of his major study to electromyographic (EMG) investigation of it, specifically seeking correlates between electrical activity of speech muscles and cognitive operations. The behaviour represented by this relationship has variously been referred to by McGuigan as "covert language processes" (1966), "covert oral behavior" (1970), or "subvocal speech" (1967). The latter term has also been used by Hardyck and Petrinovich (1970) and by Locke (1970). Lepley (1952) referring to speechlike activity during reading and writing used the phrase "implicit speech", whilst Edfeldt (1960) used "silent speech" in the same context.

The difficulty of description stems at least partly from the fact that the phenomenon cannot be directly observed, and partly from the fact that the implication of speech is obscure because of the uncertainty surrounding the boundaries of speech behaviour. While it is clear, for example, that two people engaged in normal face-to-face conversation are using speech, it is rather less clear whether whispering is speech, and less clear still whether silent mouthing of words is speech. Certainly fewer and fewer of the organs required for ordinary vocal speech are used. What then can we say of the status of the activity taken a little further to the point when not only is the "speech" silent, but the lips are closed and – to the eye – motionless? In this case can we accept the presence of speech even when we ourselves are the actors? This is the familiar case of silent reading.

Some would deny that any speechlike behaviour occurs when they read. But more commonly it is accepted as a factual experience, though not necessarily universal. Edfeldt (1960) recorded electrical activity from a number of muscles normally involved during speech when 84 adult subjects silently read text. Almost all of them showed activity greater than that of their resting levels, and the level of electrical activity was related to the difficulty of the reading task – such as known but foreign language, visual difficulty, or syntactic difficulty. Yet, when Lepley (1952) asked 200 students after a writing exercise whether they had spoken to themselves while they wrote, about half said they did not. McGuigan (1970) posed a similar question but also made EMG recordings. He found no relationship between introspections and actual speech-muscle activity. Certainly with respect to cognitive behaviour, at least of the level of complexity of reading prose, it is clear that for many, if not most people, speech muscles are implicated and that, furthermore, we are not very good at noticing it. Perhaps more surprisingly, Sokolov (1972) reported significant EMG response from speech muscles when students worked through Raven's Progressive Matrices, which is a standard non-verbal intelligence test in wide use. As the problems became harder, the EMG response increased.

Particularly for the well-researched case of reading it is not easy to avoid the inference that, commonly, some silent speech concurrently occurs. But two procedural objections have been made. The first is that, although EMG response is recorded from speech muscles during silent reading, it may reflect no more than a general increase in covert muscular activity during non resting behaviour. McGuigan (1970) clarified two aspects of this. He obtained the familiar EMG response when his subjects copied words, but not when they were drawing simple shapes, and he failed to record EMG responses when recordings were taken from legs or non-writing arms. A second objection is that, although speech muscles may be concurrently involved during reading, the apparent silent speech may be unrelated to the material read. Locke and Fehr (1970) showed this to be unlikely. Recording from the lips, they showed more EMG response when adults silently read labial words normally involving movement of the lips (map) than when the words were nonlabial (hat). Garrity (1977) has presented a very thorough review of this literature. But even were no electrical activity recordable from speech muscles during cognitive operations, the involvement of words in the operations still could not be excluded. Insofar as we hear words and articulate words, the probability that words will have correlates in imagery is high, since such correlates are present for all other sensory modes.

Whatever else may be involved, the speechlike nature of this behaviour is inescapable. At present though, since it lacks an acoustic component, we have little means of knowing how close the correlation is between silent and vocal speech. For the present we need go no further than to assert that silent speech is behaviour which is probably as common as vocal speech and which few people have never experienced. In a scholarly introduction to this topic, Sokolov (1972) appositely reminds us of man's very ancient concern with this relationship between thought, language, and words.

We ourselves will refer to this phenomenon as *internal speech*. We now assume that we can designate an activity which is sufficiently speechlike for the shorthand abbreviation of "speech" to be acceptable. But why internal rather than inner or subvocal or silent? It is largely because we do not have an agreed term. As we have seen, this is partly because we are concerned with an inferred and not with directly observable behaviour. The one we choose seems most closely to reflect our own particular conceptualization of the phenomenon in the context which specifically concerns us. We see internal speech as vocal speech which, at the moment when its presence is made known to us, has been internalized. Specifically, it is internalized in the sense that it is intended only for the ear of the "speaker". It may therefore be overt or vocal but still private – for internal consumption – in the way that reading aloud for ourselves alone may be. When children memorizing a list of words mutter them to themselves, we regard it as internal speech. More generally, internal speech is also silent – though it may be for no better than social reasons.* "Inner" speech would be acceptable to us. But Vygotsky has given his own unique connotation to that term which would be inappropriate in our present enquiry. For us throughout this study, internal speech occurs when a person manipulates, generally silently, spoken words which are required to achieve some cognitive goal. Within the limits of inference we shall see this directly when children memorize words which they have read. Because of the wealth of corroborative evidence, we will assume that this activity is closely related to that observed electromyographically.

In its limited sense we accept this as one relatively simple form of oral thinking. This in no way commits us to a view that no

* In the context of deafness, the term "silent speech" also has a quite different technical meaning when used in studies of lip reading.

thought is without a linguistic base – a proposition which seems inherently unlikely, and for our purpose, unnecessary. But, within the cognitive framework which concerns us, we do regard internal speech as thinking. Memorizing words or understanding sentences may seem far removed from the more abstract insights of advanced mathematics or the intricacies of pure logic. Intellect, though, has room for the humble as well as the high.

Here we are concerned with learning and with linguistic communication. For this, oral education of the deaf has chosen the medium of spoken words. It is then relevant to consider not only whether it provides a child with an acceptable degree of skill in communicating with other people, deaf or hearing, but whether it also provides a means of effecting cognitive operations, of communicating with one's self; whether it provides internal speech as well as vocal speech.

Again alternatives are available. To preclude children from speech does not preclude them from the capacity for thought. To preclude them from all language might. The nearest we have so far got towards evidence for the latter statement comes unsatisfactorily from anecodotes about "wolf children" and the like, presumed to be without human language. Even the well-documented case of the wild boy of Aveyron (Lane, 1977) was unable to determine the extent to which the boy Victor's paucity of abstract thought was due to a prolonged language deficit or initial severe mental retardation. But speech seems not to have an exclusive right. The evidence for this, though again largely anecdotal, is less ambiguous. Discussions with born-deaf people commonly indicate a rich mental life carried out in sign language, finger spelling, or print. The letter we quote on page 3 is one example. The celebrated Helen Keller became deaf and blind when she was nineteen months old. In later years she lectured widely and wrote several books. Her first lessons in speech took place at the age of ten years, and until then she communicated largely in finger spelling. She recounts (1956) how, in adult life, "in moments of excitement or when I wake from sleep, I occasionally catch myself spelling with my fingers" (p. 44). Max (1935) used EMG recordings to demonstrate that deaf people may use sign language in their dreams. More formally, Odom, Blanton, and McIntyre (1970) and Rozanova (1971) have shown that deaf children have no difficulty memorizing signs, and Bellugi, Klima, and Siple (1974) and Frumkin and Anisfeld (1977) clarified that they are quite capable of remembering *in* signs –

rather than recoding into words. We must therefore accept the existence and practicability of internal languages other than speech. Indeed it would be absurd to deny it since the members of every deaf community or family communicate largely in sign – and often exclusively in sign. It would then have been remarkable had this mode of communication not been internalized.

We are still quite ignorant about the chronological development of internal sign language, or its effectiveness as a medium for thinking. We would expect the latter to be closely related to the effectiveness of sign languages when used for interpersonal communications. Objective comparative studies are not easy. In formal tests, not only would the information to be communicated have to be culture-free, but there would need to be independent evidence that communicators were equally proficient in the languages compared. Neither condition could easily be met. Until such test is made there is no reason to suppose that internal sign language is not just as cognitively useful to a person fluent in that language as internal speech is to a person fluent in spoken language.

Oral education then takes on a special responsibility in its presumption that if deaf children can be taught to communicate in speech then oral thinking will develop. If this does not happen, speech will remain a superficial medium, operating perhaps at the level of basic request or command, or recognition of very simple printed declarative sentences, but with no roots into the substrate of intellect. An evaluation of oral education must not therefore stop at an assessment of, for example, lip-reading skill. It must also consider the operations of thinking itself.

The hearing child is neither taught to speak nor taught to internalize speech. On the contrary the deaf child must be actively taught to speak, just as both must be taught to read. We then might assume that if an adequate level of speech quality – as well as speech quantity – can be achieved within some measure (unknown) of time, effective internalization will also occur. We are totally ignorant of the nature of the parameters involved here, and the theoretical principles of oral education offer no formulation. While there is a substantial literature concerned with programmes for teaching speech reception and an even larger one concerned with teaching speech production, there are no discussions addressed to the question of the conditions for oral thinking. Whether or not it ever does develop is left to be determined inferentially – usually and inappropriately in terms of criteria of social or professional success.

Our own test data derive from deaf schoolchildren in England and Wales. The educational culture is classically oral. To be concerned, as we are, with modes of thinking is to be concerned with internal speech rather than with the internal representation of any other form of language. If deaf children in Britain do not think orally, it will be only by chance – and in spite of their classroom experience – if they do have readily available an alternative internal tongue. The culture is not of course totally pure. Some children come from deaf families complete with manual language; their schoolmates may acquire it in some degree. Some teachers may, from time to time, resort to signing as an instructional medium. Most will lack the ability. This particular educational system therefore presents us with a favourable framework within which, and within the limits of the reliability of our instruments, we may examine the development of internal speech in the context of intervention rather than maturation.

The deaf as language controls

We now find ourselves in the midst of a strange paradox. Virtually throughout history philosophers have sought to unravel the nature of the relationship between thought and language. There has never been any dissent from the proposition that, when cognitive operations carried out by hearing people are supported by linguistic media, then the language is spoken language. In recent years a substantial and growing body of research has come to accept that deaf people represent a perfect control for the study of the role of oral language in thinking. The basis for this – qualified by varying degrees of subtlety – is the assumption that the deaf are also orally dumb. Granted this assumption, the way is logically open for direct comparison of deaf (i.e., dumb) with hearing (i.e., speaking) people. Yet oralism, with its highly specific aspirations, has dominated the education of deaf children in the West for generations. It is then clearly legitimate to examine the empirical bases of the assumptions of researchers and to try to determine where, between them and the pronouncements of education, the truth may lie.

It has never been difficult to assert, either on the basis of introspection or on the basis of demonstrable evidence, the apparent and persistent presence of silent or subvocal speech during activities which might reasonably be considered to represent forms of thinking. But in terms of scientific rigour this is a weak statement, pointing merely to an unspecified association rather than to the nature of the relationship. It would clearly be more compelling were it possible to demonstrate the ability to "think" when internal speech was *known* to be concurrently absent. This, unequivocally, has never even remotely been achieved with normal undamaged people. But people who are pathologically already mute are something else. Better still, if they are deaf as well – were born deaf and had never heard language spoken – then surely such people would provide the perfect experimental control subjects. If internalized forms of speech were not just useful or convenient for thinking, but necessary, then these deaf-mutes would inevitably be incapable of thought as we know it. In their case, absence of internal speech would be a most reasonable assumption when they were required to carry out thinking operations which in normally-hearing people are always accompanied by demonstrable internal speechlike activity.

In spite of decades of propaganda and moral indignation by persons and institutions concerned with the education and welfare of the deaf, the notion that deafness necessarily implies dumbness remains a popular myth. The further notion that the ugly and incomprehensible sounds occasionally made by these "unfortunates" might be used as a medium of thinking in the form of internal speech seems to have been too bizarre to consider.

A century ago the psychologist William James was one of the first to realize the significance of the deaf for this area of enquiry. James was also one of the first to fall into the trap of taking at face value the popular terms "deaf-mute" or "deaf-and-dumb" as a basis for objective enquiry.

Starting from his own insights and introspections, James was convinced that internal speech played a substantial role in his thinking. Evidently too he had discussed this issue with other eminent men. Galton, for one, seems to have concurred. When James discovered an alleged deaf-mute, who nevertheless was able to write fluent, imaginative, perfectly grammatical English prose, he concluded that profound, insightful thinking was evidently unhindered by the absence of internal speech. The question that seems not to have occurred to James was to wonder whether perhaps the deaf-mute *did* use internal speech.

There are a number of technical matters involved here, and we can hardly blame James for failing to take into account technological developments which would barely have been on his horizon. The modern audiometer was still far away in time, and medical diagnosis of deafness in infants was itself in its infancy. As with so many apocalyptic stories, the truth could be substantially different from the legend. James' deaf-mute may well have been a man who, at least during early childhood, was not profoundly deaf by modern standards, but who may have become so. At that time even a moderate degree of deafness could, in the absence of an enlightened teacher, have easily led to a kind of operational mutism. If the man used vocal speech at all, it might well have been effectively unintelligible, reflecting the kind of speech sounds which he heard. Such a child, living in an age not too far distant from one which equated deafness with idiocy, would simply have stopped trying to vocalize. Few would have understood him. We do not know whether James personally knew the man, but he had clearly heard a good deal about him, including the fact that he was dumb. James (1901) therefore felt able to write, " . . . a deaf and dumb man can weave his tactile and visual images into a system of thought quite as effective and rational as that of a word-user" (p. 266). From this he argued that, " . . . the kind of mind-stuff which is handiest will be the best for the purpose" (p. 266). In other words, although speech used internally is useful, effective, and common in thinking processes, it is not an exclusive medium. James did not consider that his "deaf and dumb" man might have been only vocally dumb – and for no better reason than that, in modern parlance, his unintelligible vocal speech utterances would have received little reinforcement. Mr. Ballard, the deaf man, may well have been unwilling to speak to William James, but he may have been perfectly able and willing to speak silently to himself. James' thoughts on thinking are, in this context, probably right; his use of the phenomenon of deafness to support them is probably wrong as a general statement.

There is perhaps a somewhat compounded confusion to beset those who have since followed James into arbitrary assumption of the cognitive processes of deaf people. James assumed that dumbness necessarily accompanies deafness. From this he deduced that a deaf-mute must inevitably be without internal speech, as he is without vocal speech. The confusion in the deafness-dumbness relationship, as it pervades the scene today, spirals a little further. No one today familiar with even profoundly born-deaf people doubts that they can and do speak. Unfortunately, all too often their speech is unintelligible. Later on, we shall present ample evidence to support this statement. The additional twist proceeds to the assumption that speech unintelligible to a normally hearing listener is therefore unintelligible to the deaf speaker. This may indeed sometimes be the case. But this assumption needs to be supported by another; namely that, for internal speech to be a viable medium for thinking, it has to be totally intelligible in the sense that we use the term when we talk about the perceptual intelligibility of vocal speech. We shall show that this too is far from necessary.

A characteristic of spoken speech is that, in normal conditions of converse, words are physically easily discriminable. No language adapted for speech-hearing communication could be otherwise, and those like-sounding words which do quite often occur in a language are almost invariably identified by their context – grammatical, semantic, or social. Were this not the case, there could be no spoken language. As a result, we have immense confidence that, generally, we can at least physically decode the speech sounds that we hear. From this we have equal confidence in our ability to "hear" what we are saying to ourselves when we use speech internally in thinking.

This understanding is essentially all-or-none. So long as we opt to internalize speech in order to carry out some mental operation, the speech itself is physically clear. Even though because of the presence of ambient noise we may be uncertain as to what someone else is saying, we cannot be uncertain about what we are saying to ourselves at the instant we say it. When we complain that because of a noisy environment we cannot hear ourselves think, we really mean that the noise prevents concentration. For the noise to mask thought, it would have to be "internal" in some other way. An author then who assumes that the deaf cannot think in words because the words are unintelligible falls equally into the Jamesian trap.

Inadvertently William James set the scene for the use of deaf subjects in studies of language and thinking. In essence we are faced with the fact of the dominating position of verbal language in the processes of human conduct and human thought. It is reasonable and important to enquire how far this use of verbal language is imperative or optional. The use of deaf subjects has been seen as a welcome access to an otherwise formidable problem. Since it is implicit in this area of enquiry that the deaf are without verbal language – or at any rate significantly impoverished in an indefinable, unspecifiable, and unquantifiable way – whatever is discovered that the deaf cannot do, but that hearing people can, may be ascribed to the imperative end of the imperative-optional axis. Whenever tasks can be devised which appear to require cognitive operation and at which the deaf are as good as the hearing, then it would be reasonable to argue that those operations are not constrained by the need for a verbal linguistic medium. If it is evident that speech is associated with performance of the task, then we would have to assume that the use of speech is no more than convenient. That is, we use speech because we prefer to, or choose to, and not because we have to; not because without speech we would be unable to perform the task. So, although there are a number of studies principally concerned with the nature of the cognitive processes of the deaf for its own sake, a substantive body of work has been focussed on the nature of thinking in normal people, using deaf subjects simply as a without-speech control group. In this case there is an underlying assumption – and it is sometimes explicit – that the deaf are different from the hearing in other than hearing itself. Represented in a variety of forms, the crucial difference more frequently implicated is that the deaf lack the use of internal speech. The assumption merits extensive scrutiny.

As we noted, few of the psychologists whose work we shall shortly refer to could have believed that their deaf subjects were dumb. It is difficult to fail to elicit some kind and some degree of speech if any attempt at all is made. But many studies have been conducted which depend on the untested premise that, vocal speech or not, deaf children do not think in words. Some of these we shall discuss in later chapters, and a few examples here will suffice to make the point.

Gibson, Shurcliff, and Yonas (1970), for instance, in a study which examined the role of phonological coding in reading, used deaf subjects as controls. They argued that pronounciability of words would be irrelevant for deaf children, though not for the hearing, on the grounds that, "most of the deaf subjects spoke very little" (p. 70) and would therefore be unlikely to match words read to an articulatory plan.

Friedman and Gillooley (1977), following up the reading study of Gibson et al., also justified their use of deaf subjects on the grounds that, "... the prelingual deaf must presumably decode written materials directly to meaning" (p. 348).

Rozin and Gleitman (1977), also concerned with problems of decoding printed words, suggest that, "A different instance of phonological bypass is reading in congenitally deaf people, who have virtually no spoken language. Surely their reading performance cannot be described in terms of a phonological intermediary" (p. 66).

H. G. Furth, who has made a significant contribution to the question of language and thought largely relying on deaf subjects as the language control, states that, "... it is our contention that deaf children do not have this kind of inner language which comes from internalization of an externally transmitted language" (Furth and Youniss, 1975; p. 169). Furth (1966) had earlier attempted a qualification of this more general position: "The fact is that ... the vast majority of persons, born deaf, *do not acquire functional language competence* ..." (p. 13, Furth's italics). The qualification, though, helps little in deciding which deaf person is a suitable language control. Youniss, Furth, and Ross (1971) assessed language competence in terms of reading ability. They selected a group of deaf adolescents on the basis of a mean reading grade of 2.5 (about 8:6 years). This certainly sounds like linguistic impoverishment. But we shall show that many deaf children with reading ability as poor as this can nevertheless internalize to some degree, whatever verbal language they do have; and it may be sufficient for the particular task.

Most writers who have deduced absence of internal speech from the assumption of dumbness or quasi-dumbness or unintelligibility of vocal speech have generally been aware that degree of deafness is likely to be of significance. There are, however, no empirical data which describe a relationship between amount of hearing loss and presence or absence of internal speech, and researchers have been distinctly cavalier in selection of subjects.

Furth (1961) gives 60 dB (this is the ISO* value) as the lower

---

* The International Organization for Standardization (ISO) recommended a reference zero level for the calibration for audiometers in 1964. This standard is now widely accepted and is used throughout this work. When we cite studies which used a different standard, the hearing-loss values have been adjusted to approximate ISO levels.

limit. Furth and Milgram (1965) and Youniss and Furth (1967) accept a 70 dB cut-off. Youniss, Feil, and Furth (1965) give no hearing loss information about their deaf subjects other than that they were enrolled in a state school for the deaf. Olsson and Furth (1966) and Furth and Youniss (1965) say only that deafness was "severe".

Other important studies dependent on linguistic performance of deaf and hearing subjects are similarly inadequate. Goetzinger, Wills, and Dekker (1967) and Withrow (1968), amongst the more influential studies, fail to report the degree of hearing loss. O'Connor and Hermelin (1976) are explicit that their subjects had, "... no useful hearing ... over the speech frequency range ... and had hearing losses of at least 60 dB in the better ear" (p. 85); two statements we shall show to be incompatible. The fact is that the relationship between degree of deafness and the use of speech for thinking has never been determined.

There may be many areas of study of deaf people where narrow delineation of the degree of deafness is of little relevance. But this cannot be the case when the primary variable under discussion is verbal language. We have argued for a close association between quality of vocal speech in the deaf and probability of internalizing it. In Chapter 8 we shall show a high dependency of speech quality on hearing loss. We shall also show that there is a close association of vocal speech quality and use of internal speech. When therefore impoverishment of verbal language is taken to imply absence of internal speech, and it is the independent variable in studies of the cognitive behaviour of the deaf, the degree of deafness itself must be accorded adequate importance.

We have no doubt that many of the subjects used in these studies may well have been totally deprived of useable verbal language. We should be clear though that the paradigm which most of them adopt assumes that the deaf subjects *must necessarily* be without verbal language. Experiments then predict that, on cognitive tasks which can be performed without the use of verbal language, deaf subjects will perform as well as hearing subjects, and that, if verbal language is required, then they will not. The deaf have a place in the paradigm only if, unlike the hearing, they are known to be without language. To accept that hearing losses, when stated, of 60–70 dB meet this requirement seems distinctly imprudent. When Lantz and Lenneberg (1966) found that deaf subjects were as good as hearing subjects on a verbal memory task, they wisely commented as follows: "Deaf adults are able to do well on the memory task not because language plays no part in the task (as might have been concluded if no language variable had been measured) but because they had adequately developed and utilized the pertinent aspect of language" (p. 779).

These studies, and many similar, relate, in one way or another, to the question of what verbal language can do for thinking. All of them have made use of deaf subjects, not necessarily because they are concerned with deafness, but because as Vernon (1972) has said: "Congenital deafness is an unique experiment of nature providing a control of the major psychological variables of language development and environmental deprivation" (p. 360). This would only be true were we certain of the quality of the control. Principally we are concerned with language and, specifically for the present, with spoken language used internally as a means of, so to speak, communicating with one's self for definable cognitive objectives. Our doubt has been with the assumption that the deaf subjects used were without language. That is, without language sufficient for the experimental task.

The conditions for intelligible internal speech

Since the deaf do speak, we shall begin by discussing a model of the relationship between vocal and internal speech – the characteristics of the former which are required for the latter. To the extent that they are deaf, the vocal speech of hearing-impaired people never has the clarity, the intelligibility, of that of people with normal hearing. There is a substantial and active research effort concerned to delineate the specific characteristics of the speech of the deaf which contribute to its relative lack of clarity. We shall describe it more appropriately in Chapter 8. What is here relevant is the fact that within a spoken deaf utterance there may be, word by word, markedly different levels of intelligibility. The superficial analogy with perception of normal speech heard against a noisy background is misleading, though as the level of background noise increases, so more and more words will not be deciphered. In a situation of that kind, when we talk about a noisy background, we mean that the noise is external to the speaker. A normal speaker cannot utter "noisy" speech in this sense. No matter how much external noise is interposed between speaker and external listener, there is no evidence at all that what the speaker hears internally is other than clear speech. So, excepting the case of certain pathological conditions perhaps, our internal speech is 100% intelligible. In the sense that we are discussing it here, it is a representation of our own external or vocal speech. We speak clearly aloud and we therefore speak clearly silently. The words we say are easily discriminated – one from another.

Not so for the deaf. For the deaf, as for all of us, speech has to be produced. It requires the coordination of sets of muscles which control the organs of speech – larynx, pharynx, tongue, lips, jaw, and so on, as well as those involved in the control of breathing. Possibly by virtue of extended practice, by monitoring the speech sounds that we can hear ourselves making, early in life the physical characteristics of the words hearing people utter become highly consistent from one occasion to another. This consistency is essential – though it may not be sufficient – if a listener is to decode, or to identify with certainty, the words spoken. Both of these features, consistency and discriminability, may be absent from the spoken words of deaf people. The contributions made by these independent characteristics to the likelihood of presence or absence of internal speech we believe to be qualitatively different.

There are many good reasons why people deaf from birth should have unintelligible speech. Their limit is substantially determined by what it is that they hear (Fry, 1977). The less they can hear both of the speech sounds of other speakers and of the speech sounds they themselves make, the more they are obliged to rely on sensory information other than auditory. We must assume that the principal naturally available alternative is kinaesthetic and tactile information deriving from their own speech musculature. If, therefore, they are able, whether by training or spontaneously, to generate a consistent articulatory formulation each time that they wish to utter the same word, although the speech sound which emerges may remain unintelligible to the casual listener, it will nevertheless in fact be consistent from one occasion to another. It will tend to be the same sound; the listener may or may not recognize it. This is a matter of decoding.

Consistent speech, by definition, can be decoded – once the code has been learned. Commonly the speech of deaf people may be totally unintelligible to strangers and yet reasonably intelligible to their immediate family. The prerequisite is consistency. In the same way that we learn to recode, i.e., translate, foreign words, so too can the parents of deaf children learn to translate their utterances. Now, if a deaf person has consistent speech in the way we have been discussing, one important condition is present for that speech to be internalized. It is hard to see why not. If parents or teachers can understand, then of course the speaker can – no matter how many other listeners cannot.

But, as we have said, consistency, while necessary, is not sufficient. The speech utterances of a deaf person may be consistent; the same articulatory pattern for each utterance of the same word. They must also be different for different words. We have said that the speech sounds of words in a live spoken language must be auditorally sufficiently different for listeners to know with ease which word is being spoken. Consistency itself will not do this. Distinctiveness is essential along dimensions which, as the language has developed, are accepted as carriers of linguistic information. Intonation pattern may be as relevant as the phonemic features.

Because the deaf may have so little auditory feedback available to them, production and control of speech sounds is arduous. For most of us, there are a few words which are articulated identically and sound just the same (e.g., *weight, wait; wood, would; know, no*). In the case of the deaf learning to speak a tongue which is adapted to the sensory needs of hearing people, there is no theoretical limit to the number of such words. Because of the tremendous difficulty of articulating spoken words without the correlated auditory feedback, very many words might share a common articulatory conformation. We can all too easily imagine a case where deaf children have knowledge of a substantial vocabulary, but when they speak it, they appear in every instance to be saying almost the same word. Furthermore, they actually *may be* saying the "same" word; for them, all words may have the homophonous character that the relatively rare *weight, wait* examples do for hearing people.

We have exaggerated an extreme case merely to illustrate a theoretical possibility. What we wish to emphasize is that unintelligible speech may be consistent and still be "unintelligible" even to the speaker. There could be little value in trying to internalize such speech. More realistically, though, we can see that there might well be a small vocabulary of words which could vary from speaker to speaker, and which did have sufficient mutual distinctiveness. What we might regard as the discriminable vocabulary. A vocabulary possessing this quality could provide a basis for some degree of internal speech, and it would be determined by an intravocabulary threshold of distinctiveness. This discriminable vocabulary, though small, might still be adequate for some simple tasks. Its size and its utility would depend not only on linguistic knowledge, but crucially on quality of vocal speech as well. We would therefore expect far greater variability in the use of internal speech amongst deaf children than amongst those with normal hearing and speech. We would expect that many deaf children could not achieve the conditions we have specified at all. Furthermore, we would expect that even those who do would do so with less fluency than their hearing counterparts.

This speculative model implies first that no speech is internalized until the speakers have a threshold size vocabulary of discriminable (to themselves) words. Then, that as any new word, through use, becomes discriminable from the existing vocabulary of such words, it also becomes available for useable internal speech. The size of this vocabulary is likely to vary greatly from one deaf child to another. The same model would be appropriate for hearing people as well, with the operational difference that their speech achieves so great a clarity that a level of distortion rarely occurs which is sufficient to lead to noticeable effect. So although we see no reason why even profound deafness should preclude the use of internal speech, we suggest that an all-or-none concept is inappropriate, and that we have to think in terms of degrees of internal speech distributed in some way throughout any deaf population.

Summarizing, we suggest that, granted the presence of certain conditions, useful internal speech may develop in profoundly deaf children. They must have learned how to articulate a number of words in a manner which assigns to them discernible physical distinctiveness. Their articulation of those words must be consistent from one occasion to another. Here we can allow that some deviation is acceptable so long as it is recognized by the speaker as a deviant form and not a different word. Finally, the vocabulary of such words must comprise a set semantically adequate for a particular purpose. It is hard to imagine an analogous problem which might confront a normal hearing person; we might suppose that the development of mathematical symbols as a fluent linguistic medium takes on some flavour of its characteristics.

Internal language competence – to a degree

We now begin to see why so little progress has been made with regard to the relationship between thinking and language, when deaf subjects have been used as the essential control, and language is assumed to be verbal language. In general, the question has been posed in one of two ways. Some authors, exemplified by Furth in many studies, and especially Furth (1966), take as axiomatic that the deaf are without internal verbal language. They then ask what, nevertheless, the deaf can cognitively do, thinking of operations which are part of the normal thought processes of hearing people. Indeed, O'Connor and Hermelin (1976) wondered whether such deaf subjects might not be forced into cognitive strategies which would lead to *better* performance than the hearing. Other authors have asked what cognitive operations – normal or easy for hearing people – can the deaf, supposedly without internal verbal language, not do, or do less well (Bugelski, 1970; Conlin and Paivio, 1975; Gibson et al., 1970; Hartung, 1970; Olsson and Furth, 1966; Ross, 1969). Hermelin and O'Connor (1975a) have usefully added a concept of "elective strategy": what the deaf can, but *prefer* not to do. We have argued that a critical premise that deaf subjects are necessarily internally "dumb" is dubious. Were it false it would be sufficient to obscure real phenomena, and could well lead to contradictory outcomes in different experiments. If the principal reason for using deaf subjects is to study cognitive processes, one certain requirement is that we *know* what cognitive processes the deaf are using.

We believe that a major weakness has been to assume that internal language (linguistic competence) is either wholly present or wholly absent. But there are a number of contingent fallacies. In the first place, it has never seriously been believed that thought in hearing people exclusively requires verbal language. Here we are not thinking merely about operations involved in solving the problems of nonverbal intelligence tests. Then, we have neither an adequate taxonomy of tasks nor of people which would permit us to designate with confidence either tasks or experimental subjects as being verbal or nonverbal. With the deaf we are on even less sure ground. With few exceptions (Lantz and Lenneberg, 1966; Locke and Locke, 1971; Pettifor, 1968), no attempts have been made to determine the degree of linguistic competence in deaf subjects used in experiments. In general it has been taken for granted that the deaf subjects were without verbal language (or massively deficient) and therefore could not use it, and that the hearing subjects (reasonably) had it, and necessarily used it. We shall show that *some* deaf children, even including some who are profoundly deaf from birth in fact are able to use internal verbal language, while others, less deaf, apparently do not.

But it does not follow that a deaf person who does have internal speech available uses it exclusively in a situation where a hearing person might. We all have available more than one medium in which we can perform cognitive operations (Baddeley, 1976; 1978; Craik and Lockhart, 1972). The wide range of cognitive problems which hearing people generally handle in a speech medium may be much more restricted for those for whom speech is itself a skill laboriously learned. Far more deaf than hearing people might prefer, for example, to memorize an address by what it looks like in printed form rather than by its spoken form – though they all may be capable of using the latter. Furthermore, we have already pointed out the possibility that, for the deaf, an internal speech facility may be attenuated in operation simply because the underlying speech is "noisy". Though internal speech may be used, and even used exclusively, it may still be less effective than that of hearing people. Were this so, there is a further possibility that deaf subjects in an experiment, faced with an unfamiliar task, may choose to bring to bear more than one cognitive medium onto the problem concurrently. In trying to memorize the address, they may code it both verbally *and* visually – a strategy most of us are quite familiar with, though we may be less compelled to resort to it.

The nature of the operation must itself partly determine the choice of cognitive strategy. To take one extreme example, it is not easy for most of us to memorize a melody verbally. At the other extreme, it is difficult to count sequentially occurring events solely by means of visual imagery. Such constraints will be true for deaf and hearing alike. But there is no reason to suppose that all task constraints will be identical for deaf and hearing. From what we have said, it is much more likely that they will be different. We might speculate, for illustration, that where deaf people would rely solely on visual operations to remember a face, hearing people might also verbally code salient features such as "prominent nose". Then the probability that the verbal cognitive function of deaf people is "weak" may lead not so much to flexibility as to vacillation. On one occasion they may use a verbal process, and on another occasion, but in a similar situation, they may use a visual process.

We cannot but sympathize with the reasoning which has led to the substantial literature which has compared the cognitive performance of deaf and hearing children. But we do find it difficult to accept the assumption that any deaf child with a hearing loss either unspecified or specified to be not less than, for example, 60 dB (or 70 or 80 dB for that matter) is definitively without a capability for using internal speech to handle cognitive problems in the manner conventionally accepted for hearing people. There is no real certainty that even congenital total deafness for speech sounds necessarily precludes the development of some minimal internal phonetic experience.

The nature of the handicap – as it legally is in Britain – of deafness has been amply documented. The vast majority of the children who form the subjects of this enquiry were deaf either by the time they were born or very shortly after. Most of these children have never heard language spoken with anything remotely approaching the clarity to which the rest of us are accustomed. Many have never been able, auditorally, to discriminate one spoken word from another. Most hearing people who make the most superficial introspection about what goes on in their minds during the course of everyday life will soon realize that they are spending much time in communicating with themselves in a speechlike medium. They do not do it continuously; they do not do it every time they think of or about something; they do not necessarily talk to themselves word by word, as when we read aloud. But silent speech–like behaviour occupies a great deal of our waking, and perhaps sleeping, lives. Furth (1966), and others, have argued that it is not necessary; that much of our thinking is, or could be, carried on without this activity. If we can gain adequate control over the conditions of our observations, the deaf will, without doubt, lead us to insights into the functioning of our own cognitive processes, and perhaps, not inconceivably, to insights regarding structures as well.

In Britain, and in all other countries, most teachers of deaf children are normally-hearing people. There is no way in which these teachers can reprogramme themselves to "think" like their pupils. But even if they could, they would not at present know what the new programme should be. There are many excellent accounts of what it is like, socially, to be born deaf. There are few accounts of what it is like cognitively. Communication between teacher and pupil remains therefore on an *ad hoc* basis where a few assumptions that communication has occurred are acceptable in the way that, between hearing people, they are taken for granted. It is of the utmost importance that we do try to gain more understanding of how the deaf think – that is, the nature of the medium. In the case of hearing people we cannot evade the compelling role of internal speech. But this does not mean that our basic paradigm is a comparison of deaf and hearing children. On appropriate occasions we shall inevitably refer behaviour of deaf children to that of the hearing. But this study is concerned with cognitive processes of deaf children.

In the preceding pages we have commented critically on some of the assumptions which have governed much of the research on cognitive function in the deaf. If invalid assumption underlies an experimental procedure, questions posed in that experiment are likely to be logically invalid as well as of doubtful psychological worth. What follows is a descriptive and analytic study which tries to demarcate the limits within which we can usefully talk about presence or absence of internal speech in deaf children. Our main thrust will be to examine the extent to which education of deaf children develops in them the ability to think orally – which it claims – and to examine the consequences of the outcome for academic achievement. The result of this enquiry will force us to question the basic theoretical assumptions of educational practice, and to suggest the possibility that current forms of pedagogic intervention may irreversibly impair cognitive growth. Finally, we shall discuss implications of a programme based on a bilingual mode of instruction which would permit optimum use both of intact as well as of defective sensory systems.

The impact of an educational philosophy conjured by people enriched with the gift of hearing, upon pupils for whom auditory experience of speech may have the status only of legend, challenges intellectual curiosity. This is truly a divide of immense proportions. Yet the bridging of it is so compelling of our compassion that major enquiry seems totally justified.

2

The Deaf School Leavers of England and Wales

Educational principles

In the previous chapter we discussed what we see as the main hazards in the use of deaf subjects to clarify ancient problems of the relationship of speech to thinking. In particular we suggested that the presumption of deafness also being internal dumbness requires critical and detailed analysis. In this chapter we present a description of the population of deaf children that we used to initiate this analysis. For reasons which we shall set out, such analysis cannot be supported by the familiar few dozen subjects of the conventional studies of more limited scope. The following description therefore provides not only the usual required account of subject characteristics, but what is, as well, a substantial biological picture of the deaf children of England and Wales as it is seen in those children who are just ending their formal education.

The principal thrust of our enquiry is concerned with the role of internal speech in the cognitive performance of deaf children. Once this main variable is under control, large samples of subjects would not really be required. Without doubt, simple relationships where confounding effects of other variables might be assumed to be small could be clarified using no more than a few dozen subjects. But in a sense, leaving it at that could lead to a situation where we knew that internal speech was of major significance for the deaf, but had no idea of the factors determining which deaf children did, and which did not develop it. To complete the study in a manner which would provide both a theoretical statement and an evaluation of the pedagogic significance of that statement, we also need, were it possible, a description of the

distribution of internal speech in the deaf population we are study-
ing. This requires a far larger study than the simple elucidation of
relationships. Either we need to be certain of achieving a small but
genuinely representative sample, or we need to consider a complete population. In fact, we lacked the resources, not to mention
the will, to absorb the entire population of deaf schoolchildren in
the study. In any case it is unlikely that doing so would add much
more than the contribution of a single variable, namely age; a
variable of interest, but lacking the force of anything that can be
modified by educational procedure or could contribute more substantially to theoretical knowledge.

Once it became clear that for practical reasons an age constraint
was necessary, the choice of population was almost self-
determining. We chose school-leavers. There was a most appropriate reason for this.

A century has passed since an international conference on the
education of the deaf (Congress of Milan, 1880) formally agreed
that speech, including reception of speech by auditory or visual
means, would provide the best educational opportunites for deaf
children. In varying degree the Western world modelled its organization and practice for educating deaf children on this basic principle. The specific pedagogic philosophy was not new. It had
slowly developed as a possibility over several centuries. What was
new was the formality and the enthusiasm which in the course of
time led directly to significant changes which were structural as
well as organizational. For example, in Britain it has effectively
been impossible for a very deaf person, regardless of the cause or
onset age of deafness, to become qualified as a teacher of the deaf.
Furthermore, at the time of writing, only one college which trains
teachers of the deaf began in 1977 to offer an optional course in
manual communication. In 1947 the 1880 Congress decision contributed to the massive reorganization of deaf education in Britain
represented by the establishment, and rapid growth, of special Partially Hearing Units (PHUs). The key feature of this change was
that the PHUs were located, not in the Special Schools for the Deaf,
but in the ordinary schools attended by normally-hearing children.
Part, at least, of this reorganization was to permit deaf children to
participate in some of the educational activities of hearing children.

All countries which had well-organized educational systems and
advanced social programmes shifted the emphasis of their educational philosophies with respect to the deaf to "oralism". In Bri-

tain this was particularly true. Lewis (1968), summarizing the evidence of a governmental enquiry into the use of manual communication in the education of the deaf, reported that signing was "never" used by 85% of nursery and infant schools, 80% of junior schools, and 67% of secondary schools. Lewis made no comment on the paradox that as the children proceeded through the stages of oral education, teachers increasingly resorted to signing. In a more recent *Memorandum* (1972), the National College of Teachers of the Deaf* – the principal professional organization of teachers of the deaf in Britain – spelled out that, " . . . some profoundly or severely deaf children who are also mentally handicapped may find their only means of communication in some simple system of signs" (p. 10). This cautiously worded statement has no other interpretation than that deaf children who are otherwise normal – and we shall show that this is a very high proportion – should be educated orally.

For many decades now this policy has been reflected in practice. Without qualified teachers trained to teach other than orally, it could hardly have been otherwise. This was not just an idiosyncratic or autocratic decision by a small, if influential, group of teachers. The central Government education authority had itself precluded deaf persons from qualifying as ordinary teachers certificated to teach in any school – and one sees the logic of this. The National College of Teachers of the Deaf sprang the trap by insisting that only already qualified teachers could become qualified teachers of the deaf. Britain therefore is representative of those countries which took up the challenge of the decisions of the Congress of Milan. But there has never been an objective and quantitative evaluation of the outcome of this remarkably homogeneous educational system, with unimpeded practice backed by formalized philosophy and tightly controlled teacher training. This is especially striking since again and again the aims and outcomes of the education of normal children have been under scrutiny, most recently by Bullock (1975). It is not intended to imply that teachers of the deaf have been, or are, complacent. There is much evidence to the contrary. It seems simply that pressure to evaluate, and interest in it, has not been present or at least sufficiently forceful.

* In 1977, the National College of Teachers of the Deaf and the Society of Teachers of the Deaf amalgamated to form the British Association of Teachers of the Deaf (BATOD).

Our study therefore was launched with a dual purpose. First, to provide conventional performance descriptions, describing levels attained with reference to whatever criteria seemed available and appropriate. Second, to assess the degree to which children appeared to use internal speech, to determine factors which contribute to this, and examine associations between use of internal speech and other test performance. We wished to know what proportion of deaf children were using internal speech, how they came to use it when others might not, and whether or not they benefitted particularly with respect to certain communication skills. In pursuing these aims we examined about 600 children.

The subject population

Age

Since it was not our intention to carry out an immense longitudinal study embracing children of all ages, a definable and logically defensible subsection of population was sought. In view of the foregoing discussion on evaluation we felt that the most felicitous moment to give tests would be at the end of school life, the time when the compulsory period of education was ending. Indeed, for most children this would mark the end of all formal education. Initially we defined our target population in that way: school-leavers. But it became clear very early on that in some schools brighter children were continuing their secondary education beyond the minimum required age of sixteen. This would have been irrelevant for those parts of the study concerned with examining relationships. Where, for example, we are concerned with the role of nonverbal intelligence in reading, it would matter little whether subjects were aged fifteen, sixteen, or eighteen. But if we wished, as we did, to make a statement about levels of reading ability, then not only would it be uninformative to include in a single grouping children of widely disparate age, but it would be misleading to include a group of self-selected older children who might also be more intelligent. We therefore modified the criteria defining which children should be included in the study. With respect to age, this now became 15–16½ years at the time of testing. All children represented in the account which follows may be taken to fall within that age range, but with a margin of error in a very few cases of no more than a month or two.

Size and nature of sample

In trying to follow later sections, readers may be confused and perhaps concerned by the fact that, although we tested a single and defined population of children, different numbers of children appear to be represented in different tabulations and other expressions of results. There are a number of reasons for this.

One simple reason is that children could not be expected to complete the entire battery of tests in a single day. It would therefore have been quite possible for a particular group of children, characterized by some unknown factor, to have evaded being tested after the first day. Children are adept at this. But we would have no means of knowing whether evasion of this kind was randomly distributed in our population. Nor could we distinguish this behaviour from everyday sickness or other legitimate absence. We were well aware that children might pass on to each other information – and opinion – about the tests we gave and that this could, haphazardly, affect "show-up" rate. In the event, about 4% of the final population missed one or, at most, two tests, other than those concerned with assessing internal speech. Anyone who missed the latter tests was removed from the study. But we were reluctant to abandon potentially useful information. A child who had done a reading test, but missed the lip reading test, nevertheless provided a unit of information about reading by the deaf. Such a child would be represented in a tabulation of reading results, but obviously not one of lip reading. This kind of discrepancy would only occur with descriptive results, and the quantitative description of one variable could be based on a slightly different number of children than might another.

The less than simple explanation depends on the nature of the difference between performance and relationship. A description of performance such as reading ability is only of value when the population whose performance is described is clearly defined. The population might be "deaf children aged 15–16½ years", or "deaf children aged 10 to 11 years who live in an even-numbered house", or "deaf children whose favourite colour is green", or "deaf children who like cats but not apples". All of these categories define populations and therefore have descriptive value – if not always great intrinsic interest. The practical value of describing the reading ability of such groups becomes a matter of opinion which depends on our special interests. But if a good enough reason could be found, it would be scientifically legitimate to do so, so long as either all children in the defined categories were included in the results, or a strictly representative sample of them were.

But suppose we wished to compare – as we will – the reading ability of children in residential Schools for the Deaf with that of children being educated in Partially Hearing Units, our interest being in type of education. We are interested in performance, but only insofar as it clarifies the relationship between groups. We could present the average reading ability of the total population of each group and test whether the difference was statistically significant. But the result would have little scientific value. We cannot ignore the possibility (a) that the children in residential Schools have greater hearing loss than children in PHUs, and (b) that reading ability might be related to degree of deafness. If PHU children had the higher reading scores, we would not know whether it was because they were less deaf, or whether it was something to do with the kind of education provided by PHUs.

There were at least two ways of overcoming this difficulty, and either will be used according to the particular problem and the nature and availability of data. The first is to handle the problem statistically. There are convenient methods for comparing (e.g.) reading ability but taking level of hearing loss into account. Generally, using this method, we need to have a measure both of reading and of deafness for each child. Then, depending on the variables of interest, the numbers of children involved might vary slightly.

The problem can also be handled empirically. If we have reason to assume that PHU children might be less deaf than residential-school children, and that this might affect reading ability, we can match pairs of children. Each PHU child can be paired randomly with a residential-school child but of the same level of hearing loss. We do this exhaustively for preference, so that we establish as many pairs as the data permit. So far as hearing loss is concerned, we can then regard the two groups as equivalent, and any effects of reading that were found could not be ascribed to degree of deafness. The number of children represented in the results will depend on the number of appropriate matches that can be achieved. This of course will depend on the nature of the variables, and the way the variables occur in the two – or more – populations.

There is a third reason why numbers of children might vary from one calculation to another, and which should best be ascribed to maladministration of the research programme. After we had completed testing in the first two Schools, we decided to add a second test of speech quality to the one initally used. We do not have this second measure for 22 children. This will provide another minor source of discrepant numbers in calculations which involve this particular variable.

In all descriptive studies, which in part this is, the population described must be representative of the population of interest. This may not always be easy to achieve, and the results will be invalid to the extent that it is not achieved. There may be insoluable administrative reasons – like cost for instance, or time. While this is understandable, it will nevertheless incur a risk of yielding unrepresentative results, which will only safely represent the population actually tested and which may then not be easily amenable to reliable definition. Again, when for whatever reasons the description has to be based on a partial sample, the researcher may not know all of the variables relevant to the performance variables, and may therefore inadvertently ignore them in sampling. For example, a study which omitted children in rural areas, perhaps because they were costly to reach, might just survive a validity test if the question concerned reading habits, but would certainly fail it were eating habits being assessed.

In studies of deaf children in England and Wales there is however a further, hard to evaluate, hazard if the children of the study are older than eleven years. Two selective Schools absorb the brightest children by competitive examination at the age of eleven. Between them they accept about 13% of all of the prelingually deaf children in the Special Schools. Any descriptive study which only samples (after age eleven) from any, or even all, of the remaining Schools will have a biased population which will not represent deaf schoolchildren. Any study which includes the two selective Schools and does not include most of the remaining Schools as well will also be sampling a biased population – with the bias in the other direction. This section of as great as 13% of a population is far too large to be ignored. A number of studies have this built-in defect and we shall refer to them in the relevant chapters.

From what we have said above, it was clearly necessary to aim at total coverage of the target population. But from the outset we felt that two Schools and one department of another School should in fact be excluded. There are two residential Schools in Britain which respectively cater solely for children who are too emotionally disturbed or too severely multiply handicapped to be placed in the normal Schools for deaf children. A third School has a separate department of severely multiply handicapped children. All of these children were excluded. Many of them are unable to attempt a conventional school curriculum and would have been untestable for that reason alone. Test scores that we could have satisfactorily obtained could not logically have been regarded as normal population scores. There were 33 such children of the relevant age. Three other schools did not participate. One with only three children of appropriate age had to be abandoned for administrative reasons. A second small School was already occupied with a research project, and the education authority was unwilling to involve the children in another. The third, medium-sized School declined. We were greatly encouraged therefore by the fact that of 42 Schools approached response ranged from acceptance to enthusiasm in every case but one, perhaps reflecting the feeling of educators themselves that not enough was factually known about the abilities of deaf school leavers. The response from PHUs was very similar. Almost every Unit which had children of the age we sought agreed to permit us to test.

Children in Britain who are deaf – itself a word without sharp definition, especially at low levels of hearing impairment – may be found in three different kinds of educational establishment: Schools for the Deaf or Partially Hearing, Partially Hearing Units – to which we have referred – and ordinary classes in ordinary schools for hearing children. There is, in effect, no reliable way of counting the number of children in the last category since the distinction between deafness and normal hearing is not audiologically distinct. One arbitrary description would be: children considered by education authorities to have some identified degree of hearing impairment. At the outset, we had to decide whether or not to include such children in the study, and decided not to. This was essentially an administrative rather than a scientific decision. Hearing-impaired children are such regardless of the kind of school they are in. However we foresaw a disproportionate expenditure of research effort. Some of this would go in testing children with only a very slight and barely handicapping hearing loss. More important perhaps was a different group. In previous studies, we had frequently been told about children said to be "very" deaf, but who had achieved such oral success that they were able to profit from nonspecial education. Clearly, not to include such children would – were they numerous – have seriously biased the nature of our population. Accordingly, we polled a random 50% sample of Local Education Authorities, asking the question: How many children aged 15–16½ years with an average hearing loss of 70 dB or more and who were deafened before the age of three years, are you educating in ordinary schools? The value of 70 dB was arbitrary. Our own subsequent analyses would have suggested a cut-off of 65 dB to be more useful. Every authority replied. On average, one such child was reported per two authorities. This would mean a national total of about 70–75. Since the effort required to test these geographically widely scattered children would have added little to our principal scientific objectives, we excluded them from the study. To that extent, the descriptive aspects are incomplete. But, as we shall see from the levels of hearing loss of children in PHUs, the number of profoundly deaf children in ordinary schools would hardly reach double figures for the whole country.

In all the Schools for the Deaf and Partially Hearing in England and Wales, and excluding those we have mentioned, we found 445 children who met the sole criterion of being aged 15–16½ at the time of testing. In PHUs we found 128 such children. There are in Britain many more PHUs for children aged 5–11 years than for those older than 11 years. This reflects official policy (Department of Education and Science, 1967). Children in PHUs at the age of 11 years are assessed. Some are considered suitable for transfer to ordinary schools, some are considered to be in need of special education in Schools for the Deaf, and some remain in the PHU system. An effect of this is to increase the secondary-age School population and to decrease the secondary-age PHU population. This is reflected in the numbers of children given above.

Lewis (1968) provides some relevant demographic data for Britain covering a number of years. Interpretation of trends is confused by two opposing effects. On one hand, medical diagnosis is becoming increasingly effective in revealing the presence of deafness, while on the other hand, medical advances are reducing the true incidence. The net outcome is a steady (to 1967 at least) increase both in the proportion and in the absolute numbers of deaf schoolchildren. As one would expect, the greatest increase is for those in ordinary schools, where minor hearing impairment is increasingly recognized. The proportion of all schoolchildren of all ages who are in Special Schools seems to be fairly constant at about four per 10,000 – that is some 3,000 children. In 1967 the all-age ratio for PHU children was about the same. But for the reasons given, these proportions would not be true at age 15. Our population of 445 pupils aged 15–16½ is clearly well within expectation, and we assume this is to be true for PHU children as well. Recently, Tucker (1978), drawing on published statistics assessed the ratio of children in Special Schools and PHUs to be about nine per 10,000 schoolchildren. This latter population is about six million. In other words, when we describe our sample as being close to 100%, we cannot be far out.

At the time of testing, there were 80 PHUs of secondary level in England and Wales. A number of these catered only for deaf children with other severely handicapping conditions. Two or three PHUs declined to collaborate in the study; 22 had no pupils at the time who met the age criterion. Testing then was carried out in 48 different PHUs. Tables 2.1a and 2.1b reflect the varying sizes of School and PHU classes. Two Schools each had more than 21 children of the required age, whereas 19 of the PHUs each had only a single such child, and, as we have said, 22 had none at all.

Table 2.1a Size of Schools for the deaf

No. of children per School aged 15–16½ years	1–5	6–10	11–15	16–20	21+
No. of Schools	8	10	11	7	2

Table 2.1b Size of Partially Hearing Units

No. of children per PHU aged 15–16½ years	0	1	2	3	4	5	5+
No. of PHUs	22	19	12	5	5	3	4

Although we tested 445 children in Schools and 128 in PHUs, almost all of the description which follows is based on a somewhat smaller "basic" population. With respect to Schools, a total of 86 children have been removed from all descriptions, for one or more of the following four reasons:

1   We excluded 42 children who became deaf after their third birthday. This is an arbitrary but conventional cut-off for distinguishing prelingual from adventitious deafness. It contains the assumption that a child who can hear for the first three years of life learns enough language through hearing to give him a noticeable linguistic advantage. Since our population included a few children who had normal hearing for many years – and this was often reflected in their school achievements – we followed usual practice in excluding them. They are discussed further in Chapter 9. This value of 9% postlingually deafened children accords well enough with that of 7% given by Ries and Voneiff (1974) for a large USA population.

2   Eighteen children were excluded because English was not the language spoken at home. Either the children or their parents were recent immigrants from non-English-speaking countries.

3   For 16 children, we could not obtain sufficient information about their medical, family, or educational histories. This was usually because these were immigrant children who arrived in Britain already of school age and deaf.

4   We met 10 children who, for a variety of reasons, were untestable.

This left a basic sample of 359 School children forming the population we describe.

On the same principle, 19 children were removed from the population of 128 PHU children who were tested, as follows:

1   There were 11 children deafened after their third birthday.

2   Five children were not from English-speaking homes.

3   For three children there was insufficient historical information.

No PHU child was untestable and the sample numbered 109.

Summarizing the nature of this population of 468, they represent almost all usable children aged 15–16½ receiving Special education and regardless of hearing loss. They are all prelingually deafened and are not sufficiently severely multiply handicapped to be placed outside of the general school provision for the deaf. All of them have English as mother-tongue – and this is taken to include those from homes where signing is the normal mode of communication.

Data collection

The testing programme was initiated by means of a fairly detailed letter to schools and PHUs explaining the purpose of the study, the nature of the tests, and what would be involved in terms of child-time and school-effort. This was followed by a personal visit by the author to every School and to a good many PHUs as well. The actual collection of data covered the period from June 1974– June 1976, so that dates of birth of the subjects ranged from 1958– 1961.

All testing was supervised by a psychologist who remained at the school and collaborated with administration of tests. Otherwise all the testing was carried out by qualified teachers of the deaf. If 'there were any problems with children refusing to be tested, or with problems of discipline which might have been expected from what were in fact young men and women, they were so few as to be now quite forgotten. Some tests such as lip reading were of course carried out individually. Otherwise groups varied from 1–5 in size, but nevertheless individual instruction was the rule. Since, in almost all cases, two members of the research team were present, supervision was rigorous. This was required more to ensure that subjects continued to follow the test instructions than to obviate collusion – which was attempted remarkably rarely. Test instructions were normally given in speech. Signing and pantomime were freely used when necessary, and of particular value was the assistance given when one child clearly understood the spoken instructions and was able to translate for those who had not. The ultimate safeguards that children had understood what the test required of them resided in the simplicity of the tests, the simplicity of the instruction, the ample amount of pretest practice, and the continuous supervision. School staff were never required and were never present except very rarely as observers. Depending on the number of available children, testing was completed in two–four days per school.

As well as test results, personal information was collected both by discussion with school authorities and from records in collaboration with school staff. We wanted as much information relevant to the enquiry as possible – without being certain in advance what would be relevant – and we wanted the information to be "objective". We were greatly helped by having available the experience of Redgate (1972), reported in his study of the use of the Initial Teaching Alphabet with young deaf children. Some items, like audiograms, were self-evident. But no doubt there are many aspects of the children's background or personality which may have been relevant to their school performance but which we ignored. These were data where we felt either that only inadequate measuring instruments were available, or that the information was beyond our technical competence, or that it was too subjective. Readers may be disappointed at some of the gaps which might have led to the loss of interesting or valuable relationships. But we felt it was essential that we ourselves should have complete confidence in the "quality" of the data we did collect on each child. This, with a few minor exceptions, we achieved.

It is perhaps worthwhile at this point to join in comment on the widespread inadequacy of school records. This is not just a British weakness; Wilson, Rapin, Wilson and vanDenburg (1975) in the USA have also made this point. To cite a particularly serious example, out of 445 children in Schools who were available for testing, no audiogram at all existed for 12 of them. In no fewer than 74 cases, we have had to depend on an audiogram which was more than two years old. For prelingually deaf children, one might be safe to assume that in fact there would have been little change in hearing loss between the age of, say, fourteen and sixteen years. But in terms of school practice, it is not easily defensible. Barely 50% of audiograms were less than one year old. The significance of this is not too critical for this study. But in terms of the cardinal precepts for good oral education (Fry, 1966; 1975) the chance that a child will be using a less than appropriate hearing aid is high. Medical history is not the responsibility of schools, but we were distressed just the same at the poverty of the information frequently available to school authorities. One of the more piquant examples was that of a child whose school record indicated that his mother was "dead". In fact the mother was – deaf ! But it would be unbalanced not to record that school heads did have a gratifyingly deep knowledge of family circumstances which was frequently of great value to us in trying to understand paradoxical results in some individuals.

Audiometric characteristics and problems

In this study, we make the assumption that, in reporting on school achievements of deaf school leavers, results will need to be assessed with reference also to degree of deafness and to some extent to medical history. These are characteristics, unique to themselves, that children beginning their school life already have. Nothing that the school can do will alter the fact that deafness is, for example, postmeningitic. If academic attainments are affected by this fact, it is one which will be present throughout school life, and untouched by school programmes.

For most children, this is equally true of their level of hearing impairment. Techniques of auditory training may help children to make better use of the hearing they do have, and this may even show in a changed shape of audiogram. Like many other forms of intervention, little is known about the conditions for effecting such benefit. Some teachers have greater success than others; some children appear to benefit more than others; many children seem not to benefit at all. The true effects of auditory training are hard to establish with confidence (Bench and Murphy, 1977). Although early audiograms which may be prepared at varying ages need to be treated with extreme caution, for our School population we have been able to compare earliest with latest for some 300 children. Only in 11 cases can we find evidence of marked change (that is, 30 dB or more) in the pure-tone audiogram in the direction of better hearing. Even this could be no more than chance, since in 14 cases the change in audiogram from earliest to latest was in the other direction. Doubtless objections may be made to this superficial analysis. But it would border on delusion to assume that the 90% of assessable audiograms which show no change nevertheless do, in substantial numbers, conceal a beneficial effect of auditory training. It is reasonable to argue that conventional auditory training is aimed at improving hearing of speech rather than pure tones. It is a fact, though, that formal testing of speech hearing is exceedingly rare in Schools and there can be little evidence from records that improvement is common. We must accept that most pure-tone audiograms change little during school life.

Even in Special Schools, degree of hearing impairment varies greatly from one child to another. Particularly in comparing children's school attainment or ability to communicate this difference has to be taken into account just as much as does age. It would be meaningless to say that schoolchildren have difficulty handling sentences in the passive voice without also qualifying the statement by age. In similar vein, it is meaningless to say that deaf children have quite intelligible (or unintelligible) speech, without qualifying by degree of deafness. Any descriptors such as "the deaf", unless used in an evidently general way, are invariably misleading.

Because it is cumbersome, and frequently not possible, to refer to a child by an exact degree of hearing loss – and within narrow limits not very useful – more general descriptions have often been used. While there is widespread agreement about the kind of nomenclature which might be useful, there is much less agreement about the degree of deafness which is implied. There is for example fairly broad, though not universal, agreement that deaf people may usefully be classified by the terms *partial* (or *moderate*), *severe,* and *profound.* These terms appear to be self-explanatory, and there is no doubt that they are convenient if used with a good deal of caution.

But generally when the terms are used there is an implication that they do refer to a quantitative degree of hearing loss – an amount of deafness. Since there has never been an agreed standard definition of the degree of deafness of, for instance, a *severely* deaf person, inevitably authorities have interpreted terms idiosyncratically. A few examples will suffice. *Severe* deafness has been variously described:

O'Neill and Oyer (1970) . . . . .greater than 60 dB

Davis (1960) . . . . .60–90 dB

Dale (1967) . . . . .65–95 dB

Delk (1973) . . . . .70–90 dB

Numerous other variants can be found in the literature for this, and for the terms *partial* and *profound.* But it is probably fair to say that, for everyday use, those concerned with the deaf have a fairly good and common idea about the kind of person designated in this way. It is rather like describing something as *yellow.* The term is not very exact, but we can distinguish it from *red.*

But because these terms are imprecise labels, and because degree of hearing loss affects many kinds of performance and cognitive operation, rather more exact descriptions are required for scientific purpose. Hearing loss, usually with respect to pure tones, is measured in decibels (dB), where 0 dB represents theoretically normal hearing. But because the decibel scale is logarithmic, it cannot be handled statistically in the same way as, for instance, height or reaction time. A reaction time of 0.5 seconds is twice as fast as one of 1.0 seconds and half as fast as one of 0.25 seconds. But one person with a hearing loss of 100 dB, though deafer, cannot be said to be twice as deaf as another with a 50 dB loss. For present purposes the only significance of this is that it affects the kinds of statistical treatments of data that are appropriate. This in turn constrains the way that the hearing-loss variable can usefully be described. There are no general difficulties involved in this and common practice is to refer to an individual's hearing loss as falling within one of a number of dB bands. In other words, a more precise way of using terms like *severe* but without using imprecise verbal labels. In this case, there is no need for standardized dB bands. Each researcher is legitimately free to choose his own according to the nature of the population under investigation, and the objectives of the study. All that matters is that conventional rules of scientific reporting should be maintained. There are good reasons for this.

If statistical analysis of data with deafness as a variable is to be carried out, then "quantity" of deafness must be specified. But, in some ways more important, the researcher has an obligation to describe the subjects of his study in such a way that other researchers can – if they wish – exactly repeat the study. Specification of dB bands within which subjects fall is one way of doing just this with respect to hearing loss. In some instances, where it might only be necessary to indicate that the subjects were deaf rather than normally hearing, it may suffice to say that all subjects had a hearing loss greater than x dB, and trust that readers will agree that the limit is valid. But when different deaf populations are to be compared with respect to their differing degree of hearing loss (i.e., when deafness itself is a variable), then subjects will need to be allocated to one of two of more groupings defined in terms of different dB ranges. The present study used five such dB bands as follows:

–65 dB
66 – 85 dB
86 – 95 dB
96 – 105 dB
greater than 106 dB

In determining the specific range to be covered by each of these bands, the fact that the 66–85 dB band is "wider" than the 86–95 dB band is of little consequence. What principally matters is that children falling in the latter band are all deafer than those in the former – that is, within the limits of accuracy of audiological measurement.

Essentially the subdivision of a decibel scale is an arbitrary matter of tactics. If there is a postulate that hearing loss is likely to affect performance in some way, then the dB subdivisions must be small enough to detect trends in performance with respect to hearing loss. On the other hand, it is always important to ensure that there is a sufficiently large number of subjects in each band to ensure that appropriate statistical analysis can be carried out. But in a sense this means that subdivisions have to be decided upon before the underlying postulate about performance has been tested. One way round this has been discussed by one of our collaborators (Kyle, 1977a). There is wide agreement (Ling, 1976; Smith, 1973) that speech quality is closely related to degree of hearing impairment. Accordingly Kyle used our own data on speech intelligibility, which will be reported on extensively in Chapter 8, to find the most suitable compromise.

Kyle examined degree of deafness in relation to speech intelligibility to see how narrow hearing-loss bands had to be before no difference could be detected with confidence. The outcome of his analysis gave the subdivisions shown above. In all subsequent presentation of data and results we shall employ this classification of hearing loss.

One other topic concerned with the use of audiograms to indicate degree of deafness merits discussion, in order to avoid a possible if minor source of confusion. A given value of dB is an average of a number of values. The ability to hear pure tones, which is the basis of audiometry, is tested at several frequencies. These are described in cycles per second, representing different levels of pitch – whether the pure tone is a high or low one. Frequency or pitch is more usually described in Hertz (Hz), and in the case of suspected or known hearing impairment the degree of loss is generally examined at several frequency values known to represent the main frequencies found in speech sounds. As with hearing-loss bands, there is no theoretical limit to the number of such points at which hearing might be tested. Commonly both in Britain and elsewhere, for medical diagnosis as well as for educational prognosis, hearing is tested at the frequencies: 250, 500, 1000, 2000, 4000 Hz. The values of hearing loss at these frequencies form the picture which we know as the audiogram. But when – as we will – we talk about a hearing loss of x dB, this is the average of the hearing losses recorded at those five frequencies. We simply add up and divide by five.

An important study by Fletcher (1929) suggested that averaging over the three middle frequencies of 500, 1000, 2000 Hz was just as effective an indicator of hearing loss for most practical purposes. Researchers, in referring to the hearing losses of their subjects, sometimes specify whether the dB values they cite are averages of three or five frequencies. Although a three-frequency average is probably more widely used today, we have preferred to use five-frequency averages. This is not just perverseness.

The Kyle (1977a) study we have mentioned examined the predictive value of all of the various possible combinations that can be obtained from five frequency-values of hearing loss with respect to speech intelligibility. He found that while it is true that most of the predictive information can be derived from averaging the frequencies 500, 1000, 2000, nevertheless significantly more information is obtained when the frequencies 250 or 4000 are added. Since this extra information was invariably available to us in the audiograms provided from school records, we saw no reason to discard it and there was good reason to use it: and so we have.

This appears to lead to an unfortunate anomaly, but which in fact is more apparent than real. Since audiograms are rarely symmetrical around the middle value of 1000 Hz, the average of five frequencies may present a different degree of deafness from an average of three frequencies for the same individual. However, examination of a large sample of audiograms indicates that in fact the difference is generally small. We have found that averaging samples of as few as 10 audiograms in this way gives differences of only 2–3 dB. This is small enough to ignore.

Quite apart from the question of how to obtain an average hearing-loss value from the different frequencies that may be available, one further problem remains. It is well within the bounds of possibility to find two children with the following audiograms:

	250	500	1,000	2,000	4,000 Hz
A	80	80	80	80	80 dB
B	40	60	80	100	120 dB

Whether we average across three or across five frequencies, both child A and child B will have an average hearing loss of 80 dB. But it is evident that the shapes of the audiograms differ markedly. Not only might this suggest different medical histories (Department of Education and Science, 1967; O'Neill and Oyer, 1970) but it could also suggest that the two children might have different auditory perception. Child B has much better low-frequency hearing which would give an advantage in detecting rhythms in continous speech, but has almost no hearing for high frequencies and great difficulty in discriminating many consonants. Each child would auditorally receive very different aspects of speech, and this in turn would affect the quality of their own speech. But both are described as having a hearing loss of 80 dB.

A number of schemes have been suggested in attempts to minimize this problem. One of the more thorough has been proposed by Risberg and Mártony (1972). Based on the relationship of hearing loss at different frequencies to perception of speech sounds, 20 categories of deafness were set up ranging from A1–D5. The letter designates hearing loss in the low frequencies up to 1000 Hz, and the numeral hearing loss in the higher frequencies. Thus a child described as A1 would have a slight hearing loss at all frequencies. An A5 child would have a slight loss at the low frequencies, but a great loss at the high ones. Had it been practically possible to allocate the large numbers of audiograms that we had to a relatively small number of these groupings, we would have had a unique advantage. Although within each grouping average hearing loss might have varied substantially, children within a group could be assumed to have approximately the same hearing for speech, but discriminably different from those in other groups, some of whom could have had the same average hearing loss. In practice we found that 15 different groups were needed to allocate all of the children in this study – far too many for useful statistical analysis. We therefore followed the more conventional – if somewhat less satisfactory – course, allocating children to one of the five dB bands referred to on the basis of a five-frequency average of the latest available audiogram.

One point should be noted in the calculation of average hearing-loss values from the audiograms. When deafness at a particular frequency was so great that no audiometric response could be obtained, we followed convention and used a "value" of 120 dB for the purpose of averaging. Hine (1973) has a most useful discussion of this problem.

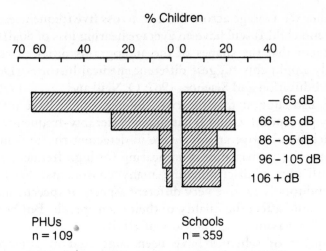

% Children

Figure 2.1.   *Distribution of hearing loss in Schools and PHUs.*

Figure 2.1 shows the number of children falling into each of the five hearing-loss bands and comprises all of the children used in the study. Of particular interest is the fact that the vast majority of children in PHUs are indeed partially hearing. It is all too often assumed that there are to be found in PHUs substantial numbers of children who are very deaf, but who nevertheless are able to benefit from opportunities for classroom integration with hearing children. The origins of what appears to be a myth lie in the official definition of partially hearing children as, "... pupils with impaired hearing whose development of speech and language, even if retarted, is following a normal pattern, and who require for their education special arrangements or facilities though not necessarily all the educational methods used for deaf pupils" (Department of Education and Science, 1967, p. 3). It will be noted that this definition makes no reference to levels of hearing loss, but is entirely in terms of theoretical assumptions regarding linguistic development. In educational circles, the term "partially hearing child" has become associated with the term "partially hearing unit". But the concepts have become confused because the above definition of a partially hearing child could, with no violation, include children with profound hearing loss. The idea then developed that there are in PHUs many children with profound hearing loss coping successfully. Figure 2.1 shows that this idea is without foundation. We shall discuss later the relative linguistic performance of children in Schools and in PHUs. But placement in PHUs is in fact largely in terms of measured hearing loss. In fact, not only do the majority of PHU children fall within the band of hearing loss which is less than 65dB, but even these are less deaf in general than schoolchildren in the same dB-band. Within this band, the median value of hearing loss of PHU children is 50 dB; for School children it is 58 dB.

We have pointed out what we believe to be the particular value of the classification of hearing loss described above. Other authors have different views. But published sets of hearing-loss data representing whole populations provide enough information to permit comparison. Figure 2.2 shows three such distributions together with our own data reorganized to match the other classifications. We have selected these distributions partly on the basis of availability, but also because they permit comparison with other countries, and with children in Britain more than a quarter of a century ago.

There is a notable similarity of the distribution we have found to that reported for the very large all-age sample in the USA. Differences from the New Zealand distribution may well be due more to sampling error than to a basic difference. A relatively small but all-age sample is likely to show exaggerated effects of specific epidemics and other disturbances to general trends. In comparing our present data with that reported by Murphy (1956) for all twelve-year old deaf UK children, it will be seen that the principal discrepancies are to be found amongst the partially hearing children. It seems not unlikely that, with the great changes that occurred in Britain as a consequence of the development of PHUs with its stress on integration into normal schools where possible, many of the children in Murphy's least-deaf group would today be in ordinary schools. In general it would seem that, over considerable amounts of time, and from one country to another, the distribution of hearing loss in schoolchildren shows striking similarity.

Of the 359 children in Special Schools – that is, excluding PHUs none of which are residential – 63% are boarders. Hine (1973), who examined the audiograms of some 80% of deaf children in Special Schools in England and Wales (and elsewhere in Great Britain), reported that deafer children were more likely to be found in residential Schools. Figure 2.3 fails to confirm this when children in residential Schools who attend on a daily basis but live at home are regarded as "day" pupils. Although the distributions are significantly different, no consistent trend is present. When the data are collapsed to form two hearing-loss groupings of 0–85 dB

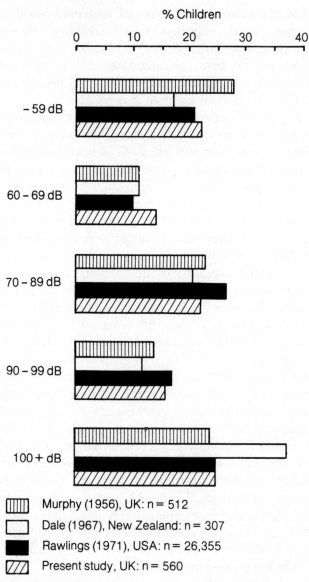

Figure 2.2.   Distribution of hearing loss in four populations.

and 86–120 dB, there is no difference in the proportions of day and residential pupils.

Causes of Deafness

There are two broad reasons for interest in causes of deafness. The

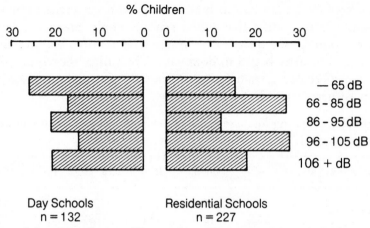

Figure 2.3.   Distribution of hearing loss of day and residential pupils.

first is concerned with epidemiology and with genetics. Our interest here is very indirect. But the second reason relates to school achievement, and we may legitimately wonder how far this is affected by the cause of the child's deafness. Not that we shall be able to throw much light on this. Our population is too small for other than some general groupings. Apart from presumed genetic cause, the single most numerous cause of deafness in our population is rhesus incompatibility. This accounts for a mere 6% of cases, and is closely followed numerically by maternal rubella and by prematurity of birth. Although, excepting genetic factors, we have an established cause of deafness for some 30% of the children we tested, this is divided amongst 10 different aetiologies. We shall therefore present only an abbreviated analysis of cause of deafness and leave the interested reader to pursue the matter in the many excellent accounts available (Fisch, 1964; Fraser, 1964, 1976; Konigsmark, 1971).

Table 2.2 shows the numbers of children in three categories of cause of deafness and according to hearing loss. Essentially we have used the nomenclature for classification discussed by Fraser (1964). "Hereditary" comprises those children who have one or both parents deaf and/or at least one deaf brother or sister. If a deaf child has a deaf parent or deaf sibling other than because of rhesus incompatibility, the chance that a genetic factor is involved must be very high. Certainly the category does not include all cases which Fraser would regard as hereditary. But allocation is quite clearly defined. We have not included children who have deafness elsewhere in the family, such as grandparents or uncles, aunts or cousins. It was clear that while schools could provide reliable information about deafness of immediate family, beyond that, guess and hearsay began to dominate. The values shown in Table 2.2 are therefore certain to be underestimates of the number of cases of hereditary deafness.

Table 2.2 Hearing loss and cause of deafness: percentage of children (n in brackets)

Hearing loss (dB)	–65	66–85	86–95	96–105	106+	
Hereditary	27.3 (35)	17.2 (22)	14.8 (19)	22.7 (29)	18.0 (23)	100 (128)
Acquired	34.7 (50)	27.1 (39)	6.9 (10)	18.8 (27)	12.5 (18)	100 (144)
Unidentified	27.0 (53)	26.0 (51)	15.8 (31)	16.3 (32)	14.8 (29)	100 (196)

It will be seen that hereditary deafness as we have defined it accounts for about 27% of the population we shall be reporting on in detail. Gentile and Rambin (1973) provide data on some 30,000 deaf children in the USA which indicate that about 30% of students are classifiable in this way. Clearly, for this category, Table 2.2 shows no marked trend with respect to degree of deafness. Profoundly deaf children are not more likely than partially hearing children to be born into deaf families. If hearing loss up to 85 dB is treated as a single group and compared with the remainder, then a just significant effect does show; but degree of deafness is not a major effect. Both our value of 27% and that reported by Gentile and Rambin are substantially below usually reported values for genetic causes of deafness of some 50% (Fraser, 1964; Konigsmark, 1971). But Ries and Voneiff (1974) estimate the incidence of hereditary deafness to be probably 45%. Konigsmark comments that not all inherited deafness is congenital, and a few of our excluded adventitiously deaf children may have inherited their deafness. More to the point though, we have taken a fairly stringent and restricted criterion of family deafness for the reasons given earlier, and then applied it to the Gentile and Rambin data, yielding the coincidence noted.

Particularly in the case of a recessive gene, and when a child has no siblings, no evident cause of deafness may reliably be available. Though of course this will not be the only reason why cause of deafness is not known. On the other hand, especially when deafness is perinatal – some 30% of nonhereditary deafness according to Fraser (1964) – the cause is hardly likely to pass undetected in Britain. An unknown proportion of the unidentified causes of deafness is therefore likely to be of genetic origin. In considering other descriptive features of our population, some evidence for this may be present. Certainly the value of 42% of the population for whom we have no identification of the cause of deafness is not too dissimilar from other reports (Fraser, 1964; Gentile and Rambin, 1973; Nordén, 1975). It might be noted that Fisch (1976) reported only 25% of congenital deafness in a British sample to be of unknown cause. But Fisch's sample of 600 children covered a period when there were two major rubella epidemics which accounted for the deafness of 24% of his population. This would distort the other proportions giving an unusually low incidence of "unknown cause". The present sample contains no more that 5% of children whose deafness is due to maternal rubella.

Table 2.2 shows that about 31% of children have some other identifiable and acquired cause of deafness. Of these about half are accounted for by rhesus incompatibility, rubella, and premature birth factors. Although no consistent trend with respect to hearing loss is present, 36% of all children with hearing loss less than 86 dB have acquired deafness. Of the children with a hearing loss greater than this, 25% have acquired deafness. This difference is significant at the 0.05* level. Furthermore, if we compare the distributions of hearing loss of the two populations for which we have a known cause of deafness, i.e., hereditary and acquired, there is a markedly significant difference (χ^2 = 16.01, p < .01). Evidently children with hereditary deafness are deafer than those whose deafness is acquired. This is a factor to which we shall have to remain alert when comparing the performance of different

---

* Readers who are not statistically minded may generally ignore all statistical statements expressed as values of χ^2, F or t. Test outcomes are also reduced to p-values. A p-value shown as p < 0.001 implies that the odds against the outcome of a particular statistical test occurring by chance would be not less than 1 in a 1000. This is a safe enough bet and regarded more formally as statistically highly significant. Throughout this study we regard odds of 1 in 20 (p < 0.05) to be the lowest acceptable. Significance levels below that are not taken to reflect genuine effects, and will be reported as not statistically significant.

groups, since cause of deafness does confound, to some extent with degree of deafness.

Little further can be said about the "unidentified" category. To the extent that it conceals children whose deafness is in fact inherited, we may find some evidence in other characteristics or in performance. But such evidence will be distorted to the extent that the designation is merely a reflection of poor recordkeeping.

One final comment on the relative frequency of various causes of deafness. We might wonder whether the different causes occur in the same proportions in Schools and in PHUs. For this analysis we have ignored hearing loss greater than 85 dB because there are so few such children in PHUs. Figure 2.4 shows for Schools and PHUs the percentages of children whose deafness is hereditary, acquired, or unidentified. There is in fact no significant difference between the two distributions ($\chi^2 = 2.13$, $p < 0.50$).

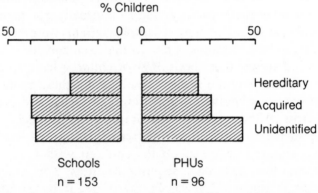

Figure 2.4.   Cause of deafness and schooling: children with hearing loss up to 85 dB.

Intelligence

What other "given" attributes should we consider? Some obvious ones like sex or multiple handicap we shall take up shortly. Intelligence is less confidently handled. We have a single data point for this. We gave an intelligence test as part of our battery. We do not know what score the child would have obtained ten years earlier. A number of factors which might lead to higher scores are known with some degree of certainty (Lynn, 1977), though none are alleged to result from educational procedures. Few authorities today will be found totally to reject environmental influences on

measured intelligence. But we know of no study that demonstrates a significant school influence on test scores, other than that
deriving from practice itself (Goetzinger et al., 1967; Heim, Wallace, and Cane, 1950).

On the contrary, virtually all studies which have made any
comparisons of the performance of groups of deaf children have
treated intelligence test scores as an independent variable which
needs to be controlled. We have done no more than follow this
convention. Erring then – if error it is – on the side of prudence
and convention, we have also regarded intelligence as "given", in
the same sense as cause of deafness is, or degree of deafness, or sex,
etc.

For many years now, there has been something of an obsession
with the question whether the distribution of intelligence in the
deaf is the same as that in the hearing. In some cases, such as the
review by Vernon (1967) which used the results from intelligence
tests to support a hypothesis concerning thinking, there was an
adequate theoretical reason. This was little concerned with the
nature of intelligence and its relationship to deafness. With respect
to the main question, we have to agree with Wilson et al. (1975)
that, " . . . a given IQ score is what a given IQ test measures, and
different tests will yield different IQs, particularly in a group of
atypical children" (p. 635). The literature appears to provide
ample support for this, though in fact very few studies can be said,
with certainty, to have tested strictly representative samples of
population. What appears to emerge is that some tests such as the
Wechsler Intelligence Scale for Children (WISC) show similar distributions for deaf and hearing children. Others such as the
Hiskey-Nebraska and Raven's Progressive Matrices do not
(Evans, 1960; Goetzinger et al., 1967; Hiskey, 1956; Levine and
Iscoe, 1955; Oléron, 1950). These tend to show the deaf to be of
lower intelligence when referred to norms for hearing children.
Or put in another, more accurate way, deaf children find these
particular tests relatively difficult. In fact, at the time of writing,
we know of only one "whole population" screening of deaf pupils
for intelligence. This is on some 20,000 students in the USA who
were given an unspecified nonverbal test. The 13,500 students
who were without additional handicap yielded a mean IQ of
100.1. Additional handicapping lowered IQ to 86.5 (Ries and
Voneiff, 1974), but it is likely that mental retardation was treated
as such a handicap.

Clearly we do have to recognize that different intelligence tests do involve different cognitive operations even when all of them are performance – or nonverbal – tests. Particularly if one is assessing the scores of deaf children, on tests such as reading, on the basis of hearing norms, it is convenient – and possibly important – that one should be able to assume that the deaf population has the same intelligence distribution as that of the hearing population on which the reading test was standardized. In our case this condition was outweighed by other considerations.

Faced with the decision to add a nonverbal intelligence test to our battery, the question was, which one? In a sense the problem solved itself. We wanted a test of accepted reliability, which had been standardized for British children of the appropriate age, and which could be administered easily to groups of children who might have little, or very poor, communication ability. Only two tests met these criteria – WISC and Raven's Matrices. Almost all children in schools for the deaf in Britain have at some time been given an intelligence test, and in the vast majority of cases, the test used was WISC. We were not willing to accept test scores from tests given by many different testers and in many different conditions. The element of uncertainty would have been unacceptable. But to have given WISC a second time – and in some cases a third time – would have violated a fundamental principle of intelligence testing. We had no choice therefore but to use Raven's Matrices in the edition of 1960. We have had no reason to regret this. No serious criticism of relevance to us has been levelled against this test; it correlates highly with other nonverbal tests (Burke, 1958; Goetzinger et al., 1967; Raven, 1960; Vincent and Cox, 1974; Wilson et al., 1975). We were never principally concerned with comparing deaf-hearing performance, and the reported distribution differences have been little more than an inconvenience. But we have no reason at all to doubt that differences amongst subjects in Raven score represent real differences in cognitive performance. The test has general acceptance as one of abstract or spatial reasoning (Goetzinger et al., 1967; Oléron, 1950; Raven, 1960). The only reason we felt unable to use the more specialized tests of intelligence of the deaf, such as the Leiter or the Snijders-Ooman, was that due to limitations on time.

The test, as were all others, was always given under the supervision of a psychologist. Instructions were given individually though children sometimes worked in groups of never more than

five. In practice we found the test extremely easy to give to profoundly deaf children, including some of very low intelligence.
Generally the instructions were given in speech and mime, following closely the procedure in the 1960 manual. Because the early
items are so easy, there was no difficulty in monitoring that the
instructions had in fact been understood. Errors occurred predict-
ably, and no child had fewer than nine items correct – and quite
evidently not due merely to random guessing.

Since the manual does not provide a conversion from raw score
to IQ, and since no effect of age could be expected, raw scores are
used in the tabulations and analyses which follow.

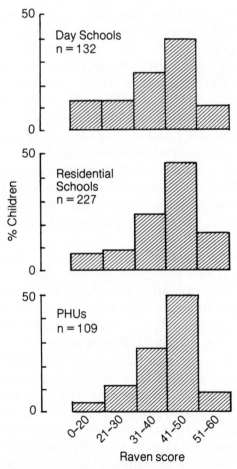

Figure 2.5.   Raven's Progressive Matrices and schooling.

The distribution of raw scores for all children (other than those whose exclusion has been referred to) is given in Appendix 1. This is summarized in Figure 2.5 according to schooling. Statistical test shows that the three distributions do not differ significantly. There appears to be no systematic allocation of children to a particular type of school based on intelligence, and insofar as performance differences may be found, this factor can fortunately be ruled out.

A number of studies have examined the relationship between nonverbal intelligence and degree of deafness. Almost all report that deafness is not a factor of significance. Montgomery (1968) also used Raven's Matrices and reported a correlation of 0.07. Evans (1960) reports a correlation for 50 children of 0.02 between the performance scale of WISC and hearing loss. Hine (1970) used WISC with 100 partially hearing children and found a correlation of 0.08 with intelligence. Oléron (1950) reported little effect and both Costello (1957) and Nordén (1975) gave Raven's Matrices to groups of deaf and hard-of-hearing children, finding no difference in mean score. One exception to this general result is a study by Rodda, Godsave, and Stevens (1974) who, using the Leiter International Performance Scale on 102 children, found a high negative correlation between IQ and hearing loss, and suggested that the Leiter test is biased against the deafer child. In point of theoretical fact, were there a well-established association between deafness and nonverbal IQ – as there is with deafness and verbal IQ – the implications would begin to ramify into assumptions about deafness and cognitive operation which would be most difficult to justify.

Our own results support the more general conclusion. Table 2.3 shows the mean raw score and standard deviation for Raven's Matrices according to hearing loss. Analysis of variance indicates that the apparent differences are chance effects and indeed no consistent trend is apparent ($F_{4,459} = 1.45$; $p > 0.05$). Profoundly deaf children are no less intelligent than those who are partially hearing, and we can safely regard the two variables as independent.

This is of immediate value in discussing the effect of cause of deafness on intelligence. Since we can now assume that degree of deafness is not a factor, in this analysis we are not obliged to break down our population into smaller and smaller parcels, and can present data based on "cause" alone. This is done in Table 2.4. It shows that children whose deafness is hereditary have significantly higher intelligence than either children whose deafness is acquired or those whose cause has not been identified (p < 0.02).

A statistical test may show that two variables are associated to a greater extent than would be expected by chance. The statistic itself, though, generally cannot indicate causal relationship. Often only speculative assessment can be made of this. So, in the present case, although statistically we have shown that children with hereditary deafness are more intelligent than those whose deafness is acquired, the statistic cannot distinguish between the possibilities that the cause of deafness determines intelligence, and that intelligence determines cause. But here, powerful *a priori* logic rejects the notion that it is intelligence which determines the cause of deafness and we therefore assume the reverse to be the case. As we shall see, decisions regarding the direction of established relationships will not always be so easily reached.

Table 2.3 Raven's Progressive Matrices and hearing loss (n = 464)

Hearing loss (dB)	–65	66–85	86–95	96–105	106+
Mean Raven score	39.2	40.8	41.0	40.3	37.4
Standard deviation	11.04	9.74	10.33	10.67	11.21

Table 2.4 Raven's Progressive Matrices and cause of deafness (n = 464)

	Mean Raven score	Standard deviation
Hereditary	42.0	9.09
Acquired	38.9	12.03
Unidentified	39.2	10.50

Sex

Fisch (1976) provides some data on the sex ratio – boys-girls – taken from the Registrar General's Statistical Reviews covering the period 1961–69 for England and Wales. For the population as a whole, there were 51.4% males. Fisch himself reported that in 1969, 56% of the 600 deaf children he saw who were born during that period were boys. Our own population, born a year or two earlier, has 53% boys. The difference between this value and that for the whole population is small, and offers little support for the popular legend that boys are more likely to be deaf than girls.

Referring to his sample, Fisch notes that girls are less likely to be partially hearing than boys. Table 2.5 shows the distribution of boys and girls according to hearing loss in our School and PHU population. Although a similar trend occurs, it is too slight to reach statistical significance ($\chi^2 = 0.69$). But as Fisch provides no information about the age of his population nor the basis for selection, special factors may be operating in his case. So far as our virtually total population of one age-group goes, we find deaf boys to be neither more nor less deaf than deaf girls.

Of the 600 children in his sample, Fisch reports 26% to be genetically deaf; the value we noted earlier for our School plus PHU population is 27%. But whereas Fisch finds these equally divided between the sexes, we find that 58% of the hereditary deaf children are boys – a value more in line with the 55% reported by Fraser (1976). Furthermore, of the 27 children in our population who have two deaf parents, no fewer than 22 are boys. Jensema and Mullins (1974) provide some data from a USA survey which show, this time in line with Fisch, hereditary deafness to be roughly equally divided between males and females, but do not isolate the case of children with two deaf parents. Without further evidence, the specific relationship between hereditary deafness and sex ratio remains unclear.

Table 2.5 Distribution of sex by hearing loss (%) (n = 468)

Hearing loss (dB)	–65	66–85	86–95	96–105	106+
Males	53	52	52	50	47
Females	47	48	48	50	53
	100	100	100	100	100

Are deaf boys and girls of equal intelligence? Montogomery (1968) tested 66 Scottish deaf children using Raven's Matrices and found boys to be significantly better. But Murphy (1956) found no difference using WISC and all the twelve-year old deaf children in England and Wales. Myklebust (1964) also reported no difference on the Chicago Nonverbal Intelligence Test, or on the perfor-

mance section of the Wechsler-Bellevue test. But in both of the
latter, numerically – though not statistically – boys had higher
scores. With hearing populations and using Raven's Matrice,
Court and Kennedy (1976) report that more studies show an
advantage for boys than for girls – but again the difference is not
great. Table 2.6 shows the mean Raven scores for boys and girls in
our population according to hearing loss. There is no difference
between boys and girls; nor is there a sex x hearing loss interaction. We have no reason to doubt that deaf boys and girls are of
equal intelligence, nor that degree of deafness is irrelevant.

Table 2.6   Mean score on Raven's Progressive Matrices and sex, by
hearing loss (n = 464)

Hearing loss (dB)	–65	66–85	86–95	96–105	106+
Males	39.2	42.1	39.7	43.0	37.4
Females	39.3	39.3	42.3	37.6	36.8

Additional Handicap

We have come to believe that of all factors which might be relevant to academic achievement by the deaf, that factor loosely
described as "additional handicaps" is most misleading, confused,
and unreliable. Yet it is one which is perhaps cited more than any
other by teachers to account for poor school performance. It
might be convenient to discuss first some data from two independent sources. The first set comes from the large Gallaudet College
survey of children in the USA (Gentile and McCarthy, 1973). The
second is smaller and relates to children born in 1954 and educated
in Schools for the Deaf in England and Wales. As it happens this
latter sample of children was, like ours, aged fifteen – sixteen, and
is described in Department of Education and Science (DES)
(1972).

In the course of the interview with the head of the School or
PHU where we were testing children, we asked the question,
individually for each child: "Does he/she have an additional handicap which effects his/her education?" – though interviews were
conducted in a less formal manner than is implied there. We put
the query in that form because it seemed to be the relevant ques-

tion, and because it reflected the phrase used by Gentile and McCarthy ("educationally significant handicap"). But in the course of elucidating replies, we had two principal and important concerns. First, we emphasized that the handicap should be significant with respect to education. For this reason a number of physical handicaps were excluded unless they had been accompanied by long school absences. Second, we did not admit unprofessional opinion with respect to the description of the handicap. Except, therefore, where the case was extreme, what for example was described as a "poor home environment" would be excluded. Nor did we necessarily accept that a child described as "difficult" was significantly handicapped. No doubt on occasion we erred on the side of caution. But teachers have their own emotional biases and we were not investigating those. We were also conscious of the fact that extremely handicapped children would usually be placed in those specialized Schools for the Deaf in which we were not testing. We also excluded visual defects from this category unless the defect was virtually uncorrectable. But we did record whether a child wore spectacles for schoolwork. Finally we excluded vague terms like "retarded", or "subnormal", or "mentally defective". Frequently such comment was no more than opinion, and in any case we had our own independent assessment of intelligence. Our criteria therefore were stringent, but it became clear that we were not in fact overzealous, thereby minimizing the educational effects of handicap.

Rather than enter into contentious argument with school heads over which handicap was or was not significant for education, we used a two-point classification. Handicap-1 represented our basic and required category. It included children who suffered from asthma, were epileptic, or spastic, for example. It excluded very slight spasticity, club foot, mild allergies, etc. These latter we recorded as Handicap-2. Anticipating to some extent, we were later able to show that, whereas the school performance of Handicap-1 children was significantly worse than children with no reported handicap, Handicap-2 children performed nor differently from nonhandicapped children.

Assessed in this way, we found that 11% of the population had at least one handicap which could have affected their education. The value reported by Gentile and McCarthy is 32%, and that reported by DES (1972) is 54%. Clearly discrepancy of this order requires examination.

The DES data are based on an interview by a medical practitioner with the child – and one must presume with teachers as
well – together with school reports. DES reports the number of
conditions found and not the number of affected children – some
children having more than one handicap. But because the difference is small (91 children with 99 handicaps) a slight adjustment to
the given values will be a close approximation to the true value for
particular handicaps.

The first four handicaps listed by DES are: vision, social problems, maladjustment, and educational subnormality. Together
they account for about 85% of handicapped children and about
45% of all children seen. Then a few non-English-speaking children are included – and such children were not part of our population at all. This leaves about 14% of children handicapped according to our classification. The difference from our 11% is no longer
worrying.

We should point out that we are not trying to force discrepant
sets of data into pseudo-concordance. We want to get as close to
the facts as possible. The DES sample is relatively small and ill-
defined. We are not told which schools were visited for instance.
Furthermore we doubt whether, in a school interview, a reliable
assessment could have been made with respect to "social
problems" or "maladjustment". Nor is there any reference to
actual tests being made to justify labelling a child as educationally
subnormal, nor to the criteria used. We do not doubt that such
children are to be found in Schools for the Deaf, but it is clearly not
easy to identify and count them unequivocally, and it clearly is
easy to make superficial allocation of difficult or poorly achieving
children.

The Gentile and McCarthy information is derived from ques-
tionnaires sent to and returned by schools. Neither interview nor
discussion was involved and the authors of the report are explicitly
cognizant of the lack of operational criteria and the presence of
subjective judgement. But they report on more than 33,000 deaf
students and this must be recognized as a major information
source.

They report that 32% of deaf students had at least one educationally handicapping condition; treble the value we gave above
for our population. This however includes two categories (visual
defect and mental retardation) which we have classified elsewhere,
and two further categories, which with the best will in the world,

we have to regard with suspicion. These are: "emotional or behavioural problems" and "brain damage". It is hard to see how assessment of the latter could in most cases be other than highly speculative, and the reasons why we excluded emotional disturbance from the list of handicaps are even more cogent when the information arrives by post. Furthermore, fewer than half of the assessments were made by either a psychologist or a doctor of medicine. Indeed only half of the diagnoses of "brain damage" were made by a medical practitioner.* Because some students may have had more than one handicapping condition, it is not possible to calculate what proportion of handicapped students would remain after these exclusions. But it is clear that the original 32% is likely to be a good deal closer to our 11%.

Finally, as we reported earlier, there were 33 multiply handicapped children in the appropriate age group who, because of their difficulties, had been removed from the normal Schools for the Deaf or PHUs and were in the specialized Schools referred to. If we add these to the number we have reported above, it becomes clear that there is much closer correspondence with the other two sources of data, when comparable handicaps are considered. But it remains true that, in our population, there are a small number of children with additional handicap, recognized by the school but not accepted as such by us. On the basis of our own tests, these appear not to be impaired academically.

In the terms of our understanding of handicap, Table 2.7 shows degree of hearing loss to be a minor factor. For the purpose of this analysis we have excluded children in PHUs. Since additionally-handicapped children are much more likely to be found in Schools for the Deaf, we are able to make a more stringent test by excluding PHU children. Then because we only have 36 such children it seems pointless to distribute them across five hearing-loss bands. So we have made the strictest test and compared children in the 0–65 dB band with all others grouped together. Even so, Table 2.7 shows that the association of handicap with hearing loss only just reaches a significant level ($\chi^2 = 4.17$; $p < 0.05$). This is of some importance because it does mean that in the same way that Schools

* Some idea of the great disparity that may occur when ill-defined conditions are assessed by people of varying ability and experience, can be gleaned from the values for emotional disturbance or maladjustment given by Gentile and McCarthy (1973) and by DES (1972). They are respectively: 9% and 25% of all subjects reported on.

for the Deaf are not disproportionately burdened with mentally retarded children with only slight hearing loss, neither is there a seriously disproportionate number of handicapped partially-hearing children. In other words, there is no great evidence that classes for the deaf are being used for children whose principal handicap is other than deafness. Evidently this does occur, but, overall, the proportion of partially-hearing handicapped children is only a little greater than those profoundly deaf and with some other severe handicap.

Table 2.7   Hearing loss and additional handicaps: number of children (n = 359)

Hearing loss (dB)	–65	66–120
Additional handicap	12	24
No additional handicap	57	266

As one would expect though, handicap is more closely associated with cause of deafness. Considering our three broad categories of "cause": hereditary, acquired, and unidentified, we find that respectively 9.4%, 16.2% and 9.7% of the children are reported to be multiply handicapped according to our criteria. In fact these differences do not quite reach a statistically acceptable level. Since it is well known that the exogenous causes of deafness are generally associated with the presence of other handicaps, we assume that failure to reach statistical significance is due mainly to the small numbers of children involved. If in this instance we stretch the criteria to include children with reported handicaps not considered serious enough to affect education, the respective values become 12.3%, 31.9%, and 13.8%. Using this more lenient criterion, exogenous causes then lead to a highly significant greater incidence of multiple handicap. It is also just possible that the multiple handicaps associated with exogenous causes of deafness tend not to be so great as to affect education. On the whole, however, the quality of these data, by virtue of the method of collection, is not sufficiently high to justify firm conclusions. But we might note that the low incidence of multiple handicap in children with inherited deafness is in accord with a similar report by Jensema and Mullins (1974) for the USA.

Children reported to have a serious handicap other than deafness are less intelligent than those handicap-free. Table 2.8 shows the mean score on Raven's Matrices for children with and without other handicap. The difference is highly significant (t = 5.02; p < 0.001). While this in itself is not surprising and is in agreement with Ries and Voneiff (1974), it points to the need for care when groups of deaf children are compared. This particularly applies to the case where children with inherited deafness are compared with other groups which might include a substantial proportion of children with acquired deafness, and therefore a higher incidence of other handicaps which, as we have seen, tends to depress intelligence. This is an issue which we shall need to consider at length when we come to talk about performance.

Table 2.8   Additional handicap and intelligence (n = 467)

	Additionally handicapped children	Other children
Mean Raven score	32.9	40.6
Standard deviation	11.92	10.15
n	51	416

Finally, to complete our picture of multiple handicap, we might note that 13% of boys have a serious additional handicap, compared with 7% of the girls, a difference which borders on statistical significance at the 0.05 level. DES (1972), again with few cases, also reported numerically more additionally handicapped boys than girls, but there the difference seems not to be statistically significant. However, Gentile and McCarthy with reports on some 34,000 deaf students provide confirmation that without a shadow of statistical doubt, deaf boys are in fact more likely to be additionally handicapped than deaf girls. Nor can this effect be attributed to sex-related epidemiology. At least within the broad "cause" categories that we are using, the Gentile and Rambin data show that boys are no more susceptible than girls to exogenous causes of deafness. What seems clearer is that when they are deaf, boys are more likely to have an additional handicap. In the case of our own data, because the numbers of children involved are small, the difference is unlikely to have much effect on performance comparisons.

In the course of testing, as a routine, we noted which children were wearing glasses. This was intended to be no more than a crude assessment of the extent of visual defect. Nevertheless, there was an unexpected and possibly alarming outcome. Some 15% of children arrived at the test wearing glasses. This compares with 10% of the several hundred hearing children of the same age that at one time or another we have used as controls. It is in line with expectation that more deaf children than hearing require glasses; what disturbs us is that the size of the difference is suspiciously small. Stockwell (1952) reported visually defective deaf children to be 45% of his sample compared with 15% of hearing children. Suchman (1968) reported visual defects in some 25% of hearing children, and 57% of deaf children. Myklebust (1964) found 51% of a large deaf sample to have visual defects.

Clearly, "wearing glassess" and visual defect determined by opthalmological examination are not identical criteria. But the figures do lead us to wonder whether these deaf children have adequately corrected vision. The numbers of children wearing glasses are too few to justify a more detailed analysis; differences between sexes, between Schools and PHUs, in terms of hearing loss or cause of deafness, were all nonsignificant. Danish, Tillson, and Levitan (1963) report that children with hereditary deafness have far greater incidence of eye defect than do children with acquired deafness. Our data do not confirm this. Considering only those children whose deafness is known to be either hereditary or acquired, we find that respectively 12.5% and 14.6% normally wear glasses for schoolwork. The difference is not statistically significant.

Handedness

Disturbed laterality, represented by left-handedness, has often been regarded as an indication of disturbed development of the central nervous system (Neyhus and Myklebust, 1969). Satz (1972) cites a number of studies showing a high incidence of left-handedness in a variety of clinical populations. He takes this to support a suggestion that brain-injured groups are more left-handed than normals, quoting a value of 17% left-handers in the clinical populations against 8% for normals. Myklebust (1964) cites Morley (1957) to the effect that left-handedness is more frequent amongst the mentally deficient than amongst normals, and many of the causes of deafness in children are not unlikely to lead to minimal brain damage. Gentile and McCarthy (1973) report that 8% of additional handicapping conditions were described as "brain damage", though as we have implied, this may be a designation indiscriminately used by teachers to account for poor learning in some deaf children. Nevertheless, that such an association may well occur is suggested by Myklebust (1964) who further draws attention to an association between "confused handedness" and disabilities in speaking, reading, and writing. The fact, therefore, that deaf children are often deaf for reasons which might also cause minimal brain damage, and have poor verbal learning ability, points to an expectation that there would be a higher incidence of left-handedness amongst the deaf than the hearing.

In her significant study of handedness, Annett (1970) draws attention to the wide range of values of left-handedness reported in the literature. She suggests that this is because of inconsistency in criteria used and she shows how different tests can yield a wide range of values even with the same population. It was beyond our own objectives to administer a complete battery of tests for handedness, but we did record which hand each child used in writing. By good fortune, Annett (1970) provides data on more than 2000 normal children aged sixteen years using the criterion (amongst others) of preferred hand for writing. She found that 10.6% of children wrote with the left hand. Our own data from a much smaller sample of hearing children yields a comparable 10.8%, and therefore seems to be adequate reason for accepting something close to this value as reliable for a British population and using this particular criterion.

We know of only two other sources of handedness data for deaf populations. Myklebust (1964) gave a series of tests for handedness to 219 children in a residential School for the Deaf in the USA. None of the tests used writing, but overall he found 12.8% to be left-handed. Since Myklebust had accepted a value of 5% from Blau (1946) as normal, he confirmed his prediction of higher incidence of left-handedness amongst deaf children. DES (1964) gives a value of 14.5% left-handers in a small population of deaf children with additional handicaps. But no specific test is mentioned, nor is a value given for nonhandicapped deaf children.

Taking Schools and PHUs together, we found 17.1% of children writing with their left hand. This proportion is significantly very much greater than the value for hearing children reported by Annett (1970). But there are major differences between different

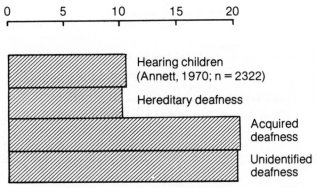

Figure 2.6. Handedness and cause of deafness: percentage of left-handed children (n = 468; deaf).

sections of our population. For the group of children designated as hereditary deaf, only 10.2% write with the left hand (Figure 2.6). For the remainder of our population, the value almost doubles. The difference between the proportions for hereditary deaf and for each of the other two groups is significant at the 0.05 level.

These results go a little further than those presented by Myklebust (1964). His main conclusion that the deaf are more left-handed than the hearing is confirmed. But added support is also given to his suggestion that neurological disorder may be associated with deafness. Those children whose deafness appears to be hereditary and who are least likely to suffer from additional neurological disorders are no more left-handed than hearing children.

The point is further underlined when we consider the children most at risk with respect to neurological disturbance, namely the deaf children with additional handicaps. Figure 2.7 shows the association between handedness and additional handicap. The χ^2 value of 5.77 is significant with $p < 0.02$. While 14.9% of the children without other handicap are left-handed, 26.7% of those with an additional handicap write with their left hands. That is close to three times the value for hearing children, and double the value cited by Satz for clinical hearing groups.

We can find few other major factors associated with handedness in our population. There is no evident effect of degree of deafness: though we might note that Gentile and McCarthy did report an

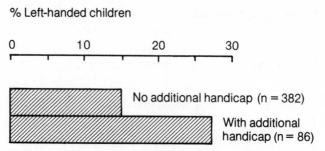

Figure 2.7.   Handedness and additional handicap: percentage of left-handed children.

increasing incidence of so-called "brain damage" with increased deafness. But, since we have in our sample no more than 80 left-handers, only very marked effects of degree of deafness would be discernible.

For hearing children, both Hécaen and Ajuriaguerra (1964) and Hicks and Kinsbourne (1976) report that boys are more left-handed than girls. The only data for deaf children come from DES (1964) on 12 cases – 8 boys, 4 girls. Overall we find no sex difference at all for handedness. But in our sample there are 13 left-handed children with hereditary deafness. Of these, 10 are boys. In the absence of any other supporting evidence, little conclusion can be drawn about sex differences in the handedness of deaf children, though the neurological implications, of course, remain.

Finally, Briggs, Nebes, and Kinsbourne (1976) summarizing the literature for hearing subjects on the relationship between handedness and cognitive function report contradictory results. They themselves in fact found that right-handers scored higher on the Wechsler Adult Intelligence Scale than did left-handers. On the other hand, in another review, Hardyck, Petrinovich and Goldman (1976) conclude that, "... the majority of studies ... strongly suggest that the hypothesis of no difference in intellectual and cognitive performance between right and left-handed subjects can be accepted as true" (p. 278). We do not know of any report on this relationship for deaf subjects. For the present population, we found no difference between left- and right-handers on Raven's Matrices; neither overall, nor for any of our major subgroups.

In this chapter, we have tried to provide a demographic snapshot of the deaf school-leavers of England and Wales. In broad outline, and where comparable criteria are used, the picture is similar to that of the USA, the only other country for which we have sufficient detail available. The snapshot describes the biologically "given" child upon whom the educational system will operate. These are the characteristics with which the children embark on their school lives, and which will be, if at all, little modified by the intervention of teachers: their degree of hearing impairment, the cause of deafness, the presence of additional handicaps, their "innate" intelligence, the sex of the child. Upon this organism, the weight of educational procedures are brought to bear for at least ten years. In succeeding chapters we shall examine the outcomes for three of the most crucial means through which these children will have to communicate with the nondeaf world – or abstain from communication other than by gesture. We shall try to assess the levels of skill they attain in reading prose, in lip reading, and in speaking intelligibly. We are well aware that these are not the only communication skills, and we are well aware that fluency in these skills is not the sole function of formal education. Whenever it is relevant and practicable, we shall relate communication performance to the demographic characteristics described above.

But description is not the principal reason for the study. Our essential concern is with the linguistic development of children with grossly impoverished input of heard language. Can children, perhaps profoundly deaf from birth, acquire modes of intellectual operation which appear to develop spontaneously in hearing children? We shall not be content to answer yes or no. The question itself is only meaningful if it is considered in terms of proportions and degrees. Otherwise the answer has to be, yes, so long as one case can be found. Because we believe that we have developed a methodological instrument for assessing the presence and use of internal speech, and because we believe it to be a highly significant intellectual operation or tool, this is what we shall examine. We shall try to elucidate, not merely whether deaf children can use internal speech, but how many children do; when they do; and whether it is as valuable to them as it appears to be for hearing children. We shall want to know what distinguishes the deaf child who learns to use internal speech from those who do not, both in terms of the prerequisites, if any, and in terms of the benefits, if any. We believe that clarification of these issues may have relevance not only for the theoretical problems of the relationship of language and thought that we discussed in the previous chapter, but also for unresolved problems of pedagogical philosophy which are at present still far from solution.

3
Deafness and Internal Speech: The Problem of Paradigms

In Chapter 1 we discussed the nature and significance of internal speech in general, discussing the role of language in thinking and cognitive behaviour, and some of the ways in which the phenomenon of internal speech has been used with respect to deaf people. It was pointed out that unintelligible vocal speech, or indeed apparent mutism, is not a reliable indicator of internal dumbness. Other languages may be internalized; verbal language may theoretically be internalized in ways which need involve neither subvocal speech nor speech imagery; words may be internally manipulated as visual images. But, more important, there seems to be no major theoretical obstacle which would prevent deaf people from internalizing whatever even minimal linguistic behaviour they were capable of achieving. So long as they understood their own internal speech – regardless of whether an external listener could comprehend their vocal utterances – and so long as so doing facilitated some useful cognitive activity, internal speech could contribute to their repertoire of thinking modes and strategies.

But this remains a speculative position. Anyone familiar with the limitations, both acoustic and linguistic, of the vocal speech of prelingually profoundly deaf children, might reasonably conclude that speech was for them no more than an extremely laborious way of communicating with hearing people; a mode too difficult to produce – and too uncertain – to make it a desirable and effective means of assisting the operations of thought. We have argued that this may be so, but need not be, and most certainly must not be assumed to be a truth in discussing thinking by the deaf. In this chapter we are principally concerned with the methodological issues which are involved when we try to answer the question: Is internal speech an option for *any* deaf people? If the answer to this is affirmative, then can we characterize what it is that distinguishes those deaf people who do use internal speech from those who do not – if indeed there are some who do not? Essentially, here we are no longer concerned with debate and speculation, but with straightforward practical matters of measurement and paradigm. How can we determine modes of thinking by the deaf ?

Historically the procedures which have been developed are within the context of broad questions of similarities and differences between deaf and hearing people. Some authors have been concerned to demonstrate similarities, starting often from quite opposite viewpoints such as Furth (1966) on the one hand and van Uden (1970) on the other. Other authors have postulated differences based on the assumption of evident linguistic impoverishment in the deaf. However, we must be careful to distinguish between quantitative and qualitative difference (or similarity for that matter). The fact that deaf children may have dramatically worse reading comprehension than hearing children of the same age may be irrelevant to the question of the use of internal speech. Hearing children aged seven years have worse reading comprehension than sixteen-year-old hearing children. But both may be using internal speech. Hermelin and O'Connor (1975a) appositely write: "We are not concerned with the question whether certain groups of children could or could not do certain things, but rather with the way in which they did them" (p. 130). This does not imply that quantitative measurement is not required. It is; but in a manner and a context which would permit us to infer from quantitative effects that qualitatively different operations are probably involved.

The use of memory

Long before the issue became one of formal enquiry, Pintner and Patterson (1917), struggling to understand why deaf children had a small memory span for digits, concluded that their subjects were unable to use "auditory images" and were dependent on visual imagery. But they were also confused by the fact that " . . . many of them used inner speech as indicated by lip movements" (p. 83). Like many later investigators, Pintner and Patterson assumed a homogeneity of memorizing process in the deaf that may not exist. This is one of the earliest reports of an awareness of the special cognitive problems of the deaf in relation to performance, and interest in more formal attempts to devise procedures which would specifically identify cognitive differences between deaf and hearing people began to develop in the 1950s.

Although Furth's classic studies were designed to examine similarities in the way in which deaf and hearing people think, in general researchers have been more preoccupied with differences. Such studies are important to the present discussion because they are concerned with mental operations which the various authors assume are verbal for hearing people. Predictions may then be made that the deaf would behave differently in some defined way. In this sense the studies are concerned with how the deaf think and provide a number of paradigms, which we shall briefly review, which could permit detection of the use of internal speech.

A good example is a study by Blanton, Nunnally, and Odom (1967). The authors' starting point was that: "It is commonly assumed that the general deficiency in language usage by the deaf is due to the inherent disadvantages of having to rely on the visual sense for language learning ..." (p. 225). This was unlike the hearing who were assumed to rely on visual and auditory senses. They therefore predicted that if deaf and hearing subjects were required to provide a word which they associated with a stimulus word, deaf subjects would be more likely to provide words which looked like the stimulus word than would the hearing subjects. This was found to be the case, as shown by the respective average number of graphemically similar responses. In another experiment of the same study, subjects were presented with a word, and then with a pair of words one of which they had to choose as being the one, "... they considered best went with the stimulus word ..." (p. 227). On half the trials the pair available for choice consisted of a semantically similar and a visually similar word (stimulus: *call,* choices: *shout, cell*). For the other half of the trials the choice words were a homophone and a visually similar word (stimulus: *four,* choices: *fore, foul*). Again, the deaf chose visually similar words more often than did the hearing subjects; but they also chose words which more often were semantically similar than visually similar. In a third test subjects were presented with a stimulus word and two others, one of which rhymed with the stimulus. Subjects had to indicate the rhyming word, and deaf subjects made fewer correct choices than did hearing subjects. In a final experiment subjects were required to memorize word pairs. The pairs were either: "meaningfully associated, (e.g., dream-bed), rhyming (e.g., tree-key), (or) graphemically similar (e.g., tour-hour)" (p. 228). All subjects, whether deaf or hearing, learned more easily word pairs which were meaningfully associated. So this result is partly at variance with those of the previous tests. But, as the authors point out, high–association words, almost by definition, are bound to be easy to memorize, and this situation seems not to be particularly useful for identifying memory codes. We believe that there is another problem associated with the first three of these paradigms; they depend for reliability on subjects' understanding of the instructions which contain inbuilt ambiguity – a luxury which with profoundly deaf subjects one risks at one's peril. But it is possible that refinement of the instruction would make this kind of test of diagnostic value. A third difficulty stems from the constraints of the English language. In the example above, *fore* is not just a homophone of *four*. It is also visually similar in the important features of initial letter and word length.

Allen (1971a) also used a paired–associate learning test to examine whether: "An early hearing loss may alter the perception, so that primary emphasis is placed upon sense modalities other than audition as information-gathering channels" (p. 69). Subjects, who had varying degrees of hearing loss from none to profound, learned lists of eight pairs of words which either sounded similar (*sign-line*), or looked similar (*cave-have*). The performance measure used was the number of trials required to learn each list correctly. The clear expectation was for "... a significant interaction between hearing ability and modality of cues ..." (p. 69). In other words, Allen expected that the deafer the subjects, the more trials they would need to learn lists of pairs which sounded alike. This would arise because very deaf subjects would be less able to use the rhyme information, and the hearing subjects would be less likely to use visual information in look-alike pairs. In fact the results were not consistent. The least-deaf group (0–25 dB loss) performed like the most-deaf group (91+ dB), and the normally hearing subjects learned no faster on the sound-alike than on the look-alike pairs. In Allen (1969), the complete sets of word pairs are shown, and it is evident that, as with the examples above taken from Allen (1971a), some modality ambiguity is present. As was the case with the Blanton et al. study, the nature of English words together with the limited vocabulary of deaf children imposes severe restrictions on investigators wishing to use this kind of test. It is not difficult to confound the very variables one is trying to distinguish.

Allen (1971b) used a quite different procedure for distinguishing amongst children who normally use words internally and those who do not. This procedure was based on the Stroop Test (Stroop, 1935). In this, the subject may be required to name as quickly as possible a set of colour patches, a set of printed names of the colours, and a third key set, in which names are printed in incompatible colours. For example, the name *red* might be shown in blue print. The subject's task with this latter set is to name the colour of the print and ignore the name of the word shown. For the above example the correct response is *blue*. A number of researches have shown that in the third condition, hearing subjects have difficulty suppressing the name of the printed word, and require much longer to go through this key set than either of the other two. Allen reasonably predicted that the deaf children in her study (hearing loss 80+ dB) would have no difficulty in suppressing printed names. In fact, they were, as a group (n = 7), able to do this more easily than the hearing subjects. But the outcome was again inconclusive. Deaf children also took far longer on the key set than on the set which had colour patches without names. Evidently for some of them – if not all – a certain amount of verbalizing was present when Allen expected that it would not be. It is a pity that Allen does not show the respective times to work through the sets individually for each deaf child.

But we might also note that the test instruction requires subjects to speak aloud so that time to name may be measured. That is, something must be named. Merely naming nameable items should not be equated with manipulating words internally in order to perform some cognitive operation. Furthermore, it is quite possible that only subjects with adequate verbal competence could understand the unusual instructions. Since the deaf subjects had a mean reading age close to their chronological age they may well have been in this category. The test therefore may be no more than a game with minor value as a tool for detecting the use of internal speech. No other investigator has reported using it for this purpose.

Rather surprisingly we can find only a single study which used free-recall learning of word lists to examine the coding strategies used by deaf subjects. A subject who said words silently to himself as each was presented would be expected to recall more of them if all the words belonged to the unique category of sounding similar (e.g., *he, sea, tree, key,* etc) – so long as he was not required to preserve the original order. In recall, there would be a distinctly limited set to choose from. But if all words sounded different, the potential set would be vastly greater, and recall likely to be worse. If, on the other hand, the subject was profoundly deaf and perhaps remembered printed words entirely by visual imagery, the defining property would be missed and like-sounding words would be no easier here than unlike-sounding ones. A study by Koh, Vernon, and Bailey (1971) which did use free recall of word lists adopted a rather more obscure set of assumptions. Subjects memorized two lists each of 16 words. One list consisted of 4 words from each of 4 categories (e.g., *mouse, bear, snake, frog: butter, pie, soup, tea*). The second list had 16 unrelated words. Koh et al. argued that " . . . the recall strategies revealed by these subjects would . . . offer an opportunity to assess the currently prevailing views that the human memory systems are fundamentally acoustic and linguistic in nature" (p. 542). Essentially the authors were expecting differences between deaf and hearing subjects in "mnemonic organization", "clustering", and "hierarchical clustering schemes". In the event, although the deaf subjects overall recalled less than hearing subjects, none of the expected organizational differences were found. Whether this was because the deaf subjects were less linguistically impoverished than assumed from their minimum deafness of 80 dB, or whether the measures were insufficiently sensitive, cannot be determined from the information provided. As we have said, the simple free-recall paradigm seems not to have been used.

At about the same time that Allen (see above) was using a paired-associate learning task with acoustically similar and visually similar pairings, Locke and Locke (1971) reported a comparable study which both extended the scope of the technique and substantially simplified it. The subjects' task was to memorize 3 pairs of consonants, and there were 18 such trials. Pairs were either "phonetically similar", (e.g., *B–V*), "visually similar" (e.g., *B–R*), or "dactylically similar in the American finger-spelling alphabet" (e.g., *B–Y*). The similarity determinations were taken respectively from Conrad and Rush (1965), Tinker (1928), and Locke (1970). Following some results by Conrad (1970), the deaf subjects were formed into two separate groups based on the intelligibility of their speech as assessed informally by school personnel. A third group was normally hearing. The rationale of the study was similar to that discussed above. "Items sharing a feature, presumably, would be recalled more accurately if that feature was relevant to the coding strategies of Ss. Thus, if Ss were coding phonetically, their recall of a phonetically similar pair would be enhanced by an awareness of the feature common to both items in the pair" (p. 143). As a memorizing exercise, somewhat inexplicably, the task seems to have been particularly difficult, since almost all of the recall data were at no better than chance level. But Locke and Locke used a procedure for analysing the nature of recall errors which was based on one proposed by Conrad and Rush (1965), and which we shall discuss shortly. They found that hearing children predominantly confused phonetically similar letters; deaf children with assessed unintelligible speech predominantly confused dactylically similar letters; deaf children with intelligible speech had confusions which fell neatly between those of the other two groups.

A study by Blair (1957) was probably the first to use a serial recall procedure with the specific intention of comparing the strategies used by deaf and hearing children. Blair tested memory span for digits when the presented sequence was to be reported either in conventional left-right order, or "backwards", i.e., from right-left. Sequences were presented in a horizontal array to both deaf and hearing children. He reported that hearing children have longer memory spans than deaf children whether report was forward or backward, but their forward report was better than their backward. The main result though was that deaf children recalled as much either forward or backward. The implication of this is that while hearing children were using internal speech to "hold" the digits in memory – a necessarily sequential process – the deaf relied on a visual picture of the array and could read it equally well in either direction. So far as we know, this study has never been exactly replicated. But two studies by Hermelin and O'Connor (1975b) and O'Connor and Hermelin (1976) come close to replication – though with one possibly crucial difference. The difference is that in the two latter studies the digits were displayed one at a time in successive locations. In Blair's study the entire array was visible for a controlled period. On the critical question of backward and forward report by deaf children, Hermelin and O'Connor (1975b), like Blair, found no difference in span, but O'Connor and Hermelin (1976) found that deaf subjects actually recalled less in the forward direction. In view both of these discrepant results and the procedural difference, the facts are hard to assess. Nevertheless, as a technique for examining coding strategies in memorizing, there is merit in this relatively simple procedure. The fact that Hermelin and O'Connor (1975b) and O'Connor and Hermelin (1976) used letters, while Blair used digits is almost certainly irrelevant. We shall comment on these studies in more detail in Chapter 5, specifically concerned with memory in the deaf.

Thomassen (1970) also used a memory span paradigm based partly on a study by Conrad and Hull (1964). Thomassen was concerned to test whether "... the difference between the recall of acoustically similar and dissimilar items ... is absent in the deaf group" (p. 74). He exposed varying lengths of letter sequence – one letter at a time – for immediate serial recall by "severely" deaf children. Sequences consisted either of letters which sounded alike (e.g., $B \ C \ T$ ... or $F \ L \ M$ ...) or of sequences which haphazardly mixed the two (e.g., $B \ F \ L \ T \ C$ ...). Thomassen found, expectedly, that hearing subjects recalled less of the like-sounding lists than of the mixed lists. But there was no difference for the deaf. Within certain limits discussed by Thomassen, this is therefore another procedural variant which could be used to distinguish coding strategies when internal speech may or may not be present.

Throughout these studies there is the assumption – almost the axiom – that normal hearing people verbally, albeit silently, name the items they are required to remember, and that deaf people may or may not – a question which is often the subject of the study. Logically from this the speculation develops that if the material to be remembered could not be named by hearing subjects, then their recall performance would, in this case, not be better than the deaf. Furthermore, if, as it has been argued (Paivio and Csapo, 1969), recall of the temporal order of items is significantly assisted if they can be named, then using nonnameable material would make the task harder for hearing subjects, but make no difference for the deaf – assumed not to name in any case. The principal methodological difficulty has been to develop material reasonably certain to be nonnameable.

O'Connor and Hermelin (1973a) used photographs of faces as

nonnameable items, and nonword consonant-vowel-consonant (CVC) items as nameable (e.g., *CIQ*). They also used an ingenious probe technique to test recall, always a problem with items which by intention cannot be named. Subjects, deaf or hearing, were shown a series of items, faces, or CVCs, one at a time. After each such presentation they were shown two of the items and were asked which had come first. The following predictions were made: (1) hearing children would be better on CVCs than on faces; (2) there would be no difference for deaf children. "Thus a materials by groups interaction in an analysis of variance might be predicted in this study" (p. 438). This was what Blair (1957) had reported. The interaction was indeed found and the prediction nominally confirmed. But in fact, the deaf subjects recalled the order of the faces better than the hearing subjects did, and the authors significantly conclude that "... it seems unlikely that retention of temporal order can depend solely on an intact auditory-vocal system" (p. 441).

Pursuing the theme of the relationship between deafness, naming and temporal ordering, O'Connor and Hermelin (1973b) employed yet another imaginative technique. A display box with three adjacent windows was used. Digits appeared one at a time, and one in each window. "In any one display the spatial and temporal order of digits was incongruent, so that they never appeared in a left to right succession. For instance, if the numbers occurred in a temporally successive order, e.g. 3 9 7, the spatial order might be 9 in the left hand window, 7 in the middle one, and 3 in the right hand one" (p. 337). After three digits were displayed, well within the memory span, subjects followed the instruction: "Write down the numbers you saw." Since subjects had no difficulty in remembering them, the issue was whether they reported them in the temporal order in which they occurred or in the spatial (left to right) order. Subjects were deaf or hearing children, and in this study autistic children were also used. Hearing children were more than four times as likely to report the temporal order as the spatial order. For the deaf children, the reverse was true by a factor of eight. In other words, the deaf children overwhelmingly retained spatial ordering and ignored the actual temporal sequence in which the digits had been presented. This appears to be an extremely convincing procedure, which is relatively simple to administer, and which would be highly diagnostic of the presence or absence of verbal mediation or internal speech.

But interpretation of the results rests on a crucial assumption. Hearing children reported the digits in speech; but because the deaf could not all speak clearly, they reported in writing. The investigators had shown in a previous experiment that for hearing children, the report mode was irrelevant and assumed that this would also be true for the deaf. This assumption remains to be tested.

There is a study by Hoemann (1978) which, although only marginally related to our immediate purpose, nevertheless suggests yet another unexploited and unexplored paradigm. This uses a phenomenon, long established in psychological literature, known as release from proactive inhibition (PI). Wickens, Born, and Allen (1963) showed that, in the course of successive trials of short-term memory for letters of the alphabet, recall steadily worsened. This is the PI effect. But when another trial was given in which the test items changed to digits, recall returned to its initial value – the release from PI. Many studies have confirmed this phenomenon for hearing subjects (Baddeley, 1976; Paivio, 1971).

Hoemann used the PI release effect when he presented letters of the alphabet to adult deaf subjects by finger spelling for three trials, obtained the customary PI, and then gave a fourth trial using printed letters. Release from PI was found – as it was using the reverse procedure. The implication is " . . . that deaf persons code Manual and English language stimuli categorically . . ." (p. 302). Now were we to draw selectively on several different aspects of the studies discussed above, we might set up an experiment in which the first three trials used the letters (e.g.) B C P T V in various arrangements, and a fourth trial used a combination of (e.g.) F M N S X. The letters of both sets are highly confusing acoustically (Conrad, 1964), but a distinctive phonetic feature obviously differs. With hearing subjects we would predict PI release when the letter-set changed. But if the subjects, for whatever reason, relied on a visual coding, at the very least, we would expect reduced release from PI on the fourth trial. We are unaware of any study that has actually made this test, but the PI release principle shown by Hoemann is provocative.

One further technique is a recognition memory paradigm used by Frumkin and Anisfeld (1977). Here a series of printed words were shown one at a time to deaf subjects. Their task was to report whether each word had previously appeared in the series. The predicted result was found. Deaf children made more false recognitions of orthographically similar but not identical words than they did to those phonetically similar. While the paradigm does seem valuable, the Frumkin and Anisfeld study seems marred by the fact that some of the orthographically similar words were also phonetically similar (e.g., *boy–toy*; *take–make*). False recognition of these words could not discriminate between visual- and phonetic-code hypotheses.

Other techniques

All of the above studies have used in one form or another measures of memory to try to determine whether (rather than to what extent) deaf subjects use a speech code or some different coding medium to aid memorizing. But there are a number of other nonmemory paradigms that have been used with varying degrees of success and varying degrees of value for our principal enquiry.

Corcoran (1966), using only hearing subjects, reported that when they were required to put a stroke through all occurrences of the letter *e* in a passage of prose – an analogue of proofreading – they tended to miss those which were not normally pronounced in saying the word. For example, in the word *there*, the final *e* was more likely to be missed than the first *e*, though Corcoran points out that the terminal position is only part of the explanation. He concludes that " . . . the *e* is more likely to be missed if an acoustic correlate is lacking" (p. 659).

Chen (1976), following up the Corcoran study and concerned with the way the deaf code printed words, " . . . hypothesized that the profoundly deaf subjects would make no significant difference in their detection of silent and pronounced *e*'s, as they would have little or no acoustic image" (p. 244). The hypothesis was completely confirmed with the additional data that probability of missing a silent *e* was shown to be a function of degree of hearing loss. Hearing subjects missed almost twice as many silent *e*'s as did the deafest group with a hearing loss greater than 80 dB. The results of a hard-of-hearing group fell between these two. This is the first study that we have so far been able to discuss which showed consistent differences within a deaf population as a function of degree of deafness. Locke (1978a) in a similar study has also reported different behaviour patterns as between deaf and hearing children in a cancellation task.

One more procedure is worth mentioning briefly. This is electromyography (EMG) from muscles normally involved in speech. Superficially it would appear to be a matter of the utmost simplicity to present deaf people with a visual display of (e.g.) digits for memorizing or some other mental manipulation, while at the same time observing whether their speech EMG response exceeded the resting level. A subject who used only visual imagery, or indeed any strategy other than silent speech, should show little change. We know of only a single such study. Novikova (1961) reports a number of case histories of children whom she describes as "deaf-mutes", and who were presented visually with tasks of simple mental arithmetic and memory span for digits. Results are shown in the form of EMG traces for unidentified individual children. Novikova states that during the presentation of the tasks there was a marked increase in muscle potentials both from the tongue and from the hand. These subjects had been taught both speech and manual language and apparently both linguistic systems were concurrently active during the tasks. The basic difficulty with this kind of technique is that of correlating muscular activity revealed by EMG response with the accompanying linguistic behaviour. There is no necessary reason to doubt that these subjects were using internal speech. But since no information is given with regard to their hearing loss, we are hardly in a position even to guess at their available modes of thinking. In spite of being called such, it is evident that they were not deaf-*mutes,* since they reported the answers to the problems orally. Furthermore, Locke and Fehr (1970) who, as we noted in Chapter 1, recorded EMG response from chin and lip while hearing children silently read labial and nonlabial words, did report some chin-lip response from nonlabial words. Thus we feel that the potential of the EMG response for the study of internal speech by the deaf remains to be developed.

We have given here a brief review of examples of procedures which have been used to examine the ways in which deaf people mentally handle certain kinds of test material. One major omission from the state of the art stands out. None of the studies cited has attempted to discriminate behaviour amongst individual deaf children. Both Hoemann (1978) and Chen (1976) used groups of varying degree of deafness and showed consistent effects. Allen (1970) used several levels of hearing loss but with inconsistent results, and Locke and Locke (1971) distinguished deaf children according to the intelligibility of their speech – usually assumed to be related to degree of deafness. In general, therefore, we have procedures which, with varying degrees of success, distinguish statistically between deaf and hearing children, and a few which distinguish, also statistically, between subjects in broad bands of hearing loss. What has not been made available is a technique which will permit a quantitative value, associated with use of internal speech, to be ascribed to individual children. This would be a value which would distinguish them from other children, and which statistically could be validly related to other personal characteristics and to other measurable behaviour. Without exception research has been concerned, in a reiterative manner, to show that deaf children do not think like hearing children – though in some situations they may perform quantitatively just as well. Yet it is hardly likely that a distinguishing characteristic would be so lacking in variance within a population that it would not lend itself to correlational and allied statistical description. In other words, the research has been concerned with whether a deaf child is different from a hearing child, but not with whether one deaf child might be different from another deaf child with respect to the same quality. Then, because research has not taken this direction, little attempt has been made to relate that quality to other behaviour. It is as if, having demonstrated that people have intelligence, we showed no interest in its distribution in the population, nor its relationship to other abilities. But initially there has to be a metric, and the following section traces our fumbling steps towards this goal.

Internal speech in individuals

Like the majority of the procedures that we have been discussing, the one we shall describe relies more or less exclusively on phenomena of memory. There is a good practical reason for this. In these fairly conventional memorizing tasks, the investigator is able to maintain substantial control over the events which interest him. It is easy to compare what was presented with what is reported; there is abundant opportunity for varying the nature and amount of presented material; scope is therefore present for testing hypotheses with reasonable expectation that the experimental subject will "do" what the design requires of him – i.e., memorize.

Yet we are only to a small extent concerned with memory in the deaf; merely as one of a number of observable characteristics. We are primarily concerned with internal speech. But we shall show how certain memorizing activity is involved with it, and how a task of memorizing can be used to detect and, to some extent, measure it. Internal speech is not visible to the naked eye nor the naked ear. It is only partly open to introspection, and not always reliably. We cannot, yet, apply technological instruments to observe its presence with certainty – let alone its content. Psychologists, and philosophers before them, have postulated a construct out of universal experience. We do not have to argue for its existence as a behavioural feature of man's life but, at the same time, we have made little progress towards bringing the phenomenon under experimental control.

We have the simplest possible operational definition that we discussed in Chapter 1. Internal speech is what hearing people use to perform specific and definable cognitive tasks. We present a problem which, psychologically speaking, might be solved in a number of ways. We observe the way that hearing people solve it. That observable characteristic we call, with immense recklessness, internal speech, because of all human behaviours speech is the closest analogy to the observed phenomena. Our purpose in this chapter has been, and is, to discuss ways in which our observations might be made more precisely and perhaps more usefully with respect to thinking by deaf children.

In the 1950s experimental psychology returned to an almost forgotten theme which had been a major research area seventy–eighty years earlier: short-term or immediate memory. For many years it had subsided to the status of a single subtest of intelligence test batteries. Psychologists knew that some people could remember longer sequences of digits than others, that these differences were stable and were correlated with other cognitive operations the power of which intelligence tests purported to measure. The "digit span" was respectable. It was used as one tool amongst others, and few psychologists looked at it more curiously than that. But in recent years, partly stimulated by D. O. Hebb's significant 1949 dissertation on "The Organisation of Behaviour", psychologists renewed their interest in why, within moments, we forget, rather than how much we can recall.

A widely used procedure in laboratories was to tape record test material, a string of digits or letters of the alphabet perhaps, which would be played back to subjects who recalled it under various

controlled conditions. In the course of our own studies, with hearing subjects we became aware that certain memory errors were
made with noticeable consistency. In particular, we noted that
letters which sounded alike when spoken (e.g., B–V) were especially prone to confusion in memory. What was bothersome for
a while was the possibility that in fact these were not memory
errors at all, but errors of listening to taperecordings of inadequate
quality. Subsequent tests in which letters were read rather than
heard soon dispelled this apprehension. Letters which sound alike
are confused in memory even when subjects read the letters in the
first place. A series of systematic studies both with letters and with
words (Conrad, 1962; 1963; 1964) confirmed the close relationship
between memory errors and their acoustic (Conrad, 1964) or
articulatory (Hintzman, 1967; Wickelgren, 1965) correlate. Independently and concurrently, Sperling (1963) reported the same
phenomenon when letters were used in brief tachistoscopic presentations.

Although this was happening in the early 1960s, as we saw in
Chapter 1, it had long been known that commonly people speak
words silently as they read them. Even in the narrower context of
memory, Woodworth (1938) recounts how, when trying to
remember names, the first one recalled often "resembles the name
sought". He gives examples such as, Cobb for Todd, Hirshberg
for Fishberg, aspasia for azalia. We can all think of many such
examples from our own experience. In fact Baddeley (1976) points
out that long before Woodworth, Aristotle had noted this
phenomenon. What has happened more recently is the systematic
analysis of the resembling features and their systematic manipulation to study processes of memorizing and forgetting.

For example, it became known with considerable precision that
if certain letters or words are particularly prone to confuse with
each other in memory, then this knowlege could itself be used to
probe further. The three spoken letters *F S X* have a number of
phonemic features in common. If they comprise a series of letters
which have to be remembered for a short while, error is more
likely than with the longer series *B J L Y* for example, which have
fewer common phonemic features (Conrad and Hull, 1964).
Conrad (1964) pointed out that " . . . the value of closely examining the nature of errors in human behaviour has been exemplified;
especially when the errors can be objectively defined, counted, and
treated statistically. An error indicates (the only indication) an

imperfectly behaving system ... The forms of malfunction may provide a short cut to an understanding of structure" (p. 83).

In effect the phenomenon that in immediate recall of words, memory errors were evidently based on features of speech – and in specifiable ways – was brought under control. Then we were able to consider what kinds of codes supported the memory processes of people who had always lacked more than minimal auditory experience – namely the profoundly deaf. It will be remembered that, as far back as 1917, Pintner and Patterson had wondered about the respective roles of verbal and visual imagery when the deaf carry out digit-span tasks. But we saw the issues as considerably wider than clarifying the reasons for the apparent weakness of the verbal memory of deaf people. We became concerned with short-term memory in the deaf, not just for itself, but also as a way into the nonhearing brain.

As a first study (Conrad and Rush, 1965), we took up where Blair (1957), Pintner and Patterson (1917), and others had left off. We compared the memory spans of deaf and hearing subjects, but we added into the study more careful control of the test material. Then we largely ignored questions of quantity of error, and concerned ourselves principally with the task of specifying the nature of the errors.

The task we used was an immediate-memory test for consonants, drawn from the set: *B F K P R T V X Y.* Using slide projection, 27 five-letter sequences were displayed, one whole sequence per slide. The subjects were 41 deaf schoolchildren at a State School for the Deaf in the USA. Their age range was thirteen – twenty years (mean: 16.5), their average intelligence measured by the Leiter International Performance Scale was within the normal range, and their better-ear hearing loss greater than 65 dB in all cases – with many of them profoundly deaf. Instructions were given by school personnel both in speech and sign. Extensive practice was provided and, by testing in groups of no more than five subjects, effective monitoring was achieved.

The main objective of the experiment was to determine whether these deaf children made the same kinds of errors as hearing children, which as we have said have striking phonological resemblance to the correct item. This objective determined the choice of the 9 letters shown above, but with an additional factor. We were concerned with the possibility that, if these children, with greatly impoverished auditory experience, did not use a phonetic memory code, were some other code predominantly to be used we might be able to identify it from the kinds of errors made. The 9 letters comprising the set, therefore, included some groupings which were phonologically similar (e.g., *B P T V*; *F X*) (Conrad, 1964), and some which were visually similar (e.g., *K V X Y*; *F P*; *B R*) (Tinker, 1928). We were well aware that these children might code by means of the manual alphabet, but at that time there was no reliable information regarding confusions within the manual alphabet such as we had for the other modalities. Locke (1970) later made the relevant study.

Since we had not previously used this specific set of letters with American children, the same test was given to 53 seventh-grade hearing children in public schools.

The question as to whether deaf and hearing children make the same kinds of error was examined by use of error matrices. When a letter is wrongly reported, the matrix shows the overall frequency with which other letters are substituted. If there are no systematic confusions between letters, then the cells in any one column of the matrix have roughly the same value; errors are distributed randomly.

Not unexpectedly hearing children recalled more than the deaf. But the 15 worst-hearing children had about the same memory error rate as the best 15 deaf children. The remaining hearing children formed the best-hearing group, and the remaining deaf children, the worst-deaf group. A principal reason for this kind of arbitrary sorting was to see whether best- and worst-deaf children used the same memory code, or whether the code used by the best deaf was in any way similar to that used by hearing children. This of course we expected to be phonetically based.

The distributions of errors in the matrices were compared by rank correlation (r) with the distribution of listening errors for the same letters (Conrad, 1964), with the following results:

best hearing: $r = 0.52$; $p < 0.001$
worst hearing: $r = 0.47$; $p < 0.001$
best deaf: $r = 0.02$; not significant

It is clear that even the best deaf were not making a sufficient number of phonetic errors to begin to approach comparability with the listening errors of hearing adults. But we did find a small but significant correlation between the kinds of errors made by the best deaf and the worst hearing ($r = 0.25$; $p < 0.02$). This suggests that some coding overlap was present which could derive from two sources. With hearing losses which went down to 65 dB, it is likely that some of the deaf children were memorizing like hearing children – though at the time traditionally our expectations of this were low. Secondly, it is possible that there were some pairs of letters which are similar both phonetically and in some other way relevant to deaf subjects. In fact, as an example, Locke (1970) showed that in American finger spelling, *T–V* have similar manual sign features, as well as the common phoneme. When we compared the error matrices of the two groups of deaf children, we found a correlation of 0.47; p < 0.001, clearly indicating substantial commonality in the errors of best and worst deaf.

This procedure adequately demonstrated – in a relatively uncomplicated way – that deaf children taken as a group memorize letters of the alphabet using coding processes different from those used by hearing children. But we were left with a good deal of uncertainty about the specific nature of the codes used by individual deaf subjects. In particular, as we saw, there was some evidence that some deaf children may have been memorizing just like hearing children. But in the course of time we realized that the more significant issue concerned individuals rather than groups. If we could sort individual children, and not merely groups of children, we would be in a more favourable stance for determining just what speech coding – internal speech – was contributing to intellectual development.

A study by Conrad (1970) used a similar procedure to that described above with a group of 36 English deaf boys aged twelve – seventeen years. The least-deaf children had a hearing loss of 75 dB, but they were in a school which selected pupils on the basis of their intelligence and academic and oral ability. Classroom instruction was strictly oral. Three main changes were made from the Conrad and Rush (1965) procedure. (1) The set of consonants used was changed to: *B C T*; *XH*; *K X Y Z*. (2) In an attempt to adjust task difficulty to subject ability – a feature which we were coming to see as necessary – subjects had test trials either of 5 or 6 letters in length, determined during practice. (3) The number of trials was increased to 45. The intention was to collect enough information from each child to make it practicable to consider the nature of individual error matrices.

Although the manual sign alphabet is probably known to most deaf schoolchildren in England, it is rarely used in the classroom (Lewis, 1968). We felt that in the memorizing situation which faced them, and especially in this particular school which expressly emphasized the importance of oral communication, children would either say the letters silently to themselves as they read them, or they would rely for remembering on visual images of the letters. The choice of letters was determined by this hypothesis. *K X Y Z* are characterized by marked diagonal features which have been shown to be relevant to legibility (Cornog and Rose, 1967; Fisher, Monty, and Glucksberg, 1969). *B C T* have clear acoustic/ articulatory common features, and though less self-evidently obvious, *X H* do have articulatory features in common (Riper and Irwin, 1958) and also confuse noticeably in a listening test (Conrad, 1964). The experiment included a control group of 75 hearing subjects.

As always, the hearing subjects showed highly significant memory confusions within the two "speech" letter-groups, and no confusion within the "shape" group. We were though, with little difficulty, able to sort the deaf children into two distinguishable groups. One group (n = 21) showed an error confusion pattern very similar to that of the hearing subjects. A second group of 15 made only chance confusions within the "speech" letter-groups, but very substantially confused the letters which look alike.

The significance of this procedure is the demonstration that, in principle, deaf children could be classified in terms of the memory code they used. By virtue of giving a rather lengthy test, we had enough error data to set up an error matrix for each subject. The advantage of this – indeed the whole purpose of the endeavour – was to be able to relate this classification to other variables. But some of this advantage was lost in the arbitrary interpretation of individual error matrices, due to the entirely practical problem of the varying numbers of errors provided by different subjects. Accordingly we sought a technique which would classify subjects strictly on the basis of objective counting.

In an earlier experiment (Conrad, 1963), we had shown that for hearing subjects, sequences of words which included homophones, which nevertheless looked different (e.g., *ruff – rough; sum – some*), were very much harder to recall than sequences in which all words sounded different (nonhomophones). With this paradigm, no interpretation of error matrices is required. Insofar as there might be coding differences amongst subjects, it would be indicated simply by relative success in recalling the two types of sequence.

A refinement of this "two-vocabularies" procedure was used by Conrad and Hull (1964). Of concern here, consonant sequences were set up, using letters either from one or other of the voc- abularies: *B C D G M N P T V* or *C D F H L N Q Y Z*. These vocabularies differ in acoustic confusability. Sequences made up from the former set would, if spoken, sound much more alike than those drawn from the latter. Groups of letters taken from either of these two sets were visually presented letter by letter using slide projection, subjects reporting from memory the order in which they appeared. The difference in recall of the two types of material was significant at the 0.001 level.

This procedure of immediate serial recall using two vocabularies or item sets was used with deaf children by Conrad (1972a). The two letter sets used were *B C D P T V* (phonetic similarity) and *K N V X Y Z* (shape similarity). Again sequence length was adjusted for each subject to accord with his memorizing ability and per- formance was measured in terms of number of correctly recalled letters. The majority of deaf children had fewer recall errors with the first vocabulary. But almost all hearing subjects found it much the more difficult.

Because it is so important for a good deal of what follows, it is probably worth while reviewing in more detail the rationale of this technique; a technique which relies on relative recall from two different sets of items to assess whether or not a subject uses internal speech in memorizing.

A number of experiments (Conrad, 1963; 1965; Conrad and Hull, 1964) had shown that, when items for serial recall were presented to hearing subjects, recall performance depended directly on the overall phonetic similarity of the items within the sequence presented. In order to understand why this should be so, we have to consider what is likely to be happening between the presentation of the test material, which in these experiments is always visual, and the time when the subjects report what they saw. Clearly some representation of the presented items – words for instance – must be held for a while in a memory store. We have to assume that the simplest representation – that is the one requir- ing fewest transformational stages – would be an exact photo- graphic replica of what was seen. When the time came to report what that was, subjects would merely "read off" from the picture in their mind. There is no doubt that in appropriate conditions and with suitable material, this is just what may happen. Paivio (1971) provides a thorough discussion of it. In such a case, were some forgetting to occur, the only information that could be lost would be visual information, because, in terms of our description of events in this case, that is the only information which is present. Were this to happen, we would expect that an erroneously recalled item would have some visual similarity to the presented item. The only alternative would be total absence of recall. Of course we have here postulated a quite unlikely situation. For simplicity of exposition, we are deliberately evading the practical fact that with nonpathological subjects this would not happen. Even if subjects could not recall a presented word correctly, they would remember that words – rather than digits – had been presented and might be tempted to guess at a word; but they would not guess that the forgotten item was a digit or a photograph of a face. An item stored *solely* in visual imagery will lead to recall errors based on visual changes from the original. Therefore, in a formal test where such changes could be identified after comparison with other possible kinds of change, we would be justified in assuming that the subject's memory was based on a visual representation of original stimulus items.

We have said that this might be the simplest representation – an exact copy of the test item. But even with very simple test items, as soon as the level of task complexity is increased by virtue of the fact that two items are presented, features other than those uniquely visual may be incorporated into the memorial representation. A short sequence of letters might form a well-known abbreviation, (e.g., U-N), or one which has some personal connotation. This could even occur with a single letter of course, such as the first letter of the subject's name. If during the interval between presentation and recall some forgetting of the sequence U-N occurs, the subject might have retained the information that an abbreviation was involved, and perhaps report it as U-K. It has long been known that this feature of meaningfulness is a significant variable in remembering (Underwood and Schulz, 1960). Baddeley (1964) has shown that even with apparently nonsensical sequences of letters of the alphabet, the more successive letters are likely to occur naturally in words, the easier they are to remember. We draw on many descriptive features to retain items in memory. Some will be idiosyncratic. But above all, as we have said, when hearing subjects memorize discrete printed words or letters or digits, though they may use visual or semantic or other

features, the predominant information which defines and distinguishes items seems to be phonetic for immediate recall.

In fact, in order to remember material of any kind, a subject will
use whatever features he can identify as being present. But he will
not necessarily give them equal weight in establishing in memory
a representation of the material (Conrad, Freeman, and Hull,
1965). By exercising appropriate control over the nature of test
items, an experimenter can gain insight into the nature of the
features which are significant for the subject. The theoretical
assumptions of an investigator might lead him to postulate that a
particular definable feature of test material will provide the
dominant cue for remembering. By presenting items with minimal distinctiveness of that feature, he can compare recall with that
for items where the same feature is maximally or highly distinct.
The hypothesis would then predict that the latter items would be
easier to recall.

This then is our paradigm for determining whether a single
feature is dominantly used as a memory code; a heavily "featured"
set of items is compared with a neutral set. For hearing subjects
and with constrained kinds of verbal material to be remembered,
we have shown that the predominant code is a "speech" code in
some form. But the paradigm can be put to more penetrating use.
The same format could be used to determine whether some subjects used a phonetic code but some others used a visual code. In
effect this was done in Conrad (1972a). There, some test items
were phonetically similar and some visually similar; the feature of
the set which was hardest to recall reflected the type of code principally used. In this way – in principle – there is no limit to the
number of hypotheses regarding coding strategies that can be
tested. The only proviso, an important one, is that the test material can, with sufficient certainty, be selected to reflect the predicted feature truthfully. In practice this means that there must
either be independent evidence for similarity, or that assumptions
underlying the alleged similarity have acceptable face validity.

In essentials, this was the procedure we used to try to determine
whether deaf children used a phonetic code when memorizing
visually presented words. That is, we wanted to know whether or
not, when deaf children read a word, they said it silently to themselves. If they had relatively greater difficulty with words which
sounded alike, we would be able to say that they did use internal
speech when reading – at least when reading for the purpose of

remembering. But we also tested a second prediction that if they did not use internal speech, they *would* use internal visual imagery to sustain in memory what they had read. These are not the only alternatives inherent in the format, but we shall discuss that issue more appropriately in Chapter 4.

4

Deafness and Internal Speech: Assessment

Selection of test materials

Our own earlier studies with deaf children all used letters of the alphabet. In the present study we used words. There are a number of reasons for this change. (1) There are only 26 letters of the alphabet. In theory, test items ought to have equal difficulty. Using vowels tends to destroy the homogeneity of the test material, because often easy-to-remember, wordlike letter sequences are produced. Even without the vowels, as Baddeley (1964) has shown, the "predictability" of letter sequences is an important variable in remembering them. The sequence *T-H-N-K* is easier to recall than *K-T-N-H* – though neither is an English word. (2) There is the likelihood, which we have mentioned, both that commonly familiar and idiosyncratically familiar abbrevations may inadvertently be set up. (3) When the test is to be given to deaf children, a particular disadvantage of using letters is that quite often the children have not been taught the conventional names of letters (*ay, bee,* etc.). So if a presented sequence is *J-F-B*, most hearing children would pronounce it: *jay-eff-bee.* But many deaf children would call it: *juh-fuh-buh.* Putting it bluntly, the deaf children would have changed the experimenter's rules of the game; they would have invalidated his assumptions. This point has nothing to do with the question of the deaf child's ability to articulate clearly; it is simply that he may have a recognized different set of names for letters of the alphabet. (4) Because of the larger number of words available to choose from, it is easier to manipulate both phonetic and visual similarity with words than it is with letters.

The ideal characteristics of two sets of words can now be defined. One set designated homophone (H) would contain words which, on the critical phonetic feature of vowel sound, sounded alike but looked different from each other. The second set of words would sound different from each other on the basis of the dominant phonetic features, but look alike. This would be the nonhomophone (NH) set. Inevitably it becomes necessary to establish somewhat arbitrary rules of similarity for both sets. Using the English language it is impossible to find more than a few examples even of pairs of words which are phonetically identical yet look different. These would be words like *way-weigh-whey* – a rare triplet. Equally, there are very few words with identical appearance but different pronunciation. One thinks of the word *wind*. But the pronunciation cue depends on grammatical context and would disappear in lists of unconnected words. It was insufficient care in choice of words requiring these properties that we suggested was a weakness in the studies by Blanton et al. (1967), Allen (1971a), and Frumkin and Anisfeld (1977), reviewed in the previous chapter.

But it is possible to set up two lists of 8 words, enough to give us the design freedom we needed, using rules which do not too greatly violate these basic principles. The NH-set was relatively easy to achieve. These were monosyllabic words of 4 letters in length, all beginning with an "ascender" and containing no others, no "descenders", and excluding the letter *i* which is "narrow". The H-set presented greater problems simply because there are far fewer in the language to choose from. The main criterion we used was that they should all be monosyllabic, have the same consonant(s)-vowel form, and as far as possible, vary in length. There was one final and major criterion which applied to both sets. The words had to be familiar to deaf children aged fifteen. It is far from easy to describe precisely what we mean by "familiar" in this context. In effect we were trying to distinguish between words which had a semantic connotation for the children, and those which were, operationally, no more than a random sequence of letters. To achieve this we carried out a substantial programme of pilot testing of lists using younger deaf children who did not form part of the main study, while at the same time consulting school heads. The outcome of this process produced the following two sets:

Every reader will object to some words in these lists, and in

Homophone (H) set	Nonhomophone (NH) set
do	*bare*
few	*bean*
who	*door*
zoo	*furs*
blue	*have*
true	*home*
screw	*farm*
through	*lane*

many cases we would agree. The process of refinement is limitless. Given the constraints of time, the English language, and the linguistic impoverishment of deaf children, we were forced to accept the lists shown as feasible approximations to theoretically perfect sets.

Hypotheses can be tested to the extent that the test material adequately reflects the theoretical requirements. The most ambitious hypothesis is that deaf children comprise two mutually exclusive populations. One population cognitively handles printed material just as hearing children of this age do, that is, by using internal speech; the other uses direct visual representation. The less-demanding hypothesis is simply that some deaf children, who can be identified, memorize words just as hearing children do. This hypothesis, though weaker because it makes no statement about part of the population, is nevertheless contrary to the assumptions of most of the literature that we referred to in Chapter 1.

To confirm either hypothesis, a subject has to recall different numbers of NH- and H-words. If we accept that the words of the NH-set are characterized by marked shape similarity, and those of the H-set principally by phonetic similarity, then the stronger hypothesis can be tested. We are clear, from the evidence of other work that we have cited, that the phonetic similarity of the H-set is reasonably assured. But in the case of the NH-set we do not have such independent evidence. The most we can say is that the words of the NH-set do subjectively look alike.* But we cannot

---

* As a matter of fact we have presented all of the words to hearing subjects both on "noisy" tape and by briefly exposed visually degraded slide projection. Subjects were merely required to identify the words from the available set. There was a very marked disadvantage for NH-words visually degraded, and for H-words when acoustically degraded.

casually exclude the possibility that inadvertently they share some other prominent feature, which for our subjects is a more relevant cue for memorizing. The most likely – and perhaps only – available feature is that based on the manual sign for the word or some aspect of its finger-spelled representation. So if some subjects use a manual memory code, and also if one of the two word-sets contains markedly more strong and common manual features than the other, we could find a difference in recall which would be wrongly interpreted. Our own examination of the two word-sets offers little support for the idea that either of them has strong homogeneity when represented manually. Nor did we see any evidence that subjects signed words to themselves as they read them. But in any case, since we know from the weight of published evidence that hearing subjects have particular difficulty with H-words, if we find a coherent group of deaf subjects who also do, we can at least accept confirmation of the weaker hypothesis. This contains all we logically need.

A test for internal speech: part 1

Each word was printed in Letraset No. 714 (96 pt.) on a card measuring 14 cm. x 9 cm., providing a display clearly legible from the rear of a large classroom. The words were also printed in the same Letraset style in two lists (H- and NH-list) on a wall chart which was permanently displayed during testing. Subjects therefore did not need to remember what the vocabulary of test words was, but only which words from the vocabulary were presented. This is analogous to a digit-span test, where it is assumed that subjects also know the vocabulary from which test items are drawn.

The first procedural step was to ask each child individually to read aloud the words on the wall chart. The point of this was to ensure that each child *was* able to make a distinctive vocal response to each word. We could then reasonably assume that such a response could, if the child so desired, become a subvocal internalized spoken response. Those few children who were quite unable to do this were discarded from the subject population. Although the intelligibility of the speech of many of the children was extremely poor, because the word-set was both limited and known to the testers, who themselves were experienced teachers of the deaf, little difficulty was encountered on this point.

Each child was also subjected to a substantial random check on the meaning of the words. He was allowed to demonstrate meaning vocally, by gesture, sign, or in any other evocative way. The least familiar words were probably *screw, bare, bean, furs*. But since the concepts represented by these words were certainly familiar, it was quite easy to establish the connection. In sum, we wanted to be fairly certain that when the children saw each card, they would accept what was on it as a printed *verbal* symbol, and not only as a pictorial display.

Test trials consisted of the presentation of 5 cards in sequence. But before that, about half of the total test time was absorbed in practice in the following way. Children were provided with a ruled answer sheet and brief, simple verbal instructions were given with appropriate mime. The group, which varied in size from 1–4 children, was then shown a single word. It was placed face down on the experimenter's desk, and the instruction given to write down what it was in the space provided. This action was then checked by an invigilator, and another word shown, followed by the instruction to write. By this point, effectively all children had learned that they were involved in a memorizing situation rather than one of copying the word while it was still visible. Furthermore they were encouraged to use the wall chart both to aid recall, to assist spelling, and to try to ensure that a response was always made. The format of the answer sheet with the test words used is shown in Appendix 2.

When these basic rules had been learned satisfactorily, the experimenter presented two cards in succession. At this stage the rule requiring correct word–order was taught. Since 2 words were within the memory span of all the children being tested, word–order was then the only free-floating variable. Several 2-word trials followed. In any trial both words were drawn from the same word-set, either H or NH, in alternate order. Practice proceeded with a series of 3-word trials, 4-word trials, and one 5-word trial, accompanied by constant monitoring and explanatory intervention when necessary. The test proper of 12 trials then followed, each of 5 words, the trials alternating between the two sets.

Since the words were displayed by means of handheld cards, presentation rate was not precisely timed, but it was approximately one word per 1.5 sec., most of which was display time. In its pilot form, the test originally had been set up using automatic slide projection and exact timing. There were three reasons for abandoning this procedure. (1) Since testing was carried out in nearly 100 locations, simple management of electrical equipment was going to be arduous. (2) Conrad, Baddeley, and Hull (1966) had shown that, over a fairly wide range of rates, in this kind of situation rate was not a factor in sequential recall. (3) The pilot testing had in any case confirmed this with deaf sujbects. So long as items are visible for long enough for certain identification to occur, and the interval between presentations not long enough for repeated interitem rehearsal, presentation rate in experiments on immediate recall seems to be unimportant.

The specific words which made up the 12 test trials were chosen from the designated set with care. To the nearest approximation, each word occurred equally often overall, and equally often in the same serial position in the trials. No prior expectation could therefore develop (on the basis of evidence, that is) that any particular word was likely to be the correct one for any particular position in the sequence.

Scoring was at the simplest level. Trials were scored word by word. An error was counted wherever a box on the answer sheet contained either no word or the wrong word for that serial position. No credit was given for correct words in the wrong place – not least because 5 words had to be selected effectively only from a set of 8. Roughly thirty minutes were required to give this test.

The decision to use 5-word trials requires some explanation. This was a very difficult task for many children. The principal reason was to provide a test which would yield a discriminating score of recall performance comparable for the entire target population. At the same time, we also wanted to be able to compare performance of deaf with hearing children. Were the test pitched either too difficult or too easy, we would have had too many subjects either giving no errors at all or recalling at no better than chance – neither outcome very informative. Pilot testing had suggested that five words were optimum.

A test for internal speech: part 2

Because a universal test of 5-item trials was given to all children, the range of errors over the population was extreme. To obtain an assessment of the use of internal speech in this test, we intended to compare recall performance of the two word-sets.

This could not be done if a child had either everything or

nothing right. We needed a "quantum" of error from each subject, while minimizing the proportion in it of random guesses. There is no satisfactory way of calculating what this "quantum" might be, and a pragmatic judgement had to be made. In any case, within broad limits, the size of the "quantum" is not critical in any way. We judged that a reliable assessment could be made given an over-all error rate of about 35% wrong words, knowing of course that some children would give more and some fewer.

We tried to achieve this desired value by giving a second test on another occasion, usually the next day. For the second test, the number of words per trial was adjusted for each child individually, and small subject-groups were made up appropriately. The adjustment was made strictly according to a rule. If on the first test, a child made more than 32 errors (maximum = 60), he changed to 3-word trials (for both word-sets). If his error rate was between 22 and 31 he changed to 4-word trials; between 11 and 21 to 5-word trials; fewer than 10, to 6-word trials. This rule was absolute. Then, regardless of number of words per trial, all sub-jects received 24 trials in the second test, the trials again alternating between the H- and NH-set. All other conditions were exactly the same as we have described for the first test except that the extended pretest practice was omitted. This second test is not a test of memory span – though it is a memory test. It was used solely to provide an adequate number of errors for the necessary compari-son, in a task of approximately equal difficulty for all subjects. In the event, the vast majority of the overall error scores fell within acceptable limits. The test words are shown in Appendix 3.

It was this second test that provided the measure of the relative difficulty of the two word-sets. Three scores are available from each child; the number of errors made on the H-set, the number made on the NH-set, and the sum of the two. From this the ratio of H-word errors to all errors was calculated. This score could range from 0 to 100. If all the errors that a child made were made on the H-set, he had a score of 100; if all were made on the NH-set, his score was 0. On the basis of the rationale which we discussed at length earlier, a child who had more H-errors than NH-errors would be assumed to be using a speech code in memorizing – to be using internal speech. Such a child would have a ratio greater than 50. For convenience we will treat this measure as an Internal Speech-Ratio (IS-Ratio), ignoring the implied deci-mal point.

Some assumptions and hypotheses

There are two principle ways of using this measure. The most attractive, at least superficially, is to consider that this variable behaves like a temperature scale or the decibel scale. That is, throughout the scale a higher value always bears the same kind of relationship to a lower value. For instance, a hearing loss of 100 dB means more deafness than one of 90 dB; and also a hearing loss of 30 dB means more deafness than one of 20 dB. The numerical difference is not necessarily equivalent behaviourally, but any value is always more deaf than a lesser value. We could assume the IS-Ratio to have this quality. This assumed property could be tested by relating the measure to other measures which we know to have the same characteristic – reading ability for instance. A linear association throughout the scale would support the assumption.

In behavioural terms, a very high IS-Ratio would carry a presumption of predominating use of internal speech. A very low value would suggest predominating use of some other internal mediating code. This code, too, would have to be related to the set of qualities which distinguished the easy-to-recall from the hard-to-recall items. In this case, word-shape; in other words, a visual code. A value around 50 would imply one of two possibilities. Either no marked coding preference, or the presence of a third code. It would in fact be remarkable were there not a "middle" group of children with weak coding preferences. But the possibility of a third code uncorrelated with either a phonetic or visual code cannot be ignored. The only serious candidate is a manual code, and we shall refer to this in appropriate context.

Our fall-back hypothesis (involving the second way of using the measure) is simply that deaf children comprise two different populations distinguished by the presence or absence of the use of internal speech. Every child has an IS-Ratio on this test. We have argued for the assumption that where this value is greater than 50, i.e., when the child has relatively more difficulty recalling homophone words, there is the implication that internal speech is being used. The simple dichotomy therefore is at that point: a value greater than 50 indicates use of internal speech – below 50 there is no such indication.

There is, though, a further problem which cannot be solved but should be discussed. We have proposed what are, in effect, two separate memory tests, each test using a different set of words. We intend to classify subjects according to relative score. We postulate that the relationship depends on the type of memory code used. Whether children have an IS-Ratio greater or less than 50 depends on which code they predominantly use. But the IS-Ratio itself depends partly on the effectiveness of the memory code used in relation to the test material. We know that homophone words are difficult for children using internal speech. We assume that nonhomophone words which look alike would be difficult for children using a visual code. What we do not know is whether the homophone words visually coded and the nonhomophone words speech coded are equally difficult to memorize. If this stimulus equivalence is not present, then logically, subdividing the IS-Ratio at 50 is incorrect. Since there is no simple, nor even complex, way of testing for this, it becomes a further assumption. However, if we have greatly erred in our choice of subdivision, the effect will be to blur rather than emphasize performance differences; we stack the odds against our finding meaningful relationships. If, on other tests, we find differences between the two groups, they may be underestimates, but cannot be overestimates.

We can try to minimize the effect of nonequivalence of stimulus by sharpening the criteria for determining which code is used. Instead of using an IS-Ratio which is greater or less than 50, we could discard children with values between, say, 40–60. Discarding subjects with this degree of profligacy would lose us far too much information. As a compromise, in subsequent analyses we have regarded IS-Ratios from 48–52 inclusive as *ambiguous*. In our "working" School population of 359 children, 46 fell into this category, and we shall refer to them on occasion.

For the major set of analyses therefore, we have established two principal groups of children designated by the assumption whether or not they use internal speech. If all this seems to the reader to be excessively arbitrary, we might urge patience. The proof of the assumed puddings will, we hope, come in the actual eating. In the next section we shall see how internal speech relates to the various characteristics of the deaf children who comprise our sample. In a sense of course the IS-Ratio, upon which so much of what follows depends, is a "private" metric – a privacy we dislike as much as anyone. On the other hand, in fairness, it is no more than a quite conventional ratio relationship between scores on two memory tests: scores which are far from private. Memory span has a long and respectable history in psychological literature.

Internal speech and degree of deafness

Figure 4.1 shows the way the IS-Ratio is distributed as a function of hearing loss. We can at once see how degree of deafness dramatically affects the use of internal speech. The baseline population is a group of 119 normally-hearing children also aged 15–16½, who were pupils at an unexceptional state school. The distribution of their IS-Ratio values is also shown in Figure 4.1. Here we see that 94% used internal speech according to the criterion we have discussed. Only 4 of these children had greater difficulty recalling nonhomophone- than homophone-words. Even for the least-deaf children the proportion who used internal speech (74%) was fewer compared with the hearing by a highly significant margin (p < 0.001). Clearly, degree of deafness is a variable of the utmost importance in determining whether or not a child develops the ability to internalize speech and to use it, at least when he reads words. There is a consistent decline in this proportion as hearing loss increases. The apparent reversal of the trend for the children with hearing loss up to 65 dB is spurious, and no more than a sampling fluctuation. Only one other study is known to us which assessed the proportion of hearing subjects using internal speech in a memory task. Locke (1978b) tested 86 adults for recall of consonants. He found 87% to be using a phonetic code; satisfactorily close enough to the value we report here.

One other feature in the data which is shown in Figure 4.1 relates to the absolute value of the IS-Ratio for those children shown to be using internal speech. The main data indicate that use of internal speech is closely associated with hearing loss. This could be taken to represent a model in which most children either do or do not use internal speech in a binary manner; i.e., the "switch" is either on or off. This however is evidently not so. Figure 4.1 also shows, for those children using internal speech, the median IS-Ratio. This also is a function of hearing loss. It implies that, even though very deaf children might be shown to be using internal speech, they do not use it as incisively as do less deaf or hearing children. All the same we should not miss the fact that, although when partially-hearing children use internal speech they use it like hearing children, substantially fewer of them actually

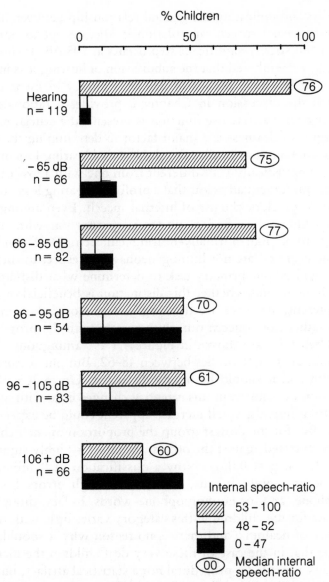

Figure 4.1. Distribution of Internal Speech-Ratio by hearing loss.

use it. This value of the IS-Ratio itself will later be seen to be an important behaviour variable.

It appears that a substantial increase in deafness can be tolerated before it reflects in a noticeable change in the use of internal speech. We shall show that the sharp change at about 85 dB is associated with sharp changes in certain performances. But at this stage, beyond indicating the general relationship between hearing loss and internal speech, speculation is idle, except to note that another statistically significant step occurs at 105 dB. It should of course be remembered that the subdivision of hearing loss into the bands that we have used also has an arbitrary element in it – although the discussion in Chapter 2 provides a rationale. But whether or not a stepwise function is present, the crucial result is that degree of deafness is a major factor in determining the use of internal speech. Statistically, the child with a hearing loss of (e.g.) 80 dB is linguistically very different from one with a loss of (e.g.) 100 dB. But it is equally clear that a profound hearing loss does not necessarily preclude the use of internal speech. Even amongst our deafest children, we find a substantial proportion who, in this context, think like normally-hearing children. Deaf children – even the deafest – are not homogeneous with respect to this variable. It will be our primary task to determine what distinguishes these children, and whether this distinction is beneficial or not.

At present, since we are thinking in terms of dichotomy, we would rather not concern ourselves greatly with the proportions of children who are shown in Figure 4.1 as "ambiguous" in the sense that their IS-Ratio lies between 48–52. But one feature does stand out and it should be briefly discussed. Up to 105 dB, the proportion of children in this category changes little with increasing hearing loss; the small increase apparent could be expected by chance. But for the deafest group the proportion of such children doubles. If tested against the others, the effect is highly significant $(\chi^2_{,1} = 12.84; p < 0.001)$. Now a classification of "ambiguous" could occur merely because a child had high errors both for homophone- and for nonhomophone-words. In fact, though, the error rate for the children in this category varies little with respect to degree of deafness, and there is no reason why it should. This suggests that in the case of these very deaf children the increased ambiguity is neither a procedural nor a statistical artifact, but may truly reflect behaviour. The data cannot tell us what this behaviour might be. A clear advantage for neither homophone- nor nonhomophone-words suggests two possibilities. One mentioned earlier is that these children are memorizing the words by means of a code which is neither phonetic nor visual – and we have suggested that it might be manual. If in this mode the two word-sets we used are about equally discriminable, then they would be equally easy or difficult to memorize. Alternatively, these very deaf children may have unusually weak preference for any coding system to a point where – perhaps haphazardly – they shift from one to the other. This could occur from trial to trial, from word to word, and even within words. Of all deaf children, these very deaf children are the ones who in terms of verbal language are most handicapped. One thing, however, is certain. Although the outcome would appear similar, in this case the "ambiguity" does not occur because children are simply guessing. Even were guessing restricted to the appropriate word-set – i.e., 8 words – the expected proportion of errors would be far higher than were actually made. At present, then, we have to consider this to be a behavioural effect not readily explained, not to be forgotten, but not greatly important at this point.

Internal speech and intelligence

If degree of hearing loss is a "given" characteristic likely to determine linguistic development, we have to consider intelligence in similar light. The fact that intelligence, in the present case, is being measured by means of a nonverbal test is not all that relevant. Almost by definition any intelligence test measures some kind of general intellectual functioning, and in Chapter 2 we pointed out that verbal and nonverbal intelligence tests are always highly correlated – also true for Raven's Matrices.

Figure 4.2 shows the average score on Raven's Matrices as a function of hearing loss and internal speech (excluding the ambiguous category). We have already seen that intelligence is not associated with degree of hearing loss. But analysis of variance shows that the presence or absence of internal speech is very significantly associated with the Raven score ($p < 0.001$). Regardless of degree of deafness, the more intelligent child is more likely to use internal speech. Garrity (1975) reported a similar association between intelligence and subvocal speech recorded by EMG. This was during a delay period between presentation and recall of words by very young hearing children.

We have found then that children who use internal speech are likely to be less deaf and more intelligent than those who do not. The combined effects of these two variables is brought out in Figure 4.3. This takes the children with internal speech, and shows for each hearing-loss band how many are in the top or bottom half

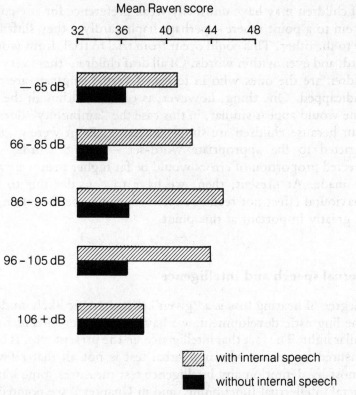

Mean Raven score

Figure 4.2.   Raven's Progressive Matrices and internal speech, by hearing loss (n = 303).

of the distribution of intelligence determined by the median value of Raven score. Apart from minor variations probably arising from the need to distribute some 200 children amongst 10 values, the relationship between these variables is clear and striking. The very deaf, not very bright child has a relatively small likelihood of using internal speech in this task. It is evident that when we come to examine the role of internal speech in academic achievement, we shall have to take care to ensure that results are not contaminated by effects either of hearing loss or intelligence.

There would appear to be no reason for disputing the proposition that the deafness-internal speech relationship has to be causally from former to latter, since absence of internal speech itself cannot be a cause of deafness. But the direction of the intelligence-internal speech association is at present obscure. The possibility that there is a codeterminant springs to mind, and the most likely

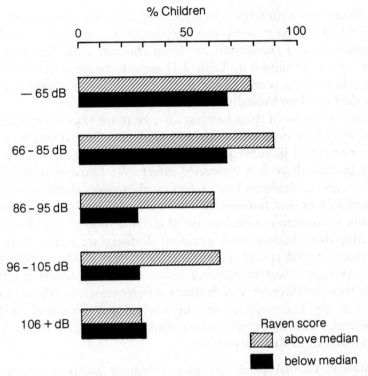

Figure 4.3.   Hearing loss and intelligence for children with internal speech (n = 195).

would be degree of deafness. But we, and many other investigators, have shown that intelligence is independent of hearing loss. It seems more plausible to assume either that high intelligence is conducive to internal speech, or that the relationship is the reverse – though not necessarily exclusively in either case. The origins of this relationship are not relevant for the pending analaysis of academic achievement. We shall though return to the point in a later chapter concerned more generally with the significance and role of internal speech. We shall also be in a better position to know if, to what extent, and when these two variables act independently.

Internal speech: cause of deafness, handicap, and handedness

In terms of the broad classes of cause of deafness that we feel safe in using, namely, hereditary, acquired, and unidentified, we find no differences with respect to internal speech. The data are set out in Table 4.1. The numerical discrepancies present cannot be distinguished from chance effects. Even children with deaf parents (not separately shown in Table 4.1) seem to be no different from any other group with respect to this variable. We might expect that deaf children brought up in normally-hearing families would, within the limits of their hearing loss, be more exposed to speech than would children whose parents were also deaf. If this is so, it does not reflect in subsequent development of internal speech. It may be that there is a concealed effect. We know that children with acquired deafness have significantly lower intelligence than do children of deaf families. We have also shown that lower intelligence is associated with less use of internal speech. It is then just possible that children with acquired deafness are more likely to develop internal speech than genetically deaf children, but that their average lower intelligence balances out the tendency. But since these intelligence and deafness differences are small, we cannot see any real support for the notion that preschool verbal experience due to family circumstances is likely to affect later development of this characteristic.

Table 4.1   Internal speech and cause of deafness (number of children)

	Internal speech	
	Yes	No
Hereditary	53	37
Acquired	54	37
Unidentified	87	36

We might note here a small but statistically just significant association between handicap and internal speech. Handicapped children are less likely than others to have internal speech ($\chi^2_{,1} = 3.90$; $p < 0.05$). This would probably follow from the fact that they are also less intelligent (Table 2.8).

One further, if inconclusive, item of evidence is worth reporting concerning the handedness of children with and without internal speech. Lenneberg (1967) points out that "congenitally deaf but otherwise healthy children whose language acquisition is delayed to their first years at school ... have a normal incidence of right-handedness which seems to emerge at the usual time and which is firmly established between four and five years" (p. 177). Our data confirm this for genetically deaf children. But, as we saw, those children with acquired deafness have a far higher incidence of left-handedness. Since handedness is associated with cerebral dominance, and speech is associated with the left hemisphere, we looked for a link between handedness and the development of internal speech, but with only the most tenuous success. Using all of our School population, we find that 47% of left-handers use internal speech, while 57% of right-handers do. But this difference does not begin to approach statistical significance. However, as Fraser (1964) has pointed out, half of the congenitally deaf population have a genetic cause of deafness. When we consider only those children with acquired deafness where we would most expect to find neurological disturbance and, as Myklebust (1964) says, therefore, "... more confusions of laterality" (p. 197), (see also Beaumont, 1976) the percentages shift to 35% and 56% respectively. Nevertheless, this difference still does not reach the 0.05 level of statistical significance. Even though the data are, so to speak, converging with the prediction, we cannot regard the relationship as any more than speculative. Bay (1975) notes that "... in the majority of left-handers, speech dominance is also in the left hemisphere, but in roughly one third of left-handers it may be in the right" (p. 22). A larger sample of subjects than we alone can provide would perhaps clarify this issue. But clarification seems never likely to be conclusive enough to be of clinical significance.

Since the allocation of children to Schools or PHUs is made by Education Authorities, we might have expected that more oral children would be found in PHUs. Because of the numbers involved, it is only practicable to compare the incidence of internal speech amongst children in these different populations for hearing loss of up to 85 dB. When this is done, the respective percentages are 77% and 79% – purely chance effects – and we have already seen that there is no intelligence difference either which might confound. Nor is there a difference between children in day or residential Schools.

Finally, there is not the slightest difference in the incidence of internal speech between males and females.

Recapitulation

This is probably the point at which to review briefly the principal topics we have covered so far, in order to set the stage for the chapters to follow. We have discussed, in its historical context, the place of internal speech as a cognitive tool, and the roles which have been ascribed to it. This led on to a discussion of the particular significance of internal speech for the deaf, its general relevance to the body of research concerned with thinking by the deaf, and its relationship with speech. Since it has been widely assumed that the deaf represent an appropriate control group for the study of speech and thought, we discussed some of the hazards of this assumption. Following a description of relevant characteristics of the population of deaf children from which our data derive, we added the feature of internal speech. Finally we described ways in which its presence or absence have been assessed and showed how this characteristic, effectively universal in hearing children, may or may not be present in the case of a deaf child, and to what extent. In particular we isolated both degree of deafness and measured intelligence as factors which significantly contribute to the development of internal speech in deaf children.

It is true for any study that outcomes depend on the hypotheses which are tested. In this way we may very well have missed other important contributors to the development of internal speech. But we are unwilling to relinquish the security of objective measurement except for occasional descriptive probes. While there can now be no doubt that the broad conditions necessary for the subsequent development of internal speech (i.e., degree of deafness and intelligence) are largely laid down at the time when deafness itself is predicated, we cannot deny that later linguistic experience might aid or hinder whatever potential is present. It is difficult enough to establish merely the bare outlines of a child's educational history; detecting the presence of relevant variables preschool is virtually impossible for other than a very few children. To try to test hypotheses concerning those parameters of less definable nature, which may be inherent in the family situation and in child-parent relationships, is certainly beyond the scope of this study. At the present time, we believe it to be beyond the resources of adequate scientific control. In exercising caution, the possibility that we may have missed crucial clues is of course inescapable. There is though no convincing pointer to what these might be.

In the following chapters we shall examine performance and the role of internal speech in school attainment. We shall ask how well children perform certain tasks, and whether using internal speech makes any difference to that performance. Inevitably, the extent of the enquiry is constrained by the availability of instruments.

We have confined ourselves to reporting on certain skills of verbal communication, namely: reading, lip reading, and the production of speech. These are the principal, and sometimes only, ways in which deaf children in Britain communicate linguistically with all of those people around them who are not deaf; family, teachers, and strangers. With hindsight we regret that we did not extend the study to include tests of numeracy, because the role of internal speech in an activity which would seem totally to preclude the need for it would have been of value. But we did make an assessment of verbal short-term memory which will be described in the next chapter.

Verbal short-term memory can hardly be regarded as a communication skill, and it reflects only a single and narrow facet of human memory. In Chapter 3 we referred to a number of studies which, in some cases indirectly, considered other paradigms of remembering. The principal reason for singling out immediate recall of words for discussion is because the data are available as part of the procedure for determining whether internal speech is used. Of course a case can be made for the importance of short-term memory in cognitive functioning, but it is not an interpersonal communication skill. Nevertheless, the data are there, and because its study has featured significantly in cognitive psychology for the past half century, and because it has also featured quite widely in studies of deafness, we shall discuss it at length.

We have referred to the question of availability of reliable and objective tests. Two communication skills have eluded us for this reason. By far the most important, and possibly more important than those we shall consider, concerns communication between deaf people. We know of no systematic and realistic studies of this behaviour. Few people are unable to communicate to some minor extent by gesture. Some deaf children have a rich and fluent manual language available to them. But in Britain manual language is very rarely taught to deaf children in school. Though there are recent shifts from this, in general schools have expected that speech will be a principal communication mode for deaf children. To *expect* otherwise would be an abrogation of moral obligation unless manual language were as central to school curricula as is verbal language. Nevertheless, we have little formal knowledge of the efficiency of either manual or speech communication when used between deaf people, as compared with that of speech used between hearing people. Apart from a rare and pilot study by Hoemann (1972), this has been a badly neglected area of research. Not surprisingly we were unable to locate a single usable test.

A second skill of verbal communication which we have not investigated is that of written language. Though certainly used as such, it is .doubtful whether writing can be regarded as having a major role in communication by deaf children once they are outside the classroom. On the other hand, a deaf child's only other way of expressing thoughts verbally depends on speech. In this mode communication of linguistic content is gravely constrained by the limits of intelligibility which are possibly, but by no means certainly, independent. The difficulty with current tests of written language skill is that arbitrary and frequently subjective criteria have to be used to develop a reliable score.

Myklebust's (1964) Picture Story Language Test is one of the best known and most widely used, and exemplifies some of these difficulties. In this test, a child writes a description of a picture. The prose is then partly scored and partly assessed. Counts are made of the number of words written, the number of sentences, and the number of words per sentence. These criteria are objective enough, but their value is arbitrary and based on a concept of linguistic ability which is debatable. For example, it is far from clear whether long sentences should be regarded as good or bad written language; nor is it clear what counts as a sentence. Myklebust (1964, Table 77) reports no difference between deaf and hearing children aged fifteen years in the number of sentences written and it is hard to know how to assess this result. Deaf children write fewer words and shorter sentences than hearing children. Some judges might think short sentences to be "good" English; these are measures with no possibility of validation. A second objective score which is used refers to "syntax". This score counts the incidence of certain specified errors such as omission, addition, word order, etc. An element of judgement rather than measurement may well enter into the decision as to whether a given word order for instance, or punctuation form, is erroneous. In particular we might wonder whether the types of error are sufficiently comprehensive. So far as we can judge, the test would give the same score to the two sentences: "The cat is chasing the dog" and "The dog is chasing the cat." In terms of sentence length or correctness of syntax they are equal. But judged pedantically they could not both be a true description of the same picture. But suppose one were a misunderstanding of the story – and therefore with correct word order? There are innumerable difficulties of this kind in attempts to allot a score on the basis of linguistic "rules". The third score is self-evidently subjective. It is an "Abstract-Concrete" score which rates a written passage in terms of whether or not the child can go beyond the visible concrete pictorial features and into imaginative writing. Several authors have noted the difficulties of adequately scoring this test (e.g., VandenBerg, 1971; Arnold, 1978).

In spite of these criticisms the Myklebust test is comprehensive and has many useful features. Furthermore, it is unique by virtue of the amount of valuable normative data reported (Myklebust, 1964). Just the same, we felt that the standards of objectivity were inadequately rigorous, and that perhaps a good deal of creative expression would not be credited. On balance it seemed that this test did not merit a place; partly because of the nature of the instrument itself, and partly because we felt that writing is usually more of a formal than a social means of verbal communication. No doubt there are other tests of expressive writing suitable for use with deaf children. But it is hard to see how any such test could evade the use of arbitrary and disputable linguistic principles, nor how it could adequately credit creativity while at the same time maintaining objectivity. These kinds of constraints, then, determined the extent, and limited the comprehensiveness, of that part of the study which measured performance.

5
Deafnesss and Memory Span

Deafness in studies of verbal learning

We have pointed out that short-term memory is not strictly a
communication skill, and that to some extent it comes into this
enquiry in an oblique fashion. Nor is it difficult to parody the
significance of short-term memory studies. They appear to some
to be barren laboratory exercises in a trivial and mechanical operation, which has little to do with the diversity and richness of
human thought. This is not our viewpoint. We see memorizing as
a fundamental brick in the fabric of the experience of learning –
and with added relevance when deafness is present. We agree for
example with Oléron (1975) who sees short-term memory as
importantly involved in lip reading. It is difficult also to see how
written prose can be comprehended without the ability to carry
forward in memory what has just been read – though that is not
the only requirement. Indeed, studies of verbal short-term memory have provoked significant theoretical analyses of the workings
of the human mind (Baddeley, 1976; Neisser, 1967; Norman,
1970; Paivio, 1971; Tulving and Donaldson, 1972).

It is not surprising that problems of verbal memory, rather than
other kinds of memory, have dominated research. Not only is it
self-evidently of particular importance in human behaviour, but
the topic has widely ramifying practical implications extending far
beyond the field of education. Furthermore, it lends itself easily to
speculation and it has proved relatively convenient to investigate
empirically. Simple procedures may be readily devised and the
essential building blocks – words – are present from a very early
age. Problems of verbal learning and memory have occupied a

commanding place in the history of cognitive psychology.

But there have always been theoretical issues which queried the degree of implication of purely verbal processes. This is not quite the truism that it may seem. At one level, for example, we may consider whether memorizing a list of printed (rather than spoken) words does involve verbal memory (rather than pictorial memory). At another level we might wonder whether verbalizing is an essential requirement for remembering order of events. We have referred to these matters, in other contexts, in previous pages. In recent years, therefore, deafness has been regarded as a tempting control in studies of learning where the implication of verbal processes is in doubt. In many cases the studies are legitimately concerned more with memory than with deafness. Deaf subjects are used because it is assumed, or known, that they use cognitive operations unlikely to be used by hearing subjects, or because it is (usually) assumed that they are unable to use certain cognitive operations regarded as central to the task and available to hearing subjects. The relevant literature displays contradictory and unexpected results to a remarkable extent.

Putnam, Iscoe, and Young (1962) used deaf students to clarify those studies which showed that hearing students, in some contexts, have difficulty learning lists of words of high similarity. In their experiment with deaf subjects they used words which varied in similarity and meaningfulness in manual sign language. The usual similarity effects held. But unusually and unexpectedly they found their deaf subjects to learn faster than the hearing – a result for which they had no convincing explanation.

Olsson and Furth (1966) made the assumption that "... verbal deficiency of the deaf could explain their inferiority on memory-performance" (p. 480). However, unexpected results led these authors to conclude alternatively: "These specific results seem to support the role of previous experience rather than verbal mediation in immediate recall" (p. 484). Chovan and McGettigan (1971), similarly assuming that "... verbal mediation is not a natural mode for deaf children" (p. 436), instructed deaf children to name aloud items to be remembered and predicted that performance would be impaired. No such effect occurred. But Conrad (1970) showed that this effect does in fact occur so long as there is external evidence for the initial assumption.

When Hartman and Elliott (1965) used a memory task which they considered would be facilitated by the use of auditory imagery, they were able to report poorer recall by deaf children than by hearing children appropriately matched. Ross (1969) on the other hand was less successful. He required deaf and hearing subjects to recall sequentially, a series of visually presented symbols, (e.g.) +-++-+—+. He equally argued that "congenitally deaf" subjects "obviously" could not use subvocal speech in this task and that hearing subjects, to their advantage, would. Since for most conditions of his study he found no recall difference between deaf and hearing, he arbitrarily concluded that the hearing subjects were memorizing without use of the "auditory-vocal" system; he could have argued that both groups used it – but did not.

In a widely quoted study, Withrow (1968), citing evidence for the importance of hearing for the perception of temporal sequence, and the importance of the latter for understanding language, asked: "What effect then does reliance upon vision to establish a language system have upon the deaf or aphasic child . . .?" (p. 34). Withrow had three lines of approach. One was to compare recall of shapes which were either those of familiar objects (e.g., apple, umbrella) or of two levels of unfamiliarity; another approach compared recall by orally educated deaf children, manually educated deaf children, and normal children; the third was to compare recall when the items were presented sequentially or simultaneously. Although the latter was central to his argument about deafness, temporal order, and language, the test could not validly be made, ". . . because it was not considered possible by the author to equate exposure times and rates" (p. 36). Nevertheless, Withrow inappropriately reports that manual deaf recalled equally well from sequential and simultaneous presentation, while the oral deaf and the hearing subjects were better with sequential. But in fact no valid statistical test could be made for the reason Withrow himself provides.

These few examples are not intended to be a review of memory studies using deaf subjects. They are cited merely to demonstrate a continuing history of confusing and inconclusive results, when a learning paradigm is used which requires a comparison of deaf and hearing subjects. In principle, these studies are based on a prior assumption of a particular quality, or more frequently absence of one in the deaf, which then suggests the key hypothesis. For Olsson and Furth, the assumption is "verbal deficiency"; for Chovan and McGettigan, "no verbal mediation"; for Withrow, "predominant spatial coding"; for Ross, "no subvocal speech"; and so on. The studies then compare performance with that of subjects for whom the assumed quality is different. The outcome of this is, as we have seen, disappointing.

Some of the explanation may simply be that the underlying assumptions were unsafe, deriving from little more than the presence of deafness and with no independent support. Indeed firm support for the use of particular mediating processes when deaf people memorize linguistic material is relatively new. It then becomes clear that deaf people may be remarkably adept at utilizing a variety of communication modes to underpin mediating strategies. Far from being without language, considerable diversity is apparent.

Use of visual coding has been reported by Allen (1970, 1971a); Conrad and Rush (1965); Hermelin and O'Connor (1975b); O'Connor and Hermelin (1976); Thomassen (1970); Wallace and Corballis (1973). Other authors have confirmed that deaf subjects make use of internal representations of manual signs to aid memorizing (e.g.) Bellugi, et al. (1974); Frumkin and Anisfeld, 1977; Hoemann, Andrews, and De Rosa (1974); Moulton and Beasley (1975); Odom, et al. (1970); Siple (1978). Locke and Locke (1971) have shown the use of phonetic, visual and dactylic coding. Conrad (1972a) has shown phonetic and visual coding. Dodd and Hermelin (1977) reported that phonological coding in the deaf is used, perhaps based on visual information from lip reading. In these studies we seem to be on much surer empirical ground.

Many of the above studies used the simple and familiar paradigm of the "memory span" which we have already described. This traditional procedure dates at least from Jacobs (1887) and, when test items consist of digits, has long formed part of test batteries. When a memory span test using digits is given to deaf and hearing subjects in a comparative study, almost always the deaf group is shown to have a smaller span. It is the relative simplicity of this technique, which permits close and easy control over factors likely to affect performance, that may permit us to clarify some of the reasons for the poor span of deaf subjects, and perhaps provide insights into some of the wider questions pertinent to the memory of deaf people.

Although there are reports of earlier studies, the classic account of memory span in the deaf is that of Pintner and Paterson (1917), who measured the digit span of 481 deaf people aged seven – twenty-six. Pintner and Paterson were able to compare the performance of their deaf subjects with that of hearing people, though the latter derived from a different study by another investigator. Nevertheless Pintner and Paterson were struck by the fact that none of their deaf subjects attained a digit span equal to that of seven-year-old hearing children. Interestingly, they rejected the argument later put forward by Furth (1966) that the relatively low-digit span of deaf people reflects an inexperience in handling digits. In an independent test of digit manipulation, hearing subjects showed only a small advantage. But the inescapable finding was that, even when deaf subjects read the digits, their memory span was much less than that of people with normal hearing. This surprised the authors. They assumed that visual imagery would take over the role of the impaired auditory function – and as effectively. They then concluded " ... that the so-called visual center seems to have failed to take upon itself the function of the auditory center and that compensation seems to be conspicuous because of its absence" (pp. 85–86). We mentioned earlier that they attributed great significance to absence of auditory imagery. This insight was perhaps facilitated by the fact that they noted that those deaf subjects who appeared to be more oral had higher spans – a phenomenon strangely neglected by subsequent researchers for some forty years.

The main result, then, of this pioneer study was that for material conventionally regarded as being "verbal", deaf subjects had a relatively small memory span; a conclusion which became widely accepted as "given knowledge". But in fact the evidence is far from unequivocal. Blair (1957) and Olsson and Furth (1966) did report longer spans for hearing subjects. Conrad and Rush (1965) in general and Wallace and Corballis (1973) also found deaf children less able to memorize letter sequences than did hearing children. But Hiskey (1956), who is much cited as reporting similarly, says only that this " ... appeared to be true ... since the different methods of scoring did not permit a direct comparison" (pp. 332–333). Hermelin and O'Connor (1975b) found no difference on a digit-span test. Thomassen (1970) and Conrad (1972a) both reported one comparison which showed no difference with disconnected letters. We believe that there are adequate reasons to account for these varying outcomes and which, when taken into account, certainly would not justify the widely accepted generalization that a short-term memory deficit for the deaf can be accepted as a theoretical necessity. The reasons, in one way or another, all reflect inadequate control over subject variables and test-material variables.

In most of the studies we have cited, a common logical format is easily discerned. Deafness, it is argued, leads to an impairment of language, implying verbal language. The logic continues that linguistic impairment predicates some other deficit – not present in hearing children. The deficit might be absence of auditory imagery, inability to subvocalize, need to depend on less efficient visual coding, defective coding of temporal order and inability to recall sequences, lack of experience of perception of sequential information, and so on. Yet in the relevant context few studies have attempted an independent assessment of language impairment itself. Most studies assume that a child who is deaf must be linguistically impaired, and we have discussed the impropriety of so casual an approach in Chapter 1.

Yet it would seem that a partial resolution of the difficulty lies in no more than using degree of deafness as an independent variable parametrically. That is, with adequate safeguards, comparison of groups of children with known differences in hearing loss is made, rather than treating the quality "deaf" as a unitary characteristic logically comparable to "hearing". That, in this context, it is not was seen in the previous chapter where we showed a close association between degree of deafness and use of internal speech in memorizing. Yet we saw in our review in Chapter 3 that this kind of control is rare. It is certainly essential, when there is no independent measure of language impairment. It employs the correct control for deafness, namely other degrees of deafness. But even then it may not be enough. We now know that internal speech is far from perfectly correlated with deafness. In any random sample of profoundly deaf children there may well be a significant proportion for whom verbal mediation is a natural memorizing mode. So in fact we also need an independent assessment of facility with verbal language, if we are to assign with any confidence the relative contributions of impaired hearing and impaired language to memory performance.

But beyond this there are other necessary and related hazards directly arising from arbitrary assumption of language impairment. The first concerns the linguistic *demands* of the experimental task. It is not difficult to think of "verbal tasks" which nevertheless make very limited demands on verbal ability. For example, almost all profoundly deaf adolescents who may appear to be almost toally without verbal language can just the same count verbally up to, say, ten. Given the task of counting a handful of coins without using vision in many cases they will demonstrably use words to do so, and will count as well as hearing controls. Between counting coins and, for example, solving the linguistic puzzles of formal education of verbal correlates, there is space for a very wide range of language competence. Any verbal task requires just so much. An overall guess that the average degree of impairment of an experimental deaf group is operationally worse than that of a hearing or less-deaf control group is rash. Tested to the ultimate, it may be; adequacy for the task is something else. Certainly no experimenters have considered the vocabularly or syntactic structures necessary for handling their experimental tasks. Even with a task as apparently simple as digit-span, we know of no proof that the deficits commonly reported in the deaf are due specifically to language impairment or to the consequences of it. There are alternative explanations as we shall see.

A second hazard of deaf-hearing comparisons in memory studies – but still concerned with experimental controls – may be briefly mentioned. Most verbal learning tasks require subjects to recall an item which they have previously seen. In the case of digits, for example, or any other small but available vocabulary of items (e.g., colours), subjects will know all possible responses. Their task is to choose specifically one of them. But, when items are drawn from an open-ended set, operationally something else occurs. In this case "forced guessing" is not a reliable instruction. If therefore a subject's mind is "blank", in the context of group experiments especially, the experimenter will find cases where no response at all has been made, and this becomes reflected in an error score.

There are two aspects to these "no response" responses. First, subjects may have a vague idea of what the correct word is, but be unwilling to commit themselves in writing. Probability of a correct response when an alternative option is no response then becomes a matter of confidence and motivation. The likelihood of a subject omitting a response may be independent of learning ability – which is what is being measured. But the experimenter has no grounds for assuming that deafness is irrelevant, and testing with a "closed" vocabularly may give different results. The effect is that hearing children who have the correct response on the tip of their tongue may at least be certain that it is a real word – and take a chance. Deaf children may also have the correct word on the tip of their tongue, but be uncertain about its lexical status. They may be unwilling to take the chance, leave a blank, and score an error. All children have remembered the word, but only the hearing child scores a plus mark. That mark represents confidence or lexical knowledge, but not learning ability.

Secondly, the larger the subjects' known vocabulary is with respect to the kind of verbal items used in the test, the more likely are they to have an item available for consideration – whether it be right or wrong. Except in the case of closed sets (digits, days of the week, etc.) deaf children will probably have a smaller working vocabulary than the hearing children with whom they are allegedly matched for comparison. So where hearing children might be able to call up a word from memory which may be right or wrong, deaf children are less likely to be able to call up a word at all. A no-response must be wrong. Unless therefore the experimenter is clear that vocabulary size is itself the linguistic impairment which is the independent variable, the outcome may be artifactually biased against deaf subjects.

Memory span and hearing loss

Because of the presence of some or all of these intrusive methodological pitfalls in most of the studies we have discussed, we still lack a reliable understanding of the verbal short-term memorizing ability of deaf children. Even with respect to the simple memory span, comparisons with hearing children have yielded conflicting results; we have opened a discussion as to why this might be so. Nor has any study directly considered the effect of degree of hearing loss itself on memory span. It is therefore not possible to compare the hearing loss-memory span function with, for instance, the hearing loss-lip reading function. Nor any other. Without such examination our understanding of cognitive function in deaf children cannot be complete.

There are other specific unresolved issues in the literature, which we hope our data may help to clarify. In particular we are thinking first of the problem of sequential memory; the ability of deaf children to organize verbal items temporally; to be able to report the order in which items occurred. Here we shall consider whether this ability is in fact dependent upon the use of a phonetic memory code. Then, second, we shall discuss certain other problems pertaining to memory codes. We believe that too little account has been taken of adaptive relationships between test materials and coding strategies available to deaf subjects. This refers to the possibility that subjects may have an above average memory span for material for which they have a reliable memory code, but may show up poorly on different material for which their "best" code is inefficient. It is possible that, tested on appropriate material, the memory span of deaf children will be less disadvantaged.

The procedure which we used was described in detail in Chapter 3 and only the briefest recapitulation is needed here. Children were shown 5 printed words one at a time and were required to write them down from memory in the correct order. There were 12 such trials using alternatively homophone or nonhomophone words; all words in each trial were of the same kind. The complete sets from which the words were drawn were permanently displayed. The major data derive from 3 scores for each child: (1) total number of errors out of 60; (2) total number of errors on homophone trials out of 30; (3) total number of nonhomophone errors out of 30. A word was scored as an error if it was any word other then the correct one for the particular serial position, and forced guessing was required.

The general format we shall use for the presentation of principal results, both there and in other chapters which describe performance, will be in terms of hearing loss. The five hearing-loss bands discussed in Chapter 2 will provide a convenient and standard framework. But inevitably we must expect, and we shall indeed show, that performance is also significantly affected by intelligence. When we come to analyse statistically the relationship between internal speech and short-term memory, we shall need to take into account the independent effects of intelligence. Main effects will therefore be examined by means of analysis of covariance, with the raw score on Raven's Matrices as the covariate. In other words, we shall look at the contribution of internal speech to memory as if all children had the same Raven score, with presentation of performance data adjusted accordingly. This will offer a truer picture of the effects of the relevant variable. By reference back to Table 2.3, which shows the average Raven score for each of the five hearing-loss bands, and especially Figure 4.2, it is easy to see how intelligence might be affecting the particular performance under discussion.

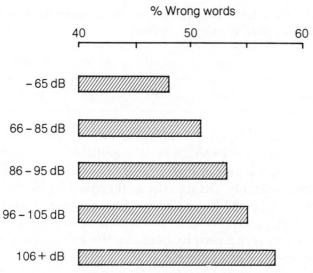

Figure 5.1.   Memory span for words and hearing loss (n = 342). Scores adjusted for intelligence.

Figure 5.1 shows the relationship between hearing loss and percentage memory errors when all errors out of 60 are used. For this and subsequent analyses of relationships we shall use only the more homogeneous Schools' population. Analysis of covariance shows the effect of hearing loss to be significant at the 0.025 level ($F_{4,337} = 2.97$). There is therefore a real, but not very dramatic effect of degree of deafness on short-term memory span for this material. Certainly the deafness effect is nowhere near as great as that of nonverbal intelligence. The covariate (Raven score) contributes far more to the differences in score from one child to another than does hearing loss ($F_{1,337} = 85.09$; $p < 0.001$). We can see the effect of intelligence more clearly perhaps in Table 5.1 which shows the correlation between Raven score and memory errors for the five hearing-loss bands. All of the values shown are significant at the 0.01 level, and there is no consistent trend with respect to hearing loss itself. None of the differences between correlations are significant.

Summarizing, although we are unable to compare the value of these memory errors with that for hearing children in a test where we are certain that *only* deafness distinguishes the two groups, there is an evident trend. There seems no doubt that hearing children would recall more than an unselected population of deaf children. We are cautious though, because further tests on the

Table 5.1 Correlation between short-term memory for words and intelligence, by hearing loss (n = 342)

Hearing loss (dB)	–65	66–85	86–95	96–105	106+
Correlation	0.46	0.46	0.60	0.49	0.36

memory scores of Figure 5.1 show that even children with a hearing loss no greater than 65 dB recall significantly more only than those whose loss is greater than 105 dB. The remaining differences could (statistically) be chance effects, though the observable consistent trend reflected by the analysis of variance should not be ignored. Apparently, as other authors have reported, memory span for words is impaired by deafness. We will now try to show that this may be a seriously misleading conclusion.

Memory span, memory codes, and test materials

We explained in Chapter 4 how, on the basis of an independent test, we have classified children according to whether or not they use internal speech in this task. Using this classification, and excluding those children whose status is ambiguous in the terms referred to, the data shown in Figure 5.1 are subdivided on the basis of this variable. Figure 5.2 presents the outcome. The difference in the size of n is due to exclusion of the ambiguous group.

The bare statistical picture is as follows. Covarying intelligence, again highly significant, the effect of degree of deafness itself disappears ($F_{4,291} = 1.89$; $p > 0.1$). When effects of intelligence have been removed and children with and without internal speech are separately considered, there is no consistent trend with respect to hearing loss. But internal speech is now seen to have a small but significant effect; except for the least-deaf children, at every level of hearing loss children using internal speech recall somewhat more than those who do not ($F_{1,291} = 4.33$; $p < 0.05$). This may suggest that the apparent effect of hearing loss on recall is spurious; that poor recall is linked not with deafness, but with absence of internal speech. Reference back to Figure 4.1 shows a far greater proportion of partially-hearing children with internal speech than those profoundly deaf. But a profoundly deaf child who does use internal speech – and there are such – may have a better memory

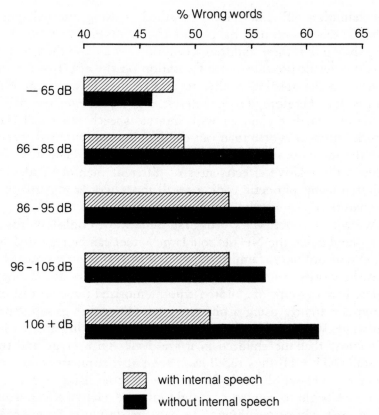

Figure 5.2. Memory span for words, by hearing loss and internal speech (n = 296). Scores adjusted for intelligence.

for words than a partially-hearing child who does not. Deafness seems to be a powerful determinant of use of internal speech; but deafness itself has little relationship to memory span, in this task. While this test has some validity, a more carefully controlled comparison, which we shall come to in a moment, suggests that other biological factors may also be relevant.

In the above analysis we have pooled scores from the two kinds of word list: homophone (H) and nonhomophone (NH). When this is done children with internal speech show the better overall recall. Now the allocation – with or without internal speech – is made on the basis of scores on a second test. Though closely similar in format, the second test has the important difference that level of difficulty is adapted individually to each child's ability. This does no more than permit us to sort children more reliably.

By definition, all children are classified as using internal speech who, in the second test, have more H- than NH-errors. We have also shown that these children recall more overall on the first test. But this result provides no information on the effect of internal speech on the absolute ability to recall either H-words or NH-words. It is therefore of some interest, and we believe importance, to know whether children with internal speech can recall NH-words better or worse than can children without internal speech; and the same question can be asked in the case of H-words. The issue is the relative effectiveness of different memory codes; do children using phonetic coding recall more words, regardless of the nature of the words?

We will consider NH-words first. Since most English words do not sound alike, the NH-set to a large extent can be regarded as a sample of ordinary, familiar English words. It is only unusual in that the words in it have high intraset visual similarity. We have defined two groups of children who memorized these words; one group apparently using a phonetic code, the other group apparently not. We do not really know what code this other group uses. We know that the children in it are deafer on average and that overall (NH + H) they recall less. If we now compare their error score on NH-words with that of the children using a phonetic code, we begin to gain some insight into the relative effectiveness of, at least, phonetic coding. The data are shown in Figure 5.3.

Analysis of variance (intelligence covaried) shows a small effect of hearing loss ($F_{4,286} = 2.87$; $p < 0.05$). But it means that even for words with the acoustic characteristics of ordinary monosyllabic words of our language, degree of deafness itself has again only a small effect. Internal speech though has a very large effect on recall of these particular words ($F_{1,286} = 19.70$; $p < 0.001$). Clearly, and not too surprisingly, an available phonetic code is of very great advantage when the words to be memorized are phonetically highly discriminable. Evidently the code takes advantage of the distinctive features in the test material. Children who fail for whatever reason to use this code appear to be penalized even when they are not very deaf. Since these words have marked shape similarity it seems likely that this group of children depend for memorizing on what the words look like.

When the same comparison is made with the alternate set of words, the H-set, a distinctly different picture is seen (Figure 5.4). Now even the small effect of hearing loss that was present for

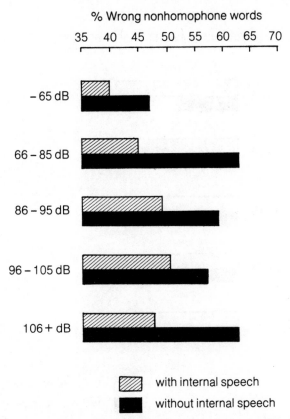

% Wrong nonhomophone words

Figure 5.3. Memory span for nonhomophone words, by hearing loss and internal speech (n = 296). Scores adjusted for intelligence.

NH-words effectively disappears ($F_{4,286} = 0.77$; $p > 0.25$). What is more, so too does the effect of internal speech ($F_{1,286} = 0.61$; $p > 0.25$).

Now what we suggest is happening here is this. Firstly, we have a group of children using a phonetic code with a set of words which have a high degree of phonetic similarity (H-words). Although this is self-evidently not the most efficient code to use with this particular set of words, it must in general be efficient for memorizing words. We make this assertion primarily because the Western world (at least) has more or less universally chosen to use it, when other codes are available. But it is ill-adapted for use with *these* words. Then we have another group of children who probably use a shape code; that is, they try to retain a visual image of the words as they are presented. Since in terms of physical appear-

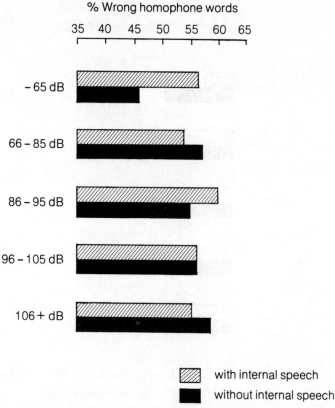

Figure 5.4. Memory span for homophone words, by hearing loss and internal speech (n = 296). Scores adjusted for intelligence.

ance, the words have fairly high discriminability, this seems to be a sensible code to use. But, evidence has accumulated (Paivio, 1971; Paivio and Csapo, 1969; 1971) which suggests that visual imagery is a poor vehicle for retaining stimuli in serial order. So here we have a generally inefficient code being put to sensible use – adapted to the material to be memorized. The outcome, as we have seen, is recall equal to that of children using phonetic coding.

Furthermore, it is not in the least surprising that there is no effect at all of degree of deafness on recall of H-words. One subject group is assumed to be using shape coding of the words, for which auditory experience or any correlate of it would be irrelevant. The other group is using a phonetic code on phonetically near-indiscriminable material – again a situation where degree of hearing loss is not likely to be greatly relevant. In the case of NH-words where there is a small but significant effect of hearing loss, it is in fact mostly contributed to by the children with internal speech. This group shows consistent improvement with better hearing. For the children without internal speech none of the differences across hearing loss reach a statistically significant level.

Another, and in some ways more direct, way of examining these relationships is by comparing pairs of children. The two children of each pair are drawn from the same hearing-loss band, and have a Raven score within a point of each other. Pairs are also matched on broad cause of deafness – hereditary with hereditary, acquired with acquired, and similarly for "unidentified". Furthermore, no child with an additional handicap is used. The difference is that one of each pair uses internal speech and the other does not. Not all of the children in the sample can be matched in this way. The number of such pairs that can be achieved depends on the distributions of the matched qualities with respect to internal speech. As we have seen, there are more very deaf, less intelligent children without internal speech, and more partially hearing, bright children with it. Matches can only be made where the distributions overlap. In the event, we can find 67 matched pairs before the data are exhausted. Since we are not using the children classified as "ambiguous" with respect to internal speech in these analyses, the population comprising the matched pairs accounts for almost 60% of the remaining total – a large enough sample, with very strict control over important variables.

The error rates for NH-words and H-words are shown in Figure 5.5. As before, analysis shows that children with internal speech recall more than those without, when the words sound different (to the normal ear) (t = 3.40; p < 0.001). But when the words sound alike (H-words) the difference is virtually zero. However, the small but significant advantage over all words for children with internal speech, which was derived from the analysis of variance, is now further eroded to statistical nonsignificance (t = 1.79). This is probably a truer statement of the real relationship, reflecting closer matching of children which has removed any differential effect of additional handicap.

If now we compare recall by children with and without internal speech, each group using its preferred code on material most suitable for that code, the outcome may surprise. Children using visual imagery recall H-words as well as children who use phonetic coding can recall NH-words. The apparent difference between 52.7% and 45.7% in fact quite fails to reach a conventionally

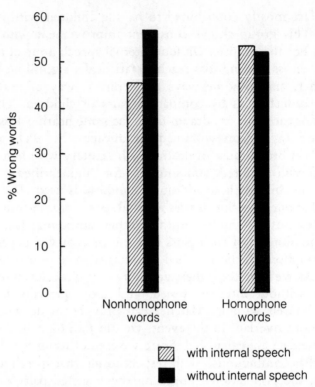

Figure 5.5. Memory span for words: internal speech and word type. (Matched pairs; n = 67 pairs.)

adequate significance level (t = 1.22; p > 0.2). We should point out that there is no theoretical reason why these two scores should be the same. Two independent factors are involved. One is biological. It relates to the effectiveness of sensory and neurological processes for particular operations. The second concerns the nature of the material upon which the operations are made. In the present case, if the two codes were equally efficient for material they each could best handle, and the two sets of test items equally discriminable with respect to the codes used by subjects, then recall would be equal. But score equivalence could occur with any number of trade-offs of the two factors. The fact therefore that the scores we have reported are similar, probably depends on an element of coincidence. The critical conclusion that we draw from the comparison is that recall of sequential order evidently can be supported by visual imagery. Had the difference shown been statistically significant, because the role of the trade-off is unquantifiable, the conclusion could not logically have been drawn – though it might still have been correct.

In point of fact, Conrad (1972a) came some way towards showing just this as well. The experiment involved immediate recall of consonants visually presented. Alternate trials used five phonetically similar consonants (e.g., C P T V B) and five visually similar consonants (e.g., X K N V Y). Subjects were either profoundly-deaf or normally-hearing schoolchildren. Recall of the visually different (phonetically similar) consonants by the deaf children was identical to recall of phonetically different (visually similar) consonants by hearing children. This result must only be taken as supportive evidence and not proof because the deaf and hearing children were neither age- nor intelligence-matched. For the particular study this was not relevant and we cite it with due caution. But the point that we reiterate is that the case against visual coding for serial recall may need revision.

It seems to be reasonably easy to find test material – "verbal" even by ordinary criteria – which can be serially recalled apparently using visual coding. Using matched pairs of children in the way we have approaches close to an ideal but imaginary paradigm in which the same child codes visually or phonetically according to experimenter instruction. This though is a paradigm which seems impossible, with an acceptable level of certainty, to achieve with normal children.

Memory span of deaf and hearing children

Since this chapter is concerned with memory span and deafness it is appropriate to have considered performance in terms of hearing loss. By and large, we have shown that degree of deafness itself has remarkably little effect on performance. But we have also shown, first, that use of phonetic coding is less likely with increasing hearing impairment, though even some very deaf children nevertheless do seem to employ it in this task. Second, that effectiveness of code interacts with the nature of the material being memorized.

The test we have evaded so far is that between deaf and hearing children. We have already discussed some of the procedural difficulties in making such a test. The problem really is how to frame the question we wish to answer, because the existence of deafness so frequently predicates other pathology. But it may be useful to define a variable which has obvious relevance to our enquiry, and such that when deaf and hearing groups are matched on it a prediction of no-difference in memory span can be made. The two groups would be distinguished by deafness and of course by innumerable other known and unknown factors. But on the one crucial variable they would not differ; and on the basis of that one similarity we would predict short-term memory to be *therefore* the same for hearing and deaf children regardless of degree of deafness. It is hardly necessary to say that the variable should also be amenable to quantification. But clearly some matching on variables likely to affect the comparison must be made; we would not use five-year-old hearing children and fifteen-year-old deaf children.

The history of this topic is burdened with the difficulties. Matching on the more accessible variables has proved fruitless. Where investigators have matched deaf and hearing groups for age, sex or intelligence, home background, and so on, differences in short-term serial recall have rarely failed to appear. The nearer we approach what might be relevant variables, the more difficult it becomes to achieve a match. Kates (1972) was forced to use two hearing groups to match deaf groups. One matched for age, the other for reading achievement. But in the latter case, the hearing children were two − three years younger than the deaf. Even so, the hearing groups were always better than the deaf on other verbal tasks.

On the basis of our theoretical formulations, internal speech suggests itself as the defining variable for memory span. We know that almost all hearing children of this age use it, and we know which deaf children do. Unfortunately, as we pointed out in Chapter 4, internal speech is a quality which occurs to a degree; it is not all or none. This has not been onerous for our discussion to this point, since we have been concerned with absolute differences in the use of internal speech, not similarities. If now we wish to compare two groups both using internal speech, we would be wise also to ensure that it was used by both groups to the same extent.

The reasons why we cannot simply take, in its entirety, that group of children we have designated to be using internal speech was discussed at length in Chapter 1. These are all children using a phonetic code – that is, some analogue of speech – to memorize words. But we have to assume that the analogous representation is degraded in varying degree. Where this degradation is great, far more words will already "sound" alike before any forgetting occurs. So, although, using our criterion, many children may be classified as using internal speech, its effectiveness for coding words phonetically will vary. It is important therefore that deaf and hearing be matched if possible in a manner which might reflect this requirement. This difficulty can be met by using the Internal Speech-Ratio (IS-Ratio).

Using these values then, we selected a population of deaf children such that the distribution of its IS-Ratio matched that of the hearing group. In order to ensure that the deaf group was seriously hearing-impaired, we excluded children with a hearing loss of less than 66 dB. The nature of the two distributions was such that not every hearing child could be matched individually to a deaf child. What we did achieve were two matching distributions using 114 hearing children and 57 deaf children. The outcome, of course, is that the means, medians, and quartiles (IS-Ratio) of the two distributions are identical. With respect to this one variable (and age), the populations are the same. With respect to deafness, they are totally different. We are predicting that, regardless of the deafness factor, the two groups will have similar memory span. In other words, we are extending our earlier discussion of degree of deafness and memory to the point of arguing that deafness itself is totally irrelevant for this particular cognitive operation.

In fact the prediction does not quite succeed. The respective error rates for recall of words of the deaf and hearing groups are: 44.3% and 38.9%, and the difference just reaches the 0.05 significance level ($t = 2.03$). But before abandoning the prediction it is worth noting that the groups are not matched for intelligence – which we have seen significantly contributes to the memory score. Intelligence test scores were not obtainable for the hearing children, but knowing the social circumstances of the population from which they were drawn, it is most unlikely that the group's average intelligence would have been less than that of the deaf group. In fact the deaf group had a mean Raven score of 45, well above the School population median value of 42. Kyle (1977b) has adduced some strong evidence to suggest that the average Raven score for a hearing population of this age today is itself several points higher than 45. Only a small superiority would have given them an advantage in memorizing large enough to account for the difference shown.

There is though an alternative approach which removes this weakness – though it may introduce another. This is to compare a group of very deaf children with a group of partially-hearing children, but in this case matched both for intelligence and for cause of deafness. Again, the distributions of the IS-Ratio would be identical.

Accordingly, the deaf schoolchildren were divided into two groups. The hearing losses of one group (partially-hearing) ranged from 50–85 dB, the second (very deaf) group had losses from 96–120 dB. Children were matched pair by pair, one from each group, on the basis of Raven score within 2 points and IS-Ratio within 5 points. Children with hereditary deafness or unidentified cause were matched only with similar children in the other group. Children with acquired deafness were matched only with other such children. No child with an additional handicap was used at all. The data permitted 51 such pairs. The only factor of substance then distinguishing the groups which might have affected recall score was degree of deafness, the weakness we spoke of being that all children in the comparison had some deafness involvement. The respective error rates for the partially-hearing and very deaf groups were 50.0% and 52.6%. This difference does not begin to approach statistical significance ($t = 0.71$). It seems then safe to conclude that the traditionally reported short-term memory deficit of the deaf probably reflects an artifact introduced by other uncontrolled variables. Lack of auditory experience does not directly impair recall in this task.

The reader will have realized that this test does little more than does the analysis of covariance discussed on p. 123. There we reported that, when intelligence was accounted for, the effect of hearing loss on recall score was small – but statistically significant. All we have added here is a more precise definition with respect to the memory-sustaining processes represented in the matched IS-Ratio. The refinement neatly eliminates that small deafness effect.

Deafness, language impairment, and sequential coding

For many people experienced in work with deaf children, there is often a deep-rooted intuitive feeling of improbability that their short-term memory is equal to that of hearing children. It appears so overwhelmingly and obviously untrue. In general, superficially at least, all their memorizing ability seems poor, and the low level of their language ability is often assumed to ramify into specific tasks.

There are, however, two ways at least in which verbal impoverishment may have no adverse effect even on recall of words. One is when the degree of impoverishment is not sufficient to impair task performance. Blank (1965) has expressed this point with precision. "Although the deaf may therefore be deficient in general language development, it is entirely possible that they possess the particular verbal concept(s) used in any experiment" (p. 442). The second way is when the child adopts a memorizing strategy which does not involve verbal language. So it is essential to know what the language requirements, if any, necessarily are; and it is essential to know what cognitive processes a child is able and willing to bring to the task. Deafness itself, in the absence of some other specified cognitive handicap, may have little relevance.

It is significant that most deaf children are educated in a linguistic environment which has evolved on the basis of normal speech. In their written mode all Western languages are phonetic and the ear becomes dominant in reading. The deaf, in general, can certainly be said to have poor memory for unselected samples of this material. In this sense the deaf are handicapped not by poor structural memory, which is hard to modify in a general way (Espeseth, 1969; A. H. Ling, 1976), but by the nature of the material they are required to remember – which may well be open to a degree of modification.

Quite apart from uncontrolled observations of classroom experience, the assumption of defective short-term memory in the deaf has also been supported by a more formal objection that deaf children are unlikely, on theoretical grounds, to be able to memorize items in sequence. There are two strands to this. One is that this particular cognitive deficit derives from the fact of auditory deprivation, especially in the form of speech. Auditory information has an essential temporal component. Deaf people therefore lack the experience of it; a lack which generalizes into formal memorizing. The concept in this form is rather vague and not readily tested. It also ignores the normal experience that deaf people have in a wide range of behaviour which is sequential in character.

The second strand needs to be given more detailed consideration. It involves the common assumption that a deaf child
impoverished in verbal language will need to depend on visual
imagery when memorizing print, and that visual imagery is inefficient for handling sequential information.

For some time (Sperling, 1960), it had been accepted that a
visual stimulus underwent rapid memorial decay unless it was
recoded into some other form (phonetic if the original stimulus
was, for instance, a digit). Many subsequent experiments have
shown this not to be necessarily true (see Baddeley, 1976). But in
any case, almost all of the relevant studies have been concerned
with single items. Unfortunately the procedural manipulations
effective for single-item-presentation studies can rarely be used
when the experiment requires several items to be presented
sequentially before the subject reports. Procedures which are both
less direct and less satisfactory may have to be resorted to.

The best-known studies are probably those of Paivio and Csapo
(1969; 1971). Their rationale was that familiar printed words
which were the names of objects could be named even if they were
presented sequentially at a rate of five per second. But if the pictures of the objects were shown at that fast rate, there would not
be time for verbal labelling; the items and their order of appearance would therefore have to be memorized in visual imagery.
This latter process was postualted to be less efficient and recall
predicted to be worse than for printed names. The observed result
was that expected. But there are several other reasons why the
pictures were possibly harder to memorize serially than their
printed names. The first is quite simply that the undergraduate
(hearing) subjects were experienced at reading print, i.e., naming
words, but quite without experience at the picture task. But,
perhaps as important, no attempt was made to secure the stimulus
equivalence of test items – a requirement we discussed above.
Nothing assures that the visual discriminability of the pictures was
equivalent to that of their names in print. Furthermore, there was
no independent evidence that the pictures were stored as visual
images. One-fifth of a second may not be long enough to name
pictures correctly. But in that time they might be named incor-
rectly – but still named. In scoring this would be indistinguishable
from forgetting. We do not see that the results therefore justify the
conclusion that "... verbal and imaginal symbolic systems are
functionally distinguished in regard to their capacity for sequential

information processing ..." (Paivio and Csapo, 1971, p. 51), nor that (visual imagery) "... is not specialised for serial-processing unless linked to an integrated (symbolic) motor response system ..." (Paivio, 1971, p. 180).

Garrity (1975) used a more direct approach to the problem, but also failed to devise adequate procedural controls. She had hearing children aged four – five years recall pictures of familiar objects, and used EMG recordings to determine the extent to which they silently named the pictures. She reported that children who named silently during a delay interval did recall more. Here again though, there is no independent evidence that the pictures were as discriminable visually as their names were phonetically. The objects depicted in the test are not reported.

One further but more convincing solution to the methodological problem was found by O'Connor and Hermelin (1973b) in a study we have already referred to. Here, deaf and hearing children memorized a sequence of five photographs of faces, report requiring no other response than pointing. The authors in this case were able to conclude that their results "... demonstrated the capacity of the deaf to store sequential order in the probable absence of verbal coding" (p. 441). Healy (1977) too, using hearing subjects in a pattern ordering task, concluded that visual coding could be used. Finally, an important study by Yik (1978) required sequential recall of Chinese words from native Chinese hearing subjects in a memory-span-type task. The interitem visual similarity and interitem phonetic similarity were independently varied in five-word sequences. While homophone-words were clearly difficult to recall, Yik also reports that subjects had significant difficulty in sequentially recalling Chinese words which look alike but have phonetically distinctive names. He concluded that "... a strong visual encoding effect" was present (p. 492).

To say the least then the evidence that visual imagery is ineffective for holding order in short-term memory is weak. More to the point we have shown that the issue should only be put within a context which includes the physical nature of the test material. In the most conventional of memory span paradigms we found deaf children, most of whom were virtually certain to be using a visual memory code, whose span for words which were easy to discriminate visually was just as long as the span of children using a phonetic code for words of high phonetic discriminability. This is not to say that visual imagery can successfully replace all cognitive functions for which hearing people use internal speech. We talked earlier about verbal language which might be adequate for counting but inadequate for more complex verbal tasks. Visual imagery similarly may be efficient for a simple memory span task, but still leave a child severely handicapped on tasks requiring more sophisticated cognitive manipulations.

We see no reason to reject the hypothesis that test items which are optionally or imperatively coded visually, or in other ways, may be sequentially recalled as effectively as when coded phonetically; *so long as* perceptual discriminability is identical in all modalities. Theoretically this latter condition is inescapable. Yet it is rarely considered and hard to achieve by design. The least likely way to achieve it is by using a single set of test items on the ground that it is the methodologically correct procedure. So deaf and hearing children are both tested on the same digits or consonants; and with total disregard for the relative visual and phonetic physical differences in the visual and phonetic modes. In the case of digits, Conrad (1972b) has provided evidence which shows that, at least acoustically, digit names are relatively highly discriminable. Compared for instance to names of consonants, a good deal more masking noise is required before they become auditorally unintelligible. Furthermore, in common print forms, the curvilinearity of most of the digits (2, 3, 5, 6, 8, 9, 0) presents difficulties for visual discrimination (Levine et al., 1973). Not surprisingly, deaf children using visual coding have always been shown to have poor sequential memory for digits. We have shown here that when care is taken with test items this need not happen.

We have shown that deafness may or may not lead to impaired use of internal speech. When it does, recall is affected only for material which – by its nature – is best coded phonetically. Other material is not affected and may be recalled just as well. But deafness need not lead to language specifically impaired for the particular task. In that case, regardless of degree of deafness, recall may be little different from that of hearing children. Recall of items sequentially does not depend on normal hearing, nor on normal language ability, nor exclusively on the use of phonetic coding, but on whether coding options available to the subjects are effective for the material to be memorized – i.e., whether the items have adequate intraset discriminability.

All too frequently, the concept of linguistic impairment has been used almost as a synonym for deafness. The concept is of value for understanding cognitive operations only when its nature can be specified as being relevant to the task in question. Linguistic demands of memory span tasks are in part specific and are partly general. If the verbal items used are totally unfamiliar, a child will be linguistically impaired. If they are quite familiar, he may still prefer to use a nonlinguistic mode of cognitively handling them. Even if he proficiently uses a linguistic mode of thinking in one task, there may be requirements in another task for which his language is inadequate. In the next chapter we shall see that reading may be a case in point.

6

Deafness and Reading

Reading is the window into knowledge. It is the first, the primary *R* of the three *R*s which dominate the earliest steps in formal education. For the profoundly deaf child entering school all too often with no communication mode more useful than crude gesture, print may provide his first linguistic insight: the concept that objects may have symbolic representations universally understood. In every first-year classroom in Schools for deaf children objects are tagged by cards bearing their names. Other than by whatever the print means to children, they have no social reference to the object. Meaning from print comes slowly and for a long time children resort to the single "word" they know, and which they use indiscriminately for all objects: they point.

At this same chronological period, hearing children of course have a large vocabulary of words accumulating at a dramatic rate, and they communicate in speech fluently, grammatically, and effectively. They may be unable to read a single word. But they do not need to see a printed word to tell them the name of an object in the classroom. They know it already. They have heard it spoken; they can themselves say it. They do not need the presence of the object in order to discuss the referent of the printed symbol. They learn that print can be spoken with consistency and communicatively. They learn how to decode unfamiliar print into familiar speech sounds. They learn to read. This is their first foreign language. At the age of sixteen years, if they are readers of average ability, they will have a reading age of sixteen years. But were they born profoundly deaf, were their reading ability about average for the deaf population, at the age of sixteen they would have a reading age of nine years whether they were British (Conrad, 1977a) or American (DiFrancesca, 1972).

Yet it is only in the last few years that research attention has begun to focus on the extent and the nature of this deficit. As an example of this neglect we may note that the *Deafness, Speech and Hearing Abstracts* did not require a special subsection on reading until 1973, although the abstracts were first published in 1960. When Ewing (1960) edited an account of an international conference on educational methods for the deaf, it contained not a single discussion on the teaching of reading. Ten years passed and the International Congress on the Education of the Deaf, held at Stockholm in 1970, again heard no paper specifically concerned with the fundamental problems involved in teaching deaf children to read. In 1964 a governmental committee was set up in Britain to consider the education of the deaf, with special reference to the role of signing and finger spelling. In a foreword, the then Secretary of State for Education and Science wrote, "The keenness of the discussion among teachers, university staffs, medical officers, social workers and the deaf themselves about the media of communication in education was an indication of their deep concern to offer deaf children the best possible education for their social and personal development" (Lewis, 1968). Nevertheless, apart from a passing reference to the use of flash cards in the USSR, having said that everyone agreed that reading was important, the ensuing report completely ignored the problem. It simply did not consider the possibility that manual language might have some role in learning to decode print – or even that it might not.

No comprehensive description and analysis of the relationship between hearing loss and reading ability has yet been published in Britain. Traditionally the education establishment has protested that every teacher already knows that deaf children are very backward at reading, and by implication such research is unnecessary. The stark fact is inescapably present in every classroom. Why then bother with expensive testing and detailed tabulation of performance? There are a number of reasons if the educational process is to advance with any semblance of order.

In principle – and preferably in practice as well – a teacher needs to know how well a child is progressing. This requires measurement. It also requires standards. It is better than nothing if a teacher knows that a child has a reading level about average for its age. It becomes more useful if reading performance can be related not only to that of other children of the same age but also of the same level of hearing loss. The more other measurable variables there are which can be taken into account, the more precise will the picture be of the child's relative ability. We have little doubt that backward deaf readers have been neglected because they were additionally handicapped in some known way, and it was assumed that their performance was all that could be expected. Classroom lore is not always the best guide for expectation – and never if normative data of large and comparable populations are available. Rare though it is, knowledge of a child's reading ability takes on new value when it can be related to population norms. In this way, individual programmes can be more meaningfully formulated, placement in programmes more appropriately made, programmes themselves can be evaluated, and progress of individual children can be compared. Knowledge that a deaf child is a very backward reader may often be the opposite of discouraging for a parent. To be told that, though aged sixteen, your deaf child has a reading age of nine years, may be less disturbing when you also know that this is above average for children of the same degree of deafness. In this chapter we shall present population data on reading which has not hitherto been available for Britain – and is distinctly sparse elsewhere.

Those data will be simple quantitative descriptions of the state of affairs as we found it at the time of testing. We shall also discuss relationships between reading and what emerge as key variables, such as hearing loss itself, intelligence, cause of deafness, and so on. But from what we have said in previous chapters, it is clear that we hope to move into some analysis of what is involved for a deaf child in learning to read. We shall examine the role of internal speech in the reading process and its significance for reading performance. We shall be able to consider how efficient reading comprehension may be in the absence of consistent phonetic mediation between visual decoding and semantic acquisition.

Contemporary data

Until recently, the most widely used source of normative data on reading performance of deaf children has been the North American survey reported by Wrightstone, Aronow, and Moskowitz (1963). The authors used the Elementary Reading Test of the Metropolitan Achievement Tests which they judged suitable for deaf children aged ten–sixteen years. Testing was carried out by the participating schools themselves, an inevitable procedure when, as in this case, more than 5000 children were screened in 73 schools throughout the USA and Canada – rather more than a 50% sample which we have no reason to doubt was a representative one.

The article presents abbreviated results as average scores according to age; the full normative data converted to school-grade equivalents form part of the instructions available from the publishers of the test. Furth (1966b), though, has provided some of this information. Of interest to our present enquiry is the fact that for age 15½–16½ years the respective mean and median grades are 3.5 and 3.4 – equivalent to a reading age of about 9½ years. But this value must be interpreted with care.

The distribution of hearing loss of these children is remarkably similar to that of our own population shown in Figure 2.2. In comparing performance, this factor can therefore safely be ignored. But excluded from the norms were children with IQ below 75, and some additionally handicapped children. This removed some 9% of the population, presumably many of the worst readers. The grade equivalent given above must be an overestimate of the true average reading ability of that population. This also of course affects Furth's (1966b) interpretation. Furth was concerned at the relatively poor reading performance demonstrated by these children. He pointed out that at the 15½–16½-year level only 12% of children had a reading age equivalent to about eleven years. In fact the true proportion is less than this once the excluded children are taken into account.

Wrightstone et al. provide little information concerning the relationship of reading ability to other variables except for age and degree of hearing loss. With respect to the former, Furth (1966b) reports that between ten and sixteen years of age, reading advances by no more than 0.8 of a school grade (that is, less than one year). Our own data, deriving only from older children, permit no comment on this. We are, however, surprised by the relationship shown between reading and hearing loss. Wrightstone et al. only give mean raw scores in this connection and did not show variances. At age 15½–16½ years for their three hearing-loss bands of, – 49, 50 – 84, 85+ dB (probably ASA), the respective reading raw scores are, 25.8, 22.1, 20.9. There are therefore evident differences with deafer children reading less well. The authors did not test the statistical significance of these differences on the grounds that they were small and, accordingly, " . . . the decision was reached that a single set of norms irrespective of children's degree of hearing loss would be practical" (p. 316). We shall present evidence that this assumed invariance of reading ability with respect to hearing loss is most dubious and therefore that norms suitable for partially-hearing children are certainly not applicable to those profoundly deaf.

These norms, in any case, have probably now been superseded by the data collected in the survey of academic achievement by the Office of Demographic Research of Gallaudet College. The principal current results concerned with reading ability derive from two separate surveys and are to be found in DiFrancesca (1972) and Jensema (1975). The former used nearly 17,000 children enrolled in programmes for the deaf in the USA; the latter used a subsample of 6871 different children. Both covered the entire school-age range. The data of relevance to us here are the results of the Paragraph Meaning subtest of the Stanford Achievement Test. This is essentially a test of a child's ability to understand connected prose. We have remarked earlier on weaknesses which may follow when test results are accumulated from many different testers as they are in these cases. But since the directions for administering this test are straightforward, and the test is widely used, the results are likely to be a reliable description of the reading ability of deaf children in the USA. Indeed, these reports are an incomparable data scource.

A rather more worrying problem is the fact that the test used is narrow span. What this means in practice is that with deaf children – poor readers for their age – the tester has to assess which level of test is most likely to be appropriate. As an example, DiFrancesca notes that his data use results of 155 students who were older than eighteen years but nevertheless were tested using the Primary I battery – the most elementary. Five different batteries were in fact used and the raw scores between different children are not comparable until after appropriate mathematical treatment. A number of such treatments have been used which are intended to bring all scores to some common base. The reliability of the ultimate-derived score will depend on the validity of the assumptions underlying the derivation. Clearly care is needed when using these data to assess the performance of an individual child. No performance test of this kind is a perfect measuring instrument, and the specific conditions (including the child-condition) in which a test is carried out are likely to contribute a substantial amount of "noise" to the achieved score. But while the need to combine scores from five different test levels in this case necessitates care in interpretation, the final outcome is very likely to be close to the truth.

Support that this is indeed so comes from a comparison of the median reading grades of the Wrightstone et al. study and the Gallaudet survey (DiFrancesca, 1972). Maintaining relevance to our own study with respect to age and considering only the older pupils, the first study's reading grade for the median sixteen-year-old (Furth, 1966b) is 3.4. For the same age, DiFrancesca reports a median of 3.27.

This would imply a reading age approximately between 9:3* and 9:6. It is evident from this agreement in studies conducted some ten years apart that the two tests are measuring more or less the same ability and that the conversion from Stanford raw scores is acceptably valid.

Jensema (1975), using Gallaudet survey data collected in 1975, shows how reading ability relates to a number of other variables. In order to handle the problem of combining scores from different test batteries of varying difficulty, Jensema first used a scaled score which relates test score to the median raw score of hearing subjects of the same grade level. Then, to examine the relationship between performance and other variables without the need to break down the data further by age, he constructs an age-deviation score, " . . . so that the entire sample . . . may be considered as a single group with scores which are comparable regardless of student age" (p. 3).

If we now consider the effect of hearing loss on reading comprehension, although normative data in the form of reading age or reading grade according to hearing loss cannot be provided, the relationship itself is clear. There is a marked decline in reading ability as deafness increases, to an extent which supports our doubt about the validity of the Metropolitan reading test norms. These, as we saw, ignore hearing loss as a relevant variable. We have no obvious explanation for so serious a discrepancy in empirical data when, in effect, the same population was used in both cases. But we assume the Metropolitan test to be less sensitive than the Stanford for a deaf population. There may be some evidence for this if we consider the reading grade by age. Between eleven and sixteen years, using the Metropolitan test, reading

* A reading age expressed (e.g.) 9:3, means nine years and three months.

advances by 0.8 grades (Furth, 1966b). Using the Stanford test, the increase is 1.12 grades. In both cases these are values for the median reader, ignoring any effect of hearing loss. In general then, the Metropolitan test appears to compress the range of scores whether age or hearing loss is considered. It seems likely therefore that the alleged unimportance of hearing loss in considering reading ability is due more to the nature of the measuring instrument than to the effects of deafness – a conclusion supported by much other evidence.

Jensema (1975) also makes a detailed analysis of performance in terms of cause of deafness. This too is in the form of age-deviation scores from zero where the value for all subjects is zero. The difficulty with this metric is that there is no way of extracting effects of other possible confounding variables such as the onset age of hearing loss or intelligence. For example, mumps as a cause of deafness shows the largest positive deviation from zero; children deaf from mumps read better than any other. But as Jensema says, mumps generally occur in older children when language may already be well developed. The data therefore have to be interpreted cautiously. One other striking example of this need shows in the relatively superior reading of the group with hereditary deafness. We saw in Table 2.2 that these children are a little deafer than others and that their deafness is almost always congenital. But on the other hand Table 2.4 shows children with hereditary deafness to be significantly more intelligent than those whose deafness is acquired; a factor likely to be an advantage for reading. There is surer ground in Jensema's presentation of reading ability and sex. We have found neither hearing loss nor intelligence difference between boys and girls. Here though, Jensema shows an advantage for girls in prose comprehension, but not in vocabulary. His general conclusion is " . . . that there is no meaningful difference in academic achievement of hearing impaired males and females, except possibly in the area of reading comprehension" (p. 4). No other major sources of normative reading data which are based on representative samples large enough for breakdown by variables likely to be relevant are known to us.

The paucity of data outside the USA is also true for Britain. In quantitative terms we know very little about reading comprehension and there are no data sources which would permit us to compare performance of British deaf children with those in the USA, taking relevant variables into account. There are a number of small-sample studies intended to be no more representative than of the particular sample used (Hine, 1970b; Owrid, 1970; Wollman, 1964). Redgate (1972) carried out a thorough study of the effect of using the Initial Teaching Alphabet with young deaf children learning to read. He presents a single table of mean reading ages based on the Southgate Group Reading Test-2 given to 698 children aged nine–eighteen years. These were drawn from 23 schools. Apart from age and the number of children at each age, no other information is given. No more than 36 children are represented up to the age of eleven – unlikely to be a random sample. Beyond that age the unusual English sampling problem occurs to which we have already drawn attention – the transfer of some 13% of the brightest children to two grammar schools. Redgate provides no information about the origin of the sample. At age 15 – 15:11 years, the mean reading age is given as 7:8. But if the grammar schoolchildren were not included this would considerably underestimate the national figure.

Murphy's (1956) unpublished study of the abilities of British twelve-year-old deaf children, though using a reliable sample of some 500 children, is probably too out of date to be of value now. The data were collected in 1952–54 when Partially Hearing Units were few and the audiological character of children in Schools for the Deaf may have been considerably different from that found today. Murphy used a word recognition test which no doubt, as he says, would correlate highly with most comprehension tests, but it does not provide meaningful reading age data. Of interest here though, he reported a significant association between reading vocabulary and degree of hearing loss – but no difference between boys and girls.

Probably the most comprehensive recent study of reading levels of deaf children in England has been by Hamp (1972). This screened children aged nine – fifteen years drawn from eight Schools for the deaf or partially hearing. Hamp considered that this provided "highly representative" (p. 206) results. This could only be true for children under the age of eleven, for reasons we have given. But since the principal aim was more to validate a new picture vocabulary test than to provide normative reading-ability data, it would matter little when considering the relationships he reports. Unfortunately, by spreading his subject population across a wide age-range, at 15+ years, the age with which we are principally concerned, only 64 children are represented.

Hamp used his own picture vocabulary test and two other comprehension tests. Interpreting the presented graphs for the age 15+ group suggests a mean reading age on the comprehension tests of about 8:10 when all levels of hearing loss are combined. But the correlation of "percentage hearing loss" (an occasionally used measure devised by Davis and Silverman, 1960) and reading was shown to be significant at the 0.01 level. He also found significant correlations between reading and intelligence. For the older group the value (0.37) is rather lower than we shall report. This may have been a statistical effect arising from the fact that two-thirds of the intelligence estimates came from teachers' ratings, measured test scores not being available.

From this brief summary of published data it is evident that large gaps in our knowledge of deafness and its relationship to reading remain to be filled. Because many factors have been reported which affect reading ability, interactive effects preclude the likelihood of a simple comprehensive statement. To date, for example, we have little idea of the relative magnitude of the contribution to reading made by, say, hearing loss together with intelligence. We know only that both are important to some extent. Jensema (1975) has shown that hearing loss affects reading, and that so too does cause of deafness. But we have shown that these two variables are not entirely independent; we do not yet know whether cause of deafness is a significant factor when hearing loss (and intelligence for that matter) has been controlled. We hope that the data to follow will help to sharpen the picture and to untangle the effects of some of the major confounding variables.

Assessing reading ability

The reading test we used for all children was the Wide-span Reading Test (Brimer, 1972). This test had two major advantages for us. First, it had never previously been used in a School for the Deaf in Britain and novelty was thus complete. Second, it is as its name implies, wide span. The single test of 80 items provides a well-standardized reading age which ranges from seven–sixteen years. There is therefore no need to make prior assessment of which of a number of different levels of test to use. Even though our chronological age-range was narrow, degree of hearing loss varied widely and we could expect a wide range of reading ability.

As with intelligence tests, reading tests measure what they measure. No two tests will necessarily tap the same linguistic ability, and no single definition of "reading" is likely to find general acceptance. The Wide-span Reading Test is one requiring sentence completion. The subject writes down on an answer sheet a word missing from a test sentence. Apart from that, there is little resemblance to other multiple-choice, sentence-completion tests. The form of the test is shown in Figure 6.1 which presents several test items mostly drawn from the more relevant early part of the set of 80. Each item consists of a pair of sentences. One sentence has a missing word which is to be found in the other of the pair. Without requiring the unstructured free generation of a word out of the head, so to speak – a characteristic of Cloze procedures (Moores, 1971; Taylor, 1956) – it avoids the linguistically constricting format of conventional multiple-choice tests.

Commonly these latter present, as alternatives, four or five words all of the same part of speech as the missing word. A problem in test-item construction is to find alternative words for

Figure 6.1.   Examples of items from Brimer's Wide-span Reading Test. (Published by permission of Dr. A. Brimer).

1	Brush up the leaves and burn them.	When logs _____ , smoke rises.
5	He tried to lift the catch on the door to open it.	He threw the key for her to _____ .
8	Put the cup on the shelf but leave the clothes in the tub.	The day was warm, _____ wet.
15	Anyone who cares for cats knows that if you scare one it can claw you and scar you for life.	The accident left him with a _____ on his cheek.
80	Medieval medicine attributed the choleric, phlegmatic, sanguine, and melancholic humours to the four chief fluids of the body.	His saturnine appearance belied his inherent optimism and the _____ view he took of this perilous situation.

each item which are equivalent in familiarity but of which only one is appropriate. Particularly in the early part of a test, which is where deaf children are likely to remain, it may be hard to evade the probability that the most familiar word is also the correct word. The test designer is heavily constrained by the nature of the English language and the limited vocabulary of poor readers. This kind of constraint does not necessarily give spurious reading ages to deaf children. If deaf children give the same responses as the average hearing child aged eight years, then they have a reading age of eight years. The possibility that deaf children might always have chosen the one word familiar to them, whilst hearing children carried out a sophisticated linguistic analysis of the sentence, cannot be a major criticism; it remains a pure speculation. The weakness of such tests is that they cannot probe far into a child's comprehension of language. The format precludes it. Even when a child is performing the test in accordance with the theoretical concepts inherent in its design, what it is in the child that is being tested seems limited. In performing the Wide-span Reading Test nothing stops a child from guessing either, nor from choosing the only familiar word. This is common to all forced-choice sentence-completion tests. We used it because it appears to us to be examining beyond mere vocabulary and into a range of syntactic forms and grammatical structures.

When we refer to a child's reading age, the value must not be used in the way we use the outcome of a thermometer reading which might be either in Fahrenheit or Centigrade. With thermometers, the same physical quality is always being measured – regardless of the scale used. But different reading tests may measure different qualities. It would be laborious to add to every stated reading age a suffix indicating the name of the measuring instrument. But that the suffix is implicitly present should not be forgotten when comparing results deriving from different tests.

One minor point with respect to this test – which was not designed with a deaf population in mind. Two items depend partly on auditory experience. One is Item 30 which few children reached. The second is Item 7. These items were excised from the test as we used it. Only a marginal effect on derived reading age would ensue.

Testing was carried out in groups which rarely exceeded four children and were usually smaller. Instructions were given to each child personally. The test as published has three practice items to be used for instructional purposes. Because of the communication difficulties of working with deaf children we found these to be insufficient, and devised three additional, even simpler items to lead children into the test proper. The general procedure was for an instructor to work with a child on the first two or three practice items and then leave the child to complete the practice set. These were then checked and any errors discussed and clarified. Once the child started on Item-1 no further help was given.*

Reading, deafness, and intelligence

Procedures which are statistically most reliable for analysing results do not always lend themselves to maximum clarity of presentation of outcomes. Readers' needs differ. One may wish to know where an individual child with a particular degree of hearing loss stands on reading in relation to other similar children. Another reader may be more concerned with the overall effect of hearing loss on reading when (e.g.) intelligence is taken into account. The principle which we shall try to follow is to test relationships by conventional statistical means, presenting only a summary of outcomes, and to interpret what this means in a less formal manner.

Figure 6.2 shows the basic data on reading ability for children in Schools – i.e., excluding children in PHUs for the moment. For each of the five bands of hearing loss it shows the mean reading age in months. Then, some idea of the range of reading ability in quartiles is shown. For each level of hearing loss, the 50th percentile represents the reading age of the "middle" child in the range. That is, half the scores are higher than that of the 50th percentile and half are lower. The 75th percentile value has 25% higher and

* The published test norms are available in two forms, depending upon whether the test is given as timed or untimed. Although we set no time-limit for completion, in fact most children would have reached their comprehension limit within the time-limit. Scoring was based strictly on the manual instructions, which define the procedure for determining, in the untimed version, when a child can be deemed to have reached his limit of comprehension. The manual provides conversion tables to permit derivation of a reading score from a raw score. This conversion requires the child's school grade to be taken into account. This is not appropriate when the test is used with deaf children, and Dr. Brimer has provided the author with another table which converts a basic score into a reading age suitable for all cases when a child begins the test at Item-1 – regardless of chronological age. This table is reproduced as Appendix 4.

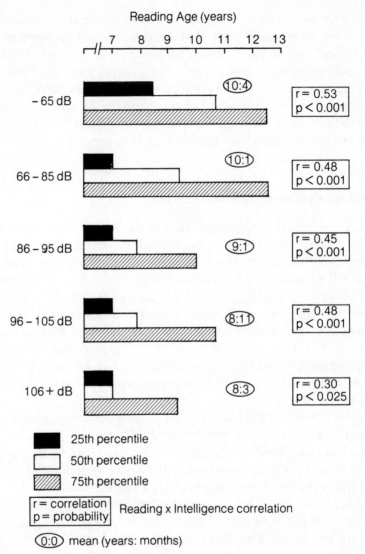

Figure 6.2.   Reading age and intelligence: by hearing loss (n = 355).

75% lower; the reverse being true for the 25th percentile value. For a given level of hearing loss, a child with a reading age at or greater than that shown for the 75th percentile is therefore a relatively good reader; he is in the top 25%. Finally we show the product-moment correlation between reading ability and intelligence. All of these correlations are significant beyond the 0.025 level. Probably not too much importance should be attached to the apparent decline in the size of this correlation as hearing loss increases. Even the extreme values do not differ significantly. It is more likely that the relatively low – though still significant – correlation for the deafest group of children is due to the increasing proportion of children who cannot read at all. That is, on the Wide-span Test, they do not get enough items correct to lift their "reading age" off the test's floor of 7:0.

It is not surprising that intelligence is a factor in reading ability and it has frequently been noted (Craig, 1964; Hamp, 1972; Montgomery, 1968). This means though that it needs to be taken into account when other relationships involving reading are considered. Accordingly, as we did with memory, the association between reading and hearing loss was examined by analysis of covariance, using the scores from Raven's Matrices as the covariate. The analysis is then carried out on "adjusted" reading scores. The effect on the mean reading values shown in Figure 6.2 is small because the intelligence-hearing loss effect was not great in the first place. The adjustment tends, slightly, to raise the reading scores at either end of the hearing-loss range relatively to that in the middle.

The outcome of the analysis of covariance is (1) that intelligence, not surprisingly, is confirmed as a highly significant factor in reading ($F_{1,337} = 74.68$; $p < 0.001$); and (2) that hearing loss itself is also significantly associated with reading ($F_{4,337} = 8.62$; $p < 0.005$). The principal effect of hearing loss lies between children with a loss up to 85 dB and those with a greater loss. The difference between the two hearing-loss bands up to 85 dB is not significant; nor are there differences (other than chance effects) amongst the three bands of greater hearing loss. But reading in both of the lower bands is significantly better than in all of the three upper bands. There does appear to be a sharp performance change around the hearing-loss level of 85 dB.

In general this result is in agreement with that of other studies where adequate numbers of children have been used (Hamp, 1972; Jensema, 1975; Murphy, 1956). Wrightstone et al. (1963), it will be recalled, did not test for this relationship and treated it as unimportant, although at all ages their data show a consistent deterioration of reading with increasing hearing loss. Montgomery (1968) in fact did report a virtually zero correlation between hearing loss and a number of vocabulary tests. But he points out that all of his sample were extremely deaf, and this would agree with what we have shown above. The only major study we know of which tested over a wide range of hearing loss and found no relationship with reading is that of Craig (1964). We have no explanation for this, and Craig himself makes no comment on it. In general it would seem that deafness is a clear factor in reading ability when the whole range of deafness is considered. Indeed it is hard to imagine any other relationship since the discrepancy in reading between deaf and hearing children is so marked.

The median reading age, when the entire school population is considered, is 9:0. The combined values covering the two age-groups fifteen and sixteen years reported by DiFrancesca (1972) for 17,000 children in the USA, yields a grade level of 3.15, i.e., a median reading age of 9:2. In spite, therefore, of the use of different reading tests and different procedures for collecting data, there is remarkable concordance. In practical terms a useful way of taking an overall view of the reading ability of these children is the presentation in Figure 6.3. Partly because there seems to be a genuine discontinuity at about a hearing loss of 85 dB, and partly to maintain adequate numbers, reading ability is shown in the form of cumulative frequencies for those children with a hearing loss up to 85 dB and separately for those above this value. The figure then shows the percentage of children reaching different levels of reading age in months. Since, with the test used, zero reading comprehension is represented by a reading age of 7:0, the lowest detectable ability shows as a value greater than this. It will be seen that of the deafer section of the population almost 50% have no reading comprehension at all – they are totally illiterate. With the same test, this would be the case for hearing children only at the chronological age of seven years. For the less deaf children, some 25% are without any reading comprehension. It is worth noting performance at the other end of the range as well. Here we can see that some 8% of the less-deaf children have a reading ability commensurate with their chronological age – a value which reduces to five such children out of 205 when deafness is greater than 85 dB. We shall look more closely at these few excellent readers later.

The analysis of covariance and the correlations in Figure 6.2 show that reading ability is associated significantly at least with hearing loss and intelligence – and we have seen that these latter variables are independent of each other. Intelligence is not determined by degree of deafness, or vice versa. To get a clearer picture

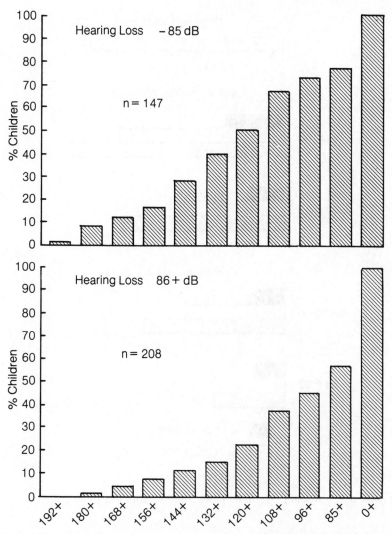

Figure 6.3. *Cumulative frequencies of reading age in months. (After Conrad, 1977a).*

of the effects of various combinations of intelligence and deafness the data have been rearranged in Figure 6.4. Again hearing loss has been divided at 85 dB and the intelligence range at the median value of the same population. Reading ages are then presented as quartiles, as they were in Figure 6.2. The figure clearly shows how higher intelligence and less deafness will lead to better reading, and how one might compensate for the other. For example, a bright,

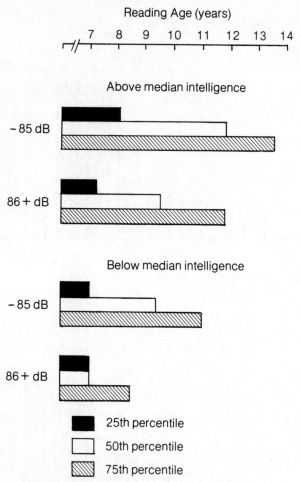

Figure 6.4.   *Reading age, intelligence, and hearing loss (n = 352).*

very deaf child may have about the same reading ability as a partially-hearing child of below-average intelligence.

Reading and internal speech

So far we have discussed reading in the conventional way, regardless of whether or not children had been shown to use internal
speech when memorizing words. Conventionally we reported a
significant association between deafness and reading. Figure 6.5
shows the outcome when internal speech is considered as well.

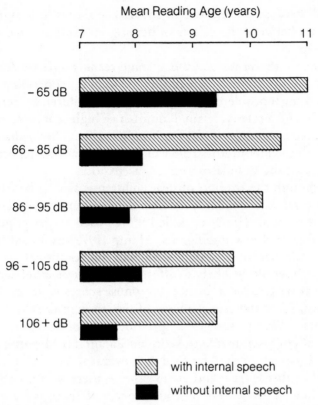

Mean Reading Age (years)

Figure 6.5.   Reading age and internal speech, by hearing loss (n = 302). Scores adjusted for intelligence.

Analysis of covariance shows three significant effects. Intelligence is again highly significant ($F_{1,292} = 45.72$; $p < 0.001$). Hearing loss is significant but only at the 0.05 level, and now there is a very large effect of internal speech ($F_{1,292} = 36.66$; $p < 0.001$). The implication of this appears to be that degree of deafness in itself is not a major factor in reading comprehension. What seems to be much more important, apart from intelligence, is whether or not the child has acquired the use of internal speech. Internal speech shows as a highly confounding factor in reading performance, as it does in short-term memory.

It is also an important absolute determinant of actual reading ability, since it can lead to a difference in reading age of up to two years, even after scores have been adjusted for intelligence. The narrowing of the gap as hearing loss increases is more apparent than real, because the analysis of covariance shows little sign of an interaction between the effects of hearing loss and internal speech on reading.

We can see therefore that the average reading ages of deaf children cited in the literature are highly misleading, concealing rather than exposing a problem. A large number of children are unable to read at all, and a relatively small number of high scores from good readers give an exaggeratedly high mean value. The median – the middle value – and interquartile values provide a truer reflection of the ability of the population under discussion.

Poor though the reading of deaf children is said to be, the true state of affairs is probably worse than generally represented. Wrightstone et al. (1963) excluded 9% of their target population because they had low intelligence. Hamp (1972) excluded first an unstated number of children who had an additional handicap "... which would be likely to affect their progress in reading" (p. 206). He also excluded a further 9% whose scores were too low to be meaningful at the criterial level of 6:6, though they were aged 15+ years. DiFrancesca (1972) provides no information on the number of children unable to score on Paragraph Meaning of the Primary I battery of the Stanford Achievement Test. But he does note that at this level – and at no other – there was no effect of hearing loss. This would of course occur if there were a large number of zero scorers.

The average value of reading ability for a given level of hearing loss depends on the proportion of children using internal speech. It also independently depends on their intelligence. We have reported a highly significant effect of intelligence as the covariate when considering hearing loss and reading, and we have shown significant correlations of intelligence with reading age at all levels of hearing loss. Thus it is clear that the level of reading ability reached by a child depends to a large extent on these three variables.

It then becomes misleading to consider how well particular children read if their reading ability is compared simply with the average for their age without taking these other factors into account. An attempt to show how serious this could be is represented in Figure 6.6. Here, to preserve numbers, we have again collapsed the hearing-loss range into the two bands – up to 85 dB and beyond 85 dB. Then, for each of these two bands, we have subdivided by use of internal speech and by intelligence. The cut-off used for the latter is the median Raven value for the School population as a whole – i.e., a score of 42. The figure then shows the median reading age of the group of children who fall within the respective hearing-loss, intelligence, and internal-speech requirements.

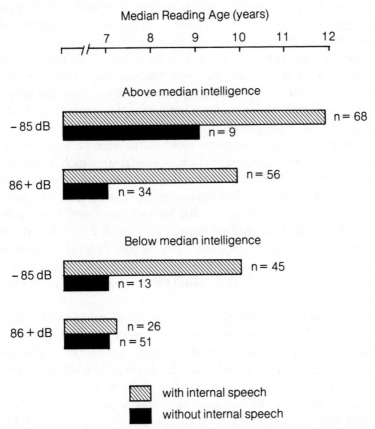

Figure 6.6.   *Reading age, internal speech, and intelligence: by hearing loss.*

The purpose of this presentation is not just to demonstrate that these three variables all affect reading. We have shown this statistically. The point is the more practical one of illustrating the hazards of incautious use of a reading age – regardless of the statistical reliability or the psychological validity of the reading test itself. It will be recalled that the median reading age for our entire population is about 9:0. A teacher might then be pleased with the performance of a particular boy, for instance, with a measured reading age of (e.g.) 10:4. But if the boy were partially hearing, above average intelligence, and used internal speech in reading, he would in fact be a relatively backward reader. Whilst, on the contrary, a parent whose profoundly-deaf child, even though of high intelligence but without internal speech, should feel encouraged if the child had a reading age of 8:4. Although well below the reading ability of the population median reader, that child reads much better than the median reader of the biologically more appropriate population. In sum, to be relatively good readers, if children are profoundly deaf, they must both have high intelligence *and* use internal speech; if they are partially hearing, they must be either bright *or* use internal speech. In general, without internal speech, children are likely to be below average readers regardless of their hearing loss or intelligence.

There is in fact an acceptably close association between reading ability and 'degree of internal speech (IS-Ratio) which is independent both of intelligence and hearing loss. We can rank-correlate IS-Ratio and reading age for each level of hearing loss, and partial out intelligence. When we do this for the first three hearing-loss bands, the partial correlations respectively are, 0.53, 0.40 and 0.57. Because of the large n in each case, all of these are significant beyond the 0.001 level. The calculation becomes impractical for the last two bands (deafest), because far too many children tie with no reading score at all.

Since we attach the minor role to degree of deafness as a factor in reading ability, and so much importance to internal speech, we might well wonder whether deaf children who use internal speech to the same extent as hearing children also read as well. In Chapter 5 we used a group of 57 deaf children, matched in this way to a hearing population, to compare short-term memory. The result showed only a very small advantage for the hearing children. Since these two samples of deaf and hearing children are matched for internal speech (IS-Ratio), and are nearly comparable in verbal memorizing, might they have similar reading ability? Most definitely they do not. We do not have a measured reading age for the hearing sample, but there is no reason to believe that it would be much different from average. Assuming a chronological average age of 15½ years, we would then expect an average reading age of the same value. In fact the mean reading age of our matched deaf sample is no more than 10:8 (also the value of its median).

This certainly suggests a very powerful direct effect of hearing loss. But a number of factors have to be taken into account which affect the validity of the comparison. One is the fact that, as we pointed out, the two groups are not matched on intelligence, though it is unlikely that the difference could lead to so great a discrepancy in reading scores. Other variables suggest themselves. For instance, medical history, with the attendant possibility of neurological disturbance; our deaf sample includes 25% with acquired deafness and 35% with unidentified cause. Then there are the innumerable and largely indefinable social and educational factors associated with deafness. These factors, though, were also present when we considered short-term memory, finding the deaf-hearing difference to be slight. Just the same, their effect can be assessed as before, by comparing partially-hearing with matched very deaf children.

We therefore made a second comparison using the 51 pairs of children whom we also introduced in the previous chapter. These children were all drawn from our deaf Schools' population – hopefully controlling to some extent for the variables we mentioned above – and were matched child by child on intelligence, cause of deafness, extent of the use of internal speech, and now also short-term memory. It will be recalled that the difference between them was that one of the pair had a hearing loss of less than 85 dB (group median = 66 dB), while the other of the pair had a loss greater than 95 dB (group median = 102 dB). The respective mean reading ages were 9:10 and 9:6 – a difference which is statistically negligible (t = 0.34).

Here we are faced with a curious and important problem. Reverting to the memory comparison, we saw that two groups of deaf children, very well matched except that one group was much deafer than the other, showed no difference. When a deaf and hearing group was matched for use of internal speech, the memory difference still barely reached statistical significance. This was taken to support a view that in itself degree of hearing impairment is not of great relevance for memorizing familiar words. In the case of reading though, while this appears to be equally true within a population of deaf children, it clearly is not when deaf and hearing groups are compared. The simplest explanation – though not necessarily the most important – is that memory was examined only for words which the children knew; this was tested for separately. But a reading test, to some extent, also tests vocabulary. A child cannot internalize words and linguistic structures that he has not experienced. Auditory deprivation will ensure deficits here. So we must assume that the less-deaf group, with less auditory deprivation, did have the greater vocabulary. But they still comprehended prose no better than the much deafer children to whom they were matched. Clearly knowledge of vocabulary and language are not the only factors involved.

Our difficulty then is that we are searching for a factor which is common to both deaf groups – the partially hearing and the profoundly deaf – but which distinguishes both of them from hearing children. One speculation to explore is the possibility that our goal may lie in the history of the early development of internal speech.

By the time normal hearing children reach the developmental point when they begin to comprehend prose at the age of five-seven years, they have also reached the point at which internal speech is well established and discernible (Conrad, 1971a; Garrity, 1975). But this is already several years after vocal speech has reached fluency. Furthermore, as soon as testing is practicable, a clear association can be shown between use of internal speech and reading ability (Liberman, Shankweiler, Liberman, Fowler, and Fischer, 1977; Mark, Shankweiler, and Liberman, 1977). We may be sure, though, that for the majority of deaf children, the first steps and many subsequent steps in reading must begin long prior to any development of internal speech. As we have already said, a large proportion of deaf children must first be taught that objects and activities have names – all well known for some time to the hearing child at that stage. If the course of linguistic development of deaf children even remotely parallels that of hearing children, then internal speech must occur after vocal speech has been established. So even though deaf children may subsequently fluently internalize the spoken words they have, to a point where on a memory test they perform *like* hearing children, this development may be very substantially retarded. Where the average hearing child breaks free of mechanical look-say (whole-word) reading procedures fairly early in reading development – or remains a backward reader – deaf children must inevitably be held prephonetic with respect to reading for many more years, assuming they ever do break free.

In Chapter 1 we stressed the importance of regarding internal speech as a matter of degree both in terms of quantity and quality. Here we suggest the importance of the extent of exercise of internal speech insofar as it is applied to reading. Liberman et al. (1977) have proposed a precise mechanism whereby this retardation may be expressed, "If he knows some letter-to-sound correspondences, and that he must scan in a left-to-right direction, he might simply search his lexicon for a word, any word, beginning with a phoneme that matches the initial letter" (p. 214). Here we see a delineation of a stage of reading in which many deaf children may remain trapped. We suggest that even those who escape into full phonetic coding of what is almost always a limited vocabulary in fact escape only many years later than hearing children. Even then, it is likely that sheer day-to-day exercise in using internal speech will sharply distinguish hearing from even partially-hearing children.

In referring to the proportion of deaf children who do use internal speech we should not forget the relative simplicity of the task used in assessment. Our reference may be closer to maximum use than minimum. The difficulty is that we need to imagine a continuum comprised of children varying in degree of deafness but starting from those with normal hearing. Now we think of different aspects of linguistic performance and wonder about the bands of increasing deafness which would be required to show noticeable performance changes. We have pointed to one discontinuity at 85 dB. There is no reason to assume that changes will occur at equal intervals. Nor should we assume that the relevant bands will be the same for all aspects of language.

If our speculation has any merit, applied to the present case, it suggests that children spanning a very wide range of hearing loss and who show little variablility when it comes to phonetic manipulation of a few familiar words may show sharp discontinuities when less familiar words are involved. The precise relationship between the developmental period at which internal speech is maturing and subsequent linguistic sophistication remains totally obscure at present.

Reverting to the deaf and hearing children whom we matched for IS-Ratio, we suggest that while this was a true match for the relatively simple cognitive operation of memorizing familiar words, the match fails to hold for the more complex operations of prose comprehension. This is obviously speculative but we shall need to return to it later.

Competence and criteria

Reading age

In the preceding pages a number of factors which affect the reading ability of deaf children have been discussed. Though degree of deafness within deaf populations seems not to be a unitary major factor, certain consequences of deafness are present. In making comparisons with hearing children we can control many relevant variables. But some remain which are so closely associated with the unique fact of deafness that control is virtually impossible. At the ultimate there is no evading the fact that, in general, deaf children are very poor readers; that is, compared with hearing norms.

What in fact are the appropriate measures for assessing the reading competence of deaf children? Throughout this chapter we have exclusively used reading age as a relative quantity to compare groups of deaf children, to compare deaf and hearing children, and for examining relationships between reading and other variables. But if reading age is to be used to assess competence, with all of the pedagogic overtones, its credentials as a criterion merit discussion.

Like most other psychological constructs, measured reading age is bound to its measuring instrument to a far greater degree than would be true for most physical qualities. Not surprisingly then, the concept of a reading age, and by implication its measurement, has often been criticized. Reading age indicates no more than a child's performance on a particular test relative to that of many other children. Daniels and Diack (1972) have pointed out that reading tests frequently assume a particular educational theory, and that a child taught to read in a different theoretical system may be penalized. It will be recalled that we were forced to delete two items from the Wide-span Reading Test simply because a phonic-reading assumption obtrudes in the case of those two items. But valid though this criticism is, with increasing age of child its force must diminish. If, by school-leaving age, the manner of learning to read determines level of comprehension, then issues of the teaching of reading are involved and not simply the nature of tests.

In the case of deaf children, the assumptions underlying the use of a reading-age index of reading ability require particularly close scrutiny. When we say that the median deaf reader has, at the age of fifteen – sixteen years a reading age of about nine years, we mean no more and no less than that on this test the same level of performance is reached by the average hearing nine-year-old. Given this information, we can, as we have said, use it to compare that deaf child with any other. No assumptions are required about the linguistic processes used in carrying out the test. We use the test because we judge it to measure some quality in which we are interested. For expository convenience we call that quality "reading". In presenting results, we have used the arithmetic representation of reading age, because it has more instantaneous meaningfulness.

By so doing – and not without forethought – we implicitly invite our readers to make a comparison of reading ability of the children discussed with hearing children, knowing that the comparison may lead to judgement. At the point when we begin to consider the reading ability of deaf children in relation to that of hearing children, we become concerned with reading competence in an especially narrow and defined way. We have adopted a criterion. We have in effect asked how *well* deaf children read *in relation to* heaing children of the same age. The question is asked not in order to clarify a theoretical issue, but to assess a practical outcome. The reading ability of hearing children merely offers one arbitrary yardstick.

This question and this device for achieving an answer are of course central to many of the studies of reading by the deaf which have been reported. Not surprisingly because, as we said, reading is the primary *R* in education. The conclusion implied in the generally concordant results, and recognized in the abundance of reading programmes, is that deaf children read very poorly. We suggest that this may be a superficial and not very useful conclusion.

We have elaborated on this elsewhere.

If reading is considered as a tool for achieving something else, such as information or knowledge, then no particular virtue attaches to any specific level of reading ability until that level has been justified as necessary for the purpose. In other words, if it is considered that adequate reading is represented by a reading age of 9:0 years, then 50 per cent of the present sample are adequate readers regardless of their apparent 'deficit'. But if the criterion is set at, e.g., 11:0 years, then one notes that 75 per cent of the children tested lack adequate reading. (Conrad, 1977a, p. 145).

The particular point we were concerned to make was that using reading-test performance of hearing children as the criterion for assessing that of deaf children requires independent justification.

Literacy

One such justification is at once available, namely literacy. This, after all, might be regarded as the first-stage purpose of reading. If a case could be made for the proposition that every child about to leave school requires the reading ability of the average sixteen-year-old hearing child in order to attain some necessary goal, then the criterion is valid and useful.

The dictionary definition of literacy – being able to read and write – is clearly inadequate in the present context. Educational programmes take it to mean ability to read to a point of some utility which is generally associated with an examination standard – which tautologically returns us to the reading-age concept. The unasked question is, how much reading is required? The curious aspect to this question is that it self-evidently lends itself to empirical answer. Readability measures (Klare, 1963) represent one possible approach, but one which has never been widely adopted; Gilliland (1972) discusses more than 30 variants. A second measure, more tedious, but perhaps of greater validity, would be to determine the average chronological age of a representative sample of children able to read a defined kind of material. In practice the tedium might be alleviated by a combination of the readability and the reading-age concepts. In fact, in spite of widespread concern with standards of literacy of hearing children, at least in Britain, this has never been generally done. We are then left with somewhat rough estimates of levels of reading which might be taken to exemplify literacy.

Furth (1966b), commenting on the Wrightstone et al. data, suggests that " ... a functionally useful ability to read ..." (p. 461) is represented by the end of USA fourth-grade reading – about 11:0. Disregarding degree of hearing loss, at the age of 15½–16½ years 88% of the sample failed to reach the criterion. The comparable value for our own sample is 75%, rising to 82% for children with hearing losses greater than 85 dB. Gray (1956), in an international survey of reading standards, took ten years as the acceptable threshold for what he called "functional literacy".

Bullock (1975) refers to a number of "official" attempts to define literacy which are models of obscurity. A British Ministry of Education pamphlet (1950) defines literate as able to read and write for practical purposes of daily life, and Bullock (p. 10) reports a UNESCO criterion that "A person is literate who can, with understanding, both read and write a short, simple statement on his everyday life."

Attempts to represent these phrases in more practical terms have been no more than suggestive of possibilities, nowhere near approaching a usable taxonomy. Bullock refers to American studies indicating that 8% of the population could not read well enough to request a driving licence, and 34% not well enough to apply for medical aid. But this kind of very specific reference material is unlikely to provide a good guide to literacy, since success is just as likely to depend on the written style of the single document as on the capabilities of the readers under test. It is not surprising, then, that values of the reading age designated as representing literacy abound. Gray suggesting ten years; Furth, eleven years; Moyle (1973), thirteen years – a level required for reading the simplest daily newspaper; Bullock (p. 11), " . . . it has often been found that . . . the lowest grade of difficulty at which complex subject matter can be written approximates to a reading age of about 15." At the other end of the scale, Bullock suggests that an illiterate person has a reading age of less than seven – a value which the Wide-span Reading Test accepts as its baseline – and a semiliterate person a reading age between seven and nine years.

Clearly there is much room for definition of reading ability in terms of goals – both linguistic and social. All we need be clear about here is that no matter what the proportion of deaf children is who fail to achieve no matter what reading age, one useful way of understanding the significance of a value is in terms of what it will "buy" for the child in terms of availability of reading material. We may merely note here the cold statistics that, using seven years as the lowest value, then 35% of our population are illiterate. Using seven to nine years as semiliterate, we have a further 20%. As we have said, Furth's criterion of eleven years for functional literacy yields us 25% of the deaf school population. If we take the most testing criterion of understanding complex subject matter, then no more than 4% of deaf school-leavers can "read". Nevertheless, the point we are trying to insist on is the need to distinguish between performance relative to hearing children and performance relative to practical goals. It is just possible that many hearing children have an ability to read far higher than they ever require, though we certainly do not wish to imply that vocational need is the only appropriate criterion.

One other point is relevant to the literacy criterion when it is applied to deaf children. It is commonly assumed that their reading ability continues to improve after they leave school. Hammermeister (1971) conducted a thorough study of the reading ability of deaf adults up to thirteen years beyond school-leaving age. Although vocabularly improved, reading comprehension did not. Evidently the impairment in comprehension was not greatly dependent on size of vocabulary – the difficulty was elsewhere in the reading process. This has to some extent been confirmed by Reynolds (1975) using an academic deaf population. Reynolds compared the reading ability of sophomores and seniors at Gallaudet College and found no improvement, though they were still some way below comparable hearing norms. Reynolds also noted that his college students thought they read better than they actually did on test. But as there is no hearing control for this latter result, it should not too readily be assumed to be related to deafness. Both of these studies, and the slow annual rate of improvement of reading with age (DiFrancesca, 1972; Hamp, 1972; Redgate, 1972; Wrightstone et al., 1963), all point to a continuing level of reading by the deaf far below that reached by the average hearing reader.

Cross-cultural comparison

In trying to form a judgement with respect to the reading ability of our deaf population, we have suggested that (1) we may relate it to hearing norms or (2) to standards of literacy. A third criterion is available. This is by cross-cultural comparison; how well do UK deaf children read when compared with those in other countries? Unfortunately, outside the USA there is little comprehensive data available which would permit comparison of any detail. Ahlström (1971) referred to the reading ability of Swedish deaf children as "very low", and Nordén (1975) reported of some 150 Swedish deaf school-leavers that they barely achieved a reading age of ten years. Vestberg Rasmussen (1973) gave a picture vocabulary test to the 109 children in the two state schools for the deaf in Copenhagen. Performance was sufficiently poor for him to conclude " . . . we are forced to admit that we cannot teach these deaf pupils to read" (p. 32). This pessimism was based on the fact that by school-leaving age some 12% of children had scores no better than those of nine-year-old hearing children. VandenBerg (1971a) tested all the English-speaking children in schools for the deaf in New Zealand and who were aged nine–fourteen years. Accepting a reading age of 11:0 as the criterion for literacy, she reported that "... not one child ... has even an approximate knowledge of the language as expressed in written English" (p. 66).

We have compared throughout this chapter with American data when they were relevant. In fact it is clear that when controlled comparison is possible – as it frequently has been – there is close accord between the outcomes for the USA and UK. Since the distributions of hearing loss of the two relevant populations are similar, the parsimonious conclusion is that the different tests used did in fact measure similar abilities. On the basis of the criterion of cross-cultural comparison therefore, it appears that UK deaf children read no worse than any other with which we can compare.

Again we have to conclude that deaf children widely read at a far lower level than hearing children of the same chronological age – the extent of the difference being some six-seven years. This is a discrepancy which is so great, and so universal, that it is hard to believe that it will be dispelled even by the most radical improvements in teaching methods which are conceivable within the framework of current theoretical and technological knowledge.

Theoretical limitations

The fact that, whenever reliable information is available, there is wide agreement concerning the limit of development of reading comprehension suggests the presence of theoretical constraints. Whether these are restricted to beginning reading, creating a retardation which deaf readers cannot recoup, or whether the relevant constraints continue to operate is still arguable.

The principal and inescapable difference between deaf and hearing children in this context is a truism; it is the absence or presence of experience of spoken language – the language which in the Western world is represented by print. Does this insurmountable difference necessarily imply the existence of theoretical limits beyond which no progress can be made? If this is so, then a criterion of performance such as a hearing-based reading age would be inadmissable – though its value for assessing relationships between reading and other variables need not be impaired. A full answer to the question would require a theoretical analysis of what is involved in developing reading skill in terms of specific processes. It might then be possible to determine which of these are likely to be – again theoretically – impaired by absence of hearing. Not only is this kind of analysis beyond the terms of our present brief, but research in this area points to only fractional consensus. We shall do no more then than to glance in certain directions.

From the very first moments of learning to read, there is a glaring difference in the size of usable vocabulary between deaf and hearing children. Hamp (1972) indicates a picture vocabulary age of about 7½ years for deaf children aged nine-ten, the youngest that he tested. This kind of test, based on correct selection of one of four pictures, cannot be an exhaustive examination of the number of words a child knows. Silvermann-Dresner and Guilfoyle (1972), for example, used a vocabularly of 7300 words carefully chosen to reflect those known to hearing children aged seven-twelve years. They considered a word to be known to children of a particular age, if 62.5% of them gave the correct response. The youngest deaf children tested – aged eight-nine years – knew no more than 18 out of the 7300 possible.

The deaf beginning reader does not learn to read in the sense that the term is conventionally used with respect to hearing children. The latter learn to decode print into already familiar verbal names which are part of their existing and well-established vocabulary. The deaf child must first learn the vocabulary. Broadly, two inefficient methods may be used. If a variant of phonic instruction is employed, the child will be encouraged to say as well as to look. But, because his speech is likely to be poor, his phonic representation may bear little relationship to the true phonemic structure of the word. Indeed, Bradley and Bryant (1978) have shown that, with young children presumed to have normal hearing, even a small defect in categorizing speech sounds may lead to several years of reading retardation by the age of ten. If, as is likely, deaf children are not grounded in the rules of grapheme-phoneme translation they will need to depend on whole-word – or fragments of whole-word – visual memorizing to acquire the knowledge that particular configurations refer to particular objects.

In the previous chapter we pointed out that children using a visual code to memorize would be penalized if the words were visually similar. The first Ladybird book of key words for initial reading (McNally, 1965) presents 92 key words. Of these, 70% have either three or four letters, that is, they look similar. Furthermore 20% of these begin with either *b, d,* or *p* – known to present problems of visual discrimination for young children. This, of course, is not a criticism of the Ladybird series, but a comment on the nature of English words. While the key words do necessarily use some common phonemes, they are not very likely to present a problem to a child with normal hearing. For instance, though the letter *b* is the most frequent initial letter, the next phoneme is different in all cases – a characteristic helpful to a hearing child, but useless to one profoundly deaf.

The deaf child, then, starts the reading process with effectively no vocabulary. Whether he struggles with phonics or with whole-word visualizing, for one reason or another, it will be inefficient when compared to the hearing child phonetically acquiring acoustically discriminable words. That this represents a true psychological barrier to normal progress seems an unavoidable conclusion. Using a finger-spelling alphabet possibly bypasses both sets of difficulty, but few deaf children in Britain are taught to read in this way.

There is, however, powerful evidence that for deaf children, even when a sentence comprises only familiar words, failure to comprehend may stem from inability to understand the syntax. A very comprehensive study by Quigley, Wilbur, Power, Montanelli, and Steinkamp (1976) used a number of novel test formats to demonstrate what had hitherto been little more than classroom hearsay. Children might be shown the following written statements, "A dog chased a ball. A cat chased a ball" They are then required to make a single sentence with the same meaning beginning, "A dog .....". Or the statement shown is, "I saw the man who the man hit the dog." Children first have to report whether it is right or wrong, and if wrong to rewrite it correctly. In a third procedure, the child is shown, "John chased the girl. He scared the girl", and then has to choose which of several offered single sentences means the same as the original statement.

Performance of deaf children aged between ten–eighteen years was compared with that of hearing children aged eight–ten years. Seven kinds of syntactic structure were examined. For example, (1) Relativization, "The man who is my friend lives down the street." (2) Conjunction, "Ellen woke up late and missed her train." This of course can be derived from, "Ellen woke up late.

Ellen missed her train." (d) Complementation, "Watching TV annoys me." ("Someone watches TV. It annoys me.") (4) Pronominalization, "The boy who hit the girl ran away," Instead of, "The boy the boy hit the girl ran away." Other syntactic structures considered were question formation, negation, and the verb system. All of the test items used words well within the children's expected vocabulary.

In general, the order of difficulty of the different structures was similar, though not identical, for deaf and hearing subjects. Both groups found relativization to be most difficult to handle and negation the easiest. But Quigley et al. point out that structures barely mastered by eighteen-year-old deaf students presented little difficulty for ten-year-old hearing children. Significantly, they conclude (p. 189), " . . . we still are willing to draw the tentative conclusion that syntactic structures develop similarly for deaf children as for hearing children, but at a greatly retarded rate."

This conclusion – and we must accept the authors' caution – is of the greatest importance. It addresses itself to the question of whether the difference in reading ability between deaf and hearing people can be regarded as being due to retardation in the deaf or to a more fundamental psychological difference. In terms of practical education we might speculate that retardation was a more tractable problem than fundamental difference. But at the same time it is also true that all developmental processes reach a developmental limit. No evidence at all has been found to suggest that the extremely slow (relative to hearing children) reading development of deaf children continues beyond the age at which it also effectively ceases in hearing children. But of course if impoverished hearing of spoken language leads to a concept of linguistic structures radically at variance with those used in prose, then improving developmental rate by conventional educational procedures will help little.

Moores (1971) has suggested just this possibility: " . . . It is evident that the language ability of deaf students differs from that of the hearing both quantitatively and qualitatively" (p. 21). Moores assessed "morphologico-syntactic and semantic differences" between deaf and hearing children using the "Cloze" technique (Taylor, 1956). This technique presents a passage of prose with every nth (usually 5th) word deleted. Subjects write in the missing words, success depending on their knowledge of " . . . grammatical and semantic dependencies . . ." (Moores, p. 3). Very young hearing children and much older deaf children matched for reading comprehension were used. The study by Moores, as well as those by Marshall (1970) and by Odom, Blanton, and Nunnally (1967), also using the Cloze technique, considered reading of deaf children to show major deficits at a syntactic level when compared with hearing children. Clearly here, too, a theoretical limit seems to have been reached by the end of school life – if not sooner – which precludes the attainment of levels which are available for the hearing child.

Finally, but by no means exhaustively, we must again consider the role of internal speech; not just as a way-in to grapheme-phoneme translation at the level of decoding print, but as a tentative step towards understanding the difficulties of deaf adolescents in understanding syntactic forms of English, which are simple for quite young hearing children.

Just what cognitive processes the "mature" deaf reader uses to derive meaning from print is largely unexplored. We know of no EMG study using deaf children comparable to those of Edfeldt (1960), Hardyck and Petrinovich (1970), Locke and Fehr (1970), etc. There is some indirect evidence that internal speech may not be used in the same way, or to the same extent, as it is by hearing people. As we have noted, Chen (1976) and Locke (1978a) reported that profoundly deaf children were no more likely to miss a silent *e* than a sounded *e* in a letter cancellation task, but that hearing children did miss more silent *es*. The suggestion is that hearing children decode via speech, but that some, at least, deaf children do not. Conrad (1971b) showed that deaf children identified as not using internal speech in memorizing were impaired in comprehension when they were required to read aloud. He concluded that this requirement interfered in some way with their natural reading processes. Deaf children who did use internal speech when memorizing were not affected by reading mode, nor were hearing children. What seems certain is that, for the population we tested, failure to use internal speech during reading impairs comprehension, and Figure 6.5 indicates the gravity of the effect. We do not know where in the reading process failure to apply phonetic correlates of print is most likely to lead to impairment. We have referred to the problems of building vocabulary. For the same reason we might assume that the mental manipulations required to extract the meaning syntactically embedded in sentences would also be hindered if the words were held in an inefficient form. Insofar as this is true, the absence of an appropriate medium must impose a theoretical limitation to development.

Learning to read is an immensely complex skill. Some of its elements have been identified. There is little expert consensus with respect to a complete description of the component parts; nor with respect to the relative importance of the generally agreed parts. It would be surprising were the fact of hearing impairment to have equal relevance at all stages. When significant biological factors are accounted for, our evidence is that speech is not a *requirement* for relating print to a semantic lexicon. Nor does it appear to be necessary for creating that lexicon. Morkovin (1960; 1968) and Moores (1972) have described how enviable vocabularies have been acquired by preschool Russian deaf children using finger spelling as the medium, and Evans (1978) reports a better-controlled account for English children. The status of internal speech at higher levels of integration seems more debatable. It clearly has an advantage over visual coding of words, as Liberman et al. (1977) have also shown for hearing children. But in their case, and ours, we must doubt whether all the children in the studies had been taught to read using a method which capitalized on their preferred coding strategy. Certainly in the case of deaf children other modes of handling words need to be examined.

But for hearing people, whose only other sensory-based coding medium is probably visual, the evidence appears to be that internal speechlike transduction provides unique advantages for many people. In a delightful discussion on the history of silent speech in reading, Pugh (1975) points out that at one time reading was normally vocal. The increase in literacy and the consequent great increase in the number of readers made vocal reading unsociable, while the increase in the available reading material presumably rendered the relatively slow vocal (word-by-word) reading uneconomic of time. But why did the ancient scholars read vocally in the first place? Was it just because they were so often reading to an audience? Our data suggest either that there were more funda-mental reasons.

The principal impact of our analysis of reading performance is the need to understand the very great deficit which is present at the time deaf children leave school. A reading ability equivalent to that of nine-year-old hearing children does not permit compla-cency. This is not a parochial matter. Deficits of this order are widespread. But it would not be difficult to argue – and it would be true – that, wherever this six-seven year retardation occurs, broadly similar educational traditions underlie teaching methods. Oral education leaves too many deaf children close to illiterate. The inability of so many children to acquire a facility for oral manipulation of words has been a neglected area of pedagogic discussion. It may also surprise that, while degree of hearing loss over a wide range has so small a reflection in reading ability, the discrepancy between our least-deaf children and those with normal hearing is still very large indeed. Some of this must derive from selection factors, so that we would expect to find good partially-hearing readers in ordinary schools. Yet Ling (1975) and others have reported contrary evidence, and the very slight hearing impairment needed to affect speech reception (Hood and Poole, 1971) provides a warning. It is clear – and not an overstatement – that we do not know how to teach deaf, or even partially-hearing, children to read.

In the course of testing 468 children in Schools and Partially Hearing Units, we found 18 children who were prelingually deaf and had a reading age comparable to their chronological age. These children have certain unifying characteristics. Every one has a score on Raven's Matrices above the median for the population as a whole and 14 of them are in the top 25%. All show marked use of internal speech in memorizing words. Three children have acquired deafness, that is 15%; for the population as a whole the value is nearly 40%. Of the 18, 13 have a hearing loss which is less than 86 dB; most of them are not very deaf. This means that there are five such readers – a little over 1% – who are also profoundly deaf. These children, their teachers, and their parents (both also deaf in two cases) must surely be saluted.

7
Lip Reading

We have seen that few deaf children reach levels of reading proficiency which are average for their hearing peers. It is widely accepted for the latter, that although reading is a primary means of advancing linguistic knowledge especially during the earlier school years, it also depends on an existing language base. Printed words and grammatical sequences of words are referred to the linguistic data bank established and developed first through hearing and subsequently through the addition of speech. If hearing children reached school age with normal hearing but with no understanding or use of spoken language, we can be sure that rectifying this deficit would become an urgent prerequisite for learning to read.

Profoundly-deaf children reach school age in just this state. To what linguistic data bank then will they refer those printed words? In other words, what is their mother-tongue? Insofar as they are profoundly deaf, and also in the 95% of deaf children born of hearing parents, it is highly likely that such language as they do have will have been acquired through lip reading. But the fact is that, unless they have participated in formal training, they will have virtually no verbal language; even if they have had such training they will still reach school age with only the minutest knowledge of lip-read language.

For a hearing child in a normal language environment, comprehension of spoken language proceeds in a relatively orderly and facile manner. For the deaf child, comprehension of spoken language through lip reading presents an unnatural and difficult cognitive problem. We shall come to the nature of this problem shortly, but perhaps the most devastating – and quite obvious –

feature is that while speech sounds are omnidirectional, the lip reader *must,* in advance of an utterance, be observing the speaker's face. Where for the hearing child in a normal family situation speech sounds are part of the natural environment, the equivalent for the deaf child is not just auditory silence but, for the most part, linguistic silence. Even if a hearing child is not listening, speech may be volubly present. If deaf children are not looking, no matter how much family chatter there is, their personal environment may be totally without language. For most deaf children, school is where they first seriously begin to learn to understand what is to be their mother-tongue. Unless they are born into a signing family (deaf or hearing), lip reading will be the primary means of understanding what is said.

Some authors (Frisina, 1963) have suggested that auditory information is useless for lip reading when hearing loss reaches 90 dB, but, as a general and more conservative statement, by the time the loss reaches about 95 dB we can be fairly sure that no usable speech will be heard (Erber, 1975). Figure 2.1 shows that at present some 40% of children in Special Schools in England and Wales have this degree of deafness, and the figure is paralleled elsewhere.

This refers to the case of the profoundly-deaf preschool child with minimal usable hearing for speech sounds. But comprehension of speech is disturbed long before levels of profound deafness are reached. Hood and Poole (1971) have reported that discrimination of speech sounds begins to be impaired with a hearing loss of as little as 31 dB. In formal tests using single words, a number of authors have shown with hearing subjects that very little noise is required before the first weak phonemes are masked and may only be identified visually (Erber, 1969; O'Neill, 1954; Sumby and Pollack, 1954). As degree of hearing loss increases, a child will need to rely more and more on visual cues for understanding speech.

Lip reading and linguistic ability

Because it is generally accepted that facial gestures may have an important role in understanding speech which is imperfectly heard, the act is often described as *speech reading,* implying a role to parts of the body other than the mouth and jaw (Berger, 1972a). Nevertheless, both the terms *lip reading* and *speech reading* carry an implication of exclusive visual behaviour, and insofar as they do, neither adequately reflects what generally happens when the behaviour occurs outside of artificial laboratory contexts. Here we shall use the former for no better reason than that it is in common use in Britain and has a more ancient history; Berger (1972a) recounts that three centuries ago the English Dr. Plot was writing on "labiomancy".

It is more important to distinguish between lip reading in the virtual absence of correlated auditory information and speech comprehension when both vision and some residual hearing are together involved. The degree of involvement of lip reading in speech comprehension is bound to depend to a large extent on degree of hearing impairment, and we shall inevitably use both terms somewhat arbitrarily. Many partially-hearing children do not depend on lip-read – but on auditory – information, and since we cannot tag each child with precision, it would be rather misleading to pretend, terminologically, that we could.

It is clearly misleading, though, to imagine that deaf children rely entirely on speakers' lips for face-to-face communication. There can be no doubt that watching a speaker's mouth concentrates the mind, and centres attention on the major source of information – the area where the gestures accompanying phonology occur. But it is highly likely that other facial gestures make some contribution. Indeed it is self-evident that verbal communication involves meaningful and complementary gestures which are not only facial but may extend to the whole body. While there is this element of self-evidence about the occurrence of additional gestures, we usually know very little about their precise value. Common experience indicates, for example, that raised eyebrows may be more expressive of a communication that any conformation of the lips. But we do not really know whether other than oral gestures do in fact enhance or supplement, or whether they are used as alternatives when the mouth proves inadequate, or whether they are irrelevant occurrences, or even whether they might be distractions from the difficult task of "reading" the lips. Berger and Popelka (1971) reported that lip reading was more difficult when only the speaker's lips were visible and the rest of the face masked, but knowledge here in general is scanty. Since the angle of sharp visual acuity is small and movement of the lips and organs in the oral cavity are fleeting during speech, it is perhaps surprising that there appear to be no formal studies concerned with where deaf lip readers are actually looking while they are lip reading.

The distinction between pure lip reading and comprehension of speech in general is essentially pragmatic. This chapter is principally concerned with everyday behaviour. Our purpose is to enquire into the ability with which deaf school-leavers can understand normal speech, when their residual hearing is available and they use a hearing aid if they so wish. We shall therefore try to evaluate performance at the skill of speech comprehension rather than lip reading, with level of hearing loss as one of the independent variables. In this we shall be concerned with normal communication between people.

Even if the speech utterances used in a lip reading study are very common words, a confounding variable may be introduced which is itself associated with degree of deafness. The relationship between degree of deafness and linguistic competence is well established, as we saw in the previous chapter. At the same time, many authors have pointed out that lip reading ability is also dependent on linguistic knowledge (Berger, 1972a; Craig, 1964; Evans, 1965; Myklebust, 1964). Not surprisingly therefore, studies concerned with the effect of degree of deafness on lip reading ability frequently confound linguistic ability. Whether the procedure uses silent speech (Evans, 1965) or vocal speech (Myklebust, 1964), whether the subjects wear hearing aids or not (Craig, 1964; Montgomery, 1966a), it is unclear whether language knowledge or the ability to "read" lips is being measured.

The fact is that we cannot expect hearing-impaired children to be able to lip read words which they do not already know. But even if they do know them, they may still be unable to lip read them. Most tests cannot distinguish between these two possibilities, though there are procedures which probably evade or at least minimize this problem. When Erber (1974a) tested children with hearing losses ranging from 52–127 dB for their ability to comprehend simple spondaic words, two precautions were taken. First, the children familiarized themselves with the words some time before testing. Second, during the test the set of 25 test words was provided to the children who merely had to choose one. But it would be hard to generalize results from a procedure as formalized as this to the case of everyday conversation – and Erber does not presume to do so. There seems, in sum, no simple and certain way in which lip reading achievement can be evaluated for ordinary discourse even relatively, which is uncontaminated by language factors. In a moment we shall describe a somewhat less than simple procedure which to some extent does avoid the difficulties described above.

The validity and use of lip reading tests

There are a number of excellent reviews of tests which have been used to assess lip reading ability (Berger, 1972a; Farwell, 1976; Jeffers and Barley, 1971). Berger (1972a) pointed out that no test had, at that date, been standardized in the USA; the same is true for Britain, though something probably close to a standardization (but unpublished) has been made for the Donaldson Lip-reading Test (Montgomery, 1966a; 1968). It is equally true that, for deaf children, no large-scale and comprehensive evaluation of lip reading ability has been published. There would in any case be a serious problem of validation if the results were to have value as an absolute standard. Here we refer to the question of what achieving a particular test score would mean to a child in terms of absolute ability to use lip reading as a means of communication. As we shall also see in the next chapter with respect to speech intelligibility – where the issue is perhaps in sharper focus – a high score may indicate an excessively easy test just as well as a high level of skill. For the present therefore we are obliged to use lip reading or speech-comprehension tests as no better measures than are the tests themselves.

One possible solution to the problem of validity – the degree to which the test represents how well a child comprehends speech – would be by validation against ratings. A rating made by an appropriately "programmed" judge could tell us just this. We did use rated judgements in the case of speech intelligibility. But, for our purpose, similar ratings of lip reading would have weakness. Our concern is with everyday behaviour. We want to know how well children can understand what is said to them. But, as we have said, this depends on their language competence and their hearing loss, as well as on their skill at decoding the visible elements of speech. We doubted whether we could "programme" judges in many different schools to weight each of these factors consistently. Except in special contexts we feel that lip reading ratings are likely to be unduly ambiguous.

Using the Donaldson Lip-reading Test, Montgomery (1966a) reports a correlation of 0.76 with ratings by some seven judges on

55 children, and in a later study (Montgomery, 1968) a similar correlation for some 70 children. These are highly significant and satisfactory correlations, but they are based on relatively small numbers of children and all judges did not rate all children. Simmons (1959) compared the ratings of five judges with scores from two different filmed tests (Utley, Mason) and also reported significant correlations. Sudman and Berger (1971), on the other hand, cite several studies which showed low correlations when filmed tests were used.

In fact, widely used tests of accepted validity are rare. Though both seem now to have passed out of favour, the two most popularly used in the USA have been those devised by Utley (1946) and by Craig (1964). Neither would have been entirely suitable for English children. For example, the Sentence Tests in Utley include such statements as:

"My *folks* are home",
"I flew to *Washington*",
"They went *way* round the world".

Most deaf English children would never have met the italicized words in those contexts. The original filmed test has been criticized as being too difficult in that form (Jeffers and Barley, 1971) and in any case the accent is American.

The more recent Craig Lipreading Inventory includes both a word- and a sentence-recognition test and the subject chooses as his response one of four pictures which also have printed captions. The test is intended to be given live. Apart from a single word (jello) the language is probably appropriate for English children. There are though a number of features of this test which we felt were unsuitable for our needs. The four alternative answers for each item are linguistically highly formal. For example, Item 22 of the Sentences offers the following choices:

A woman is washing a chair
A woman is carrying a chair
A woman is washing a shirt
A woman is carrying a shirt

This format is unvarying throughout and appears to have little validity with respect to ordinary language. The test also seems to be rather easy for children using residual hearing. Craig (1964) reports correct scores on Sentences of nearly 70% for children aged roughly six-sixteen (no age distribution is given). Finally, with four alternatives the heavy guessing component would tend to reduce the true range of performance difference between children.

However, apart from the limited availability of suitable tests, other problems are present in the case of a national investigation of ability. These reduce to three. (1) Whether the test should be given in silent form or whether use of residual hearing, including the use of hearing aid, be permitted. (2) Whether the test should be given in film or videotape form, or given in live speaker-to-child form. (3) If the test is to be live, who are to be speakers, remembering that some 600 children were to be tested.

We have already suggested that where concern is with a child's ability to communicate, there is little value in silent lip reading tests. In daily life a child does use residual hearing. It is only when precisely this variable factor obtrudes into the aim of the study that artificial exclusion may be justified. There are, for instance, a number of important studies which have substantially clarified problems of phonemic decoding by vision alone – the core of lip reading (Berger, 1972a; Berger and Popelka, 1971; Erber, 1972a; 1972b; 1974a; Winkelaar, Arnold, and Johnson, 1976). Another example is the study of Byers and Lieberman (1959) who examined the effect of rate of speaking using the Utley film in silent form. In fact they found little effect of rate as between 40–120 words/minute. But in this case generalization of the result to normal listening conditions would have little validity, since there are no grounds for assuming that the presence of residual hearing would not interact with rate of speaking. There seems little point therefore in assessing lip reading as a practical skill without the use of normally used hearing aids, unless the object of the study is to make a direct comparison of performance with and without the aid.

In essence this question of silent or vocal testing has to be answered in terms of objectives. If our interest in lip reading is concerned with theoretical problems of visual perception and analysis, then clearly sound frustrates the aim. But if we are concerned with lip reading performance as a communication skill, then excluding sound frustrates that aim. For our purpose, we judged that if children freely used whatever hearing remained to them we could more usefully regard their scores as a reflection of their speech comprehension ability.

Our second problem concerned the question of personal testing. A standard filmed or videotaped test has many obvious attractions. All children have exactly the same test. If the sole purpose is to obtain a pure relative measure of performance, then the disadvantages are largely technical – though possibly considerable. In our case, and with most other large-scale studies, cumbersome equipment would need to be transported and set up in very many schools with varying facilities. Face-to-face testing requires no more than two chairs, a table, and a quiet space. But there is nevertheless a problem, the dimensions of which are unclear. When using a filmed test, there has to be an assumption that what is tested is in fact highly correlated with the skill which the child uses when he lip reads in ordinary social conditions. Jeffers and Barley (1971) gave the Utley test both filmed and live to 68 hard-of-hearing adults. Though they report that the observed correlation of 0.64 " . . . indicates that the live version is testing the same skill as the filmed version" (p. 339), we are less confident. A correlation of 0.64, though significant at the 0.01 level, is really not greatly predictive. More serious perhaps is the reliability with which we can generalize results from hard-of-hearing adults to severely- and profoundly-deaf children. Winkelaar et al. (1976), using 19 subjects, reported a correlation of 0.75 between scores of a videotaped and live test (again Utley). This too is significant at the 0.01 level, but here the subjects were hearing college students and the presentations were both silent. Berger (1972a) cites several studies which reported conflicting evidence on the question of whether two-dimensional speakers are harder to lip read than live speakers. Simmons (1959), Caccamise, Blasdell, and Meath-Lang (1977), and others have suggested that depth cues contribute important information and that therefore the two kinds of test are really measuring different aspects of receptive speech. Since the aspects of receptive speech that we ourselves are considering are those most likely to be captured by the presence of a speaker, and taking the factors discussed above into account, we preferred to use live speakers talking naturally. This brought us to the problem of who were to be the speakers.

Berger (1972a) also refers to studies in which different speakers were compared for lip-readability. Generally no difference is reported when the speakers are trained. Erber (1971), in a study of distance as a factor in lip reading, used two speakers yielding highly concordant results. Just the same, it is universally assumed, and attested to by deaf people, that there are in fact large differences in the lip-readability of different speakers. Sheavyn (1976), who is herself profoundly deaf, was a member of the British governmental committee set up to examine the role of signing in education (Lewis, 1968). She reports poignantly that there were only four members of that committee out of twenty-four whom she could lip read comfortably. This is common experience for deaf people. But we do need to distinguish between the casual speaker probably unaware of the extreme difficulty of lip reading and the trained professional. Such objective evidence as there is suggests that when the speakers are informed, concerned, and speaking in·good physical conditions, speaker differences may not be important.

Ideally we would have employed a single trained speaker. But, with a study in which testing was intensive throughout two years, this was impractical. We used three female speakers, all with long experience of deaf children. Independently of the main study, we compared their lip-readability. For this we used the Donaldson Lip-reading Test and children not involved in the main study. The three speakers were tested in pairs, each pair facing a single lip reader who was profoundly deaf. Speaking conditions were natural but good. The speakers alternated between items on the test. After more than a dozen deaf boys had been tested in this way for each pair of speakers, it was clear that there was no speaker effect at all with respect to these particular speakers. For the main population, therefore, the speakers were used according to administrative convenience. Subsequent post hoc checks on appropriate large samples confirmed that this was justified; no speaker effects were found, though we must reiterate that these speakers were fully aware of the problems of lip readers.

The Donaldson Lip-reading Test (Montgomery, 1966a; 1968) was used for the main study, but with certain significant modifications. The test comprises 10 pages, each a photomontage of 6 – 9 black and white pictures. The speaker makes a statement; the lip reader points to the relevant picture. The general style is that of the Craig test, but there are more alternatives and the difference between them is less formal. The first item uses sentences like, "Show me the dog" and seven different familiar objects are available. Later items use more complex formats; (e.g.) "the mother reads to the boy", and the page shows a variety of situations and objects using boys, fathers, mothers, and other scenes. As the test increases in difficulty, comprehension of almost all the spoken words and frequently their syntactic relationships is tested. In the original test each page is used 4 times, making a test of 40 items.

The Donaldson Test was designed to be used with children of all school ages. We found that the first 10 items in particular were too easy for fifteen-year-old children, providing little useful information. To make the test more discriminating, we added a further 6 items at the end, which also used the Donaldson booklet but which were more heavily biased towards syntactic understanding rather than vocabulary. A second modification concerned the usefulness of the individual items. When enough data had been collected, we examined the reliability of each item as a predictor of lip reading ability. Eight of the items were found to be inconsistent in this respect and were discarded from subsequent analysis – though the complete test was always given. The final score then had a maximum of 38. It would be truer to say only that the test used was based on the Donaldson.

Although the test has been used effectively as a pure lip reading test for profoundly-deaf children not wearing hearing aids (Montgomery, 1968), we treated it as a test of speech comprehension. We therefore expected better comprehension from partially-hearing children, and degree of deafness was an important variable. Then, since our overriding concern was with communication and not principally with visual perception, if children arrived at the test wearing a hearing aid, they used it during the test. Only when we knew that children normally did wear an aid but were not when they arrived for testing, did we suggest that they fetched it. As far as possible we tried to examine children under conditions n which they normally perceived speech. For the same reason, the test items were presented in ordinary conversational manner. Children were not told whether their answers were correct.

Earlier in the chapter we discussed the difference between lip reading ability and language ability and the fact that they are easily confounded in conventional tests. We tried to minimize this effect in the following way. When the child had completed the test described above, it was repeated, but this time children silently read the items which were typed on individual cards. This provided a measure of language comprehension using what was, in almost all cases, the child's more effective communication mode. Almost all children returned a higher score when they read the items. This agrees with similar results from Gates (1971), and from White and Stevenson (1975). We were then able to derive a second score. This represents the proportion of items that a child can read and which he can also lip read. For this measure, items which cannot be correctly print-read are discarded. We shall call it a Speech Comprehension-Ratio (SC-Ratio). Within the limits of what language the test samples, the SC-Ratio reflects true ability to understand speech when we know that the underlying language is comprehended. We can distinguish what a child cannot lip read from what he does not linguistically understand. The SC-Ratio is a far more valid measure of speech comprehension than is the simple lip reading test score.

Lip reading, language comprehension, and hearing loss

The simple relationship between speech comprehension and hearing loss is shown in Figure 7.1. Speech comprehension is of course markedly influenced by degree of hearing loss (p < 0.001).* This, though, in itself tells us little more than that children with more hearing also understand more spoken language. More informative

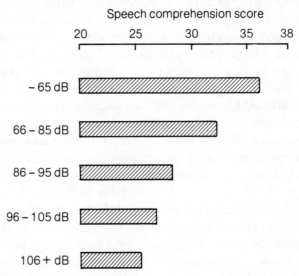

Figure 7.1. Speech comprehension (maximum = 38) and hearing loss (n = 358). Scores adjusted for intelligence.

* Because distributions of all performance scores used in this chapter are markedly skewed, statistical analysis is on transformed data.

is the relationship between hearing loss and SC-Ratio shown in Figure 7.2. Again though, hearing loss is a highly significant variable ($F_{4,346}$ = 23.50; p < 0.001).

If, regardless of degree of deafness, all children, using whatever aids and residual hearing they have, could equally understand through speech whatever they linguistically knew, the values shown in Figure 7.2 would be the same. Were this the case, it would mean that profoundly deaf children could comprehend speech just as well as those of partial hearing – so long as the linguistic content was within their competence. Evidently this is not so. Over the whole range of hearing loss, there continues to be a decline in what children can understand through speech (Figure 7.1). Not just because they know less language; they also lip read less of what they do know.

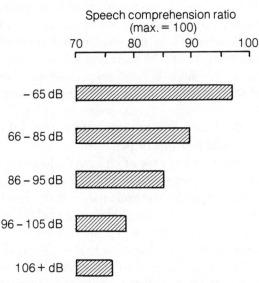

Figure 7.2.   Speech Comprehension-Ratio and hearing loss (n = 351). Scores adjusted for intelligence.

These measures which we have been discussing are totally bound by the particular test we use to assess the ability. They tell us very little directly about how well a child will be able to cope with everyday conversation. The problem is similar to the one we had with reading; it is the problem of criteria. Figure 7.1 shows that very deaf children can understand about 65% of what is said to them. But, without doubt, by making the test item more or less difficult this value could easily be shifted. On this issue Figure 7.2

helps no more. It tells us that very deaf children understand through speech about 80% of what they know. It still does not tell us what they know. Nor can we gain much help on this latter point by reference to the print-reading score. Nor do we know whether, if they knew much more language, they would still be able to lip read 80% of it. There is no objective standard to which test performances can be related. In practical terms, solving this problem in a formal way is virtually impossible. But we offer two suggestions which may help.

Think of the case of hearing people listening to speech in normal conditions. With unimpaired hearing, we must assume that they can understand everything that they linguistically know. That is, if they do not understand a spoken statement, neither would they were it written. Partially-hearing children, whose hearing is imperfect but far from gravely impaired, may be expected not to do so well. We now count the proportion of children with hearing losses up to 65 dB who can in fact understand through speech almost everything – let us say 95% or more – of what they can understand in print. We find 93% of such children. This means that nearly all of these partially-hearing children comprehend the language they know through speech, more or less as well as do hearing people. Evidently vision can effectively substitute if necessary for their mild hearing impairment.

Now however consider the case of children whose hearing loss is beyond 95 dB – those very deaf – and ask the same question: what proportion have speech comprehension at the level of their linguistic knowledge (95% or more)? Here we find no more than 16%. For the vast majority there is a gap, of varying size, between what they can understand and what they know. While all hearing children and 93% of slightly deaf children can understand (through speech) whatever they know, only 16% of profoundly-deaf children can. This provides a dramatic idea of the deficit incurred when most of known spoken information has to be derived visually.

The second suggestion involves a direct comparison with hearing children. Essentially what is being evaluated here is the effect of some ten years of training and practice at lip reading by deaf children. We took a group of 75 hearing children aged fifteen – sixteen years from a state school. White noise was passed through headphones to a degree where no speech sounds at all could be perceived. In this condition they were in fact more "deaf" than probably any of our deaf population, since their "deafness" was literally total. They were given one practice run through the Donaldson test followed by a test run. We omitted the print-reading version because three tests would have begun to strain patience. We gave the latter test to 43 different hearing children from the same school. Otherwise the test conditions were identical to those used with deaf children. For comparison, we used all of the deaf children with a hearing loss greater than 95 dB who were in Schools for the Deaf. An earlier article (Conrad, 1977b) reporting this aspect of the study compared the hearing group with a subsample of deaf children selected to be free from additional handicap and with an intelligence distribution fitted to that assumed for the hearing children. The results were so close to those for the entire profoundly-deaf group that it seems simpler to present them now for the more complete population.

Table 7.1 shows the outcome of this comparison. The speech comprehension scores for the two groups are, coincidentally, identical. It is difficult to assess the auditory benefit derived by the deaf children from whatever residual hearing was available to them. In varying degree, some element of the prosodic features of speech are likely to have provided a little information. But at the very least we cannot say that they lip read better than untrained and inexperienced hearing children; a conclusion also drawn by Berger (1972a). Indeed Lowell (1959) reported that noise-masked hearing students lip read better than deaf students. Clearly though, a good deal of the absence of difference, when logically we might have expected it to be present, is not simply that, as Vernon (1976) has suggested, hearing subjects can use their knowledge of syntax

Table 7.1 Speech comprehension by deaf and noise-masked hearing children

	Speech comprehension (max. = 38)	Print-reading (max. = 38)	SC-Ratio
	Mean	Mean	
Deaf	25.3	32.0	79
	n = 150		
Hearing	25.3	36.7	
	n = 75	n = 43	

"... to fill in by guessing ..." (p. 100). Hearing subjects actually know linguistically more. They have a greater range of vocabulary and syntactical form against which to match visually perceived oral gestures.

In this sense, then, it is possible that the deaf children were able to make better use of the visual features of unheard speech than were the hearing. That is, they were able to lip read a greater proportion of what they could print-read than could the hearing children. Were this so, we would have to conclude that the deaf children's experience to a degree had benefitted them, and that lip reading can be taught to some effect. Because we have two different groups of hearing children, this comparison of the SC–Ratio is not strictly possible. But, as important perhaps, is the difficulty of assessing the value to the deaf children of their residual hearing. If the print-reading value of 36.7 for hearing children can be taken as a reasonable approximation to the general case, we can make some estimate. In total silence, the hearing group lip read 25.3 items correctly. What score would they need, to achieve an SC–Ratio value of 79 – equal to that of the deaf children? In fact no more than 29.0 (36.7 x 0.79). This is a value we showed in Figure 7.1 to be close to that recorded from deaf children with hearing losses of 85–95 dB. On this speculative basis the conclusion that deaf children are benefitting from training seems less assured. It appears that with just a little more auditory information, hearing children might well be able to lip read the same proportion of speech material that they linguistically know, as do those profoundly deaf. It is unfortunate that technologically there is no reliable way of noise masking the hearing children in a manner strictly comparable to the way that deaf children are naturally noise masked – and even less reliably so on an individually matched basis. Whatever weight we are willing to attach to these various scraps of evidence, it is hard to see an outcome which gives more than marginal advantage to all of the educational effort and practice in lip reading which is enjoyed by deaf children.

In sum, using a fairly natural conversation environment, and the natural contribution of residual hearing, we find a highly significant effect of hearing loss on the ability to understand spoken utterances. However, as numerous authors have pointed out, linguistic factors are likely to make a substantial contribution to this relationship. When we do take this into account, we still find a significant hearing-loss effect. Deaf children have great difficulty interpreting even known oral information when it is predominantly visual.

Compared to reading, very little attention has been given to the central educational issue: how well do deaf children lip read? As we have seen, this question breaks down into two parts. First, how to teach lip reading as a perceptual skill involving both vision and residual hearing. Second, how to provide the language to be lip read. Obviously there is an element of vicious circle here which is not present in the case of prose reading. There, the rudiments can be learned, and proficiency may then develop with exercise of the skill. This is not true for lip reading when lip reading itself is the principal means of acquiring the mother-tongue – circularly, a requirement for effective lip reading. Because of these difficulties, the quest for appropriate criteria for evaluating pedagogic programmes remains paramount.

The fact is that we do not know, in an absolute sense, how well deaf children lip read. Neither Berger's (1972a) nor Farwell's (1976) review mentions any evaluative study. Two official British reports concerned with the health of deaf schoolchildren consider this problem (Department of Education and Science, 1964; 1972). In both studies a single observer is said to have assessed a large sample of children's ability to communicate through lip reading and speech using a three-fold classification. Although results are given for speech intelligibility (see Chapter 8), none at all are reported for lip reading. This remains an open and challenging issue.

Lip reading and intelligence

When comparisons have been made, it seems that deaf children lip read little, if any, better than untrained hearing children. Can we then really say of lip reading that it is not a skill; that there is nothing useful that can be learned; that teaching programmes are irrelevant; that practice gains nothing after an initial start? Were this analysis true, there would be little reason to expect degree of intelligence to be related to lip reading performance. After all, except when intelligence is extremely low, we do not expect it to be related to the quality of speech of hearing children – though we do expect an association with reading. Farwell (1976) writes, "Most researchers reported low positive but nonsignificant correlations between speech reading and I.Q" (p. 24). Berger (1972a) also, but rather diffidently, inclined to agree with Pintner (1929) that, beyond a very low intelligence level, there is no association. Were this the case, we would indeed be close to a conclusion that lip reading has no part in a formal teaching curriculum and that there is nothing to be taught nor learned. Lip reading would happen or not, according to factors independent of intellectual ability. This may be true – but seems improbable.

Farwell might have cited – but did not – Craig (1964); Montgomery (1966a; 1968); Neyhus and Myklebust (1969); Quigley (1969), all of whom reported significant correlations between lip reading and intelligence. Costello (1957), with some insight, found a significant correlation for partially-hearing children, but not for the very deaf. Yet Costello used a live-speech test and Raven's Matrices – as did Montgomery, whose result was contradictory. Evans (1960; 1965) used silent speech and WISC, as did Craig. In one of his studies the correlation just failed to reach the 0.05 significance level, and only just reached it in the other. It is not easy to find clarifying characteristics amongst these conflicting reports, though no one has reported a negative correlation.

With no evident key factors to account for what are unacceptably discrepant data, we add our own with some reserve, encouraged by the size of our sample and by the fact that we used the same lip reading test and the same intelligence test as did Montgomery. As it happens, we strikingly confirmed the relationship he reported. Montgomery's two studies (1966a; 1968) using profoundly deaf children reported respective correlations of 0.50 and 0.42. Table 7.2 shows that for each of our five levels of hearing loss the correlations between Raven score and lip reading vary between 0.38 and 0.57. All are significant at least at the 0.01 level. The apparent trend – the lowest correlations appearing for the most- and least-deaf groups – might have some interest, but in fact none of the differences between the correlations is significant. Clearly the more intelligent children do have better comprehension of speech, even when they hear quite a lot. But the relatively low level of the correlations indicates that other factors make a substantial contribution to performance. With these values very close to Montgomery's, the very least we can say then is that, for these tests and this method of administration, a significant and consistent association may be fairly confidently accepted. But it does seem that the degree to which lip reading relates to measured intelligence may substantially depend on the specific tests used and perhaps the conditions in which they are used as well.

A certain proportion of the value of these correlations must be accounted for by linguistic knowledge. Using our SC-Ratio we can consider the role of intelligence when children lip read only those items which we know they can print-read. There is no point here in using data from children who have usable amounts of residual hearing if we are concerned principally with intelligence and visual decoding of speech. If we then take the 144 children with a hearing loss greater than 95 dB, the correlation between Raven score and SC-Ratio is 0.36 (p < 0.01). This confirms that, the more intelligent a child is, the better use he can make of his knowledge of the language of the test. But the low value of the correlation gives it little predictive value. This, together with the other evidence we have cited, suggests that lip reading is a skill which is likely to be difficult to teach formally.

Table 7.2   Speech comprehension and intelligence: product-moment correlation (n = 358)

Hearing loss (dB)	–65	66–85	86–95	96–105	106+
Correlation	0.38	0.42	0.57	0.56	0.44

Lip reading and internal speech

Not surprisingly, in conditions of ordinary conversation where a child can use whatever information is within the limits of this auditory perception, as deafness increases, his ability to comprehend speech falls significantly and systematically. But whether the predominant percept is visual or auditory, it is linguistically meaningless until it can be referred to a preexisting store of information, and recognition occurs. Does it then matter in what form the linguistic units are stored? Is a visual perception of facial gesture as readily identified in a store of such images as a predominantly auditory perception is identified in a store of auditory images? We know that many deaf children do not manipulate words in phonetic form. We might therefore suppose that the phonetic correlates of visual oral information would be of relatively little value to them. Their store of linguistic units simply would not contain that kind of information. For these children it is the visual picture of speech that must be sought in the language store. We do not for a moment believe that this simple story is a complete account of the psychological facts. It does no more than provide a rationale for reexamining our data in terms of our established assumptions of the presence or absence of internal speech. But also our expectations are fairly obvious. Just because the oral gestures of speech are highly correlated with their phonetic characteristics, we would expect that a child whose language store was basically phonetic would be able to extract more useful information from nonauditory components of speech than would a child for whom the phonetic correlation was irrelevant. We can test this prediction by recasting our data according to whether or not a child uses internal speech in memorizing words.

Figure 7.3 shows this for speech comprehension. Analysis of variance, with Raven score as a covariate, shows hearing loss and internal speech both to be highly significant (p < 0.001). Clearly, in general, absence of internal speech does impair speech comprehension, and the adjustment indicates that this is not simply an effect of intelligence. But again we must remember that this measure represents the absolute amount of speech information that the child understands through this medium. It does not tell us a great deal about the role of internal speech when we are interested in the speech comprehension process itself; whether the absence of internal phonetic representation impairs the ability to understand that language which is known. We saw from the reading data in Chapter 6 that these children are linguistically inferior. But are they also inferior in lip reading what they linguistically know?

Figure 7.4 shows that they are. Again, hearing loss and internal speech are highly significant (p < 0.001). But a further effect was also present. For children with internal speech there is a consistent decline in the SC-Ratio value. In other words, the deafer the child the greater the discrepancy between what he knows and what he can comprehend through speech. The child with a slight hearing loss behaves as he should, like a normally-hearing child; he can understand the speech used almost to the full extent that he knows the language spoken. With increasing deafness we see a reflection of the changing balance between auditory and visual information; but because of the internal speech facility, it is always referred to a phonetic internal representation.

For children without internal speech there is a marked difference. Once deafness reaches a level of 65 dB, the gap between

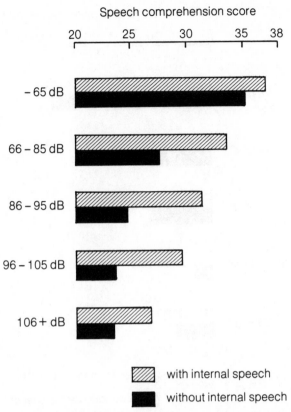

Speech comprehension score

Figure 7.3. *Speech comprehension (maximum = 38): by hearing loss and internal speech (n = 302). Scores adjusted for intelligence.*

performance and knowledge is already as wide as it is for those profoundly-deaf children who do use internal speech. But then there is no further change. Without internal speech the child with a loss of, say, 70 dB extracts no more linguistic information than does the child with internal speech whose loss may be up to 120 dB. Even a substantial degree of residual hearing seems to be of little value in the absence of an adequate store of language held in phonetic form. For the child using internal speech on the other hand, even small amounts of auditory information referred to a phonetic store seem to be of linguistic value. At the very profoundest level of deafness (105–120 dB), there is no difference in the SC-Ratio between children with and without internal speech. Both groups would be relying more or less exclusively on the visual components of speech. One group would refer perceptions

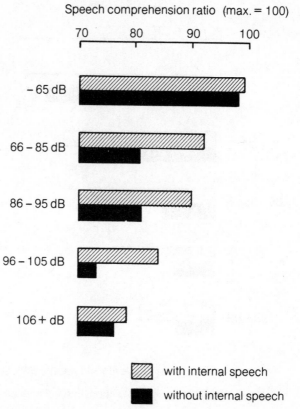

Speech comprehension ratio (max. = 100)

Figure 7.4.   *Speech Comprehension-Ratio: by hearing loss and internal speech (n = 296). Scores adjusted for intelligence.*

to a phonetic base, the other group to a base dependent on some other imagery – probably visual. The processes seem to have equivalent effectiveness, and it would be futile to speculate further in an area where our ignorance is so great.

Both Costello (1957) and Myklebust (1964) were aware that there should be an association between lip reading and "inner language", and believed that they would develop reciprocally. Costello, too, expected a close relationship between both and the ability to solve the problems of Raven's Matrices. Having failed to find a significant correlation between Raven score and lip reading in her deaf group (mean dB = 97) she suggested that, "Apparently, the verbal system of which speech-reading is comprised, was different from the inner language system used by the (deaf) children" (p. 139). For this reason she argued that the kind of intellectual processes which such children used for the problems of the Matrices were quite different from those required for (verbal) lip reading. Costello's problem, echoed by Myklebust (1964), derived from the assumption that inner language was acquired via lip reading and that the symbol systems (verbal) of the two would correspond. The data from Raven's Matrices forced her to modify this, and to recognize that some other nonverbal inner language was available to her subjects. Because her subjects were fluent signers she suggested that the inner language would be manual.

We believe that the most seminal feature of the data in Figure 7.4 is the fact that even with a good deal of hearing (66–85 dB loss), children without internal speech seem relatively unable, or unwilling, to use that hearing to understand speech at least when an alternative information source (oral gestures) is present. Children with similar hearing loss, but using internal speech, lose much less of what they know. Presumably they regard the visual information as secondary. If this analysis is correct, we have to wonder about the pedagogic implications for fifteen-year-old children for whom a substantial proportion of heard speech is meaningless. Not because the language is beyond them – they understand it in print – but because they seem to have an incompatible internal representation of it, which has developed not only without benefit of, but in spite of classroom instruction. The outcome is that they learn less language than other children far more deaf (see Figure 6.5). What is perhaps more serious is that, notwithstanding their better hearing, they understand no more of it in conversation.

We can show this more sharply and in a more practical way. We can again ask what proportion of children can lip read 95% or more of what they can understand when they read it in print. This is shown in Figure 7.5. We must be careful when comparing children with and without internal speech using the Figure 7.5 data because children with internal speech have higher Raven score which, as we saw, does have some relevance. But we can consider the effect of degree of hearing loss. Those children who do use internal speech show a consistent and fairly steady decline in performance down to a hearing loss of about 100 dB. We assume this to reflect their increasing need to rely on visual information which is difficult to interpret. But for children without internal speech there is an extremely sharp drop beyond 65 dB. In other words, performance no longer reflects just hearing loss. Regardless of

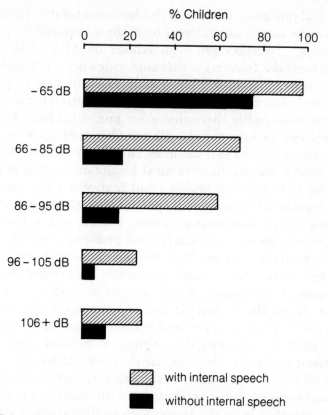

Figure 7.5.   Percentage of children who can comprehend in speech 95% of what they can understand in print: by hearing loss and internal speech (n = 296).

internal speech, all children in the 66–85 dB hearing-loss band are partially hearing. Purely audiologically they would be receiving similar auditory input and needing to rely to a similar extent on visual cues. But very few of the children without internal speech are fully able to utilize the auditory information they receive; they are audiologically partially hearing, but profoundly deaf for comprehension of speech.

The cognitive problems in lip reading

We are left with two broad questions: why is lip reading so difficult, and why are children who do not use a phonetic code particularly handicapped? We know that lip reading is difficult, not because we or any other researcher has produced convincing evidence, but principally because deaf people themselves tell us so. The problem of devising an absolute and objective criterion of performance or effectiveness remains unsolved. But when we do compare hearing children with those deaf children who have least residual hearing, the outcome shows none of the advantage that would obtain were other skills examined for the effects of ten years of instruction and experience.

Some aspects of the problem are obvious. Soundless speech is grossly impoverished in distinctive physical features. Far too many of the morphological units which subsume comprehension of spoken language are "homophenes" – visually like other words – either because they share important visual characteristics, or because there are none (Berger, 1972b). No instructional programme can change this. True, additional aids of various kinds apart from direct finger spelling have been suggested and used. At the present time, "cued speech" (Cornett, 1967) is probably the best known. This supplements ordinary speech with manual gestures in the case of phonemes which lack a distinctive visual correlate. Faced with two apparently identical oral patterns, the lip reader may refer to a concurrently presented finger configuration to aid identification. Objective and adequately controlled evaluative studies of cued speech are hard to find. We suspect that it is too difficult for most deaf children and it has not been sufficiently widely used for the necessary screening survey to be practicable. Ling and Clarke (1975), using 12 deaf children, reported somewhat better performance when speech was cued than when cues were removed. This could be due merely to the removal of a familiar aid as much as to intrinsic benefits of cueing. Clarke and Ling (1976) also reported that when cueing was removed, lip reading was impaired. More to the point, the earlier study noted the overall very poor lip reading performance even with cues. Above all, cued speech requires a cueing speaker – as do other manual aids – so detracting from its everyday value.

In an attempt to overcome both the poverty of visual distinctiveness of English phonemes and at the same time to obviate the need for a speaker able to cue speech, Upton (1968) developed an ingenious device for which some success has been claimed. Fuller details are also available elsewhere (Pickett, Gengel, and Quinn, 1974). In brief, a body-worn microphone passes the acoustic characteristics of speech to a microcomputer. This transduces relevant features to visual form which are displayed on spectacles worn by a lip reader and optically projected to the distance of the speaker's lips. The speaker then merely speaks in a normal way. The lip reader augments his knowledge of lip reading with the formalized computer-generated visual pictures to help him identify those phonemes which lack visual distinctiveness. Again, adequate evaluation is still awaited – and particularly with reference to a random sample of deaf children.

For the foreseeable future the vast majority of deaf people trying to understand speech will have to depend upon unaided lip reading together with whatever residual hearing they have. In practice, the problems of visibility can be alleviated but not yet obviated, and substantial and excellent research has clarified such parameters as illumination, angles, speaking rate, distance, and so on (Berger, 1972a; Erber, 1974c). Essentially though, lip reading is difficult because speech is not very visible.

A contingent aspect of the difficulty of lip reading is linguistic. Hearing people first learn language by hearing it, so making it available for speech communication. Congenitally deaf people may have first to learn language by lip reading it before it can be used for communication. Because lip reading is an extremely difficult skill, relatively little language is learned, greatly reducing its effectiveness as a communication mode. Above all, had deaf children the knowledge, redundancies of spoken language would permit guessing to fill the gaps in visibility. Lip reading itself apparently fails to provide this knowledge.

If the primary source of information to lip readers is visual, why then are children without internal speech worse lip readers than those who do use phonetic internal representations? This is not simply an issue of impoverished language; our SC-Ratio shows that children without internal speech lip read less of the language they know. Something else has to be involved.

There are far too many gaps in our knowledge for reasoned explanation. Essentially we have to speculate about the cognitive steps involved in the search for identification of a pattern of oral gestures. For the child whose internal representation of language is predominently phonetic, the steps are easier to see. The pattern he sees is an analogue of what the speaker says. If the lip reader has this analogue available as an internal representation, the transform is not difficult to infer since it may be similar to the processes used by hearing people to recognize speech sounds. The difference is

that the deaf lip reader must depend on the imperfect visual correlate and is deprived, in varying degree, of the accompanying
sound. It is common experience though to observe lip readers
re-forming seen words into their phonetic origins (Erber, 1974b;
Numbers, 1939) in the way that hearing children "sound out"
unfamiliar printed words. In both cases the reference to an internal
lexicon is tangible. For these deaf children, then, the process may
be similar to that used by the hearing when listening to speech, but
deprived of acoustic information and therefore less successful.

How though can we conceive of the processes when there may
not be a phonetic internal representation? As we said earlier, since
the input is visual we would expect an alternative representation to
be visual, though we must continue to emphasize that this is
entirely inferential. But an internal representation which has been
historically derived from the sensory information available from
speaking lips (and other consistently accompanying facial gestures)
will also reflect the ambiguities of that information. Inevitably, the
penalty will extend beyond mere vocabulary and into syntactical
aspects of linguistic comprehension. Then, insofar as short-term
memory for visually processed items perceived sequentially is in
fact less efficient than for items held phonetically, a further handicap is present. We discussed this in Chapter 5 and in fact cast
doubt on the suggestion, especially when the process has
benefitted from extended practice. But the outcome, as we then
argued, may depend on stimulus discriminability. In this case, not
the perceived stimulus, which is the same for all children, but the
recoded stimulus held in memory. Even without the memory
factor though, a visual lexicon of oral patterns (of English in our
case) upon which a child without internal speech might depend
will be a less effective substrate for lip reading; the patterns will
lack clear discriminability. If of course the internal representation –
and there is no conceivable theoretical model without one – is
neither phonetic nor visual, decoding performance is likely to be
poorer still. We must accept that a child whose mother-tongue is
sign has linguistic units internally represented in sign. When a
fluent signer lip reads, unless he is bilingual, he needs to translate
from visual to manual patterns – with additional likelihood of
degradition of information.

If this discussion of hypothetical processes seems too abstracted
from the everyday issues of practical lip reading, we should constantly remember performance levels which, by whatever criteria

we draw on, are unsatisfactorily low for a primary mode of communication; and that at present there is little valid theory likely to support an educational breakthrough. For this reason alone we must continue theoretical discussion and even speculation.

There are certain aspects of lip reading as a skill which are unique in ways which have relevance to few other skills, and which present problems for the researcher trying to understand the nature of the skill, or to assess levels of performance at it. The first of these is that a deaf person has no alternative but to lip read the speaker. Unlike the hearing person listening to speech, it is pointless to wait until there is less noise, or to evade noisy environments. The perceptual problem will remain. People with normal hearing rarely lip read as a conscious mode of communication; the additional visual cues are present and research shows that they contribute something of value to comprehension. Lip reading is something which happens to the hearing; deaf people do it. A practical effect of this distinction is that we do not know what good lip reading is. We can rate it, but we lack any absolute frame of reference. All hearing people are excellent hearers of speech and little distinguishes one from another. Deaf people vary immensely in their lip reading ability. Nor, psychometrically, can lip reading be compared to reading print. Hearing people, like the deaf, vary greatly in their ability to read. But there are conventional standards which permit us to describe a person, deaf or hearing, as a "good" reader. There are no such standards for lip reading. The apparently simple enquiry as to how well deaf people can lip read – that is to say, to what extent they can overcome their handicap – is beset with problems. We can easily test whether one deaf child lip reads better than another; we can examine the role of illumination or speaking rate. Less easily can we assess the degree to which education facilitates satisfying social integration when lip reading has to be a principal vehicle. In the context of oral communication, while lip reading is essential, there has been little convincing attempt to validate teaching procedures nor to evaluate performance against realistic criteria.

A second unique feature of lip reading also has direct relevance to the educational process and concerns the question: what is to be taught? We have no more than a superficial theoretical knowledge of what lip reading cognitively *is*. Thinking for the moment solely of the visual aspects of the skill, the sensory display of primary information which the lip reader observes is a set of gestures of the lips, tongue, and jaw which are totally arbitrary with respect to their function of presenting speech *without* sound. The nature of the gestures is such that they are highly correlated with speech sounds which accompany them. It is just this correlation which permits a hearing person to use the visual information in noisy conditions. But for profoundly-deaf people the correlate is absent, and may never have been present. It is certain that, were we to design a language which could only be expressed through facial gesture and could only be received visually, we would develop a means of communication far more efficient than lip reading unheard speech.

While the acoustic characteristics of heard speech which are crucial for identification are substantially known, though they are far from simple, there has been little progress towards a comparable understanding of the parallel cognitive processes of lip reading. We do not know what it is that a good lip reader does which a poor lip reader does not. Because of this, the history of teaching lip reading has been a series of lurches from one fashionable technique to another – none based on a tested theoretical formulation of the process.

Lip reading is a skill, with features not always comparable to more familiar communication skills. It is against this background of ignorance of the process that we have to try to assess the achievements of education, and try to understand determining relationships. The facts of residual hearing and amplification of speech, crucial though they are, may do no more than confuse. We do not know what the deaf person actually hears, and we do not know just when he uses auditory cues and when visual – and he himself probably will not know this. The one certainty is that with increasing deafness a point is quickly reached when discrimination of spoken speech-sounds becomes noticeably imperfect and other sensory processes become necessary.

Much research has shown that lip reading does not provide prelingually deafened children with easy access into language. The inescapable problem of the lack of visible distinctiveness at the level of phoneme, syllable, or word, will not easily be overcome, and we must seriously doubt the wisdom of insisting that lip reading English remains the vehicle for learning a mother-tongue.

8

Deafness and Speech Intelligibility

While the epithet "deaf and dumb" is vanishing from the English language with grim lethargy, the soubriquet "dummy", in Britain at least, remains an inner-urban label for a profoundly-deaf child. Yet at least from well before the end of the seventeenth century it was clearly understood that the absence of speech by the deaf was no more than a consequence of hearing loss (Jordan, 1961). John Conradi Amman published his treatise on articulation by the deaf in 1692. Yet, as we noted in Chapter 1, two hundred years later William James himself continued to associate deafness with dumbness as if there were an organic relationship.

Unable to hear words spoken, without specific instruction deaf children failed to reproduce the sounds of speech in the course of their natural development. The Congress of Milan formalized the growing awareness that this could and should be changed. One of the more bizarre paradoxes which have followed is seen in the dilemma of many of its adherents. On one hand, as Ling (1976) points out, educationists have taken the comfortable position that speech is unimportant in education because it is "language" which really matters. Since linguistic expression requires a vehicle, this attitude appears to limit oral communication to reading and writing, or to assume absurdly that, if vocal utterances are linguistically rich, the sounds will necessarily be understood. These consequences are rarely those intended since they represent a denial of the cardinal principle of oral education. The attitude derives from despair in the classroom that no more than a few profoundly-deaf children will ever be readily understood through their speech. Nor is the argument invoked with respect to lip reading where standards of performance are more ambiguous.

The alternative horn of the dilemma is represented in the influential views of, for example, Whetnall and Fry (1964), who simply see no problem. This view asserts that given the correct conditions there need be no difficulty in teaching a deaf child to speak intelligibly – a view which the authors support by a number of case histories. This latter position at least is open to evidential consideration and we shall look at it later when we have clarified what seem to be the determining or limiting factors. The fact is, as we shall show, it has proved to be disappointingly difficult to teach most very deaf children to speak in a manner which would permit them to converse freely. The concept that unintelligible speech might conceal a richness of linguistic thought may well be true; to the extent that the thoughts are expressed in unintelligible vocal speech we shall never know. The evidence from levels of reading skill does not greatly encourage. In fact, the continuing search for technological aids reflects both recognition of an un- solved problem and awareness that more natural educational pro- cedures have failed to fulfil the heady promise of unrealistic con- gress decisions. At the end of a deaf child's school life, few teachers are other than deeply pessimistic about the utility of the child's speech. But, given the vast amount of school time appro- priated in the belief that oral communication is an attainable goal, failure may have consequences for intellectual development reach- ing far beyond the everyday needs of social communication.

Problems of measurement

In determining a method of approach to evaluation of speech qual- ity, a number of conflicting decisions have to be made. The prin- cipal one concerns the instrument of measurement itself. Conflict arises from the fact that means and ends are not easy to reconcile. There can be little doubt about the objective. We need to know how well we can understand what a deaf child says to us. Natur- ally we want our evaluation to be as objective as possible. But we also want it to be realistic. This realism needs to be in terms both of measurement and of what is measured.

At first sight, a procedure developed by John and Howarth (1965) has attractions. Children describe, in their own words, a series of pictures. The speech is taperecorded and played back to a panel of listeners themselves unfamiliar with the speech of deaf children. The listeners attempt a verbatim report and the score is represented by the proportion of words correctly understood. This is attractive because the speech samples reflect the child's own natural language. The utterances are spontaneous and so there is no recourse to a prepared text devised by the investigator which the speakers need to read. But there are problems. Certainly the naturalness of the language enhances realism. But then language becomes a confounding variable which in this instance is not the central concern. One effect is that different children will provide speech samples of linguistically different kinds and of different length. When length is excessive it can of course be cut short. It is less easy to increase it in the case of a shy child, a reluctant child, or, using the word in its everyday sense, an inarticulate child. In other words, if words are to be recorded they have to be spoken. There is no doubt that listeners learn to understand speech. The more there is available the more likely they are to understand it. Markides (1977) makes this point in connection with ratings of spontaneous speech and recommends samples of 50–100 words from each child. As descriptions of pictures this may be beyond the capability of many deaf children. When Markides himself (1970) required young deaf children to describe pictures, the average output per child was no more than 14 words.

The kind of output matters also, and particularly when a point is scored for every correctly identified word. Language contains lexical redundancies; many words may be omitted without destroying sense, and many words are "given" by their grammatical context. When the order follows the expectations of the listener, parts of speech proceed in orderly sequence providing opportunity for guessing. Grammatically, the speech of deaf children is characterized by "deafisms" – syntactical structures which do not resemble those of English. Word order is not necessarily what a naïve listener would expect, and this largely linguistic factor could well affect the ease of identifying individual words. This method of generating speech samples seems to us therefore to provide excessive opportunity for nonspeech characteristics to obtrude into measurement. Furthermore, the score itself has a built-in element of ambiguity. It is the proportion of correct words. But only the speaker knows with certainty what he has said. Ultimately the score becomes based on concordance rather than accuracy. With speech quality reflected by the kind of ratings we will show, the applicability of this method is probably limited to partially-hearing children.

One solution to the scoring problem is to use prepared formal speech statements. In this case the identity of the words is unambiguous. The investigator can manipulate the nature of the utterance, controlling its length (Magner, 1972), or the phonetic or prosodic character of particular key words (Smith, 1973). The score again may depend on the number of correct words or syllables (Magner, 1972); or it may depend on the number of correct key words (Smith, 1973), so eliminating confounding effects of linguistic redundancy. But now the speaker has to read formal sentences and there can be no pretence of spontaneous speech. There is a real risk of confounding speaking ability with reading ability. Nor is this a simple matter to disentangle. Quigley (1969) had deaf children reading word lists and reported a significant correlation between reading ability and speech quality. This might be causal. But is just as likely to be reflecting a general verbal factor. If statements are to be read, then clearly the listener must receive what is written because that is what the score is based on. The investigator has to decide how much reading practice directly on the test material the speaker may have – and how much speech correction may be given. On this point, Ling (1976) appositely draws attention to the use of orthographic-phonetic relationships in teaching speech which may affect the nature of reading-aloud speech. A further possible disadvantage of the formally read statement, compared for example with picture description, might be the absence of linguistic context. In conversation a listener generally has, or develops, some idea of what the conversation is about – the topic. This delimits the size and nature of the vocabulary which the listener expects. The speech used with unconnected "blind" sentences may be more difficult when the listener has to determine context from a single short sentence.

Some of the problems which seem to be inherent in the search for an objective easily quantifiable score can be obviated by the use of ratings. Here we no longer ask the listener: what did the child say? We merely ask: how well did you understand it? We take for granted both the listener's veracity and confidence. Errors from this source can be largely controlled if several raters all judge the same speech samples. Not all that many are needed. John, Gemmill, Howarth, Kitzinger, and Sykes (1976) report that increasing the number of raters from 5 to 25 has little effect on the ultimate assessment. Markides (1977) recommends 5–10 listeners; Quigley (1969) used 4; Levitt (1976) used "several". Most authors report a high level of agreement between raters so long as they are themselves drawn from a fairly homogeneous population.

But there are disadvantages of this procedure as well, if relatively few listeners are to rate a large number of speakers. When the speakers are using formal material – reading sentences for instance or describing pictures – a large amount of different, but equated material is needed. It is of considerable importance that listeners should not know in advance what is being said – or talked about. Exceptionally this may be permitted if the listeners are trained and required to assess defined phonetic or phonological features. Alternatively large numbers of suitable listeners need to be assembled in small panels, and it may be impossible to ensure that different panels use the same subjective scale. A child's speech rating should not depend on the luck of the draw of a particular listening panel.

The purposes of each enquiry will determine the compromises which will have to be made amongst these various procedures, each with advantages and defects. Over and above these detailed points, we must recognize that the numerical value of a scaled score as compared with an overall rating is highly dependent on the nature of the words spoken, and has no absolute validity. When children are reported to have a speech intelligibility score of (e.g.) 20%, the value permits us to relate the quality of their speech to that of other children in the same test. It tells us nothing about the ease with which a listener will be able to converse with them, since different test material might easily yield a different score. On the other hand, if a child is rated as "barely intelligible" on a five-point scale, we have information of different utility. If the material has a reasonable degree of realism, the designation has some absolute validity. It indicates a direct reaction to relevant speech, and is a meaningful description.

Scores based on ratings scales of four, five, or six categories, though, have limited value for parametric analysis. The categories cannot be assumed to form an equal-interval scale as objective right-wrong scoring can, and statistical treatment of data becomes limited. Large numbers of children will all have the same score because few different scores are available, and it would be rash to assume that all children rated as "barely intelligible" by different raters in fact have identical intelligibility of speech.

For our own purpose neither ratings nor objective scoring alone was sufficient and we used both methods – ratings of spontaneous speech and scaled scores of formal utterances. In view of the fore-going discussion on methodology we can claim no special merit for this approach. It seemed to us to be least inappropriate as we picked our way through these numerous hazards to reach accept-able compromise.

The intelligibility of deaf children: a brief survey

A survey of the simple facts concerning the ability of people to understand what is said by a deaf child requires litle space – there are few formal studies to consider. This is somewhat surprising because the performance criteria are relatively clear. There is almost a self-evident standard since we are all familiar with the concept of intelligible speech and, just as important, we are equally aware of degrees of unintelligibility; listening in noisy conditions for instance. When, methodologically, we ask the simple question: what did the child say? – opportunties for valid measurement are far less equivocal than in the case of reading where standards are more arbitrary, or of lip reading which is largely beyond the experience of hearing people. Just the same, though methodological discussion is appropriate, procedural dif-ferences seem not to affect the broad outline. It is simply that the outline has been poorly sketched in. The majority of speech intel-ligibility studies are probably more concerned with assessing the outcome of a training programme, or with a relationship to some other variable, than with absolute judgement of how easy the speech is to understand. Ling (1976) cites, for example, a number of studies concerned with the treatment of specific language defects where before-and-after intelligibility testing might be appropriate. John et al. (1976) used an intelligibility test to com-pare the speech quality of children in day and residential Schools. Quigley (1969) used one as part of a comparison of two broad educational procedures: conventional oral plus manual against "Rochester" – finger spelling in specific conjunction with speech.

The reports of the British Department of Education and Science (DES) (1964; 1972) to which we have referred provide brief details of how intelligible to a single (medical) layman the speech of deaf children sounds. The information comes from conversational interviews with samples of schoolchildren born in a single year. The earlier study (n = 359) must have been close to a complete

UK sample, while the later (n = 167) was more restrictive and less representative. Three grades of intelligibility were adopted: Intelligible, Partly Intelligible, Unintelligible. The 1964 study reported that about one-third of the children with a hearing loss greater than 80 dB had speech which was unintelligible. The comparable figure for 1972 was 23%. It is not possible to determine whether the apparent improvement represents a true pedagogic advance, technical improvement in hearing aids, or merely a sampling effect. Neither is it clear how strictly criteria were defined or applied. Indeed, the 1964 report states that 54.7% of all children had speech rated as "Partly Intelligible". Nevertheless, "It is doubtful whether the speech of many children in this group could be readily understood at the first attempt by anyone unfamiliar with the speech of deaf children" (p. 66).

Markides (1970) recorded samples of spontaneous speech from 110 children in four Schools for deaf and partially-hearing children. These were subsequently listened to by a panel of teachers of the deaf and by a lay panel unfamiliar with the speech of deaf children. The listeners wrote down verbatim what they thought each deaf speaker said. The untrained listeners were able to report correctly only 19% of the speech of 58 "deaf " children described as having a mean hearing loss of 95 dB. The teachers did better; they understood 31% of the words. Both panels of listeners also provided subjective ratings of intelligibility on a six-point scale (as well as other speech characteristics). Regardless of degree of deafness, the lay listeners found the speech of 64% of the children to be either "very difficult to follow" or "unintelligible". Here the teachers were only slightly more effective. Their comparable value was 59%.

Levitt (1976) reported on ratings of intelligibility of virtually all children born in 1962 and enrolled in "state-operated or state-supported schools for the deaf in New York". Raters heard taped descriptions of short picture sequences spoken by the children, and were provided with a five-point scale for assessment. Roughly 75% of the children were placed in the categories either "Speech cannot be understood" or "Speech is very difficult to understand." No hearing-loss data is provided in the report, which is evidently of an interim nature. It may well be that the sample studied was on average far deafer than that used by Markides or the Department of Education and Science.

By far the most thorough American study is that reported by

Jensema, Karchmer, and Trybus (1978). Their data come from a representative sample of nearly 1000 children in Special education, for whom speech ratings were provided by teachers. A five-point scale of intelligibility was used as follows:

Very intelligible

Intelligible

Barely intelligible

Not intelligible

Would not speak

Their results show a highly significant effect of hearing loss. We might consider that the last three ratings shown above represent speech which would be of little practical conversational use. Up to a hearing loss of 70 dB, there are 14% of such children; in the 71–90 dB band there are 45%, and for children deafer than that the value is 77%.

The overall impression derived from these studies is that the pessimism of teachers is amply supported. With the speech of very deaf children so difficult to understand, the possibility of underlying linguistic excellence may seem academic in the context.

A test of speech intelligibility

For the present study we adopted the following procedure. First, each school head was asked to rate the intelligibility of children in his school using the following scale:

1   Wholly intelligible

2   Fairly easy to understand

3   About half understood

4   Very hard to understand

5   Effectively unintelligible

The rating was not of a particular sample of speech, but was based on the head's general experience of a child. The descriptions are very similar to those used by Levitt (1976) and also by Markides (1970) – the latter permitting six alternatives. Recognizing that teachers are skilled in interpreting the speech of deaf children – and especially their own pupils – we added a qualification. This was that the rating should be made with inexperienced listeners in mind. It will be appreciated that different children were assessed by different raters who would be likely to centre the scale at different imaginary points. We hoped that the simple descriptions of speech would minimize this and, in effect, traded this weakness against the strength offered by experienced teachers with extensive knowledge of their own pupils.

Then a formal intelligibility test was given, which drew on a number of features of other published tests. In essentials, children read 10 sentences onto tape using one of 4 different available versions. The tapes were played back to listening panels consisting generally of housewives unfamiliar with deaf speech. Panels varied in size from 4–6, and each panel listened to 4 children, none of whom used the same test version. Listeners therefore heard 40 different sentences, 10 from each child. During listening, the panel were provided with copies of the sentences being spoken, but each sentence had 2 words deleted. The listeners' task was to insert the missing words, having available both the spoken version and also a formal linguistic context. The test is therefore one which is closer to discourse than are tests using word lists, and involves fewer scoring assumptions than tests in which all words identified have equal weight. As has been commonly reported, there was close agreement between listeners but, just the same, the scores of the listener in each panel who was least successful were excluded from the derived average. This reduced the interlistener variance in a manner "favourable" to the speaker. Since 2 words were to be identified from each of 10 sentences, the average score out of 20 was used as the measure of intelligibility. Prior to hearing any test material, listeners heard each speaker count to 10. This provided a brief introduction to the kind of speech sound to follow.

The sentences themselves were based on text in children's story books appropriate for a much younger age. In fact, the test as administered used 4 versions each of 15 sentences. For the purpose of scoring and after listening was completed, 5 sentences were removed from each version with 2 objectives in mind. Principally it is prudent to eliminate sentences which on statistical test are found to have poor predictability for speech quality. These are sentences which might be easily understood when spoken by otherwise poor speakers, but hard to understand when the speakers otherwise were good. In a simple sense these are maverick sentences, which if left in have the effect of reducing scored differences between children when genuine differences in speech quality are present. The second objective was to equate the 4 versions for overall difficulty, to prevent a version-effect from contaminating scores. We were then left with 4 test versions of equivalent difficulty and in which each item had acceptable reliability. Each sentence contained about 10 syllables.

The words deleted from the listeners' score sheet were chosen on the basis of certain broad guidelines.

1 The location of the deletions in the sentences covered beginning, middle, and end positions.

2 Different grammatical parts of speech were deleted in approximate proportion to their usage in the source material. More nouns, for instance, were deleted than were adverbs.

3 Word length was taken into account, so that more monosyllabic than polysyllabic words were deleted, again to reflect as closely as possible the original material.

4 Where possible, no word was deleted if the remaining context ensured that if the listener simply guessed he would, with a high probability, be correct.

The guessing probabilities for item 4 derived from prior testing of "listeners" who heard nothing, but were given sentences each with 2 blank spaces and were merely required to guess at what they thought the missing words might be. Words which then proved to be easily guessed right were modified. Examples of sentences are shown in Appendix 5, where some awkwardness may be discerned because of these constraints.

Experience with deaf children had convinced us that, when speaking prose, too many children would be totally unintelligible and obtain zero scores, not easily handled statistically. Reducing the spoken material to a closed set of items highly familiar both to speakers and listeners would be likely to provide a more sensitive measure in these cases. Accordingly all children read a set of 10 two-figure numbers before reading the sentences, and a different set of 10 at the end. These numbers were restricted to 21–99. Since a point was allotted if a listener correctly reported 1 digit of a pair, each child had a score out of 40 for numbers. Subsequent analysis showed very high correlations between intelligibility scores based on words and on numbers. Tested separately for each of the five hearing-loss bands, the correlations ranged from 0.69 to 0.82. The lowest – though highly significant – correlation came from the children with hearing losses greater than 105 dB, where speech was least intelligible.

Further analysis showed two minor points, but of some methodological interest. Listeners returned higher scores on the second set of numbers, indicating that they had learned something about a child's speech. But there was no practice transfer between speakers. A child whose taped speech was heard last derived no benefit, nor did the first child suffer. Listeners seemed to learn specific features of a single child's speech, but, in the period of this listening session, learned little about deaf speech in general.

When speech material is read from text rather than being spontaneous, there may be the problems arising from reading difficulties that we referred to. In the event, as we shall show later, intelligibility scores could have been little affected in this way, partly no doubt because of the simplicity of the prose. But few deaf children will be able to provide a perfect spoken rendering on first reading an unfamiliar sentence. Quigley (1969) gave his subjects extensive practice at reading the words he used prior to taperecording and corrected substantially. In our case, we felt that this kind of speech training was inappropriate. But we did allow one dry run in the course of which children could ask about pronunciation. Beyond that no aid was given.

Speech rating, speech intelligibility, and deafness

How easy would it be then for people unfamiliar with deaf children to understand what they say? The simplest evaluation can be seen in the proportions of children allocated to the five rating descriptions by their own teachers:

Wholly intelligible	14%
Fairly easy to understand	20%
About half understood	18%
Very hard to understand	25%
Effectively unintelligible	23%

(Children in Special Schools only: n = 331)

Evidently there would be little difficulty in holding a conversation with about one-third of these children. But it would be extremely difficult to do so with nearly half of them. This is altogether too simplistic a description since the figures shown must conceal a continuing effect of degree of hearing loss. This can be seen in Figure 8.1 where the distribution of ratings is shown separately for each band of hearing loss.

Essentially, as hearing loss increases, there is a steady decline in the proportion of children with reasonable speech and a steady increase in the proportion of those with whom conversation would clearly be difficult. Whatever model of heard speech such children use, it is, to say the least, highly degraded. The descriptions of points 4 and 5 on our intelligibility rating scale might also then very well represent a description of what very deaf children hear of speech.

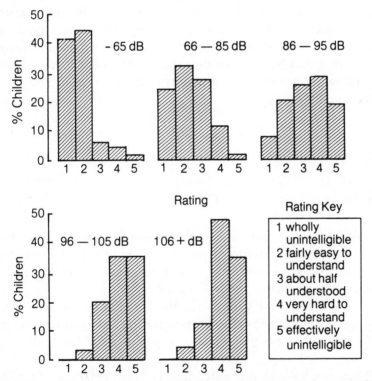

Figure 8.1.   Teachers' ratings of children's speech and hearing loss (n = 331).

The values given above are well in line with other comparable information available from large-scale studies. It will be recalled that when Markides (1970) used untrained raters, he reported 64%

of children to be at least "very difficult to follow" – rather more than we have shown. The DES Reports (1964; 1972) respectively gave about one-third and 23% as the proportions of children with "unintelligible" speech. This latter, more recent figure, which is probably the more appropriate comparison, is identical to the proportion we found. The Levitt (1976) data seem out of line in that considerably more children were rated at a level equivalent to our points 4 and 5. But such differences between British children and those of New York may be concealing demographic factors of which we are unaware. Comparison with the more numerous data from Jensema et al. (1978) is more difficult because their rating categories do not so easily match those we used – and this is especially true for their "would not speak" rating. If, though, we consider their three categories, "barely intelligible", "not intelligible" and "would not speak", to represent roughly similar speech to that represented by our last two, "very hard to understand" and "effectively unintelligible", comparison can be made. Adjusting our hearing-loss bands to fit those in the American study, we find the following percentages of children with speech no better than barely intelligible:

	Present study	Jensema et al. (1978)
−70 dB	6.3	13.8
71–90 dB	31.4	45.0
91+ dB	73.5	76.8

The difference in results is significant only for the 71–90 dB band ($p < 0.05$). Particularly for the major group of very deaf children, there is close agreement that some three-quarters have speech of little use for ordinary communication.

Summarizing these various results there can be no escape from the conclusion that speech communication between hearing and profoundly-deaf people remains a problem of immense magnitude.

When we look at the outcome of the objective intelligibility tests, we must interpret with care because we are considering speech which, though related to that which teachers rated, is nevertheless different in a number of respects. The teachers were taking a general view of the speech that children themselves freely generate. In the intelligibility tests, children are saying specifically what we want them to say. That intelligibility scores as absolute values have validity only for the material that we oblige children to use is dramatically reflected in Figure 8.2. Respectively for each hearing-loss band, these plot the median score – together with interquartiles – for two-figure numbers and for sentences (words). The difference is striking – if predictable. It is much easier for deaf children to speak numbers intelligibly than prose. Two factors at least are involved. The numbers are drawn from a finite set

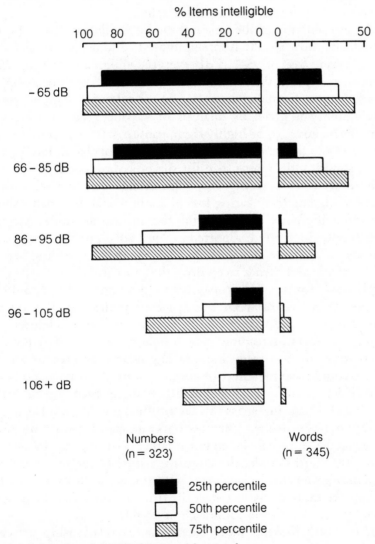

Figure 8.2.   Speech intelligibility and hearing loss.

thoroughly familiar to the listeners and a rather small set at that. If merely prosodic features of the speech can be discriminated, so that listeners know which of the sounds represents each digit, the choice lies between only eight possibilities for the first sound, and nine possibilities for the second (the digit zero was not used). But we should also recognize that the speakers may have had greater practice at speaking numbers than at many of the words in sentences. These influences do not invalidate the results so long as we are clear that their use has these limitations, and that the statements have more statistical than absolute value.

An examination of the range of the intelligibility scores shows, informally, how closely is intelligibility tied to degree of deafness. At a hearing loss of 95–105 dB even the children in the top 25% have worse speech than those in the bottom 25% for the 66–85 dB band. A more formal appreciation of the role of hearing in speech intelligibility is given by analysis of variance. The hearing-loss variable is shown to be highly significant ($p < 0.001$). Both for the numbers and the sentences, at every hearing-loss band, intelligibility is significantly worse than for the preceding band.

Somewhat discrepantly from the ratings data we see only a small change up to a hearing loss of about 85 dB, but then a sharp fall in intelligibility occurs. Using the not too dissimilar Magner (1972) test, Boothroyd, reported in Stark (1974, p. 39), showed an exactly comparable relationship; a small effect of hearing loss to about 85 dB and then a steep drop down to around 105 dB. One explanation for the discrepancy between ratings and test could lie in the difference between the speech samples being evaluated rather than in the nature of the evaluation. When children are saying numbers or reading very simple prose, the relatively few alternatives in one case, and the linguistic redundancies in the other, could have the effect of compensating the listener for what is real deterioration with increasing deafness even for partially-hearing children. In a sense this factor shifts the threshold at which recognition is possible. When teachers rate speech using a memory of generalized speech behaviour, rather than on the basis of a currently heard sample, the linguistic nature of the material rated becomes irrelevant. In this case, with respect to hearing loss, the ratings are more likely to reflect the true function. But the general form of the association cannot be in doubt.

It is worth looking more closely at the relationship between teachers' ratings of speech and test scores. In Tables 8.1 and 8.2 we

Table 8.1 Relationship between rated speech intelligibility and test scores for sentences (n = 322)

		Test scores Number of children in quartile:			
		I	II	III	IV
	1	40	7	0	0
	2	34	27	6	0
Teachers' rating	3	6	25	22	9
	4	1	17	30	36
	5	0	5	22	35

Table 8.2 Relationship between rated speech intelligibility and test scores for numbers (n = 326)

		Test scores Number of children in quartile:			
		I	II	III	IV
	1	38	9	0	0
	2	31	30	5	0
Teachers' rating	3	9	26	22	8
	4	4	12	33	35
	5	0	4	22	38

have broken down the latter into quartiles regardless of hearing loss, and we then show the distribution of ratings within each quartile – that is, the number of children allocated by teachers to each of the five possible alternatives. It is evident that the association between the two methods of assessment is very close indeed. Nearly all children who, on test, comprise the best 25% of speakers are also rated 1 or 2; almost all of the worst 25% are rated 4 or 5.

Nevertheless, there is an aspect of this relationship which seems to have received little attention in the literature. It is generally reported that the two measures are highly correlated and our own

results support that. But different assumptions underlie the two
kinds of estimate. In particular, a listening panel may not directly
know how deaf a speaker is. There may be inference from the
quality of speech, but not knowledge, unless – unusually – it is
provided. In the case of the raters we used, this was not the case.
They were familiar with the children. We wondered therefore
whether teachers' ratings are influenced by their knowledge of
how deaf a child is.

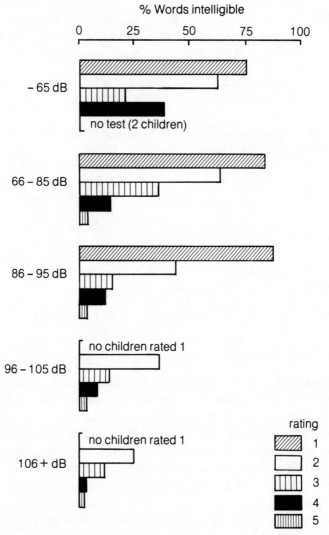

*Figure 8.3.   Speech intelligibility: ratings versus test score (sentences): by
hearing loss (n = 331).*

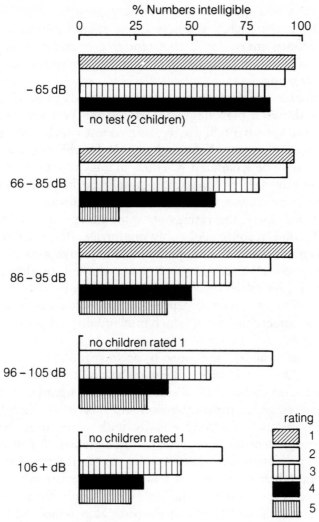

Figure 8.4. Speech intelligibility: ratings versus test score (numbers): by hearing loss (n = 331).

In Figures 8.3 and 8.4 we show the intelligibility test scores for sentences and for numbers according to hearing loss and according to teachers' rating. We would expect in principle that, for a given rating, intelligibility score should be constant and not affected by hearing loss. We ask teachers to rate speech, not deafness. However, it would seem, and analysis of variance confirms it, that for a given rating intelligibility scores tend to decrease with greater deafness – an effect which is significant at the 0.05 level. So, while the effect is not great, it is discernibly present. What may be happening is that, while teachers are in general reliable raters of speech (Montgomery, 1975), they tend to give credit for degree of deafness. They seem to uprate very deaf children and downrate the partially-hearing.

One matter which we have referred to needs to be discussed. We have shown a high degree of association between degree of deafness and speech intelligibility, using a test which requires children to read sentences. Knowing that deafer children are poorer readers, it may be wondered whether, in this case, the poor speech of profoundly-deaf children may simply be because they have more difficulty reading the test material. Two features of the data discount this. First, the ratings are quite independent of reading ability. Second, reading could only minimally affect the test scores for spoken numbers. We do not have an objective measure of the ability of these children simply to name printed numbers, but it must surely, by school-leaving age, be uniformly high. So while reading ability may overall depress intelligibility scores, it seems unlikely to affect the way in which intelligibility relates to hearing loss.

Insofar as reading and speech performances are correlated (Quigley, 1969), it is more likely to be due to a general factor associated with verbal skill. We do indeed find significant correlations between prose comprehension and speech intelligibility for sentences. But we also find equally high correlations between prose comprehension and speech intelligibility for numbers. Ultimately the issue can be clarified by statistical formality. When prose comprehension scores are treated as a covariate in an analysis of variance of speech scores, the highly significant effect of hearing loss remains ($p < 0.001$); in other words, after removing (statistically) any effect of reading, hearing loss itself remains a dominating influence.

All other performances that we have assessed have been significantly influenced by intelligence. Yet several authors have reported that intelligence does not seem to be associated with speech intelligibility (Markides, 1970; Myklebust, 1964; Quigley, 1969; Smith, 1975). Ling (1976) also notes that "Intelligence does not appear to be as important in speech acquisition as it is in many other aspects of education" (p. 158). Montgomery (1968) shows a significant but only a small correlation between teachers' ratings of "voice production" and score on Raven's Matrices. In spite of this accord there is something superficially implausible in the notion that a skill absorbing much school time should uncharacteristically carry no intelligence component. We discussed this matter in connection with lip reading, and it is equally relevant here. It is hard to think of skills which are not learned more efficiently and more swiftly when aided by higher intelligence.

In fact our own data are not greatly divergent from those of other studies. While intelligence test score shows as a significant covariate in the analysis of the effect of hearing loss on speech intelligibility, as Montgomery reported, the relationship is of little predictive value. The correlation coefficients we obtained at each level of hearing loss are shown in Table 8.3. The weakness of this association is further substantiated if we examine the intelligence of children according to their rated speech quality. While there is a consistent decline in the average Raven score from those rated "wholly intelligible" to those rated "effectively unintelligible", even at the extremes the difference is not statistically significant. The fact that intelligence seems to be so unimportant has educational implications which might cause concern. We are led to wonder about the effectiveness of training procedures which seem to have little more impact on bright than on dull children. Alternatively, we are led to wonder whether speech can be taught to deaf children any more than it is "taught" to hearing children. Rather startlingly, Jensema et al. (1978) report a zero correlation between rated speech intelligibility and age between four – twenty-three years. This completely confirms an earlier study by Babbini and Quigley (1970). The latter found no improvement at all in the intelligibility of 163 deaf children over a five-year period, though prose comprehension and lip reading improved significantly.

Table 8.3 Correlation between speech intelligibility and intelligence, by hearing loss

Hearing loss (dB)	–65	66–85	86–95	96–105	106+
Sentences	0.14	0.42*	0.33*	0.38**	0.14
Numbers	−0.01	0.21	0.39**	0.31**	0.13

* Significant correlation: $p < 0.05$
** Significant correlation: $p < 0.01$

Vocal speech and internal speech

In Chapter 1 we briefly discussed a speculative model in which we proposed a specific relationship between quality of vocal speech in the deaf and the likelihood that it could be usefully internalized. We emphasized two essential conditions. First, that there must be consistent speech sounds; and second, that they must also be discriminable. The nature of the empirical relationship between speech intelligibility and internal speech is therefore of interest. But we have in the meantime seen that both hearing loss and intelligence are significant factors in determining whether or not a child does use internal speech. It is possible, then, that any effect due to speech intelligibility may be no more than the working through of deafness and intelligence, the former especially relevant for speech. Our present problem therefore is to examine the association between intelligibility and internal speech, regardless of degree of deafness and regardless of intelligence.

In the event, the model is well supported. Again, using formal statistical test, we treat hearing loss and internal speech as independent variables, covary intelligence, and examine the effect on scores of speech intelligibility. Whether we use scores for sentences or for numbers, there is a highly significant effect of internal speech. The relationship is shown in Figures 8.5 and 8.6. The main effect can be seen more simply perhaps if we use the 67 pairs of children who have been matched for hearing loss, intelligence, and cause of deafness that we introduced in an earlier chapter. The difference in intelligibility between these groups is shown in Figure 8.7. For both sentences and numbers Wilcoxon tests show differences significant beyond the 0.001 level.

The model of course requires that quality of vocal speech causally determines its internal use. These analyses show no more than an association. The direction of the relationship cannot be determined experimentally and essentially it has to be argued logically as it did in the case of reading – but for the reverse direction. In fact we would expect an association between vocal speech and internal speech to have generality beyond the case of deafness, and the evidence that it does helps to clarify the issue of cause and effect.

Locke and Kutz (1975) reported a study using hearing children who misarticulated certain words (*wing-ring* and *sack-shack* confusions), but who could detect the difference when they were correctly spoken by the experimenter. In a short-term memory

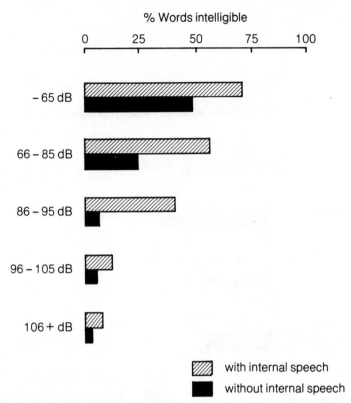

% Words intelligible

Figure 8.5.   Speech intelligibility (sentences), internal speech and hearing loss. (n = 296). Scores adjusted for intelligence.

experiment which did not require spoken responses, the children confused those words in memory. Saxman and Miller (1973) also report a study in which they found that hearing but "articulation-deficient" children had poorer recall of sentences than children with normal speech. There is a clear implication that these children internalize the words in speech and then have difficulty in distinguishing them for recall. It seems hard to accept that a degraded internal representation develops independently of vocal speech and then subsequently determines how the children speak. Goodglass, Denes, and Calderon (1974) examined verbal mediation in a task in which adult hearing subjects memorized nameable pictures. An aphasic group showed clear evidence in the errors they made that they did not use internal speech, unlike the nonaphasic controls who did. Again, the only reasonable assumption here is that it was not the absence of internal speech that led to the aphasia, but that the direction of the effect was the reverse.

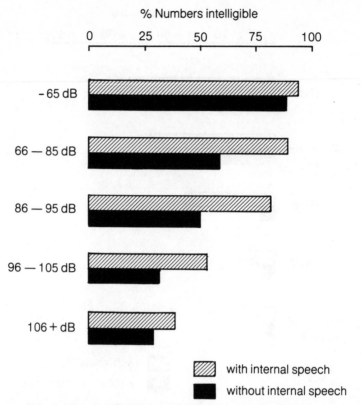

*Figure 8.6.   Speech intelligibility (numbers), internal speech and hearing loss.
(n = 296). Scores adjusted for intelligence.*

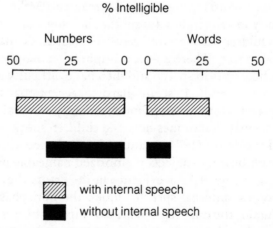

*Figure 8.7.   Speech intelligibility and internal speech (matched pairs: n = 67
pairs).*

There is also a good deal of evidence from developmental studies which shows that vocal speech developmentally precedes internal speech (Conrad, 1971a; Flavell et al. 1966; Hagen and Kingsley, 1968; Kendler, 1964). We have to assume that a child cannot internalize speech until he has some vocal speech to internalize, and the normal course of development from babbling through to the meaningful use of words in social and communicative contexts has been well enough documented (Lenneberg, 1967). Vocal speech seems to be well established by about the age of three years. All of the studies cited above are in agreement that internal speech or verbal mediation cannot be observed prior to a child reaching a mental age of four–five years. We can see no way in which deafness could reverse the direction of this development.

The model also requires an association between quality of overt speech and quality of internal speech. Our internal speech ratio (IS-Ratio) provides a measure of the latter. It represents the degree to which homophonic words are difficult to memorize serially, and we take this to indicate the degree to which phonetic coding is useful. The more degraded the internal speech the less useful will it phonetically be. We would therefore expect that the higher the speech intelligibility score, the larger the IS-Ratio, *regardless of degree of deafness* or of intelligence.

If we examine this association separately for each hearing-loss band, we virtually remove the effects of deafness itself from the relationship. We can then correlate IS-Ratio scores with speech intelligibility scores and eliminate the effect of intelligence by partial correlation.

Table 8.4 shows the values of the rank partial correlations. For hearing losses up to 85 dB, the score of speech intelligibility for sentences was used; at greater losses, the score for numbers was more sensitive since there were no zero scores and only two at the possible maximum. It will be seen that for every level of hearing loss, the correlation is significant. The fact that they are relatively low in absolute terms is of less importance to the model than that the significance levels are mostly high; the model certainly does not exclude the influence of factors other than vocal speech for determining quality of internal speech. Indeed, intelligence has been specifically removed from the statistical analysis.

The association is further confirmed by the teachers' own speech ratings. Figure 8.8 shows the percentage of children using and not using internal speech classified according to their rated speech. More important here, it also shows the respective median values of the IS-Ratio. For those children who do use internal speech, it is clear that not only is intelligible vocal speech closely associated with presence of internal speech, but it is also associated with its quality, which is seen to decline as speech is rated worse. Furthermore, those hearing-impaired children who nevertheless have rated speech which is "wholly intelligible" are as likely as hearing children to use internal speech – and to the same degree. But we also see that for children without internal speech, the IS-Ratio is independent of speech quality, as it should be.

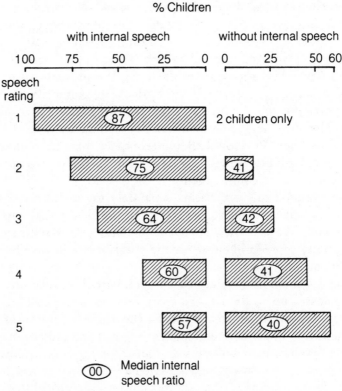

Figure 8.8.   Speech ratings and internal speech (n = 327).

None of this discussion of the proposition that quality of vocal speech determines the effectiveness of speech internalized excludes the possibility that internal speech is also directly and independently determined by degree of deafness. We have seen the influence of hearing loss on internal speech as it operates through speech quality. Then we have seen (Table 8.4) that regardless of hearing loss, speech quality remains a significant factor for internal speech. But the direct pathway from hearing loss to internal speech may still be additionally relevant.

Table 8.4   Correlations between Internal Speech-Ratio and speech intelligibility, by hearing loss (intelligence partialled out)

Hearing loss (dB)	−65	66–85	86–95	96–105	106+
Rank correlation	0.47	0.31	0.69	0.42	0.32
Significance level	0.001	0.025	0.001	0.001	0.05
Number of children	53	71	52	73	56

In fact there is a strong suggestion – no more – that it is not. If we assume for the purpose that children with the same teacher-rating of speech do have similar speech quality, we can look at the independent role of hearing loss on the IS-Ratio. We can take those children with the same rating and rank-correlate hearing loss and IS-Ratio (partialling out any effect of intelligence). That is, we hold constant both speech quality and intelligence. When we do this, not one of the five correlations reaches the 0.05 significance level. An association seems not to be present. Figure 8.1 indicates that a single speech rating may extend over a surprisingly wide range of deafness, providing meaningfulness to the correlations. But, since a nonsignificant association cannot prove the absence of an effect, we can only regard this outcome as helpful to our argument rather than conclusive. In other words, we still have no evidence that degree of deafness does act independently of speech quality to determine the usefulness of internal speech.

It may though be wondered how it is that 17 of the children whose speech is rated by their teachers as "effectively unintelligible" nevertheless do appear to use internal speech. In fact, this presents no difficulty for the model. We have said that to be internalized speech must be consistent and discriminable – to the speaker. Evidently the speech of these few children is unintelligible to their teachers; we need only accept that it is not unintelligible to the children themselves. In some of these cases – and we are only discussing a total of 17 children in this category – we cannot rule out the possibility of error in measuring the IS-Ratio. But there are also 3 children amongst this small group whose internal speech facility, in spite of their unintelligible speech, is almost certainly genuine; their reading ability is actually equal to that of hearing children of the same age.

These various analyses provide support for the hypothesis that quality of vocal speech determines, independently of degree of hearing loss, the extent to which a child develops useful internal speech. This we have seen has a significant effect on other communication skills. We must though beware of leaping to pedagogic conclusions. Internal speech is demonstrably a valuable cognitive tool. It appears to be highly dependent on the presence of intelligible speech. Not only therefore is good vocal speech of immense value in the broadest social sense, but it evidently provides a means by which children can communicate with themselves. There are, however, two major obstacles in the way of regarding these results as support for exclusively oral education.

No data presented here exclude the probability that other communication modes than speech – were they available to a child – would also be internalized and be available as a cognitive tool. We shall return to this in some detail in a later chapter. The second obstacle, which is of course related, we shall discuss here. We have seen that the development of internal speech depends substantially upon the acquisition of good quality vocal speech. But we have also seen the massive contribution made by degree of hearing loss itself to that very acquisition of vocal speech. There is what we might see as a reception-production barrier that has to be breached if deaf children's own speech is to be any better than the speech sounds they hear. Fry (1977) expresses this with great clarity. He refers to a deaf child, " . . . shaping his own sounds to the best of his ability until they make a match with those he hears from other people" (p. 143). As Montgomery (1966b) has pointed out, speech production is a good guide to speech reception. We noted earlier how little deafness is necessary before speech reception becomes impaired. Less formally but more directly, Johnson (1962) reported on the rated speech of the children with hearing impairment in ordinary schools. Even of those with hearing losses of less than 50 dB, only 25% were without noticeable defect. The comparable value for our own combined Schools and PHU populations (rating of 1) is 41%. When we reach levels of profound deafness, Erber (1974b) reports that "Children, in fact, seem to perceive little more than the gross time and intensity patterns in

acoustic speech signals" (p. 179). To the extent that those innumerable and often ill-defined cues for perception of speech that we
all take for granted are unavailable, speech will be impaired, as
Erber says, to a point where little intelligible remains. The crucial
and elusive problem has been, and is, how to teach children to
make sounds which they cannot hear when others make them, and
when they frequently cannot hear their own attempts. Unless success in this can be assured, quality of internal speech will also be
constrained to a point of uselessness. So, although internal speech
is desirable, specifically oral education guarantees its development
no more than it does the development of intelligible vocal speech.
The value of oral education in this context depends largely on the
degree to which it can overcome the reception-production barrier.

Speech training and the reception-production barrier

There is, in oral education, an urgency about speech training
which far transcends the teaching of reading. Our own experience
of these two communication modes differs. We readily accept that
we must all learn to read and that there are degrees of literacy,
recognizing that even a low level nevertheless permits some access
to communication and culture. Speech, on the other hand, is not
usually taught to hearing children. We accept that virtually
everyone speaks "normally" – i.e., perfectly. The smallest
impairment is immediately perceived – the slightest lisp; the faint
r/w slurring. Conceptually we pass instantly from good to defective speech. With hearing children, we accept that some will read
better than others. But the concept of better or worse speaking is
strange. The level of intelligibility of the speech of deaf children,
though, is an unremitting challenge to educationists, with the outcome of their efforts directly perceived. During the past century,
there has been ever increasing pressure on the reception-
production barrier, first relying on the intuitive skills of teachers
aided by some understanding of the anatomy of speech production, and in more recent years by developments in phonetics,
speech pathology, and the psychology of speech perception.
Amplification shifts the threshold of course, but does not change
the fundamental nature of the problem. In addition, and especially
during the last forty years, advances in electronics have offered the
temptations of acoustic speech received visually.

Whether working with no more than intuition, patience, and devotion, or with the aid of a powerful computer, the problem ever present is what of speech should be taught? Within what has emerged as an extremely complex psycho-acoustic phenomenon, what are the crucial features to be extracted and given priority in training? If a child has no useful hearing, it is pointless to say "make a sound like this." If we knew how the sound was made – the necessary articulatory configurations – this might help. But it becomes clear that not all sounds are of equal importance for the production of intelligible speech. There is, therefore, substantial research effort concerned with analysis of speech sounds and with analysis of the sounds of "deaf speech" to see where the mismatches occur and to determine their relative importance for intelligible production and thence training.

Nickerson (1975) has provided a valuable summary of the characteristic ways in which the speech of deaf people differs from that of normal speech. Deaf speech shows poor timing. It is generally slower than normal speech, distinguishes less between stressed and unstressed syllables, pauses in unusual and inappropriate places, lacks rhythm, and suffers from inadequate breath control. Patterns of intonation are poor; deaf speakers lack pitch control, frequently breaking into falsetto, while appropriate changes in pitch are often neglected, leading to flat monotonous speech. Nickerson summarizes research on many articulatory problems. Articulatory movements may be defective with respect, for instance, to transitions, nasalization, production of diphthongs, and so on. Improper placing of the tongue is frequent, distinction between voiced and unvoiced consonants may be missing, and consonants completely omitted. Deaf speech frequently features unexpected changes in loudness. Clearly the list could be greatly extended. Calvert (1962) reports that he has found 52 different adjectives which researchers have used to describe deaf speech.

It would be too much to expect teachers to concentrate their efforts on all of the distinguishing features which have been isolated. Indeed, it might waste effort since Smith (1975) points out that, for example, not all phonemic errors affect speech intelligibility. Nor when a significant articulatory error has been determined is the way to correction always clear. Povel (1974) notes that there are many ways of producing the same speech sound, differences which may have their origin in what he calls "neural commands".

Nevertheless, though far from complete, we do now have, and have had it for some time, a very adequate description of the ways in which the speech intelligibility of deaf children needs to be modified if it is to resemble more closely the kind of speech with which we are familiar and which is of high intelligibility. In the preceding pages, we have presented an account of the recent outcome of training as it pertains to Britain, and Jensema et al. (1978) have reported similarly for the USA. Ling (1976) summarizes: "Advances in acoustic phonetics, speech science, psychology, hearing aid technology, and other related fields appear to have made no significant impact on standards of speech production" (p. 11).

Apparently, not only do profoundly-deaf children not speak more intelligibly than in the past so far as we know, but there appear to be no convincing accounts which show specific training programmes (as distinct from nontransferable inspirational teaching) to have made a discernible improvement in intelligibility sustained over a period of time. Even though we seem to know what modifications are needed, and in such refined detail that the actual step of "process shaping", as Povel calls it, ought to be trivially easy, some crucial element is missing. It is true of course that any single training programme generally concerns itself with a single or narrow range of speech features. It may be that speech production is a prime example of a skill where the whole is not usefully described by the sum of the parts. But we prefer to examine another aspect.

Speech training is necessarily based on the assumption that pupils will imitate something and remember how they did it. Essentially they are trying to imitate a speech sound which they cannot hear. They can hear something and no doubt can imitate that. But that sound is not what the teacher accepts as adequate. Training therefore entails provision of analogues of speech sounds. The most widely used analogues are either articulatory or visual – a distinction which determines the psychological processes involved in utilizing them, and we shall discuss them separately. Other analogies, such as tactile vibration, have also been used to present to a pupil a description of a sound in nonacoustic form, but the application is limited to relatively coarse characteristics of the speech signal. Much of what we say about visible speech applies equally to tactile speech (see Kirman, 1973).

Speech sounds are "produced", and require a speech musculature. Different organs, each controlled by a different set of muscles, are involved – and possibly required – in the production of different aspects of speech sounds and in the transitions from one sound to another. Activation of specific groups of muscles and in particular sequence lead to the emission of a speech sound in definable relationship; though this does not mean that there is a rigid one-to-one relationship between speech-motor pattern and speech sound as Povel (1974) noted. In appropriate phonetic context, extremely small variations in articulatory pattern may result in clearly perceived different speech sounds – as in the difference between voiced and unvoiced consonants for instance.

When hearing people speak they have three principal sources of information to indicate to them whether they have made the speech sound they intended. One is the quality of the sound which can be heard: acoustic feedback. The other is articulatory or kinaesthetic feedback from sense organs within the muscles. The third comes from tactile sensation when one surface touches another. Normally we are unaware of articulatory or tactile feedback, but may become so by paying more attention, or when we detect that the sounds we make are not those intended – through anaesthesia for instance, or inebriation. More generally we rely on acoustic feedback to monitor that we are making appropriate speech sounds, and there is some debate as to whether or not we also make fine corrections based on what we hear. We hear our own speech partly through the air – as we hear other voices – and partly through sound conducted through the solid structures of the head, that is, bone conduction. Little is needed to mask the former. When it happens, covering one's ears for example, though we notice the difference in sound quality, we have no difficulty in adapting to the somewhat changed feedback and external listeners detect little change in our speech. But if we are willing to sustain the extremely great – and dangerous if prolonged – intensity of sound required to mask bone-conducted sound, several dramatic events generally occur. The first is that we become immediately aware of articulation in a way not normally experienced. Suddenly there seems to be a great deal of movement in the throat. At the same time there is a change in speech quality. We speak more loudly, presumably trying to overcome the noise mask, but we are unaware of the change. We also articulate in a more precise than normal manner – as if, deprived of acoustic feedback, we strive for more articulatory information. Finally, we lose control of pitch to some extent (Elliott and Niemoeller, 1970) and singing is very severely impaired.

During the short periods of time (minutes) for which this kind of experiment is possible, though noticeably changed, speech remains intelligible (Schliesser and Coleman, 1968), and with the off-set of masking at once returns to normal. Clinically, a comparable condition is present when a hearing person with normal speech rapidly becomes profoundly deaf through accident or disease. Here the condition may be permanent, and a swift deterioration in speech quality occurs. Few systematic studies of this phenomenon are available, but it is rare for intelligibility to deteriorate to a point where speech becomes unintelligible. The loss of quality goes so far, and then seems to stabilize. Remembering that we have been discussing feedback from several sources, it is tempting to speculate that once articulatory and tactile patterns have been established through the use of acoustic feedback, deprived of the latter the adventitiously deafened person is able to fall back onto the remaining information which has always been available though not consciously used. It seems likely that speech can be sustained by articulatory and tactile feedback, but lacking those characteristics preeminently and perhaps exclusively derived from acoustic monitoring.

What is important here is that we learn to make speech sounds by hearing them, and then by matching them, acoustically. We do not make exact acoustic matches. Small children do not sound like grown men, and the difficulties of acquiring the accents of a foreign language are notorious. Part of the mismatch may simply arise from ignorance of how to make the desired sound. We can hear it, but we cannot observe the accompanying articulatory pattern. Hearing children, then, learn to make speech sounds by hearing them spoken, by developing articulatory patterns which they are not taught, but which permit them to imitate the sounds to a degree of approximation which is acceptable for communication. If they forgot how to articulate, they would lose speech. The born-deaf child cannot hear speech well enough for imitation to be intelligible. In a broad sense, speech training attempts to teach these children how to articulate.

A number of unsolved problems have so far frustrated any noticeable advance. The first, as we have noted, is simply that we do not know which are the significant speech features for high intelligibility. Nickerson, Kalikow, and Stevens (1976) showed that a number of specific speech features, such as velar and pitch control, can be improved without improving intelligibility.

A second problem is that deaf children have to learn to execute articulatory patterns of which they can perceive only fragmentary portions which may not carry the most relevant information. They can see whether the instructor's lips are parted or closed, and may be able to observe some tongue positions. But thinking no further than the oral cavity, they are required to detect events which are rapidly changing and often invisible. Nober (1967) analysed articulatory errors made by deaf children, and reported that those consonants which are least visible in terms of articulatory placement (linguavelar) have the highest error ratings. Insofar as a child depends on an articulatory model of speech sounds, the "copy" can be little more than a crude approximation; the requisite information cannot be consistently provided.

Thirdly, we do not know how well the kinaesthetic information deriving from speech can be remembered. Evidence of the fragility of newly learned articulatory control is suggested in a study by Nittrouer, Devan, and Boothroyd (1976). Intensive auditory training of deaf children over a period of eight weeks showed posttraining improvement in speech quality. Seven months later, though, intelligibility was back to its original pretraining level, requiring a further twenty-five training weeks to recoup the loss. The fact that adventitiously deafened adults retain some degree of intelligibility suggests that, while conformations for fine control are forgotten, coarse movements of the speech musculature may remain retrievable. We are then led to wonder whether the gross control which can be remembered can in fact provide information for speech which is more useful than that available from severely deficient residual hearing. That it may not be is suggested by the close association that clearly exists between speech intelligibility and degree of hearing loss.

Summarizing very briefly, we argue that children born profoundly deaf have only a very degraded acoustic speech model. Their speech must therefore be based either upon this or on remembered articulatory (and tactile) patterns for which there can be no external model. Ultimately then, the reinforcement during learning has to be verbal or some other secondary and symbolic, rather than direct, kind. There will inevitably be long periods of time without this reinforcement, during which speech patterns are sustained only by memory of what they did before. We doubt whether in general there is appropriate neurological organization to support this feat of memorizing. At all events the attempts to teach speech by use of the articulatory analogue have been fairly consistent failures.

Speech training by visual feedback

The evident resistance to conventional training methods of this most pedagogically sensitive of oral skills has led to a growing research exploration of the use of the visual analogue of speech. The particular theoretical attraction of the visual analogue is that the speech model it can present is, within the limits of phonetic theory and technological knowledge, rich, complete – and visible. Even better, it may be highly selective of chosen particular features of speech, and so avoid, bombarding a learner with information not yet relevant.

The historical development of these devices and descriptions of those in current use is provided in many excellent reviews (Boothroyd, 1975; Levitt, 1973; Pickett, 1968a; Strong, 1975). They range from the simple illumination of a lamp in response to any speech sound, through instant displays of amplitude and frequency characteristics, and on to detailed spectrographic analysis including temporal components. But knowledge of the complexities of speech perception has increased, while experience indicates that deaf children can only use information from highly simplified displays. The focus of attention has therefore shifted away from the simpler devices towards those technically more sophisticated. These are capable both of presenting subtle features of speech, and in the form of a perceptually simple display. Then the ability to "freeze" the picture on a cathode ray tube display brings an opportunity for matching to a model which is not present even in natural speech. Because of these advances, together with the substantial progress in analysing the nature of the defects of deaf speech, hopes have been raised for the technologically based breakthrough of the reception-production barrier.

Perhaps it is too soon for pessimism. But Pickett (Pickett, 1968b) reminds us that as long ago as 1874 Alexander Graham Bell used pictures of speech wave-forms to train deaf speakers. It is of course true that the more sustained impetus has come in recent times with the development of the cathode ray tube and the computer. But it is increasingly evident that success will not come easily.

A critical problem is perhaps highlighted in one of the rare well-documented evaluative studies to have been reported. Nickerson et al. (1976) developed a computer-aided device which could extract a number of different parameters of speech and display them visually in ingenious ways likely to be interesting to children. In this way training could reasonably be presented as a game – or at least as a pleasurable activity. Some 40 children at the Clarke School for the Deaf in the USA received daily 20-minute training sessions for 7–14 weeks. No control group was used but progress was logged by experienced teachers, and assessments from taped records of formal and spontaneous speech were made both by ratings and using Magner's (1972) objective test. Although improvements were reported for specific features of speech production, the authors reported that, "Measureable improvements in overall intelligibility of unrehearsed speech were not demonstrated for most students" (p. 130). The problem highlighted is one we referred to earlier, namely that the overall intelligibility of speech may be poorly represented by the sum of its parts. It is too early in the history of evaluative studies to know whether this is an insoluble theoretical problem, or whether it is in fact amenable to further, as yet unspecified, research.

A further problem which might be illustrated by reference to this study – though we intend no direct criticism of it – concerns evaluation. The study required 20 minutes per day of student time, together with a good deal of teacher time, together with use of a costly device. We do not know whether, in operating the normal curriculum, more or less pupil-teacher time would have been employed, nor do we know what outcome to have expected from a similar schedule of training but using conventional and cheaper methods.

A number of devices of varying degree of technical complexity and cost are now being installed in schools for (so-called) evaluative studies. We hope that when success is claimed – as it will be – it will be based on adequate control and use of valid criteria for assessing performance. The essential questions that must be asked with respect to any novel training device are largely obvious. Has the device in fact improved speech? Over what period? With how much practice and at what total cost? Then there are questions of measurement; the validity of the measuring instruments themselves. Do they have established test-retest reliability? What degree of improvement is regarded as acceptable? In a sense we have to become involved in cost-benefit analysis. Equally important, we need to beware of studies which use small selected samples of children; we need to be sure that children have not been discarded from the study because of lack of progress. There may well be great merit in a device which benefits only particular children. This is no bar so long as the characteristics of the child-device interaction are understood.

These are largely practical matters with which any serious evaluation study of any programme must concern itself. There are perhaps more critical theoretical issues. A child is confronted with a visible pattern which is a very accurate analogue of certain features of speech. Whether the picture is an analogue of vocal tract shape or intonation pattern of a short phrase is not important here. The picture has probably been generated by a teacher and "frozen" on the display. The child must say something which will produce a matching picture. Every attempt presents a visual indication of discrepancy – and if the rules have been learned, what articulatory changes are needed to reduce it. Displays of some speech features are easier to match than others. It is part of the art to optimize between ease of matching pictures and usefulness for speech intelligibility of the sound represented. But the act itself of matching pictures using articulatory conformation as the controlling organism is demonstrably feasible.

Trial then proceeds trial until the match can be made swiftly and with accuracy. Up to this point training by visual analogue has the very great advantage over the articulatory analogue of classical speech training, that in principle the resulting speech sound is likely to be of better quality – closer to the target. With classical methods, the target is not present; when visual feedback is used, it is. But from then on in the process, we are faced with a critical psychological problem. How do children generate the sound when there is no picture to match? What is there for them to remember? Remembering the picture is useless; without the device they cannot generate a matching picture. All they have available is what is fed back from their articulatory organs – the memory of tongue position, how they breathed, the position of the velum, and so on. Here we are right back at a point necessarily reached when training is based on an articulatory analogue. We are again faced with the question: how well can articulatory patterns be remembered? What determines recall of different components of the pattern? What is the relationship between ease of recall and functional utility in speech?

The history of speech and indeed of music tells us that the auditory system is beautifully adapted for remembering extremely fine nuances of sound. Yet Nickerson (1975) reports that there is little articulatory feedback from the velum, for instance, control of which affects nasality. In fact we have barely begun to develop a taxonomy of the feedback characteristics of the various muscles involved in speech and the relative contributions that they make towards intelligibility. We know of no controlled study which has examined speech intelligibility six months after the end of visually aided training. Povel (1974), using a visual display to correct defective speech for simple vowels, retested three weeks after training ceased. There was maintained improvement for the specific words which had been used in training, but actual deterioration in speech from the pretraining level when reading prose.

The history of speech training for deaf children is littered with failed hunches. Continuing technological advance will suggest new approaches leaving the psychological problems unchanged. We do not know which of the various directions are likely to be more rewarding than skilful teaching supported by no more than hearing aids, technically improved, more easily maintained, more continuously worn. But saying that implies that the most useful prosthesis is still likely to depend on auditory feedback of speech. Technologies reach limits, and it is possible that in terms of usable amplification and correction of distortion the modern hearing aid is close to it. If that is so, other developments here will not improve speech beyond auditory limits, but more children may reach that limit. Prosthetic devices based on alternative feedback systems will probably need to incorporate a facility for continuous provision of the feedback, exemplified in one form by the Upton spectacles to which we referred in Chapter 7. But that would merely be a beginning. Extensive research will be required to determine optimum display characteristics, trading off aspects of visual perception against utility of those articulations which can be so aided. The critical problems will remain psychological.

The role of the physical quality of vocal speech is decisive if insistence on oral education is maintained. Faced with the conspicuous evidence of varying degrees of unintelligibility by school-leaving age, it is comforting to be deluded into a belief that nevertheless these children have good language. Orally, they do not. Whenever verbal linguistic ability can be assessed, it is shown to be grossly impoverished. It is futile to ignore the close association that there must be between linguistic ability and its internal representation, and this requires a medium no less than does its vocal expression. Children with unintelligible vocal speech in general have unusable internal speech which cannot – and evidently does not – support fluent and rich linguistic forms. We have also seen the indisputable dependence of speech quality on degree of deafness. We are confronted here with an inflexible chain between deafness and oral language which continues to defy technological assault.

9

A Language for Thought: II

With the analysis of the ability of deaf children to communicate in speech we can essay an overall assessment of the degree to which the goals of the underlying educational philosophy have been achieved. We should consider these young adults, about to leave the shelter of school for the rougher realities of an economic environment, in terms not of what they biologically are, but of what they can technically do. Are they equipped to operate in the linguistic environment of a society less protective and less tolerant perhaps than the benign classroom? In particular, we may now more profitably ask whether at the end of their formal education they are in fact oral; do they have adequate ability to understand speech, and to be understood when they speak; do they understand written English? Above all, we are in a better position to make a statement about their modes of cognitive functioning. Here we may ask the key question: do they think orally? The answers, especially to the last question, will determine the way in which we, as scientists rather than as educators, view the mind of the profoundly-deaf child. Is it without language? Is it without verbal language? Many studies have assumed that the answer, at least to the latter question, is affirmative; that the poor quality of speech and the evident low level of literacy are such that these children represent a population ideally suited to serve as a control in the study of intellectual processes; a population alleged to function fundamentally differently from normally-hearing people.

Descartes considered that a man without language was no better than a beast. No natural law prescribes the medium in which the language is contained. Though all hearing people have oral language as their mother-tongue, the first tongue they are ever aware of, and the one in which their first linguistic communications are made, for most this comes to be inadequate as an exclusive medium. Not only may we deviate from the oral form of verbal language in intellectual operations, switching into a print mode when it is tactically more appropriate, but the nonverbal languages of mathematics and sensory imagery are also available. Sokolov (1972) discusses this in some detail, pointing out the considerable variety of the modes in which intellectual operations are carried out, particularly for the more specialized problems of mathematics and physics. Oral thinking is primary, but not exclusive. What is certain is that we cannot conceive of language which cannot be internalized. For most of us this is our first environmental language and it is oral. It is the language which we acquire without being taught; the one we hear and later speak – and later still internalize. This is the language which oral education seeks to provide to children whose hearing is impaired or even grossly defective.

Deaf children as experimental subjects

In trying to assess the degree to which deaf children think orally, we do not delude ourselves into imagining that an analysis of the use of phonetic coding in memorizing a familiar set of words represents a comprehensive statement of the matter. It clearly does not. It is no more than a detectable response to a particular – and defined – cognitive problem, for which we have the base of a hearing norm. But it is a good predictor of performance of more complex intellectual operations such as reading and the solution of the abstract problems of Raven's Matrices. For this there is ample independent evidence using quite different methods such as speech electromyography that internal speech is heavily involved.

The procedure we have used we recognize as a compromise. It provides information which is consistent and in accord with that from other methods. It seems inherently unlikely that a deaf child who is able to think like hearing children will choose an alternative and in general less effective mode. It seems just as unlikely that the proportion of deaf children using internal speech in short-term memorizing will be exceeded when the operations of thinking are more complex, and (of course) where hearing children would think orally. We are not concerned with the question of when oral thinking is used, but only whether deaf children can think orally in a situation where a hearing child would. That specifically is a principal objective of the philosophy of oral education. If it is not reached, no superstructure of external oral communication could survive. Even in the limited terms in which we can phrase the issue, it is valid and important to consider the extent of the use of internal speech by deaf children, knowing that the values we find will be closer to the maximum than to the minimum figure.

The quantitative details are set out in Chapter 4. Here we need only summarize and emphasize. Up to a hearing loss of 85 dB a relatively favourable outcome can be seen. More than three-quarters of such children in Schools for the Deaf are using internal speech – and there is a similar figure for children in PHUs. Those who do not tend to be children of lower intelligence. True, the comparable value for hearing children is 95%, but it would be absurd to expect equivalence. Furthermore, looked at in more detail, the usefulness of the internal speech of those who use it is very similar to that of hearing children. If we look at the degree of phonetic coding represented by the median value of the Internal Speech-Ratio, it is about 75 both for hearing and partially-hearing children. But here the warning we expressed earlier is relevant. This high level of internal speech seems to be confined to the simple memorizing task. It is not reflected in reading ability, where even this relatively orally successful group of children is some four years behind the hearing norm. Finally we cannot ignore the absolute size of this favoured group; it is no more than one-third of the Special School population and little more than a half of all children receiving special education.

When a hearing loss of about 85 dB is reached, a striking difference emerges. Here some 60% of children seem not to use internal speech, and we have to suppose that the value would be greater when tasks are orally more demanding. We say this with some confidence because, whereas the partially-hearing children using internal speech do so on average to the same degree as their hearing peers, this is not the case for these deafer children. Here the median value of the IS-Ratio, considering only those who do use internal speech, is now 65. We have no means of translating the IS-Ratio scale into effective performance and cannot easily judge what a difference between 75 and 65 would mean for oral thinking. But reference to Figure 6.5 shows that for reading it could be considerable. In brief, once a hearing loss of 85 dB is reached, no more than 40% of children can be said to be orally thinking even at the relatively simple task of short-term memorizing.

Ewing (1960) and others have stressed the crucial importance of oral thinking for deaf children – as it is important for others. Nor can oral language be accommodatingly regarded as an independent activity which might reflect some level of oral competence without resort to concepts of oral thinking. Sokolov (1972) has expressed this succinctly: "Whenever we delay communicating our thoughts ..., we first fix them in our mind with the aid of inner speech, formulating a mental plan or a synopsis of some sort for our future statement" (p. 65).

If it is desirable that deaf children should be able to communicate orally, then oral thought is a prerequisite. Until we have a theoretical model which might provide a basis for expectation, our evidence is neither encouraging nor discouraging. Looked at pragmatically it is not easy to be encouraged. The majority of children with severe to profound hearing losses have either no internal speech or only enough for the simplest mechanical cognitive operations.

We return here to our earlier paradox. The main stream of educators of deaf children have insisted on their success at inculcating oral thinking. We shall discuss this in some detail in the final chapter. Many psychologists on the other hand have argued that the absence of oral thinking makes congenital deafness an appropriate control in studies concerned with language in cognitive behaviour (see Chapter 1). We now have some guide to the balance of truth within the paradox. The fact is that any unselected population of deaf children is likely to contain some who do use internal oral language in a formal test and some who do not. Nor is there a simple tag which, as it were, visibly adheres to experimental subjects as they come through the laboratory door. Degree of deafness is certainly one criterion, but in itself a most unreliable one. Even at the profoundest levels of deafness – greater for instance than 105 dB – some 25% of children in our sample used phonetic coding to remember words, giving them an advantage over very much less deaf children who did not. Many investigators, as we saw, relied specifically and solely on an audiological criterion; in some cases using a cut-off which might virtually guarantee that half of their allegedly internally "dumb" subjects were approaching the oral (internal) level of their experimental hearing subjects. Other investigators have simply accepted the designation of "profound" or even "severe" deafness as sufficient evidence, but, we now see, with no greater validity.

Quality of vocal speech provides a much more reliable indication of internal speech. Though taken alone it is also an uncertain guide. We have reported here on children whose speech was rated unintelligible by their teachers but who evidently and profitably used speech internally.

Clearly when either quality of speech or degree of deafness determines the criterion, investigators are underrating the value of articulatory mechanisms for supporting phonetic processes; again, interestingly, in direct contradistinction to the practices of conventional as well as the more novel forms of speech training. It is indeed the case that quality of vocal speech is a good predictor of internal speech; but it is the speaker who makes the judgement of relevance, not the listener.

It is not surprising that many of the studies we referred to in Chapter 5 which used deaf children as controls for the use of oral language yielded results often inconsistent and unexpected. Most deaf children live in oral homes; most deaf children are taught by oral teachers using traditional oral methods. In Western societies today it could well prove to be difficult to find a deaf child, otherwise normal, who was totally nonoral. There does not appear to be an intrinsic characteristic associated with deafness which permits a statement that a particular child, in no situation, can think orally. When deaf children are to be used as controls, some external criterion is essential, and it needs to be one which has relevance to the specific behaviour under study.

We do not find that the presence nor the degree of internal speech stands in a constant relationship to performance when compared with that of hearing children. When deaf and hearing children are matched with respect to degree of internal speech, their ability to remember familiar words is very similar. When the same children are compared on reading, there is a highly significant difference. This does not necessarily imply that deaf children may not be suitable controls. The contrary is the case. The example of reading permits an insight into the cognitive operations in reading just because there is evidence for a process adequate in one task (STM) but not in another (comprehension) where close relationship is a reasonable assumption. Particularly, when the behavioural requirements of a task can easily be defined, but the underlying cognitive requirements are hypothetical, care is needed. The benefit then of well-specified deaf subjects as controls was exemplified in Chapter 5. We were able to show how the interacting factors of type of material and coding medium influence memory span.

A model of oral language performance

We see then that oral education of deaf children may sometimes be accompanied by the development of oral thinking in the form of internal speech. But by school-leaving age success is not conspicuous. We cannot even be sure that those partially-hearing children who do usefully internalize oral language do so because of specific pedagogic intervention. Hearing children do not need to be taught to think in words. There is no obvious reason why the presence of some small degree of hearing impairment should be incompatible with the natural development of the process. When hearing loss is not great, the term "oral education" may be no more than a misnomer for a set of procedures which merely do not obstruct developments which will occur unaided – an argument we shall return to.

What is more to the point is the failure of the philosophy to provide much usable internal speech for the majority of children with a hearing loss greater than 85 dB. When fewer than half of the children for whom the intervention is intended seem to profit, and when no alternative is substituted, success is hard to justify. To regard the partially-hearing child who clearly thinks orally as an oral success carries an implication that there exists an alternative pedagogy which would deprive the child of the use of that residual hearing. There is of course no such pedagogy.

At the very heart of the oral philosophy is a denial of the true significance of deafness itself. It is commonly said that audiological deafness is not important; that early diagnosis, early use of hearing aids, parental understanding, abstention from nonoral communication modes, and so on will not repair, but will overcome, the effects of physically damaged organs. If deafness can be overcome or ignored, then indeed there would be no handicap.

The evidence we have presented, and which is confirmed by other studies we have cited, is totally at variance with this proposition. Without doubt, there is a crucial relationship between degree of deafness and quality of speech – and much follows from that.

The various analyses we have presented show the extremely close dependence of intelligibility of speech upon hearing loss. This is true whether speech is rated by teachers or assessed by objective test. This evidence can be seen in Chapter 8, and need not be repeated. The effect can easily be summarized.

No fewer than 92% of the children whose speech is rated as wholly intelligible (Rating 1) have a hearing loss of 85 dB or less; beyond that level of deafness we find only a handful of children with really good speech. At the other end of the scale, more than three-quarters of children whose speech is rated as unintelligible (Rating 5) have hearing losses greater than 95 dB. Figure 8.1 shows that at that level of hearing loss there is not a single child whose speech is wholly intelligible. The picture that emerges from objective testing is similar. If we consider the children who form the top 10% in terms of quality of speech, 9 out of 10 of them have a hearing loss less than 86 dB. At the other end again, practically all children (97%) forming the 10% worst speakers have a loss greater than 95 dB. This association is so close that we cannot evade the conclusion that, no matter what behaviour is not affected by deafness, the intelligibility of a child's speech most certainly is. Because of the substantial confirmation from other sources, it would seem not only that the hearing loss-speech quality relationship is indisputable, but that the levels of intelligibility achieved by current forms of intervention cannot support an educational theory which depends so heavily upon the attainment of good speech. In many ways, what follows from this has even more serious implications.

Central to oral education is the belief that it is conducive to the development of oral thinking – the predominant mode for hearing people. The extent to which oral education fails here is a valid and critical criterion for evaluating the entire philosophy. Even were it possible, the position would not be helped by pointing to children without internal speech but with good reading skill, for this could have been achieved using nonoral cognitive processes. It is much more crucial for the *theory* of oralism that children should leave school thinking orally, but with poor reading, than with good reading based on nonspeech mediation. Cognitively, that is acceptable, but not as a consequence of oral principles.

Again the facts are harsh. In the simple task of word memorizing, almost all hearing children use internal speech. But beyond a hearing loss of 85 dB fewer than half of the orally educated deaf children do. We have sought the locus of this failure in the close association that we find between internal speech and quality of vocal speech, arguing the presumptive case that the former is determined by – or follows from – the latter. The degree of association is inescapable. Almost all children rated as having wholly intelligible speech also have internal speech and their Internal Speech-Ratio is as high as that of hearing children. For children with speech rated as unintelligible, not only do no more than 25% develop internal speech, but, when they do, its quality is poor (Figure 8.8). Using the scores from the speech intelligibility test we again showed a close association between speech quality and the extent to which internal speech is used. Of the utmost importance, this relationship does not depend on the fact that degree of deafness determines quality of speech. For a given level of speech quality the correlation between deafness and internal speech is insignificant (p. 229).

We see then clearly developing the following model, which is illustrated in Figure 9.1. Degree of hearing loss directly determines the quality of a child's vocal speech. That the extent of this involvement is great is now obvious. Of other factors present – and we suspect a multiplicity of minor factors – intelligence we know is not very important.

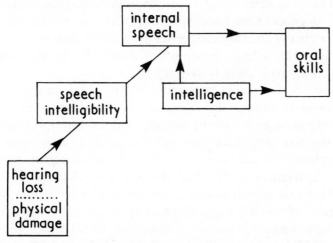

Figure 9.1. An oral model of communication skill for deaf children.

The model of oral competence then proceeds from vocal speech to internal speech. But there is also an established association between internal speech and intelligence. Here the direction of the association is more obscure – and indeed it may to some extent be reciprocal. Evans (1966) has suggested that impaired language due to deafness may impede the development of abstract reasoning; Zangwill (1975) has made a similar suggestion with respect to hearing aphasics. We have though proposed that a high level of intelligence may to some extent augment the contribution made by speech of relatively poor intelligibility. It is not difficult to see that bright children might be able to detect useful phonetic features of their internalized speech which remain subthreshold for others. It also seems fairly certain that this intelligence-internal speech association is a direct one, independent of both hearing loss and speech intelligibility. Unfortunately, at this time we do not have scores on Raven's Matrices and IS-Ratio for the same hearing children. We cannot therefore test the tantalizing possibility that variations in the IS-Ratio of hearing children with normal speech might be correlated with intelligence. Hermelin and O'Connor (1975a) have, though, shown that hearing subnormal children seem not to use phonetic coding when hearing children of normal intelligence do. Although we accept that there may be some reciprocal interdependence between intelligence and the development of internal speech, at least when vocal speech is imperfect, the model shown in Figure 9.1 emphasizes the hypothesis that internal speech is more determined by intelligence. Since the former is so heavily dependent on vocal speech quality, we would otherwise expect a greater speech-intelligence association than we, or others, find. By the same logic, hearing loss would also be represented in intelligence; again there is no evidence of this.

Figure 9.1 also shows how other empirical relationships which are present in our results conform. The analysis of the factors which are associated with lip reading was discussed in Chapter 7. Since the test permitted the use of residual hearing, degree of hearing loss is of course a major contributor to performance. So too, in agreement with other studies, is intelligence. Independently internal speech is also involved here. As we pointed out, Myklebust (1964) has suggested that lip reading provides the linguistic input necessary for the development of internal speech, and Dodd (1977) has independently argued a similar case. Were this so, there would be a direct route from degree of hearing loss, through lip reading to internal speech, which bypassed the contribution from vocal speech. But we have seen that this route is untenable since, except through speech intelligibility, hearing loss is not associated with internal speech. We propose therefore that the principal contributions to lip reading within the confines of this model are hearing loss, intelligence, and internal speech. This implies in principle that children will not become good lip readers unless they already have adequate internal speech.

The case of reading is somewhat different. Unlike lip reading, the effect of hearing loss is attenuated because it is involved only through a number of other processes. We saw in Chapter 6 that, when internal speech and intelligence were controlled, hearing loss itself plays only a minor role in reading skill. The reason why we have found so few profoundly-deaf good readers is because in an oral model of communication skill, vocal and internal speech are so important. Only when high intelligence – significant for reading as for much else – is present can the handicap imposed by poor quality internal speech be partially compensated. Reading in particular is a skill for which absence of hearing could be irrelevant to a degree impossible for lip reading. This is vividly seen in the case of suddenly deafened adults. Their reading is unimpaired, but comprehension of speech is totally disrupted. Initial acquisition of the respective skills need not implicate processes which sustain developed performance; the parallel between the congenitally and the adventitiously deafened person is therefore limited. The basic point is that when initial teaching of reading is forced into a nonoral mode there is no good evidence of inevitable failure. In fact, the evidence from nonorthographic languages is to the contrary (Rozin and Gleitman, 1977); Chinese children learn to read. The children we are considering have been taught as if they did have an internal oral facility.

Because, by definition reflecting the theoretical assumptions, oral education allocates to speech a commanding role, the model shown in Figure 9.1 suggests why it has resulted in levels of oral performance which have isolated deaf people from their social environment in a manner exactly contrary to the pedagogic aspiration. Oral education, far from being a positive intervention with recognizable gains, may be no more than a passive barrier between the needs of deaf children and alternative intervention. The insistence on speech as the appropriate means of communication in effect demeans the fact of deafness. During the era of dominance of oral education there has been no technical way of evading the devastating effects of the sensory deficit with which the child is endowed. A hearing aid removes a proportion of children from these effects. These are the children who then may not require Special education. Our concern is with those who do – a concern shared by oral educators.

Disregarding deafness does not remove it. But its relevance to communication may be modified. In deaf homes, communication flourishes without great recourse to speech; deafness has relevance for communication only when it is allowed to preempt the route to thought. When thinking is not oral this need not happen. Adequate speech is imperative for oral thinking, and deafness precludes this beyond doubt for most children whose loss exceeds about 85 dB, and for a disturbing proportion of less-deaf but also less-intelligent children. Any alternative language mode which is independent of auditory function merits discussion and investigation. The crux of our criticism of oralism is twofold. It does little for partially-hearing children that would not in any case occur given the privileged educational facilities, such as very small classes, which it enjoys. But more important, for the majority of children requiring Special education, not only does it provide only minimal oral skill, but there is a risk that the obstruction of alternative procedures may have adverse consequences of a far-reaching nature.

Neurological development without speech input

In evaluating the cognitive and communicative performance of deaf children, there is no evading the basic handicap of deafness. Regardless of the criteria we adopt to assess performance, and regardless of whether or not the average deaf child reaches the theoretical limit imposed by his handicap, the low level attained is a continuing challenge both scientifically and socially. But, in advancing the qualifications of theoretical considerations, we must also recognize two levels, one based on the immutable presence of the sensory deficit, the other on the more tractable nature of the rehabilitative philsophy which aims to exploit what is not impaired – including, of course, what remains of hearing. While it is right to identify the problem, it is equally right to examine the consequences of the remedy. If performance is poor, must it be so because no theoretical formulation could further improve it? Or is it poor partly, or even principally, as the outcome of the particular treatment?

The model of performance which has emerged from the data demonstrates the crushing burden of the biological characteristics which accompany deaf children throughout their school life – and which no known forms of intervention can significantly modify beyond what appear to be the relatively minor effects of hearing aids. Conventional oral education has confronted this biology with the weapon of speech to express thought and to receive it in its visual correlate as lip reading. We have seen that the oral philosophy is indeed coherent in that the quality of speech that a child can deploy does contribute in a major way to linguistic ability and communication skill. Not surprisingly, just as with hearing children, its impact lies in its ready availability for symbolic function that we have called internal speech. The chain of events that we postulate to be causal pivots on speech. On one side are the biological irreversibles (defective auditory pathways, other physical damage, the constants in intelligence), on the other side the behavioural outcomes. If the former so constrain the operation of the pivot, there seems little prospect of improvement in performance that is so patently necessary. We now need to consider the possibility that the designation of speech as the gateway to other language skills and effortless communication with hearing people may be theoretically incorrect for the early stages of formal education – to a degree where it may be irretrievably damaging.

We should emphasize that in this context we are referring to the physical characteristics of speech – its intelligibility – and not to the nature of the language which may be expressed in speech or other medium. We are at a relatively simple level where the quality of the speech sounds heard are reflected back into the quality of the speech sounds uttered – and which then reflects the quality and cognitive usefulness of the speech when it is internalized. We are observing remarkably simple and clear relationships which seem only minimally to be influenced by others factors. We have doubted whether speech can support this key role for deaf children. Here we go on to consider whether, if it cannot, biological consequences are trivial or profound. We will not clarify these matters without understanding the way speech normally develops, both structurally and functionally, and what deviations may be inevitable in the absence of hearing.

Biology and environment

Lenneberg (1972) has described with elegant simplicity the way in which biological endowment and environmental influences nourish each other even at the most basic stages of development. "The physical development of the brain, its structure and its function, follows its own inherent program, provided that it is supplied with appropriate building blocks: proteins" (p. 34). In all growth and development we see this essential and continuous interaction. It underlies not only the shape and size of the body and its organs but, "cognition also grows by its own, inherent program, but in addition to being dependent upon physical brain growth, it requires its own building blocks: sensory input" (p. 35). All developing function requires an innate programme interacting with specific environmental conditions, and speech is no exception.

The hearing child is born with a well-developed – though not complete – neurological structure specified for hearing and subsequently speaking. It is born into an environment of sound, including speech sound. The auditory processes, from those of the peripheral ear to the neuronal networks of the auditory cortex, endlessly transmit and process sensory information which continues to shape the underlying structures and further specifies the characteristics of the relevant environment. This orderly progression of interacting events will lead through cooing and babbling to the first speechlike sounds and the utterance of the first identifiable meaningful words at about the age of eighteen months. Long before then, Menyuk (1975) notes that even at the age of two or three months infants appear to be listening and responding particularly to the speech of the person closest to them; the environment is not only present but used selectively.

As time passes, it is not only the observable verbal behaviour of the child which is changing. The brain itself continues to respond to the incoming sensory information and continues, physically, to organize its structures and processes. Even in the newly born infant, the left planum temporale, which is part of the posterior speech zone of the brain, is larger than the right (Wada, 1969; Witelson and Pallie, 1973). Later it can be readily demonstrated that the dominance of the left hemisphere for processing speech is more or less established fact.

A variety of techniques have been used since the pioneer work of Kimura (1963). Kimura herself used taperecordings of groups of spoken digits played simultaneously into both ears of normal children aged four–nine years, "... to gain indirectly some information about the age at which speech becomes lateralized in the brain" (p. 899). Lateralization was determined by noting that digits which have been heard in the right ear (i.e., processed in the left hemisphere of the brain) were better recalled. Other researchers have used consonant-vowel syllables (Berlin, Hughes, Low–Bell, and Berlin, 1973; Dorman and Geffner, 1974) or words to which children responded by pointing to pictures (Ingram, 1975). There is now substantial agreement that cerebral dominance for verbal language is established by about the age of four years and continues to develop for some years towards puberty. It is interesting that Geffner and Hochberg (1971), who reported results which confirm this general picture for middle-class (New York) children, found that in children of lower socioeconomic groups – though of the same school grade – establishment of cerebral dominance was delayed until age seven years. This differentiation may have particular significance for us. There are still few accounts of cerebral dominance considered in relation to intellectual development – a relationship we would expect to follow from Lenneberg's model. But one study by Bakker (1973) not only shows a general relationship between cerebral dominance and reading ability in hearing children, but suggests that different stages of reading development require different degrees of dominance: "Early reading seems to require no dominance: fluent reading necessitates maximum dominance" (p. 25). This was confirmed by Sadick and Ginsburg (1978), who studied children aged five–eight years. They postulated that earliest reading is predominantly spatial in character, while at a later stage more verbal elements associated with left-hemisphere dominance take precedence.

Though the physiology of speech and language is still poorly understood, it becomes clear that the period from birth, and possibly even earlier (Bench, Collyer, and Mentz, 1976) up to the age of about four or five years is an extremely busy one with respect to neurological development of the structures as well as the processes involved in the development of speech and verbal language. At the beginning of this period we have an infant barely responsive to speech, but who hears. The brain shows considerable functional plasticity persisting during this prelingual stage. Lenneberg (1967) summarizes a number of cases of such children who had suffered from massive lesions in either hemisphere. Regardless of which hemisphere was involved, the development of speech followed a similar course. But in a series of cases of children who suffered brain damage after speech had developed but before the age of ten years, almost all of the children with left-hemisphere damage failed to regain normal speech. When the damage was in the right hemisphere, half subsequently spoke normally. Thus we see, during these early years, an immensely influential interaction via the auditory mechanisms of verbal environment and neurological structure. By the time the child is at the age of three–five years, he has fluent speech and advanced linguistic knowledge. He also has a supporting· neurological substrate which, though not yet at the end of its formation (though Krashen (1973) has suggested that the limit is in fact reached by five years), does not readily reorganize itself when damaged. One other behavioural feature becomes observable about this time; the child begins to internalize speech, a process which continues to develop in parallel with the consolidation of cerebral dominance at least until about eleven years (Conrad, 1971a).

Biology and impoverished auditory environment

The child born deaf presents a striking contrast, some aspects of which we outlined in Chapter 1. The essential element in the contrast is stark. Except in rare cases of gross malformation there is no evidence that the neurological structures specialized for the development of speech and language are not identical to those of hearing children. But, in varying degree, these are structures without link to the environmental sources of their essential nutriment; the genetic potential for speech is present, the sensory input is not.

It is not surprising that there is constant emphasis of the need for early diagnosis where deafness is suspected. Yet we saw earlier that in the USA fewer than half of the children born deaf were so diagnosed before the age of three years. There is little reason to assume that worldwide this is a below-average figure. It is not difficult to see why diagnosis is so often delayed. Apart from social factors referred to earlier, the proportion of deaf children who are born to deaf parents, that is, parents most alert to the presence of deafness in their babies, is tiny. Most genetic deafness is recessive and it is evident that there is little awareness of risk in those families carrying a recessive gene for deafness – particularly with respect to the first child. Where deafness has a prenatal or perinatal cause, in most cases deafness is merely one of the possible sequalae and not necessarily the most common. Though the milestones of verbal and linguistic development are orderly in their sequence, the rate at which any particular child progresses has wide variation. It is easy then to see that, without routine and still unreliable audiological screening of babies, literally years of delay in diagnosis is inevitable, and even routine screening on a national scale involves very considerable technological and administrative problems. The deafer the child in fact is, the easier it will be to detect and the sooner will a hearing aid be provided. Unfortunately, the deafer child is less likely to benefit from an aid than one less deaf – and correspondingly more difficult to detect.

At the present time we have to recognize that the majority of children deaf at birth or shortly after will pass the first critical years of their lives in relative verbal silence. There is no way, at least until their deafness is identified and possibly not even then, that the expectant neurological structures can draw in the auditory stimulation so essential for further development. We have to consider whether, without this necessary input, growth will cease or be gravely retarded. At present we do not know with certainty whether the effect of early auditory deprivation continues indefinitely to restrict the growth of verbal function. Furthermore, there is no reliable consoling support for the notion that compensatory mechanisms using other and intact sensory pathways will develop beyond the range found in children without deprivation. Nor do we know with any certainty in this case the nature of the parameters which govern the structure-environment interaction. It is possible that structural and functional growth continues normally until a threshold deficit of sensory input is reached, at which point growth is totally inhibited. The alternative is for a close correlation between organic and functional development on one hand and sensory deficit on the other. Such evidence as we have supports the latter. As we have noted, even very small degrees of hearing loss reflect in observable impairment of speech.

In the next chapter we shall show that substantial linguistic retardation also occurs with only quite slight hearing loss. Here our concern is to consider the possibility that it predeterminedly must. Our current state of knowledge presents a picture of rapid interactive development of sensory input with functional and structural organization. Though both the underlying neurology and the nature of the relevant input are even less clear, we may be reasonably certain that, parallel to the developments which surround the speech function, those necessary for the emergence of language will also be present. Just as children are not taught speech, neither are they taught the rules of language. "There is," Lenneberg (1972) notes, "no evidence that we can make a child use the productive rules of language unless he has abstracted the rules himself and applies them of his own accord" (p. 38). But this process of abstracting linguistic rules from his language environment will no less depend on the ordered development of the relevant neurological organization than will the acquisition of speech.

The child born deaf proceeds through infancy and into childhood deprived in varying degree of the benefits of one crucial sensory channel, and in most cases deprived thereby of a language environment. In the absence of an appropriate external intervention what changes in neurological function might we expect to ensue? There appears to be no reported case of postmortem histological examination of a profoundly-deaf child. But the few animal studies that have some relevance support Lenneberg's general description. There is no way of exactly reproducing the analogue of human deafness in animals – that is, with verbal and linguistic isolation. But there is accumulating evidence that absence of sensory input, which experimentally can be achieved, leads to progressive organic degeneration which may extend far beyond the peripheral damage and towards cortical areas. The visual function lends itself readily to studies of this nature. Brindley (1970) describes several in which lesions in the retina of monkeys led to degeneration in neural pathways which critically crossed synapses. Just the same, Cowan (1970) discusses a number of studies of cats in which destruction of the cochlear with consequent cessation of afferent impulses has also led to transneuronal atrophy in structures some way from the periphery. A study by Batkin, Groth, Watson, and Ansperry (1970) showed that rats withheld from birth from environmental sounds had substantially lost their hearing after four months, implying at least some functional degeneration if not organic. Stein and Schuckman (1973) blocked the auditory meatus of neonate rats for a minimum of 32 days. Subsequent testing showed normal response from the visual cortex, but that from the auditory cortex was severely impaired, clearly indicating a degeneration of function as a result of sensory impairment. Furthermore, the effect was not present when adult rats were used. Kyle (1978), summarizing the results of a number of such studies, concludes that "... there is serious cause for concern that auditory deprivation can be damaging to cortical processes later required in auditory-based behaviour" (p. 39). We are necessarily cautious in generalizing from animal to human behaviour, though it is probably justified at the sensory level. To ignore data from animal studies, or to dismiss them as irrelevant, would, in the context of deafness in children, be the height of irresponsibility. We have to accept from the available evidence – tenuous though it may appear – the risk that the absence of appropriate sensory input implied by congenital deafness can permanently disrupt neurological organization. The consequences for human behaviour are even less understood at present, but the threat of them cannot justifiably be ignored.

As we noted in Chapter 1, the rare, well-documented cases of children reared accidentally in environments, not of auditory, but of total, linguistic and social deprivation, have provided us with a further source of information concerning the integrative nature of the environment-organism relationship. A detailed study by Fromkin, Kreshen, Curtiss, Rigler, and Rigler (1974) of a thirteen-year-old girl who, from the age of about twenty months, had been tied isolated in a small room provides important insights. On admission to hospital the child (Genie) was mute – apart from showing many other physical disabilities. Genie learned to speak, but some years later was still severely mentally retarded. She was unable to cope with items of the Leiter International Performance Scale – a nonverbal test of cognitive function – beyond the seven-year level. At about fifteen years of age she performed on Raven's Matrices at a level below that average for normal nine-year-olds. But her impairment of cognitive and linguistic function was shown to have a neurological involvement as well. Genie dramatically showed disturbance of cerebral lateralization for verbal items. Unusually, although she was right-handed, Genie processed spoken words in the right cerebral hemisphere. The authors point out that, "this would be tantamount to a kind of functional atrophy of the usual language centers, brought about by disuse or suppression" (p. 101).

Let us restate the crux of the problem in the context of deafness. Several years may, and usually do, elapse before a child born deaf is formally involved in a programme of intervention aimed at ameliorating the effects of the handicap. In Britain, and in many other countries as well, the intervention has taken the form of oral education. That is to say, the development of cognitive function has been encouraged by emphasizing the use of speech and its lip read form to link the child to its linguistic environment. Generally these programmes have either ignored or discouraged other non-phonetic media. Since most deaf children are born into hearing homes, this type of treatment is an extension of the child's prevailing environment. But the treatment now becomes more formal and directed like all education, and also more intensive as use is made of techniques for amplifying speech and for teaching articulatory patterns. At the same time, a more structured linguistic environment is made available; infant classrooms prolifically display printed names of objects and activities, and teachers specifically draw attention to correct grammatical usage of words.

The question we now need to consider is whether this is a biologically appropriate treatment. If it is not, it certainly cannot succeed in its educational and social aim. But what is more important is whether it leaves the child biologically stationary or even actively encourages further structural and functional degeneration. This could occur both because of the vast reduction of sensory and linguistic input compatible with the requirements of normal neurological function, but also because stimulation which would be compatible with alternative neurological organizations is withheld. We know that particular neurological structures are uniquely specified for the development of particular functions in the presence of relevant stimulation. Since a child who is hearing-impaired during the critical early years may have no better than a grossly defective channel for transmitting that information, in the light of the evidence presented in previous pages we are led to postulate a disturbance of function which may well be irretrievable. Clearly, until deafness has been diagnosed, no intervention will be made. Our concern is to discuss what, at that point, the intervention should be.

Deafness and cerebral dominance

We have remarked on the absence of direct histological evidence of auditory deprivation – at the cortical level. At a functional level the problem is more tractable. Specifically, Myklebust (1966) proposed that, " . . . lack of audition interferes with the neural processes responsible for the development of cerebral dominance" (p. 145). Here evidence is more plentiful. Clearly we are not going to expect all deaf people to show gross right-hemisphere dominance for verbal material regardless of degree of hearing loss. What we do expect though is a pattern of dominance different in general from hearing subjects.

The methods for determining hemispheric dominance, which we mentioned briefly for hearing people and which involves listening, obviously cannot be used when subjects are deaf. Studies which have so far been reported all use the "split-half visual field" technique. In this, a subject visually fixates a central point while test items are exposed for a few milliseconds either in the left or the right half-field, or simultaneously in both half-fields. Familiar words or letters or pictures of manual signs have been used as test material. The subject is required to report what he has seen. Since the duration of exposure is too short for eye movement to be of value, the visual information upon which identification depends is transmitted only to the specified hemisphere. However, identification of linguistic material will not just involve the visual areas of the brain; information must also be referred to areas concerned with processing language. Cerebral dominance is assessed by reference to whether more correct items were exposed to the left or right half-field, and this is compared with results from hearing subjects at the same task.

McKeever, Hoemann, Florian, and VanDeventer (1976) tested 18 congenitally deaf undergraduates and found very little cerebral asymmetry for printed words. Their 18 hearing control subjects on the other hand showed the expected dominance of the left hemisphere for this material. The authors conclude that, " . . . the deprivation of auditory experience results in markedly reduced asymmetries of cerebral information processing capacities" (p. 419). Manning, Goble, Markman, and LaBreche (1977) also exposed pairs of words, one to the left half visual-field and simultaneously one to the right to congenitally deaf students. A similar result is reported; much weaker left-hemisphere dominance for words than in hearing subjects. Phippard (1977), using lower case letters of the alphabet, introduced another variable. While 28 deaf students aged eleven–nineteen years were drawn from a school which used both oral and manual methods of instruction (Total Communication), another 10 deaf students were used, of about the same age, but drawn from a school which was exclusively oral. Hearing subjects as usual showed left-hemisphere dominance for letters. The students in the Total Communication programme showed no asymmetry, largely in agreement with McKeever et al. and with Manning et al. The "oral" deaf students, however, showed significant right-hemisphere dominance. Phippard surprisingly attributes this result to the possibility that these "oral" subjects coded the perceived letters visually rather than phonetically. But there is no independent evidence for this. It may well be that exclusion of manual language further shifts the balance of dominance away from the hearing pattern.

Since we have shown that in some cases even very deaf children may develop the use of internal speech, we must interpret these results with care. While they are in general concordance, when results are presented as group averages, it is possible that finer detail is concealed. The linguistic ability of subjects is not reported on in any of these studies, and they may have included varying proportions of genuinely oral students. The difference between deaf and hearing is striking in all cases though. The particular point that we wish to stress is the support which these data provide for Lenneberg's model of input-structure interaction. Sparse though these studies are, they cannot encourage a hope that children who are seriously auditorily impaired can evade some disturbance to the development of neurological function. The general picture that emerges is that, while lateralized cerebral function for speech develops during the earliest years of life of hearing children, possible through a shift away from right-hemisphere involvement (Berlin et al., 1973), this may not occur in the case of children who are hearing-impaired.

The detail here is far from clear. Only a very small proportion of deaf children are raised in a sign-language environment. Their relevance in the present context stems from the fact that, while they are deprived auditorally, they need not be linguistically deprived to the same degree as equally deaf children dependent on spoken language input. The study of brain function in this population is important for the contribution it could make to the question of whether the dominance of the left hemisphere for language extends to the case of nonphonetic languages. In other words, whether the dominance reflects a speech function or a language function. None of the three studies we cited provides the necessary information about the subjects used, beyond indicating that they were born deaf. We do not know whether any had sign as a first language, nor, if so, from what age. This is of considerable theoretical importance. If, in fact, all language, regardless of the mode, is principally processed in the left hemisphere, the exclusive emphasis on speech is also likely to impair subsequent sign-language development. Furthermore, early emphasis on nonauditory language might enhance subsequent potential for the oral mode by virtue of the opportunity for more normal neurological development.

Evidence for the possibility that the left cerebral hemisphere is specialized for language regardless of the nature of the language medium would, by its nature, be hard to establish. Nevertheless, the few rare reported cases of left-hemisphere stroke in deaf patients tend to support rather than reject this possibility. No more than a handful of such cases are known to us (e.g., Critchley, 1938; Douglass and Richardson, 1959; Kimura, Battison, and Lubert, 1976; Sarno, Swisher, and Sarno, 1969; Tureen, Smolik, and Tritt, 1951). In all of these cases sign language was disturbed, suggesting a common locus for all language processing. Even if, as Hardyck, Tzeng, and Wang (1978) have suggested, the precise role of cerebral dominance with respect to language processing is shown to be less clear than has been supposed, the intimate relationship between sensory and linguistic input on one hand, and cortical organization on the other, seems assured.

We may be faced then with an increasing divergence of function which depends on irreversible structural changes, and contingent upon auditory deprivation. The extent of the disturbance is bound to be related to degree of hearing loss and we have little insight into the quantitative nature of this relationship. No published study to date has related dominance findings to degree of deafness in useful detail, nor to any other personal characteristics or individual cognitive ability in the case of deaf subjects. Insofar as neural organization becomes less and less adapted for efficient processing of oral language, an environment which excludes linguistic modes which do not depend on hearing may continue to impoverish cerebral language functions. In the absence of a biologically relevant input we should not ignore the possibility that the "functional atrophy" discussed by Fromkin et al. (1974) may come to involve structural atrophy as well.

Effects of onset age of deafness

The pattern is elaborated by what is known about the effects of adventitious deafness. Conventionally a child deafened before the age of three years is regarded as "prelingually deaf" and it is generally accepted that the postlingually deaf child has a much greater command of oral language and better academic performance. Clearly a person who becomes deaf in later life, when language is thoroughly established, does not lose that knowledge with the onset of deafness. Equally clearly we would expect a gradient relating linguistic performance and onset age of deafness. Common experience, rather than detailed research, has suggested that an age of three years represents a distinctive point.

Research is hindered by the relative scarceness of adventitiously deaf children still at Schools for the Deaf. Just the same, a report by Jensema (1975), using the large population of the Gallaudet Survey, completely confirms the consensus view. Children whose deafness occurred after the age of three years had, on later test, much better reading comprehension and vocabulary. Our own data agree with this. In our sample of children from Schools and PHUs we have about 20% who were not congenitally deaf – a figure very similar to that reported by Jensema (1975) – comprising 62 children whose deafness occurred before the age of three years, and 44 children deafened later than that. When tested many years later, the children who heard up to, but not beyond, the age of three years performed a little worse than the congenitally deaf children. This would be explained by the presence of other handicaps and by the absence of the brighter genetically deaf children. They also performed a good deal worse than children deafened later.

What is important to us here is that the effects of normal exposure to auditory language for a period of three years appear to become totally erased. When we recall that by this time, according to Lenneberg (1966), some of them would have had a vocabulary approaching 1000 words, and many would show, "spontaneous construction of sentences with five words or more" (p. 226), the subsequent loss is dramatic. It seems that cessation of auditory input has an almost immediately damaging effect. The change occurring at this age is strikingly shown if we consider which children subsequently use internal speech. There is little point in including partially-hearing children in this analysis, and we report only on those with a hearing loss greater than 85 dB. Classifying them into three groups according to onset age of deafness: congenital, birth to three years, beyond three years, we find the following respective proportions using internal speech: 47%, 46%, 93%. The last value is approximately what we found for hearing children.

It is evident from these data that a normally-hearing child at the age of three years, although apparently showing marked linguistic competence, nevertheless holds this competence in fragile form. In particular, cerebral dominance is only just becoming detectable, and it will continue to consolidate for a number of years. As Lenneberg (1966, p. 248) puts it in a note: "... little cortical specialization with regard to language though left hemisphere beginning to become dominant." Children who become deaf after this stage of development, though they may show language deficits, will think like hearing children. But even three years of normal auditory input may be nullified if deafness is permitted to interrupt the organization of neurological function.

Implications for education

We may now begin to see that an insistence on an oral language environment for a child who has had minimal auditory experience from birth or shortly after is a hazardous and perhaps irreparable gamble. At the time when formal education begins to be the major linguistic intervention for most deaf children, neurological organization may have become poorly adapted to process the phonetic features of speech. Little of the speech signal may reach the cortex and to assume that articulatory correlates of speech will find a brain with the necessary neural development begins to seem unlikely in the face of the research evidence. We have already discussed the visual problems of deciphering lip-read information and, in the virtual total absence of usable input from this linguistic source during the first few years of life, it seems highly improbable that after four–five years of age a favourable neurology will be present. Beyond a level of deafness which we cannot specify with accuracy – but which measurable cognitive performance indicates is not great – the provision of inputs which cannot be processed are all too likely to hasten the atrophy of those functions which are desperately needed. Apart from functions dependent on auditory inputs, there is no evidence, apart from specific pathology, to suggest that the deaf infant will not develop neurologically normally, since all other sensory pathways are intact.

We have no reason to assume that speech has exclusive rights as a linguistic medium and there is much evidence from studies of reading nonphonetic languages that the brain can just as well handle language visually. Lenneberg (1972) has in fact proposed that graphic language is a suitable mother-tongue for profoundly-deaf children. While we are not convinced of the merit of English graphics as a first language, the case for utilizing sensory pathways and cortical functions which are in creative interaction does seem compelling.

Discussions with people born deaf certainly suggest that, in principle, print is a viable first language. But Frisina (1959), for example, notes that deaf children would be " . . . expected to use vision for perceptual and conceptual purposes many years prior to the age at which this type of functioning is demanded of the average hearing child" (p. 95). The evidence we cited in Chapter 6 illustrating the slow growth of vocabulary in the young deaf child supports this. In particular, as we pointed out, printed English words are seriously lacking in visual discriminability and the varied history of teaching reading by the whole-word method is not encouraging here. But the least attractive feature of a graphic first language would be the difficulty of achieving spontaneous communication — a feature we would have thought essential. Finally the expressive form of graphic language is barely within the child's motor competence much before the age of four years.

The more obvious alternative both to speech and print is manual sign language, and in the final chapter we shall discuss its relevance in a number of contexts, both theoretical and pedagogic. There is now a rapidly growing literature on various aspects of sign language, including social (Schlesinger and Meadow, 1968), linguistic (Bellugi and Klima, 1975; Brennan, 1975; Stokoe, 1960), cognitive (Bellugi et al., 1974; Siple, Fischer, and Bellugi, 1977), communicative (Stuckless, 1976), educational (Evans, 1978) configurative as analogous to phonemic (Lane, Boyes-Braem, and Bellugi, 1976) and so on. Essentially we see sign language as a means of bypassing the ineffective auditory system so as to provide those neurological structures which are specified for language processing with a compatible and adequate stimulus input.

Effects of early signing

We have discussed the problem of providing direct evidence of damage when a child is deprived of linguistic input during infancy and early childhood. An alternative approach would be to consider the case of children who because of deafness were excluded from spoken language, but who did have what we might regard as natural access to nonoral sign language.

Our prediction would have to be that their subsequent linguistic development would outstrip that of children growing up in a largely alinguistic environment. The ultimate comparison of course would need to be between two different languages – manual and oral. No such test has ever been made and the theoretical pitfalls involved are all too obvious.

There is, though, some benefit to be derived from this natural experiment. Children whose mother-tongue is sign later enter schools which have a predominantly oral culture. There, as a second language, they learn to speak and to read, let us say for convenience, English. Were the presence or absence of language in infancy irrelevant to later development, we would expect no difference between them and nonsigning deaf populations. In fact a test of this nature has a further advantage. It is axiomatic in oral education that early signing actively impedes subsequent oral skill. Insofar as such a test is possible, then a number of hypotheses can explicitly, or by implication, be tested. Deaf children whose first language is sign are generally those whose parents are also deaf. The effect on school performance of these children has become a research interest, not because of the neurological issues we have raised, but as a response to the pedagogic pressures. The outcome though will serve us as well.

Stuckless and Birch (1966a) record that 93% of deaf parents used sign language with their deaf child, while 11% of hearing parents did. The proportion of deaf children with deaf parents is small. In our entire sample, we found 27 cases – about 5% of the total. Rawlings (1971) reports a value from a very much larger sample of 2.5%. But since she also reports that information was not available for 37.7% of children, there is room for error. Though our enquiry may have missed a few cases, it is unlikely that parents were described as deaf who were not.

All parents are in communication with their children effectively from birth. Parents with normal speech will predominantly and increasingly use speech. If their children are sufficiently deaf little verbal information will pass at an age when hearing children would be developing rapidly in their understanding and use of speech. If the parents are deaf, not only will deaf children hear little, but what speech they do hear will be highly distorted. So, as Stuckless and Birch found, deaf parents usually use sign language at least in situations where hearing parents would use speech. We say at least, because, whereas hearing parents do not have an elaborate nonverbal language, deaf parents do and may be less restricted in the linguistic complexity of their early communications. There is some evidence that children of deaf parents do use sign language meaningfully sooner than hearing children use speech (Ahlgren, 1977; Brown, 1977; McIntire, 1977). Furthermore, by the time such a child enters school the (sign) language may be as fluent as the verbal language of a hearing five-year-old would be (Schlesinger and Meadow, 1972). But if deaf children have hearing parents, and particularly if their siblings are hearing as well, not only are they unlikely to have any knowledge of sign language, but their verbal language will be extremely impoverished. The specific issue then has been whether these markedly different early linguistic environments subsequently affect school achievement at oral skills.

The basic, and possibly insoluble, methodological problem has been to define an appropriate control group against which to compare the experimental group – the deaf children with deaf parents. The cause of deafness of the latter group is genetic. It is well established that the measured intelligence of children with hereditary deafness is higher than that of children whose deafness is either acquired or where the cause is not known. In Chapter 2 we showed significant differences in the Raven scores. Furthermore, it is equally well established that children whose deafness is not hereditary but acquired also have a greater incidence of additional handicaps, often with presumption of minor brain damage, but in any case, with an implication that the handicaps reflect directly in lower intelligence. We noted on p. 63 nearly twice as many additionally-handicapped children with acquired deafness than with hereditary deafness.

It would seem from this that the more appropriate control for deaf children with deaf parents would be deaf children with hearing parents, but where the cause of deafness is nevertheless hereditary. But there are difficulties here as well. When genetic deafness is present in a family but the parents are hearing, other siblings may be deaf. Even if the parents do not sign, the siblings may well sign amongst themselves – the language having been incidentally acquired at school. The effect of this depends on the hypothesis under test. If the hypothesis predicts an advantage of some kind for the children of deaf parents, signing siblings in the control group will reduce differences. If the hypothesis is confirmed, it is in a sense confirmed against the odds and its support is strengthened. If the hypothesis is not confirmed, there may still be a true, but concealed, difference. But if the hypothesis is for no difference, the test may be invalid. The ultimate test is probably between deaf children with deaf parents, and known genetically deaf children with hearing parents, but using only the first born without access to sign language. To date this control has not been used. Failing this, the prudent solution has, historically, been to match on all variables which might conceivably be relevant and to hope that then factors associated with cause of deafness will be nullified.

One of the earliest studies was that by Quigley and Frisina (1961). In fact the part of their study which is relevant to our present problem was incidental to their main enquiry which need not concern us. That related to performance of children in day and residential education. In the course of it they separated 16 children in day schools with deaf parents, whom they compared with 70 deaf children also in day schools but with hearing parents. The children with deaf parents had worse speech quality but, not surprisingly, better finger spelling which seems to have helped their vocabulary. But they were not significantly better on "educational achievement" which would include reading comprehension (though they had slightly higher scores), and there was no difference in lip reading.

Stuckless and Birch (1966a; 1966b) greatly refined the same procedure. An extensive enquiry yielded 38 children with deaf parents known to have used sign language with their children from the earliest age. These were compared with 38 deaf children with hearing parents who had only used speech. The pairs of children were carefully matched for age and sex. They were matched on IQ within 10 points, which is within the limits of test reliability; no children with additional handicaps according to school records were used; and the pairs were matched for the socioeconomic status of the family. Though educational disadvantages of lower socioeconomic status have become widely recognized, as we saw, once intelligence is taken into account this factor seems of little importance. But, using it, though again reducing the number of possible matches, adds face validity which in this polemic area of research seems wise. All children were prelingually deaf and all had hearing losses greater than 70 dB (probably ASA, i.e., about 80 dB ISO). Though the average hearing loss of the two groups was similar at about 105 dB (ISO), no closer match on this variable seems to have been made. Children were drawn from five different schools but were also matched on "educational attributes" of the schools. We cite these details to indicate the thoroughness of this study, and because it became a model for a number of later enquiries. Curiously, the cause of deafness of the children with hearing parents was not taken into account.

In discussing the results from this and other studies we shall confine comments to matters concerning communication skills where our own data may make a contribution. In the Stuckless and Birch study the principal outcome was a significant advantage for children with deaf parents, in reading and written language, both at the 0.01 level. In fact the Metropolitan reading test used showed the difference to be half of a grade – about six months of reading age. The Craig Lip-reading test also showed a small but significant (0.05) advantage for children with deaf parents. But there was no difference in speech intelligibility using phonetically balanced discrete words. With minor exceptions, other studies have reported similar results.

Meadow (1968) added further refinements to the matching procedure in a study which used 59 matched pairs. In addition to most of the variables used by Stuckless and Birch, she did ensure that the children of hearing parents did not have deaf siblings, virtually guaranteeing that no signing was used in the home. There is no indication that their deafness was genetic. But she also additionally excluded children deaf as a result of maternal rubella, Rh incompatibility, or anoxia – all specific conditions which might affect normal brain function. It is not clear what the basis was for matching degree of deafness, but the children with deaf parents were as a group rather deafer, and all children had a loss greater than 80 dB (probably ISO).

Again there was no difference in rated speech intelligibility, and in this study lip reading – also rated – showed no difference. Rated written language was better for children with deaf parents, and

Stanford Achievement Test reading score highly significantly favoured those children. Here, the advantage was more than two years of reading age. In this connection, there is a disquieting feature of the IQ matching which might be relevant. Originally 59 pairs were matched. Meadow reports that, using WISC, 45 pairs were matched within 10 IQ points. But in 12 cases the discrepancy extended up to 15 points, a further case to 17 points, and one case had a 20-point difference between the two children forming a pair. Overall, after matching, the children with deaf parents were slightly more intelligent, but by no more than three IQ points. Reading scores however were available only for 32 of the 59 pairs, and the average IQs for these is not reported. It is clearly logically possible that the children used for the reading comparison included all of those with the most discrepant IQs – though we also do not know which group might have benefited. We would like to make clear that this criticism probably reflects no more than a reporting defect – since the study has many excellent features. What in this case adds to the disquiet is that Meadow also used a test which rated "intellectual functioning" (Meadow, 1967). On this test, the children of deaf parents were rated significantly higher, implying at least the possibility of higher IQ.

Vernon and Koh (1970) grasped the problem of the appropriate match for medical history more firmly. Rather than exclude particular categories of acquired deafness as Meadow (1968) had done, they opted to match children with deaf parents to children with hearing parents but, " . . . whose family pedigrees clearly indicates genetic deafness . . ." (p. 527), and who did not know sign language. But no information is reported about the hearing status of any siblings of the control children. Using a single school, 32 pairs were then matched for IQ within five points, and age – which ranged from eleven-twenty years. Degree of hearing loss seems to have involved no closer matching than that all children had losses greater than 70 dB (ASA). No average or median hearing-loss data for the groups is reported. Once again, rated speech intelligibility and rated lip reading showed no differences between the two groups. Again in line with other studies, reading comprehension (Stanford) showed a significant advantage for children with deaf parents. At age fifteen – sixteen years (n = 11) the difference was slightly more than one year of reading age. In this study, though, there was no difference in rated written language.

Although the conventional oralist hypothesis in these studies would be that early signing would impair later school attainment, paradoxically they have also been criticized from the opposite standpoint. That is that, in effect, they compare children with preschool signing experience against children with no preschool language experience at all – when a more appropriate control might be against children with preschool oral experience. Vernon and Koh (1971) considered this in another study. It was unfortunately somewhat poorly controlled. All children were drawn from the California School for the Deaf, Riverside. The oral preschool group had also attended the Tracy Clinic Oral Preschool. But not all Tracy Clinic children proceeded to the California School for the Deaf, Riverside. Indeed 44% did not. The sample who did may or may not have been representative of all Tracy Clinic "graduates", and with a 56–44 split, no assumption of such is justified.

A much more thorough coverage of this particular point – as well as others of relevance to us – is provided in a study by Brasel and Quigley (1977). Four groups each of 18 children were used. The 2 groups of particular interest here were designated Manual English (ME) and Intensive Oral (IO). These groups had matched and high IQ (121 v. 119), and all children had a hearing loss greater than 90 dB. The ME group had deaf parents who signed using the grammar of English from the children's infancy, but on average they did not start school until about 4½ years of age. The IO group had hearing parents and started oral school at a mean age of less than two years. Oral communication was also intensive in the home – the parents themselves having been trained in the oral method. At testing, the average age of the groups was 14:8 but with a large matched range (ten – nineteen years). On the Paragraph Meaning Subtest (prose comprehension) of the Stanford Achievement battery, both groups were well above the national average, partly perhaps reflecting high IQ. The ME group had an average reading age of 13 years (Grade 7), the IO group, about 11:4 years (Grade 5.3) – a significant difference. The Quigley et al. (1976) Test of Syntactic Ability (TSA: see Chapter 6) was also given. The ME group were significantly better on 4 of the 6 subtests, and never worse. A third group of somewhat lower IQ (114) had deaf parents who used American Sign Language. This group read about as well as the IO group and showed no differences from them on the TSA. The fourth group were regarded as Average Oral and performed worst on all tests. It is clear that the advantage for signing groups could not have been due to extended early language experience, but to the nature of that experience. The added importance of Signed English for reading skills will be developed in our final chapter.

Summarizing these results, we see that for the principal inter-personal modes of communication, speech and lip reading, early experience of (sign) language does not help (nor greatly hinder), but, where print is involved in either reading or writing, on balance it does help. The only seriously discrepant result is that Quigley and Frisina (1961) found children of deaf parents to have worse speech. It is though far from clear how their 16 children with deaf parents were matched for degree of hearing loss to the 70 control children. The authors simply say that there was no significant difference. For their main experiment this was taken to mean that all children had a loss greater than 75 dB (ASA). Because of the very close association between hearing loss and speech quality which continues well beyond that level of deafness, we have doubts about the reliability of this particular result. On the other hand, Smith (1975), as part of a much larger study, also reported that 8 profoundly-deaf children with deaf parents on average had worse speech than 12 such children with hearing parents. Apart from degree of hearing loss, no evidence is presented to suggest any other matching, though all were less than eleven years old (Smith, 1973). In view of the uncertainty regarding selection and the small sample size, we are cautious about this particular evidence as well.

Our own results with respect to this issue can be expressed with brevity. When we compare children with both parents deaf against other groups of deaf children, matched on Raven score within two points and hearing loss within 10 dB, we find no differences at all. In different tests we have been able to compare 25–27 same-age children of deaf parents with 2 separate groups where in each case the parents were hearing: children with hereditary deafness and children with acquired deafness, but excluding those with an additional handicap. Since we have no data for written language, the only serious discrepancy with previous studies is with respect to reading – where we find no difference.

But apart from the Quigley and Frisina study, there is no published evidence at all which indicates that early signing inevitably impairs subsequent oral ability. No published study which has adequately controlled the relevant variables has reported results contrary to those discussed above. Considered as a theoretical scientific problem rather than as a matter of doctrine, it is hard to see why early signing should impair since most profoundly-deaf children reach the threshold of formal education more or less speechless, and proceed through training programmes which do not consider whether the child's parents are deaf or not.

The results do pose certain problems though. All American studies show children with deaf parents to have an advantage in reading, but no consistent advantage for other verbal skills. But we have been unable to replicate the reading result in Britain. Superficial explanation of this latter could be sought in differences between test instruments. This can be neither decisively supported nor challenged, though in general levels of reading ability in our study are very close to those reported for the USA. So the fact that there appears to be some difference with respect to the effect of deaf parents between American and English children suggests explanations which are more likely to be administrative than theoretical. It is noteworthy that all of the American studies used children who were in Schools in which signing was extensively used in the classroom – as well as speech. In Chapter 2 we cited evidence from Lewis (1968) which amply demonstrated that few Schools in England and Wales regularly employed manual methods for educational purposes. The children who formed our sample were about eight years old at the time of the Lewis enquiry and would therefore in most cases have been taught to read by nonsigning teachers within a phonetically oriented framework. Without, at that age, realizing it, children with some command of sign language, but little if any of English, might well have been in a situation where they were obliged to learn a set of linguistic rules bearing no relationship to those already known. They would not necessarily know that translation was an option – and few teachers would so inform them. In a sense, they would be forcing a current, which most of their American peers would not to the same extent. Bornstein (1978) discusses this kind of mismatching of subjects more fully. He refers to poor "language linkage" between home and classroom, with children of deaf parents particularly handicapped.

In fact we believe that the contentious context of the American studies has effectively obscured a far more important theoretical problem associated with an early signing environment. It has been entirely proper for researchers in this field to ensure that children in their experimental and control groups were matched for intelligence. The principal concern was the effect of early linguistic influences and not the role of intelligence. Since no one would risk an assumption – which we and others have shown would be false – that intelligence was insignificant in the development of verbal skills, it needs to be removed as a contributing factor. What has received virtually no consideration is the possibility that the principal effect of learning sign language at an early age is in fact to advance intellectual development; or at least the kind which is measured by conventional intelligence tests.

Early signing and intelligence

We have noted in a number of places that several studies of the intelligence of deaf children have reported children whose deafness is hereditary to have a higher measured IQ than those with acquired deafness. The average IQ of the latter population is usually found to be below the hearing average, the difference often assumed to be due to neurological deficits which may accompany aquired deafness (Myklebust, 1964). It will be recalled that Meadow (1968) excluded certain of these children for this reason. In general, it has been easy to define physical conditions which might be expected to be associated with lower intelligence, especially when a simple average was used as the descriptive statistic. An alternative suggestion was mooted by Vernon (1972). Having referred to the possible effects of "environmental deprivation", he continued that the higher IQ of genetically deaf children suggests, "... perhaps a genetic syndrome typing hereditary deafness to IQ" (p. 372). This suggestion has not been widely accepted, perhaps because too many different genetic syndromes have been implicated in hereditary deafness. Fraser (1964) points out that many of the syndromes involving deafness also include other defects which would tend to discount a purely biological explanation of the observed IQ effect.

Curiously, in view of the interest in deaf children with deaf parents, little specific interest has been shown in the intelligence *per se* of this group. Apart from an unpublished communication from Dr. Schildroth,* there seems to be only one other study on

---

* Personal communication. Data drawn from Gallaudet Survey.

this. Brill (1969) also reported higher nonverbal IQ for deaf children with deaf parents who signed at home than for those with hearing parents who did not. It is not clear, however, whether this latter group were genetically deaf or included all aetiologies. Dr. Schildroth's data equally do not make this distinction. As we see it then, three groups of deaf children can be distinguished with respect to intelligence. Those with acquired deafness who are below average with respect to both deaf and hearing populations; those with genetic deafness who must be close to average; those with deaf parents who are above average for both the deaf and hearing populations. Dr. Schildroth reports an average IQ for several hundred such children of 107. Our own results support this. The average Raven score for children with deaf parents is significantly greater than that of children who have hereditary deafness but hearing parents (see Figure 9.2).

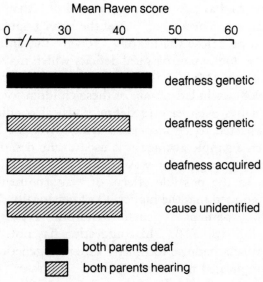

Figure 9.2.   Raven's Progressive Matrices (maximum = 60), by cause of deafness and parents' status.

With at least three independent reports this phenomenon has to be taken seriously. How can we account for the apparent fact that deaf children with deaf parents are possibly more intelligent than hearing children and certainly more intelligent than other genetically deaf children? Balow and Brill (1975), referring to the Brill (1969) study, suggest that " . . . as a result of learning to communicate, ... (at an early age) ... cognitive growth and the development of thinking processes begin earlier" (p. 259).

We find this an attractive speculation. It implies, in effect, a converse to the hypothesis that linguistic deprivation, as with other kinds, may lead to retarded cognitive development (Fromkin et al., 1974; Lane, 1977). Here it seems that access to a medium of linguistic communication, which is available before oral language is, may sooner affect or assist whatever those processes are which are involved in the relationship between language and cognition. These children do not learn sign language because they are particularly intelligent, they are more intelligent because they have learned a language sooner.

Another suggestion which might be regarded as complementary derives from studies of bilingual hearing children. In a review of studies of the cognitive effects of early bilingualism, Lambert (1977) concludes: "All of these studies ... indicate that bilingual children, relative to monolingual controls, show definite advantages on measures of 'cognitive flexibility' " (p. 16). Specifically, for instance, Peal and Lambert (1962) reported that bilingual children carefully matched to monolinguals were ahead in measured verbal and nonverbal intelligence. It should be noted that most of this work has assumed that bilinguals have two languages from an early age. In the studies of deaf children we have discussed, though we are virtually certain that the children of deaf parents signed from a very early age, we do not usually know whether they also, early, had some degree of oral English. By the time they were tested they certainly did have; English was the language of the tests. At present there is little information with respect to the way age of bilingual development might come to affect cognitive growth. It seems certain that children of deaf parents are more likely to become bilingual much earlier than other deaf groups. We do not know whether the difference in intelligence is present before they learn English, or whether it is a consequence.

Regardless of the validity of explanations, the undoubted fact is the higher IQ of this particular group of children. But if the explanation we have advanced is given credence, then matching pairs of children for intelligence destroys the very effect we are purporting to examine. Instead of testing for the effects of early signing on oral skills, we should be testing for its effect on intelligence. The effects of intelligence on oral performance should specifically not be separated from the effect of the early linguistic environment.

Intellectual development *is* the main effect. The correct study then becomes the kind of comparison which has been made – with all of the appropriate controls *except* intelligence. If the oral abilities of deaf children with deaf parents are seen to be greater than the appropriate control group, a criticism that it is because of higher intelligence must logically also offer an explanation of why intelligence is higher; but it must be an explanation which is independent of the experience of early signing.

When we make the above comparison using our own data, the outcome of course depends on which group we use as a control. We can follow Vernon and Koh (1970) and use other deaf children with hereditary deafness but hearing parents; here we risk including children with signing siblings. Or we can use children with acquired deafness but exclude those with known additional handicap. Or we can adopt a somewhat unconventional control using children whose cause of deafness is not known, but where it is known that all immediate members of the family are hearing, and there is a reasonable assumption that deafness was not acquired. It seems simplest to make all three comparisons; matching now excludes intelligence, but does of course include degree of hearing loss.

We have 27 children with deaf parents available for matching, none of whom has an additional handicap. These are matched to children from 3 different populations:

1   children with hereditary deafness but hearing parents.

2   children with acquired deafness and hearing parents.

3   children with unidentified cause of deafness but hearing parents.

The groups are already age-matched, and no child with an additional handicap was used. Since the groups were not matched for intelligence, a very close match – within 2 dB – was achieved with respect to hearing loss – of particular importance for speech intelligibility. No other matching was considered, since we have found no other significant variable for which matching is practicable. To add to reliability, though, for each of groups 1 and 3 above, we were able to select two independent samples for matching to the group of children with deaf parents.

The results of these comparisons for speech intelligibility, reading, and lip reading are respectively shown in Figures 9.3, 9.4, and 9.5. There is no difference in the speech intelligibility of children with deaf parents when compared to any of the other 3 groups.

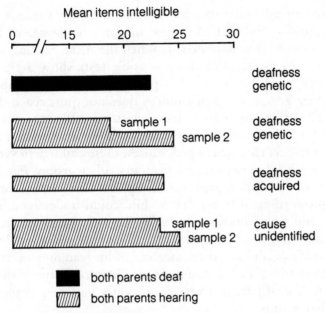

Figure 9.3.   Speech intelligibility (numbers: maximum = 40), by cause of deafness and parents' status.

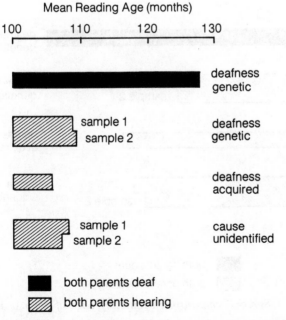

Figure 9.4.   Reading age, by cause of deafness and parents' status.

We have already seen that intelligence has only a minor role in speech quality and that the major influence is degree of hearing loss, here very closely matched. When the mean reading ages are compared by t-test, 4 of the 5 possible tests show a significant advantage for children with deaf parents. One of the comparisons with other genetically deaf children does not quite reach the 0.05 level. The effect, of course, does reflect the difference in intelligence. So in spite of the possible effects of a communication disability with respect to teaching procedures, these children nevertheless do leave school better readers than any other group. Finally, the measure of lip reading used was the Speech Comprehension-Ratio – the proportion of items that a child could understand in print that he could also lip read correctly. This discounts the linguistic advantage of the children with deaf parents indicated by their better reading, and is a truer measure of lip reading as a decoding skill. This time, all the comparisons (Mann-Whitney) show the children of deaf parents to be significantly better lip readers than any other group.

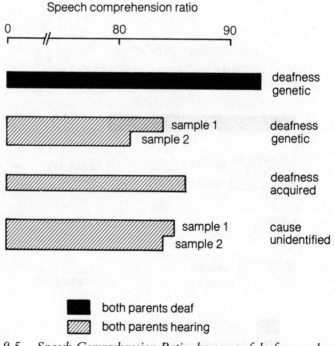

Figure 9.5.   Speech Comprehension-Ratio, by cause of deafness and parents' status.

Those studies which have matched intelligence as well as other variables have, in a sense, provided what we believe to have been unnecessarily cautious results. Since they have been based on a variety of samples of children drawn from different schools in different parts of the USA, it is not surprising that some discrepancies show. But the overall conclusion points to unambiguous rejection of the proposition that early signing impairs subsequent oral performance. Quite simply, it does not. A negative proposition is not readily disproved. But a good deal of research, most of it carefully controlled, has failed to provide any acceptable support.

Criticism of the kinds of studies we have cited has often been made on the grounds of their *ex post facto* status (Nix, 1975; Owrid, 1971); that is, the results are derived retrospectively from chance conditions which an investigator takes advantage of. The hazards of such studies are clear. In particular there is a risk that the results are due to one or more, usually assumed to be environmental, factors which were not controlled. Lowell (1976) for instance has pointed out the possibility that deaf parents are more motivated in their child rearing, knowing in advance the damaging social effects that deafness can bring. Owrid (1971) has suggested that studies using children in residential Schools with a signing tradition penalize nonsigning children – though he does also note that Stuckless and Birch used only day pupils. Nor is it clear how this factor could so greatly affect intelligence. When though a criticism of a retrospective study is made based on failure to control a variable, the criticism has little validity unless it also makes an evidential case for what the relevance of that variable might be. Any study controls a finite number of variables leaving an infinite number not controlled. The careful investigator controls for those factors for which a reasoned case of relevance can be made and where control is possible. With an infinite number of uncontrolled variables no study is secure. But insecurity is not the same as invalidity, and these studies can only be invalidated through the *ex post facto* criticism, when a variable not controlled can be demonstrated to be relevant to the outcome. In the case of studies of the effect of early signing, this remains to be done, and the conclusion that early signing is not detrimental has, for the present, to be accepted.

We have criticized these studies using deaf parents on the ground that researchers have been oversecure because they have controlled a variable assumed to be independent but which we have argued is not. We believe that level of intelligence is arguably a consequence of early signing and not independent of it. Though this is of immense importance in its own right, in the present context it has little relevance. Intelligence plays a very small part, for example, in the development of intelligible speech which may depend more on imitation than on learning. But the linguistic conditions for the development of cognitive ability most certainly merit the widest discussion.

It is important that before entering that discussion we try to clarify this point. The standarization of intelligence tests requires that the person with "average" intelligence in the population to which the test applies has an average score. When test scores are expressed as intelligence quotients (IQ) to take account of age effects, conventionally an IQ of 100 is nominated to be the average score. In theory, the average IQ of any unselected population – that is a population without a bias with respect to intelligence – will be 100. When a population has a genuine average IQ which is above or below 100 we search for "selective" factors which may be in relationship with intelligence. When the factors are psychological, they may be impenetrably obscure.

For instance, we have confirmed what has often been reported, that multiply handicapped deaf children have lower intelligence test scores than other deaf children. In this case we assume that multiple handicap is the crucial selective factor which shifts the average IQ of this population to below 100. Indeed, when we look for such selective factors, it is generally because the IQ is lower than average. But the present case of deaf children with deaf parents is an unusal opposite one. Here we have to seek factors which are associated with higher than average intelligence – not only average for unselected deaf populations, but possibly for hearing populations as well. Because we so often associate lower intelligence with underprivilege of some kind, in the case of these particular deaf children it is natural to think in terms of overprivilege. But the apparent definitively selecting variable is that of having two deaf parents. Whatever privilege this characteristic brings, it has to be one which can reasonably be associated with higher intelligence. Our problem is to formulate hypotheses which might suggest a causal relationship. The options are neither self-evident nor numerous. We start with a characteristic which few people would regard as desirable, yet it brings, or is accompanied by, an immensely desirable quality – higher than average intelligence. Furthermore, it is almost a defining characteristic of this quality. Our population of 27 deaf children with deaf parents includes no fewer than 24 who are above the average value for the deaf population as a whole. This means that whatever it is about parental deafness it is something common to almost all such relationships.

Sign language as an option

It may seem inconsistent that after continuously urging the advantages of internal *speech* for cognitive function, we now apparently desert that view. There is, though, no real contradiction. Because of the emphasis of social attitudes and educational philosophy, profoundly-deaf children in Britain have little choice. Some may acquire at a relatively low level a knowledge of spoken English and we see a reflection of this in their internal speech. Most, as we have pointed out, have failed to develop the necessary competence and their internal language seems to be restricted to printed English, clearly less effective for understanding prose for example. Internal sign language is simply not a genuine option for most of these children. It is the language neither of home nor of school authority. They are not taught sign language, nor taught in it. Only those few children brought up in a signing environment are likely to have enough competence in sign to use it internally. We have seen that it is in fact these children who are likely to be the most effective in English – their second language. Nor would it surprise if, by the age of sixteen years, these children also preferred internal speech – reflecting the language of the classroom – in academic contexts.

Just the same, quite apart from the anecdotal evidence of deaf people, Bellugi et al. (1974), Odom et al. (1970), and others, have shown that internal sign is as practicable as internal speech. It is a living language with forms wherever there are communities of deaf people. But, above all, as a medium of communication it presents no special problems to deaf infants. The hand configurations are as visually distinctive as the speech sounds of English are phonologically distinctive (Ahlgren, 1977). The gross movements of simple signing are almost certainly easier for children to form than are the precise articulations of speech, and follow naturally from the gestural behaviour common to all infants. Vocabulary comes easily. Several hundred of the early-learned signs are iconic – they are visually associated with the objects or activities they symbolize (Stokoe, 1978). Brown (1977) has drawn attention to the wit which may be present in a sign – giving pleasure to a young child. It is a language with grammatical rules which children acquire at least as easily as hearing children acquire the rules of English (McIntire, 1977); Schlesinger and Meadow (1972) describe two-word pivoting in sign by a child aged seventeen months. Sign language can provide an easily learned mother-tongue, which may serve not only a communicative function but, much more important, it may preserve and develop the crucial neural organization for language upon which second-language learning must be based.

We see the principal case for sign as a first language for deaf infants as biological rather than social. Because during the last century it has tended to be a clandestine language, the growing research effort concerned with it in no way approaches that which has been applied to spoken language. We do not therefore know its full potential in terms of linguistic richness. But even supposing, in an environment of greater freedom of expression, its potential is great or small, that worth must be considered against the great ease of acquisition by deaf children. Speech has evolved as a biologically adapted communication mode for hearing people. For the deaf the choice may be between an easily learned but relatively impoverished language and a rich one which we, and others, have shown to be exceedingly difficult to learn. As long ago as the early part of the seventeenth century, J. P. Bonet, who published the first manual for teachers of the deaf, noted that mental growth could be retarded if the tempo of language learning was slowed down to the pace required by speech learning (cited by Levine, 1963).

Up to the time deafness is diagnosed, most children will grow up in a quasi-oral environment. It is quasi-oral to a degree which will be a direct reflection of degree of their hearing loss. Speech, not much of which may be heard, will go on in the home. It should be obvious that we do not propose that when children are exposed to sign language, speech in their presence should cease. Children will derive most linguistic benefit from the language with which their sensory capacities are most compatible. We have shown that early signing cannot be said to impair subsequent skill at English, and at the very least it will have provided an enviable, and otherwise unattainable, vocabulary. Deaf children will need to learn their societal language. It is evident that for the majority it is exceedingly difficult for this to occur as a first language. But it is highly plausible that a (second) spoken language will be more easily learned upon the base of fluency in a tongue dependent on intact sensory and neural structures. It is interesting to reflect that the sourbriquet "brain damaged" is so often used to explain the poor oral performance of a deaf child. True, the cortical damage inflicted by meningitis, for instance, is quite different in nature from the disturbance of function that we have been discussing. Nevertheless, it is ironic that in so many cases insistence on a speech medium may produce just the effect which in the other context is considered an indication for changing from oral to manual methods.

Geschwind (1967) has written that, "often the only means available to us ... to see the hidden foundations of highly complex activities is to study the brutal experiments of nature on the nervous system of man" (p. 103). Congenital deafness is indeed a brutal experiment. There is much we can learn from it. Deafness offers insights into problems in neurology, cognitive function, linguistics, social relationships, and other areas where research is active. We cannot value too highly the contribution that deaf people can make, simply by being deaf and willing to collaborate. But here our first responsibility is to deaf children as people; to their education, and so to the development of their intellectual and emotional potential. We have shown that intensive and highly personal education leaves them seriously deficient. We have tried to probe beneath the surface of test scores to glimpse and begin to identify the weaknesses in the substructure at several levels of behaviour. This analysis has led us – forced us, since we began our enquiry with the openmindedness of ignorance – to a conclusion far from novel, but nevertheless independently reached. In the final chapter we shall discuss and elaborate on the practical implications of this conclusion.

10
The Education of Deaf Children

Ends and means

Superficially, the hurly-burly of the classroom is far removed from the transmission of nervous impulses across synapses. Yet, unless instruction is to be entirely haphazard, it is guided by varying degrees of adherence to a set of principles. When the pupils are characterized by a pathological condition, the pathology both constrains the range of practicable educational objectives and preempts the means of reaching them. Pedagogic principles cannot ignore the pathology which limits the tactical options and so determines the strategic goals.

This is particularly true for the education of deaf children, and consensus with respect to principles is still elusive. The great universities of Europe had been established for some five hundred years before the first Schools for deaf children began to appear in the second half of the eighteenth century. Specific objectives were not formalized until the International Congress of Teachers of the Deaf in 1880. Resolution I notes,

Considering the incontestable superiority of articulation over signs *in restoring the deaf-mute to society* and giving him a fuller knowledge of language ...(our italics).

The Congress also agreed on the tactics – the methods to be used to achieve this goal. Resolution VI declares,

That ... they (the deaf and dumb) make use exclusively of speech.
That speech and lip-reading ... are developed by practice.

In effect, then, the objective of deaf education became integration into normal society by means of providing the deaf with society's language. But, in particular, manual methods of instruction which had played a dominant part in deaf education were voted out, and instruction through speech was formally voted in. In this way, educators of deaf children challenged head-on the fact that their pupils could not hear what they said.

It is interesting that the continuing debate concerning the tactics of education, and in particular whether nonoral instruction is acceptable, has obscured the significant and humanistic Congress decision that the era of society's rejection of the deaf-mute was to end. At least since that time, this objective has remained unquestioned. The questions have surrounded the means, as generation after generation of deaf children passed into, through, and out of school either unable or unwilling to take their place as integrated members of the society which believed it had provided the theoretically best solution to the problems of their handicap.

The data we have presented in preceding chapters suggest that the question of willingness is irrelevant: deaf children remain unable to participate in full social interaction because they leave school unable to meet the language demands which that interaction requires. In a sense, stating the issue in that general way represents a minimal statement. In a time of great migrations of people throughout the word, we are familiar with the concept of ethnic enclaves in much larger and dominant host cultures. If the deaf had a common language of their own which did not involve speech, could they not form one more such enclave? The difference between an ethnic group and a deaf group using a common but nonsocietal language is that 95% of deaf people are part of normally-hearing families. As a responsible society we therefore remain confronted by the crippling inability of deaf children to learn the language we write, or speak, or hear.

It is remarkable, as Furth (1971) points out, that the massive language deficits of deaf children have been, until very recently, largely overlooked. Furth implies a conspiracy; "For understandable reasons this fact is not usually broadcast ..." (p. 69). We prefer to recognize delusion rather than deceit. What is certain is that educators have been singularly reticent about the quantitative discrepancy between their aspirations and achievements. Charitably, we may assume that in spite of the rapid growth of the means of psychometric assessment of the past half century, they did not know. That option is no longer open and has been under growing pressure of erosion for some years. Indeed, the more common response of teachers faced with indisputable evidence for widespread illiteracy amongst their pupils, is agreeement, together with a plea for administrative remedy. Outside the USA the possibility that the pedagogic theory might be incorrect is still regarded as hostile criticism. In this chapter we now take the nature of the end product – the levels of achievement reached in the basic skills of verbal communication as given. Hitherto we have been careful not to assume that either the theory or the practice of education has been faulty. We considered at length questions of criteria that might be applied, other than the mere evidence of gross deficit. But in the previous chapter we sketched in a model for the development of verbal skill which depends heavily on the immutable burden of hearing loss itself – the characteristic that oral pedagogic theory has undertaken to challenge. Here, then, we are forced to consider the way that the still worldwide, prevalent philosophy sees itself, as empirical reality becomes increasingly documented and increasingly evident to society outside the school gate.

For most of a hundred years much of Western education and education modelled on Western ideas has depended on a relatively homogeneous set of principles collectively known as the oral philosophy of deaf education. In Chapter 6 we briefly referred to the major abandonment of these in the Soviet Union during the early school years. It is far from clear from available sources how widespread the changes were, and there is a total lack of comparative performance data outside the Soviet Union which extends beyond generalities. In the USA as well, growing discontent with levels of academic attainment has led to a nationwide reconsideration of educational principles and the reinstatement of manual methods of communication in schools. There, the traditions of the early teachers had never really been lost, and manual communication remained strong in some schools and at Gallaudet College, the principal institution for higher education for deaf students.

In 1968, the Maryland School for the Deaf introduced a formulated programme of "Total Communication" in which sign language and finger spelling of words, as well as speech, were incorporated into classroom teaching. The 1880 Congress of Milan rejected, but could not eradicate, the use of signing in schools, since it is the indigenous language of deaf families. The concept of Total Communication not only gave it status, but systematically coemployed it as a desirable instructional medium. Only now are

the first children to have been wholly educated in this way beginning to reach school-leaving age. One isolated school would have
poorly represented so great a change. But other schools have followed. Garretson (1976) reported that by 1976 almost 75% of all
school programmes for deaf children with an enrolment of 100
children or more had reported the introduction of Total Communication. During this time, the Office of Demographic
Research of Gallaudet College has continued to collect data on
academic achievement from which we have extensively quoted.
These data will now cover an increasing number of children for
whom manual as well as oral instruction has been standard. We are
now, therefore, on the threshold of a unique comparative study
which could clarify this critical issue during the next decade. The
comparison will not be pure, since achievement depends on the
child's home environment and the success of teacher training for a
method, as well as on the validity of the method itself. Nor will all
schools be equally rigorous in the application of principles – never
the case for strictly oral principles either. Nevertheless, an historic
change of some moment is in train.

In Britain, and in other European countries, the formalized
introduction of manual communication in classrooms is barely
nascent. The outcome of American experience, with its unique
and efficient documentation, will – whatever it is – have extensive
consequences. In most European countries adequate documentation has been lacking. The striking concordance between comparable values for the USA and for the data we have reported here
suggests that the similarities of educational philosophies in the
USA and Britain have evolved a genuine norm against which
future innovations might be judged, and which is virtually independent of minor programmatic variations. This agreement in
those results which are available for comparison is also important
because it supports the supposition that, regardless of national
variations in resources and priorities allotted to education of deaf
children, in terms of whole populations, we do seem to be faced
with an inherent set of limiting factors. In fact, the growing dissatisfaction has been based largely on pragmatic issues – it simply
seems not to have worked. Insofar as there is a coherent theory of
Total Communication, it is based on little more than that there is
no reason not to employ all the forms of language input that deaf
people can utilize, together with empirical support against the
criticism that this would prejudice linguistic development. We

have suggested a stronger argument; that there are sound theoretical reasons why manual – or some form of visible – language must be made available as a mother-tongue to some hearing-impaired children. This conclusion – though not the theory – has been vigorously contested, and the current low academic standards either excused, denied, or ignored.

Social factors in school attainment

The success of any national educational system is likely to reflect unevenness which depends either on the overall design, or on specific social characteristics of pupils beyond school control. In examining outcomes, therefore, we need at least to glance at some of the more obvious features which might lead to perturbation in overall performance. In the context of dominant oral education it seems particularly important to determine, first, whether deaf children already handicapped might be less responsive to a linguistically demanding programme, if they also live in what we might assume to be linguistically underprivileged homes. Secondly, we may consider whether specific administrative arrangements are more benign than others.

There are of course many factors which distinguish one child from another and which might be relevant to the child's ability to learn to communicate verbally. We know of course that degree of hearing loss and intelligence may be implicated causally. These are qualities which we have, perhaps dogmatically, regarded as "given". No doubt part of the score of an intelligence test derives from non-innate sources; the extent must be debated elsewhere. Less debatable perhaps is that social factors, both through maternal health and through selective eugenics, provide a social contribution to incidence of deafness. Rawlings and Jensema (1977) report that deaf children are more likely to be born into large than into small families; and into poor rather than wealthy families. But no one has ever seriously proposed that degree of hearing loss is of exclusively social origin. When we use the term "given", we imply no more than what is effectively unamenable to educational intervention. There are a number of other such factors which, when two children are equally deaf and equally intelligent, may still serve to distinguish their academic performance. We shall report on those for which we have quantitative data; we do not imply that others are unimportant. In a sense, then, formally we postulate a factor likely to affect performance and test the hypothesis. Procedurally we shall consider matched pairs of children. Each pair will have approximately the same level of hearing impairment, similar scores on Raven's Matrices, and will also be matched according to the three main categories of cause of deafness. The two children of each pair will be distinguished by the presence or absence of the condition under test. In this case, since it is matched, any degree of deafness is admissable.

Home circumstances

In discussing children with their teachers, we obtained a certain amount of background, including social, information. This was sketchy, partly because we were unwilling to extend the scope of the enquiry beyond our brief, partly because teachers' knowledge was limited, and not least because our scientific competence did not extend into sociological enquiry. We therefore restricted questions to matters where it would be reasonable to expect accurate and classifiable answers. One such question concerned the occupation of the child's father. Two clear categories of relevance are "manual worker" and "professional". By excluding discussion of other designations, we hope to have achieved separate but fairly homogeneous groupings. The point of making this comparison is based on the admittedly naïve, but commonly accepted, assumption that, in socioeconomic terms, the former are relatively less "privileged". The question is whether this shows in school performance. Children of professional fathers are no more likely to be found in Partially Hearing Units than other children and, since we shall match for hearing loss, all children in the study have been used. Of these 38% are "manual" (i.e., socially, not linguistically in this context) and 11% "professional", the remainder being hard to classify with certainty.

Two factors may initially be noted. The first is that significantly more "manual" children are in broken homes; this we shall discuss in a moment. But here it seems prudent to compare only children, whether "manual" or "professional", who are living with both parents. The second is that "professional" children are more intelligent. While their mean Raven score is 43.5, that of "manual" children is 38.9. The difference ($t = 2.72$) is significant at the 0.01 level. If we ignored this difference, we would no doubt show that "professional" children do better at school. But we are concerned here not with intellectual distinctions but with effects due to home circumstances regardless of a child's intelligence. The matched pairs comparison takes care of this. The data provide 37 such pairs.

When the matches referred to have been made, there is not the slightest evidence that the occupational status of the child's father – and presumably the kind of home environment – affects level of verbal skill. Using speech intelligibility scores, 18 "professional" children are the better of the pair against 17 "manual" (two ties); for reading the division is 16 against 17 (four ties). Wilcoxon tests on speech comprehension (lip reading), and on the proportion of printed items understood in speech, both yield negligible z values. Finally, "professional" children are no more likely to use internal speech. Again, performance seems to be dominated by degree of deafness and intelligence.

The second condition we examined which must be considered as a relevant feature of a child's home is the psycho-social stability. The information comes from a question which simply asked if the child's parents were living together – with the child. Where this was not the case the child was categorized as living in a broken home. The oversimplification here is obvious. The category includes death, as well as divorce or other separation. We also recognize that cohabiting parents do not guarantee an emotionally satisfactory environment. The conclusions are therefore valid only with respect to this loose definition of a broken home. But while we do know that few of the broken homes are due to death, and the majority to a broken marriage, we have no information about the happiness or stability of the two-parent homes.

Here again we used all children in the study, and found 44 children living in broken homes. There is no effect of deafness itself. A profoundly-deaf child is just as likely to be in a stable as in a broken home. The average intelligence is also the same. Nor is there a difference in cause of deafness. There is no tendency, for example, for families with genetic deafness either to hold together or to break up. Nor is the presence of a handicap additional to deafness associated. In short, we find no biological differences at all. When these 44 children were appropriately paired with 44 children in stable homes, once again we found no differences in performance. Our first thoughts on this were that the sample was too small to show possible real effects. We therefore tested the 44 children from broken homes against a different second matched set of children from stable homes. The results were identical. It is possible that this criterion is too coarse to detect the kind of disadvantage conventionally, if superficially, associated with broken homes as environments for children. It may be, though, that on average there is in fact no disadvantage with respect to the indications we considered. Indeed there is some support for this in Ferri (1976), who reported similar results in a study of hearing children in one-parent families.

Schooling

Of all factors which contribute to a child's academic performance, none is more amenable to the effects of educational intervention than school itself. In Chapter 2 we mentioned three types of special schooling available to deaf children: day, residential, and Partially Hearing Units in ordinary day schools. Now we consider whether the type of school particularly contributes anything to success. The broad advantages and disadvantages of boarding have been continually debated from many viewpoints. Our data can only inform this debate with respect to academic performance. But even here only in principle, and we discuss the matter partly to draw attention to the practical problems of such comparison.

If we think first about a day/residential comparison we immediately meet a number of methodological difficulties which obstruct direct interpretation of results. Principally, these derive from the administration of a national educational system for relatively few children requiring Special education. Where, for example, a large city can justify day education for its deaf children in Special Schools, rural areas may not. The social characteristics of children in day and residential schools may therefore be different in relevant ways, though we have seen that in fact the distributions of both hearing loss and intelligence do not differ. In view of the highly significant contributions to performance made by these variables and our failure to find a difference with respect to some quite important social factors, this particular administrative aspect may not greatly matter.

Children, though, change schools. We have no control data for hearing children but, in our sample, fewer than 50% of children remain in the same school throughout their school life. Changes occur for a variety of reasons. There is the conventional sorting at different ages common to many large educational systems, with some special features associated with education of deaf children. A number of deaf children, especially if they also have additional handicaps, may be administratively difficult to place in the most appropriate environment. Then families move from one locality to another. We have found no fewer than 55 different educational "treatments" amongst the children we tested – many unique for a single child. Most unfortunate perhaps, for reliable comparison, is the fact that a number of children, in changing school, change between day and residential Schools, and PHUs as well.

At least one moderately uncomplicated comparison can be made. That is between children whose entire school life has been in day Schools – though not necessarily the same School – and children whose education has been exclusively residential. Those few day pupils who were in residential Schools have been treated as day pupils in this comparison. Respectively, the numbers involved are 86 and 112. Test then shows not the slightest suggestion of an advantage for either type of School at any level of hearing loss. No differences occur for speech intelligibility, or for reading or lip reading.

Cross-cultural comparison is not very meaningful here. The factors which determine whether a deaf child is in residence or not are likely to be nationally specific in varying degree. Hamp (1972), though, in his study of reading by deaf children in England, reports a significant advantage for children in day Schools. But his data came from only three day Schools and three residential Schools, and there is little reason to suppose that the results would generalize. Both hearing loss and intelligence also appear to be confounded in the scores which Hamp presents – though all of his subjects were very deaf. But he does not take account of the possible effects of child mobility that we have found so common. His conclusion, therefore that " . . . even the most severely deaf children are able to progress better when linked to a family environment," (p. 211) seems premature.

Partially Hearing Units

Statutory educational authorities in Britain, whose numbers and geographic distribution of deaf children justify the establishment of day Schools, have less need to use the facilities offered by residential Schools than do authorities relying principally on PHUs for Special education. In the former case, there may be appropriate reasons for placing the child away from home, but degree of hearing loss need not be one of them. Apart from other considerations, the latter authorities do need to consider this factor. In Chapter 2 we referred to the difficulty there is in determining the criteria which different authorities use when placing a child in a PHU or in a residential School, and Hemmings (1972) has noted that where one authority placed 2½% of its deaf children in residence, another sent 45% to such Schools.

While it is clear that the majority of children in PHUs are in fact partially hearing, there are also considerable numbers of partially hearing children in residential Special Schools. Most of these presumably live in areas where Special day schooling would be difficult, and in these cases a deliberate decision has been made to board a child – even though he may be partially-hearing – rather than place him in a PHU; the authority being legally obliged to provide suitable education. Though many of the problems that we discussed in connection with day-residential comparisons are present when comparing PHU and residential schoolchildren, the implications in terms of a national education policy are perhaps more critical. It seems worth while therefore, while not forgetting the difficulties, to try to assess what it is that distinguishes these two groups of children: partially-hearing children in residential Schools and partially-hearing children in PHUs.

Since nearly 90% of children in PHUs who were of school-leaving age had hearing losses no greater than 85 dB, we have restricted our comparison to residential schoolchildren of similar hearing loss. A glance at Figure 2.5 will show that scores on Raven's Matrices for the two types of school have slightly different distributions. In particular, there tend to be proportionately fewer children in PHUs with very low and very high scores. The latter may reflect the fact that the selective grammar schools are residential, but the difference is small.

The remaining more obvious biological and social factors, which might have been thought to influence placement, seem not to do so. The children in residential Schools are not more likely to come from a broken home of the type discussed earlier. Nor are they more additionally handicapped. The distribution of cause of deafness – genetic, acquired, unidentified – is also the same. But here we might note one curious distinction. Within this range of hearing loss, in our entire sample there are 8 children with 2 deaf parents. None of these are in PHUs; 6 are in residential Schools, and 2 in day Schools. With numbers as small as this, any interpretation will be suspect. But Hemmings (1972) reports that PHU teachers complained that their "children travel on the same buses as children from the nearby special school, and pick up habits of signing from them" (p. 464). It is just possible that for this reason children with deaf parents likely to sign at home tend not to be placed in PHUs.

Again, the simplest type of analysis seems to be to match pairs of children on the basis of intelligence (Raven score + or − 1) and hearing loss (+ or − 5 dB). This provides 47 such pairs, 1 of each at the time of testing being in a PHU, the other in a residential School. Since the general make-up of the groups comprising the matched pairs is very similar, we can reasonably assume that the principal factor which might affect performance will be the type of schooling. Because none of the children forming the comparison is very deaf, the lip reading test is one simply of speech comprehension, and it is not surprising that here no difference shows. But neither is there a significant difference for reading. The one skill in which PHU children do show a significant advantage is in speech. Tested for the intelligibility of their spoken sentences, the PHU children are clearly easier to understand ($t = 4.24$; $p < 0.001$).

The decision about placement would, for most of these children, have been made at about the age of eleven years. During the interval between then and the time we tested, little formal speech training would have been undertaken. With the run up to public examinations, most school time would be devoted to academic or handicraft subjects. The marked superiority in the speech of PHU children suggests either that placement was principally made on the basis of that criterion or that the PHU environment, with its opportunity for social as well as educational integration with hearing children, has a marked role in improving speech after the age of eleven years.

There is no *post hoc* way of deciding which of these alternatives is nearer the truth. But the implications differ. If in fact speech quality were not a factor in placement at age eleven years, but PHU education itself improves speech, we have failed to uncover any unifying criteria on the basis of which children are selected for education away from home when an alternative is administratively available. Indeed, an ethical issue arises, and it might be wondered what bases there are for – in effect – penalizing the children placed in residential Schools when they appear to be little different from those placed in PHUs and, apart from speech, academically as able.

On the other hand, as we noted earlier, of all the communication skills, speech quality is the most immediately obtrusive whether to an interviewing education or medical officer, or to a teacher whose recommendation carries weight. This would not be an inappropriate criterion; integration with hearing children would clearly be facilitated for those children whose speech was more intelligible to their hearing peers. But it seems not to be "official" policy. The Department of Education and Science (1967), considering the placement of older deaf children, suggests that, "He must be able to learn through listening, looking and reading ..." (p. 15). It does not refer to speech. Nor do we find PHU teachers singling out speech quality as a placement indicator. Certainly the term "language ability" is sometimes cited. But we saw that when it is reflected in reading, PHU children are not better. In brief, it would appear that either children are selected – regardless of what principles selectors imagine they use – on the basis of their speech quality, and then subsequent integration does little for them academically; or placement depends on a large number of idiosyncratic concepts leading to the discrepancies reported by Hemmings (1972), and to the disadvantage with respect to speech of children placed residentially.

The defence of oralism

The oral philosophy embraces a mixture of pedagogic and rehabilitative principles – the distinction not always sufficiently recognized. The more general rehabilitative aspects reflect sound educational and medical practice which today would be regarded as essential to all educational programmes regardless of their distinguishing features. All programmes for the education of deaf children urge earliest possible diagnosis and, when applicable, prescription of a hearing aid. The technical development of the hearing aid has been quite independent of educational thought, stemming principally from the needs of hard-of-hearing adults. Then, since few children are totally deaf, acoustic treatment of classrooms is universally accepted as important. This will reduce echo, reverberation, and extraneous noise from which a child might have difficulty filtering out those attenuated speech sounds permitted by the hearing which remains. All systems of education consider that guidance of parents of deaf children is important for the emotional development of the child. The acceptance of deafness in an infant becomes a problem which the entire family has to overcome since the natural pattern of social interactions may be violently disturbed. The desirability of these and many other rehabilitative features are part of the development of social medicine. A wider understanding of the problems of deafness happens to have emerged during a period when oral education has been dominant, but the association is coincident rather than consequent.

The essential pedagogic character of oralism does involve unique principles. Foremost is that the medium of instruction is speech without recourse to sign or gesture. The speech may be "natural" in that the environment of instruction which is aimed at is similar to that of hearing children. In this case the teacher speaks with normal conversational modulation. But it is recognized that the imperfectly-hearing child will depend for verbal content, not only on prosodic features of discourse, but on lip reading as well. For this reason, some schools of oral thought prefer a less natural but more precisely articulated manner of speaking, so as to emphasize the features of speech visible at or in the mouth. Sometimes the natural gestures which normally accompany speech are used. Other teachers, giving more weight to the theoretical requirements of strictly aural-oral communication, restrict manual gesture to an unnatural minimum. Totally barred is formal signing or finger spelling, but great use is made of written language to reinforce spoken language, so as to aid establishment of the phonemic relationships between print-read, lip-read, and heard forms, and to emphasize intonational patterning and the syllabic stress which is available to the hearing child acoustically. The 1880 Congress of Milan rose to the cry of, "Viva la parola!", and the speech medium, aided by whatever amplification of speech can be provided by technology and financial resources, dominates.

Oral pedagogic principles would insist that the oral environment be maintained outside the classroom as well: at play, in dormitories, at home. The practice of course varies. Because signing is a vernacular language amongst deaf adults, its presence is virtually impossible to eradicate within a school community. At the very least children with deaf parents must be refused admission. Few schools go to such lengths. Many though insist on nonmanual communication as a matter of discipline. On school premises we were once assured by a profoundly-deaf girl that she was unable to understand sign language – only to discover later that both her parents were deaf and that signing was in fact her mother-tongue.

More commonly, and especially in the case of nonselective Schools, signing may be used outside the formal classroom. At play, where children need to communicate over long distances, speech will be useless to deaf children. They will gesticulate as will hearing children and, if more meaningful signs are known, they will be used as well. But even inside the classroom, as we noted earlier, although speech may be the official language of instruction, some teachers will use gestures and whatever sign they may know when communication by speech is self-evidently inadequate. In Britain, few teachers are skilled signers – the conditions of teacher training have precluded it – and regardless of communication modes used outside classrooms, speech does dominate formal instruction, and has done so for many generations of pupils. Yet, as we have seen, little progress is made during school life in the oral essential of lip reading, and speech production remains poor and frequently unintelligible. Inevitably, oral education is coming under increasing attack.

By its nature, when oralism fails to create an orally thinking child, it also fails to provide the child with alternative modes of thought. It lacks imaginative variety of procedures appropriate to the needs of a population characterized by extremes of endowment far greater than that found in ordinary schools. In Britain, when Schools for deaf children report on the use of manual instructional methods, it is usually reported for the latter part of school life when it has become obvious that there has been only minimal communication between teacher and pupil for many years. Even then signing is used by teachers lacking proficiency and often having learned what little they know from their own pupils. Partially-hearing children, able to use the same cognitive operations as their hearing teachers, advance very slowly but steadily through school curricula. But, as a generalization, the majority of deaf children remain in a private cognitive world which only touches, from time to time, that of their teachers. Whatever the "stuff" is which forms the substrate of their internal language, it is not speech.

It is easy to confuse rather narrow issues of academic standards with broader matters of social well-being. Discussing the oral-manual controversy, Lowell (1976) for instance asks what the agreed objectives are, whether, "performance on the Stanford Achievement Test, happiness, lip-reading skill, ability to earn a living, manual fluency, mental health, the size of the bank account of a family, or the intelligibility of speech" (p. 33). We have no way of knowing what the specific relationships are amongst these aims, but our task of assessment is simplified by his inclusion of the basic communication skills which have been central to our enquiry – and which no educator has minimized. Yet there has been little informed discussion of appropriate standards even for those abilities for which adequate measurement is readily available. Instead there is a curious polarization of attitude which seeks both to excuse the evident low standards and at the same time to deny that, for the majority of deaf children, they are in fact low. This is a recipe for inertia.

For instance, Watson (1976), speaking from the standpoint of training teachers of the deaf, remarks that, " . . . one is dissatisfied with the terminal attainments of pupils being educated by oral methods only" (p. 6) and urges the need to make the system work better. This is not a novel insight into the problem. Twenty years earlier, Lumsden (1953) had also made similar comments regarding standards: "It is said that they cannot speak intelligently, that they cannot write . . . that they cannot read . . ." (p. 71). Twenty years or more before that, Ewing (1930) commented that, "From time to time the criticism is made that 'oralism' is not what it was twenty years ago" (p. 53). Not only is there current dissatisfaction with standards of attainment but there has been for at least fifty years – but accompanied by no discernible shift in theoretical emphasis.

Reeves (1976) provides an exhaustive list of defects in the oral education of deaf children in Britain. These include inadequate numbers of especially trained teachers and high staff turnover, failure to diagnose deafness early enough, insufficient parental guidance, lack of amplification equipment of all kinds, both individual and group, together with inadequate servicing of what there is, poor facilities with respect to other classroom equipment, and poor design of purpose-built premises. This kind of shopping list is common in defence of oralism and its main interest is that it contains no item which bears on requirements for specifically oral education. As Reeves later says, "The same impoverished conditions will of course equally impair the progress of manual principles" (p. 16). Yet, while this is true as a generality, the relative effects of attempting to correct these various deficiencies are probably not equally significant for pure-oral education and for education which uses manual communication as well. Two items may be singled out for note.

Firstly, failure to diagnose deafness early enough becomes a particularly important defect when linguistic development is crucially based on the auditory channel. It delays the application of special intervention and especially provision of a hearing aid. But we should be clear that "early diagnosis" can become a delusory catch-phrase. Certainly special attention must be paid by welfare services to children at risk: those where there is a genetic risk and those cases where there has been a specific pre- or peri-natal risk. This kind of care may easily reach its practical limit even in an advanced society and still miss a substantial number of children. As we noted, most genetic deafness is recessive – only a few deaf children have a deaf parent. The presence of deafness in a family will not necessarily be visible to medical services at the birth of the child, and even reasonable enquiry of parents may not reveal it. With the greatest care likely to be provided by generally overworked medical services, a substantial proportion of risk cases is likely to be missed. A very high state of alertness will be needed, because many of the conditions which may result in a child being born deaf are statistically far more likely not to – though other defects may be expected. Fewer than one child per 1000 receives Special education because of deafness, and for only half of them is the deafness inherited. The specific causes of deafness of the remainder are numerous, and there seems to be ample opportunity for an at-risk infant to escape adequate test. The statistical improbability that deafness is present will in fact represent an optimum condition for missing such very rare events.

When the risk to the child has occured specifically during the pregnancy, the difficulties are compounded. Not only is the statistical element again present, but actual occurrence of an event which could cause deafness in the child may have been undetected or forgotten. In conventional practice, only after deafness has been diagnosed is the cause retrospectively established. Particularly amongst the socially more deprived sections of a community, the chance of detecting deafness shortly after the birth is exceedingly small. Once that opportunity is lost, audiological testing is unlikely to be sought until it is clearly evident that normal speech is not developing.

Since it is widely recognized that medical detection of at-risk children during early infancy is far from effective, mass audiological screening of all infants has often been urged (Downs and Storritt, 1967; Ewing, 1957). Ling (1975), though, points out that newborn infants have a very limited response repertoire and are likely to make the same response to an internally generated stimulus as to an external acoustic one. This could easily lead to classification of normal hearing when it may not be. Ling concludes that, "A simple screening test remains a feasible solution ... but it does require further development" (p. 128). In practice, as we reported earlier, at least half of the children who were in fact born deaf will not have deafness diagnosed before the age of three years. Now, while this critical period of auditory deprivation is serious for all children, it must be particularly so for those who are then expected to acquire exclusively oral language depending on the defective sensory system – including the possibility of damage extending into essential higher neural centres. With respect to early diagnosis of deafness, then, the inherent practical difficulties which extend beyond adequate financial provision could be regarded as particularly serious for effective operation of the principles of oralism. It might seem less inappropriate if, at that point, a linguistic intervention which substantially included visual inputs were undertaken. Were it possible to relate academic oral performance to age of diagnosis of deafness while controlling other relevant factors, we would be on surer ground. No such data are known to us.

A second broad condition claimed to impede the application of correct oral principles, particularly in the early years of education, is insufficient provision and maintenance of equipment for amplifying speech in classroom contexts. Generally this refers to group hearing aids which permit a teacher talking into a portable microphone to move around without changing the intensity and quality of sound reaching pupils. At the same time, the pupils themselves may be listening through headphones providing higher fidelity of sound, more contoured to their individual impairment, and with less ambient noise, than a personal hearing aid could offer.

Here again this is a sensible requirement for optimum communication, whether it be purely oral or oral augmented by signing. But the absence of any additional linguistic input in the former case – other than writing which is common to all systems – gives special significance to speech amplification. Yet poor facilities of this kind can be a hazardous excuse for poor oral standards. The benefits of amplification do not stand in a one-to-one relationship with degree of deafness. Indeed, the relationship is complex and far from fully understood. In general, as deafness increases, the contribution of amplification to auditory perception of speech diminishes. A point is reached when further amplification provides no further useful information, and may in fact cause physical pain. There is no theoretical way of specifying this point for any individual – though the pain threshold may of course easily be determined. But this does mean that claims for better equipment of this kind need to be justified by some audiological specification. This oralism has conspicuously evaded. Ling (1975) has expressed this authoritatively: "... even the highest possible level of sophistication in auditory programming cannot compensate fully, or even mainly, for severe or profound hearing impairment" (p. 134). No one can reasonably underestimate the need for optimum speech amplification, whether inside or outside classrooms. The issue is the educational cost when practice cannot reach best.

We have discussed here one pole of the defence of its record which oralism makes. The defence is largely based upon the claim that inadequate provision is made for correct application of the theoretical principles. On the contrary, we have suggested that many of those provisions are applicable to any style of education of deaf children and have no unique relevance to oralism. We have further suggested that certain conditions which would be particularly critical for oralism to succeed either cannot be met realistically or are invalid without further specification. No set of educational principles can survive for long when the conditions claimed to be essential for their implementation cannot be met realistically. Not only are the material resources of any society limited and subject to priorities, but the resources of knowledge and technology are limited as well. A viable educational principle must be capable of adapting, not merely to the special requirements of its clientele, but to the constraints which are imposed upon it by the socioeconomic system in which it operates. Until quite recently, oralism, solidly entrenched in the Western world, has not needed to defend its academic record. This is no longer possible. Curiously, there has never been the defence that, given the nature of the handicap, no more was possible than was already being accomplished. This might have made a sound theoretical case. It would, though, no doubt, sooner have opened the way for alternative theories. Rather, it deluded itself into believing that it had achieved success. Oralism created the legend of "oral success".

The concept of oral success

A classic defence of oralism relies on the example of deaf individuals who have become outstandingly successful members of society in spite of their handicap. While we do not doubt the value of these cases, they are extremely rare, and certainly far too few to sustain an educational system intended to encompass the majority of deaf children. The evidence of the detail we have presented can hardly be taken to reflect the achievement of a successful pedagogic theory. Inevitably adherents have searched for less vulnerable criteria than those deriving from measurement and statistical analysis. The greyness of, for instance, widespread illiteracy may occasionally be illumined by an outstanding individual, who then comes to be regarded as the norm – the average product of the system – or at least to represent the standard which most deaf children can attain. "I can only offer the evidence of many many successful oral, deaf persons", Lowell (1976) writes, 'If it could work for them, why not for everybody?" (p. 31).

These "oral successes" are people who, in spite of grave hearing impairment, nevertheless have achieved a level of oral communicative ability which virtually frees them from their hearing handicap, so that they achieve a social or professional status equal to the more successful hearing people. A certain mystique is involved here. It is not simply that these special people represent the top end of a normal distribution of ability – balancing extremely retarded people at the other end. It is rather as if some grace had been bestowed upon them in a way which marks them out. But, at the same time, they are regarded not as out of this world, but very much as shining examples of the heights that most or many deaf children can reach – so long as their educational treatment is equally correct. Ewing (1960), for example, referring to children who from an early age suffer from " . . . profound, subtotal, or in a small minority of cases, total deafness" nevertheless reports that, "A good many of them have gone far in achieving high occupational status" (p. 2/3). In assessing oral education, here we are on somewhat surer ground. These orally successful people exist – they do not await the arrival of the ideal educational conditions. They can be named and pointed to – and therefore their abilities can be observed and evaluated.

There are no agreed quantities which define an orally success-ful child, and there is the obvious danger that criteria become articles of negotiation, shifting according to whether or not they provide confirmation of the cherished hypothesis. There is the further problem concerning the point in time at which evaluation is made. Almost always – and with justification – oral success in an oral society only becomes evident when occupational status has been established. However, insofar as oral ability at school-leaving age can be accepted as a close correlate of subsequent oral success, the data we have may be of value; we have only the problem of agreeing to criteria.

More specifically, the problem is one of validity of criteria. The particular performance we assess must have some self-evident connotation of oral success and the *cachet* or authoritative external approval. We must also have a means of assessing it quantitatively using a measuring instrument widely accepted as valid for that skill. We believe we can meet these requirements with respect to speech intelligibility.

Clearly the ability to be understood through speech is by definition central in any concept of *oral* success. Fry (1975) has asserted that "there are many instances of children with very con-siderable losses of hearing, of the order of 80–100 dB, who ... have also learned to produced speech that is readily intelligible to the ordinary listener" (p. 148). But when we have isolated the true oral successes we still need some way of distinguishing be-tween statistical success and oral success which can be used as a model as Lowell has claimed is possible. Someone has to be top; ten children have to be top ten. This could be merely an outcome expected from the nature of nonspecific individual variation. A top group could also be characterized by the presence of specific innate and definable factors, which when present are likely to place their oral performance at the highest levels. Thirdly, they could be top principally because of exposure to a particularly favourable programme of intervention. Both in the sense of oral success used by Ewing and by Fry, and particularly in the more everyday use of the term, it is clear that "oral successes" are such because of some prescribed treatment. If oral successes are born and not made, then the concept can have no part in a philosophy of education.

In trying to identify and clarify oral success, two methods of approach are available – statistical and clinical. Using the first method, we formulate hypotheses concerning factors which might contribute to oral success. Then using what knowledge we have of our available population, we can formally test the hypotheses. In using the clinical approach, we first find the oral successes, and we then look at them, in which ever ways are open to us, searching for characteristics which they share to a degree not found in the remainder of the population.

In our study we have used a measure, the definition of which happens to correspond closely to Fry's requirement; and the measurers themselves have impeccable qualifications. We have teachers' ratings of speech made with reference to ordinary listeners, and which consist of a statement of how readily the speech might be understood. We might therefore be justified in arguing that orally successful children are those who (1) are sufficiently deaf for the term "success' to be relevant, and (2) are rated by their teachers either as 1 or 2 on our scale; that is, their speech is either "wholly intelligible" or "fairly easy to understand." Beyond those ratings, speech becomes increasingly difficult to understand. With regard to degree of deafness, our classificatory system suggests a level of greater than 85 dB as convenient for investigation. In any absolute sense, we see little point in attributing oral successfulness to partially-hearing children, preferring to restrict the enquiry to the more testing level proposed by Ewing. We may then count the number of such children and leave it at that.

Speech quality then is an appropriate point from which to start. We have noted that there are very few deaf children in Partially Hearing Units. In our PHU populaton there is only 1 child with rated good speech and whose hearing loss is greater than 85 dB. The early medical history of this child was not known to the school she attended and we have excluded her from this particular enquiry. All subsequent discussion then refers to children in Schools. We also noted in Chapter 8 that speech ratings were not obtained from the first 2 Schools at which we tested. At one of these, all of the profoundly-deaf children had very poor speech scores on measurement. At the second School, only 1 child had a hearing loss greater than 85 dB; his measured speech score was only slightly better than the median for the whole population. Our enquiry then concerns 198 children, the remainder not reaching the 86 dB criterion of deafness.

Within this population of roughly 200 children, 21 were rated by their teachers as either 1 (n = 4) or 2 (n = 17). We can provisionally regard these as "oral successes". Although we cannot be certain about their earliest degree of deafness, 19 were born deaf and the other 2 deafened shortly after. Their good speech does therefore seem to be a genuine achievement meriting further enquiry.

There is a widespread assumption that the role of the School itself, since speech is necessarily taught, is an important contributing factor. If all Schools are equally successful, then the factor disappears. On the other hand, if all of the successful 10% came from a single School, the evidence in favour of the particular techniques of this one School would be compelling. The matter is complicated by the already noted fact that only about 50% of children spend their entire school life in one School. But a School factor remains a possibility. In fact, to achieve oral success, it is not necessary to avoid changes of School. More of our "oral successes" – 14 out of 21 – change School than remain single–School children. Furthermore, at the time we tested, these 21 children were in 12 different Schools and, between them since the age of five years, they had passed through 24 different Schools. The 4 children who achieved a rating of 1, had all passed through several. There is not the slightest evidence therefore that a unique School factor itself contributes enough to the speech quality aspect of oral success to merit serious consideration.

We should perhaps examine our criteria for oral success in more detail. Our 21 successes were chosen on the basis of their rated speech. But orally successful children who achieve "high occupational status" will do so only if all of their oral skills are exceptional. We know that performance scores of oral skills show substantial correlation with each other. But for the term to have useful meaning, orally successful children should be outstanding at all oral skills. Because we have no absolute standard for lip reading we have no means of determining from our data which children are outstanding. We can say who is best, but this establishes nothing absolute. With reading we do have certainty. How would we assess children rated as having very intelligible speech, but who were unable to read? They might conceivably be orally successful but be undetected, very rare dyslexics. But they might also be children whose deafness was slow to develop so that their speech was close to normal before their deafness became profound. In any case, it is clear that such children would be unlikely to achieve the occupational status that Ewing designates.

The children in our study who have a reading age commensurate with their chronological age will have test scores at least at the fifteen-year-old level. We would expect general agreement to the proposition that reading at that level would be outstanding performance for a profoundly-deaf child, though merely average for a hearing school-leaver. We could of course set the criterion lower. But first we need a solid – and valid – peg to tie performance to, and then we need to remember that the concept of oral success aims high in exceptional children. To satisfy the claims that are made for such children we must accept severe criteria.

Only 5 children with a hearing loss greater than 85 dB have a reading age of more than fifteen years. Of these, just 1 also has highly rated speech quality; 1 out of 198. In fact the success concept is little supported by degrading the criteria. Accepting a reading age of fourteen years adds only 3 more children. Whatever the reasons for the particularly good speech of our 21 oral successes, for most of them, their prowess is restricted to speech.

The concept of the exceptional child who, in spite of the handicap of profound deafness, nevertheless succeeds in establishing himself socially and economically on a par with successful hearing people has become fundamental to the credibility of the philosophy of exclusively oral education. As with other intensely demanding systems of conduct, legends are needed – heroic figures, who are heroic not by chance circumstances of history, but because all those concerned, directly and indirectly, with their education have conformed doggedly and devotedly to the rules. Explicitly then, where one has trod others may follow.

We have found virtually nothing to support this legend. Nor have others. Jarvik, Salzberger, and Falek (1963) report a study in which, using all reasonable means, the whole of New York State was searched for "deaf persons of outstanding achievement". Since this study included everyone who had left school, the population involved would have been of substantial size. Though the method lacked precision, because of the self-containedness of deaf society, it is unlikely that many qualified people would have been missed. The authors found 14 such people who had become deaf before the age of three years. Of these 14, 8 attended college and 3

obtained an advanced degree of MA or PhD. The authors conclude that, "Few if any ... would qualify as persons of outstanding attainment amongst the hearing" (p. 140). It would be idle and
bigoted to pretend that profoundly-deaf people do not have potential for success in our society. We will indeed argue the opposite in
a later section. Every society has outstanding people. Some of
them will be deaf. But we should not too readily assume that their
success is a direct consequence of an educational theory. Adopting
an admittedly fairly tough but also realistic standard, the single
genuine oral success we have uncovered provides no basis for
extravagant claims. There is a second and less radical form of the
myth of oral success that we now want to discuss.

The unsuccessful "minority"

As objective information about school achievement has become
more widely available, assertion of the universal benefits of oral
education has become increasingly suspect as teachers themselves
view the outcome of their own endeavours, and parents of deaf
children become aware of the discrepancy between promise and
fulfilment. Protagonists of oralism have accordingly introduced a
qualification into their now more muted claims. Oralism is
regarded as the correct form of educational intervention but with
an excluder. This appears in the quotation from Fry on p. 305,
while van Dijk and van Uden (1976) also state only that "A great
number of deaf children are able to learn to speak intelligibly" (p.
72). These authors, then, conventionally qualify the statement by
reference to the late age at which hearing aids are prescribed – a
defence to which we have already referred – and to the harmful
contagion of signing, which we shall come to shortly. Again, Ling
(1975) also reports that "With adequate training, most hearing-
impaired children can be taught to speak intelligibly" (p. 137). So,
while caution is justifiable, we are inclined to detect the insertion
of a loop-hole into these claims.

Usually a casual attempt is made to specify which kinds of
children constitute the minority who do not benefit from oral
education and require some other treatment – invariably then
stated to be manual communication. We regard these attempts as
casual advisedly, since they include the more obvious characteristics always likely to be found at one end of a distribution of cogni-

tive ability. For example, an authoritative statement taken from a Memorandum of the British National College of Teachers of the Deaf (1972) says that "It may be, for instance, that some profoundly or severely deaf children who are also mentally handicapped may find their only means of communication in some simple system of signs" (p. 10). Watson (1976) cites children with "low ability", or "additional handicap" and a general category who appear, " . . . to have some specific disorder which seemed to be militating against the satisfactory development of oral methods of communication" (p. 6), though he does not otherwise specify what the disorder might be. Van Dijk and van Uden consider that some deaf children fail to profit from oralism because of "dyspraxia" which may be detected by a test of finger dexterity. Markides (1976) cites additional handicap, severe subnormality, "and other disorders" not specified either, as characterizing the "small percentage" of deaf children who, " . . . do not benefit from oral methodologies" (p. 310). John and Howarth (1973) exclude children with "apparent or *concealed* additional handicaps" (p. 103) (our italics); Lowell (1976) those with "neurological involvements". In this way an insubstantial and unsubstantiated image is created with minimum specificity of an elastic population of children who must first be discarded before oralism can be properly evaluated. Mindel and Vernon (1971) refer to these children as those who have been failed by the oral method.

Nevertheless, the signing alternative, which is then usually suggested as a last resort, is also regarded as dangerous, almost hostile; teachers feel superstitiously threatened by its use. We noted earlier Hemmings' (1972) comment that teachers in Partially Hearing Units felt this way. It is explicitly voiced by van Dijk and van Uden: "Even when the parents are very successful in teaching their deaf children to lip-read and speak at a very early age, this success is often threatened when . . . the child comes in contact with children who make a lot of signs" (p. 74). As we have seen, there is not the slightest evidence that fluently signing children are behind others in language skills. Elsewhere, van Uden (1970) again catches the feeling of threat when he refers to signing children, " . . . building up a primitive own world-view, different from ours . . ." and which will make the teaching of "our oral language" more difficult (p. 75).

There is an unresolved paradox in the role that oralism does see for signing in schools. It is regarded both as a dangerous influence from which children should be protected, and also as suitable for an alleged minority of children who do not benefit from oral instruction. It seems strange that the children most in need of help for the development of their communicative ability are offered no better than the educationally "inferior" and "harmful" alternative. Whatever the dangers of sign language are for the bright, deaf child, we have to assume that they will be equally or more potent for those even more cognitively handicapped.

Oralism has never systematically accepted the need to resolve this paradox. Nor does it provide or attempt to develop principles for educational provision when these radically different options are available – and accepted as being available. Instead, an ad hoc collection of conditions is permitted which when present exempt the teacher from using oral methods and from teaching oral skills. Little unifies these conditions other than that they all use labels which reflect deprivation of some kind. Oddly, no data have then ever been presented which relate to the ability of these children to learn sign language.

The one attribute which might have been thought to be a bar to full oral education – that is, profound deafness – is not usually cited. We say this in view of the data on rated speech we presented in Chapter 8. On the contrary, a number of authorities have referred to profound deafness specifically as being compatible with oral methods. Apart from Fry's (1975) reference to children with losses up to 100 dB, Furness (1972) refers to losses in excess of 85 dB. Van Dijk and van Uden (1976) are explicit that the "deaf" children who can learn to speak intelligibly have hearing losses greater than 90 dB. Nicholas (1976) refers to children with losses "from 90 dB to 130 dB", but nevertheless receiving oral education, " . . . with emphasis on sound perception training" (p. 28).

In fact, there is a notable confusion with respect to how deaf "deaf" is if speech is to be intelligible. In an earlier account Fry (1966) had also argued that even small amounts of hearing could be used in the development of speech by appropriate methods. He stated that, " . . . we may say that the amount of speech a child develops depends not so much on the amount of hearing *per se* as upon the use he is able to make of his hearing for language learning" (p. 201). He then presented 3 illustrative audiograms of children who " . . . all acquired excellent speech . . ." (p. 202). Averaging across the conventional five speech frequencies, these 3 children have better-ear hearing losses of 62, 64, and 65 dB respectively. Excellent speech with this level of hearing loss accords well of course with our own data, but helps little when much greater losses are involved. Ewing and Ewing (1964) also provide audiograms of 2 children who early acquired good speech. One shows an average loss of 77 dB, the other of 65 dB.

It is true that the contribution of deafness itself to the development of different oral skills varies considerably. But contrary to oralist doctrine it does contribute massively to the key oral skill, speech; and the effect threads through the quality of vocal speech and into the development of oral thinking. But this does not lead us to propose that there is a specifiable level of hearing loss beyond which it is pointless to teach speech. Almost the contrary. We see the issue not as when should speech not be taught, but what conditions merit the additional use of other – and we are thinking principally of manual – media. The oral protagonist is locked into a vulnerable paradigm which precludes level of hearing loss as a factor in determining which child might require alternative treatment; because oralism is designed to defeat deafness. The concept of a notional "minority" unable to benefit from oralism appears to border on fantasy, as soon as attainment is objectively looked at. Furthermore, impairment of oral skill is evident not just with profound hearing loss, but with quite minor loss of hearing.

Partial hearing and oral deficit

Jensema et al. (1978) report that of children with losses no greater than 55 dB, only 51% had speech rated as "very intelligible". Extracting a comparable value from our own data, i.e., for losses up to 55 dB, we find 41% rated by teachers as "wholly intelligible", both for Special Schools and for PHUs. Johnson (1962) examined the speech quality of deaf children considered to be suitable for education in ordinary schools. He used the total population from one education authority in England – yielding 68 children with a hearing loss greater than 30 dB. Of the 16 children whose loss was 30–49 dB, only 4 were given the top speech rating. VandenBerg (1971b) also examined deaf children in ordinary schools in New Zealand of whom three-quarters had a hearing loss of less than 51 dB. Of her sample, 44% were given the top speech rating by their own teachers. We clearly see here the very marked effect of even quite small degrees of deafness in a skill which is closely associated with level of oral thinking.

Comparable retardation can be seen for other oral skills. Our own data show the least-deaf group to be already some five years behind in prose comprehension. To date, the relevant value for the USA in terms of reading grade cannot be extracted from available sources, but from the evidence it seems likely that again it will be close to our own. Elsewhere, Kodman (1963) and Quigley and Thomore (1968) both reported deficits of up to three years in attainment of children in ordinary schools with losses of 40–55 dB. Goetzinger (1962) shows language retardation of up to one year in children with losses of only 30–35 dB. Ling (1959) reported on the reading ability of children with losses which were less than 25 dB. Most of them were in ordinary schools, and probably would be today. As a group, the children were above average intelligence, but reading was still retarded by fifteen months. Vernon and Billingslea (1973) discuss deaf children in ordinary schools in Maryland, USA, the majority of whom also had a hearing loss of less than 25 dB. Again "educational achievement" showed an average retardation of a year.

When even the very minor losses that we have just been discussing can result in all too easily detectable retardation of oral ability, it seems inherently unlikely that identical pedagogic procedures could permit profoundly-deaf children to realize their cognitive potential. Clearly children who are just mildly hard-of-hearing are unable to cope in the ordinary classroom at average performance levels. When hearing loss reaches no more than 50 – 60 dB, the additional advantage of Special education with small class sizes and specialized equipment still leaves them massively educationally impaired and vocationally gravely handicapped.

Sign language

We have shown how closely educational achievement is constrained by biological endowment. The case for reexamining principles with the hindsight knowledge now available from many sources seems irrefutable. A system which can justly be said to achieve so little must offer itself for reconsideration; a few anecdotes count little against so great a weight of quantitative evidence. In fact the only change for which there is at present sufficient experience to merit examination is that which involves the addition of manual communication.

Essentially, use of sign language has its impact educationally as a means of evading hearing deficit. It emphasizes a visual mode of language which, unlike lip reading, provides a linguistic signal which is easily perceived. No special equipment is needed to converse in sign language and, though lacking the omni-directionality of speech for a normally-hearing person, it is probably usable over greater physical distance than speech. It may well be that the hearing world has opted for spoken, rather than sign, language, only because sign is useless until attention has been gained, and because sign requires exclusive use of limbs ideally adapted for other essential functions. What for the moment we might call "signing" rather than "sign language", is a system of gestures principally centred on the hands and used for interpersonal communication. In its most rudimentary form, therefore, its use is common experience. Signing used by deaf people may also purposefully use arms, facial gesture, and fingers.

Here we might separate out finger spelling itself. Finger spelling is a means of representing letters of an alphabet of a spoken language. The words represented are not a native part of vernacular signing, but it is used when no sign is readily known to the people conversing. The extent of the use of finger spelling during conversation varies greatly depending on the content of conversation and the people engaged in it. The English language and most others (Carmel, 1975) can be used without any speech at all simply by finger spelling each word. It began to be used formally as a medium of instruction for deaf people in the early part of the seventeenth century in conjunction with reading, as a preliminary to teaching spoken language. Most finger-spelling alphabets are represented using the fingers of one hand. But two-handed alphabets are in use in Great Britain (though not Eire) and many areas which once formed the British Empire, in Yugoslavia which shares many configurations with the British system, and for some letters in the Italian system. As an exclusive mode of communication, finger spelling is generally regarded as too slow, though surprisingly fast transmission rates can be achieved by highly practised users. We noted earlier the extensive use of finger spelling during the early stages of education in the Soviet Union to teach vocabulary, and for one hundred years (since 1878) finger spelling together with simultaneous speech has been used at the Rochester School for the Deaf in the USA (the "Rochester Method").

Where finger spelling – like Morse code – is an exact translation of the alphabetic elements of another language, signing is generally an autonomous gestural system with morphological and grammatical forms independent of the spoken language of the society to which the deaf sign-users belong. The history of the earliest development of signing is as obscure as we would expect for behaviour which is so natural. The fact of gesture as a medium of communication needs no discussion. In recent years, though, a rapidly growing body of research has been concerned with whether we could validly talk about "sign *language*" – the question of whether the system of communication by sign is based on the kind of rules which linguists regard as determining characters of a language; the "... use of a finite, though complex, set of units and rules which allow the generation of an unlimited variety of sentences" (Bonvillian, Nelson, and Charrow, 1976).

The majority of these studies have centred on American Sign Language (ASL) and conclusions reached with respect to ASL may need qualification when applied to British Sign Language (BSL) or any other. One reason for this is that ASL has retained that essential characteristic of a living language, free and rich usage. Signing is a principal medium of instruction at the major colleges for higher education, and at Gallaudet College facility in ASL is a requirement for teaching staff. The outcome of these studies leaves us with little doubt about the linguistic status of ASL. Cicourel and Boese (1972a, p. 226) refer to its "... capacity to generate a system of manual signals that makes distinctive use of physical space for generating a non-oral system of communication."

Following on Stokoe's (1960) description of grammatical regularities, Lane, Boyes-Braem, and Bellugi (1976) have made a detailed analysis of the systematic way that space is used in ASL, defining four parameters of which a sign may be composed: shape of the hand, location of the hand, orientation of the palm, and movement of the hand. In a sense this description is an analogue of the description of phonetic features of spoken language. So much so that, pertinently, Bellugi et al. (1974) showed that signs which shared common features, like words which share common phonemes, are difficult to recall serially. Far from being the crude pantomime which sign language detractors have suggested and which could only represent the simplest communicative concept, ASL at least is capable of expressing remarkable linguistic nuance in a systematic manner.

The vocabulary of sign languages has often been assumed to consist of relatively few iconic gestures. Unquestionably there are many such signs with observable relationship to their referents (Charrow, 1974), giving rise to the notion that there is an international sign language which is universally used by deaf people. Battison and Jordan (1976), though, report that deaf people from different cultures have considerable difficulty understanding each other – the case with spoken languages – and that only the small proportion of signs of different sign languages which are iconic tend to be shared. Sign languages, like spoken languages, have ancient origins and individual histories. When at one time there had been commonality, as in the case of ASL and the sign language of Paris from which it was borrowed in the eighteenth century, Woodward and Ertin (1975) have estimated that today only about 25% of signs are still common. The fact is that, depending on the degree to which a sign language has been allowed to flourish in a society, it may have a substantial and effective vocabulary undergoing, as we would expect, continuous change and development. Bellugi and Klima (1972) point out that ASL has a vocabulary permitting discussion of topics such as religion, politics, and ethics, and lends itself to humour, poetry, and even whispering. In many ways it may have a richer and more expressive vocabulary than many spoken languages. ASL, for example, can represent nuance as between chronic and passing sickness, serious or minor sickness, feigned or genuine sickness.

A further potent area of confusion concerns the syntax both of ASL and BSL. It is commonly argued that sign language should not be used in schools because it is "ungrammatical". Stokoe (1971) has clarified this in pointing out that some signs may be produced concurrently when the words of spoken languages are always sequential. Fischer (1971) notes that a sign may be repeated, without necessarily indicating a plural, and that meaning may depend upon the rate of repetition. What perhaps most facilely strikes the hostile observer is the fact that the grammar of, for instance, BSL does not follow the rules of English. As Brennan (1975) notes, "Once stated, the absurdity of the claim is immediately apparent: we do not expect Russian, French, Turkish or Gaelic to conform to English norms, so why BSL?" (p. 474).

It would be as well to recognize that there is indigenous in probably most countries, and certainly in Britain, a vernacular sign language which is *the* language of the deaf community – a community of people whose degree of hearing-impairment bars them from natural and easy social intercourse with hearing people.

Some learn sign language from their deaf parents as mother-tongue in exactly the same way as do hearing infants. Some learn it later as an acquired language though they may be more fluent and comfortable in it than in their society's spoken language. It becomes their mother-tongue. Language is persistent, and even in schools which formally ban its use, sign is still used surreptitiously. In most schools in Britain it is openly the language of the playground and dormitory. It may contain a good many finger-spelled words which are English words, but usually it is not simply English in translation: it is itself.

In spite of suppression, and a good deal of repression, children persist in passing to each other the mysteries of this medium, which, from these unformalized origins, continue into adult life. In view of the levels of skill reached in the alternative modes offered by schools, we need hardly be surprised. The fact that ASL is in daily use as a medium for higher education suggests that, like other organic growth, climate is a significant factor. In practice in Britain, the manual language in common adult use is a pidgin sign language which is neither pure vernacular nor an exact form of signed English. It borrows freely from both and from finger spelling. Nevertheless, anyone who has addressed an audience of profoundly-deaf people via a signing interpreter is left in no doubt about the general effectiveness; even quite technical material spoken in English generates questions and discussion as relevant as would obtain were the audience hearing. We must therefore consider whether manual communication can provide easier access to oral language than does its exclusion.

Bilingual education for deaf children

Two considerations which we have adequately discussed are of the greatest relevance. The first is the dominating way in which degree of hearing loss limits the quality of vocal speech, and in consequence limits the degree to which internalized speech becomes available as a vehicle for thinking. The second consideration is the possibility, and perhaps the high probability, that insistence upon exclusively oral language at a very early age in fact results in a developmental deprivation of linguistic input which may well put young children at unacceptable neurological risk. At the same time we see every justification for persisting with the objective of a high standard of oral language ability by the end of school life. We do not have an instant blueprint for realizing this goal. But there does seem to be an *a priori* case for discussion of formal bilingual education, using a sign and oral language, instead of the current repression of the only language in which deaf children rapidly acquire facility and in which they so obviously feel comfortable. Cicuourel and Boese (1972b) express the problem succinctly: "The oral teacher of the deaf may assume that she is teaching the child his native language because he is learning to use his vocal cords. . . . But what (she) is actually doing is teaching this deaf child a second language" (p. 40).

Bilingualism in children is common enough. Migrations of peoples: Europeans, Mexicans, Puerto Ricans to the USA, Asians to Britain, Europeans and North Africans to Israel, have amply demonstrated the ease, both cognitive and emotional, with which children fluently use two languages. It is the monolingual person who is startled when a child from a Chinese-speaking home addresses us in pure Cockney-dialect English. Indeed, Hornby (1977) notes that "for a large percentage of the peoples of the world, speaking more than one language is a natural way of life" (p. 1). Schlesinger and Meadow (1972) point out that genuine bilingual pathology – at one time a popular misconception – only occurs when the bilingualism is accompanied by an emotional crisis of identity. True manual-oral bilingualism is virtually unknown amongst deaf people – and for obvious reasons. But it is common amongst hearing children of deaf parents, for whom sign is often mother-tongue, with oral language developing as a second language. Many of these people become professional interpreters. Mayberry (1976) studied 8 such children aged three-seven years, all of whose parents used sign language. Even at that age, none of the children was considered to be defective in oral ability which was sufficiently acquired outside the home. Charrow and Fletcher (1974) looked at the converse case. They compared the way in which deaf children with deaf parents, and deaf children with hearing parents, respectively learned English – both groups being compared with hearing foreign students. Not only were the students with deaf parents better readers than the other deaf group, but, on a formal test of English as a foreign language, it was clear that like the foreign hearing students, they had learned English as a second language, and apparently had benefitted thereby.

It is now beyond dispute, not merely that deaf infants in a

signing home learn sign language as a first language, but that they learn it in the same cognitive manner and at least as fast as hearing children learn their first language (Bonvillian et al., 1976; Brown, 1977; Klima and Bellugi, 1972; Schlesinger and Meadow, 1972). Most of these studies have been made in the optimum linguistic conditions of a signing home where both parents were deaf and sign the primary language. For the vast majority of deaf children these conditions do not hold; very few hearing parents are likely to be fluent users of sign language. Curiously, well-documented accounts of progress by deaf children in learning sign language in circumstances when it is taught by hearing people are rare, though it is happening in many places. Evans (1978) provides a very detailed account of the introduction of one-handed finger spelling into a residential School for deaf children in England; children aged seven-sixteen years made very substantial progress within one year. Fenn and Rowe (1975) report a study of 7 deaf children aged about ten years who were also mentally extremely subnormal and had varying degrees of spasticity. Initially none had linguistic ability beyond single-word signs. At the end of a six-month programme using the Paget-Gorman Sign System, they reported that the children could understand and express a wide variety of semantic structures. In fact though, we do not need more studies to demonstrate that deaf children easily acquire sign language. To assume neural structures and organization specified only for spoken language is patently untenable. The fact that both deaf and hearing children with deaf parents fluently use sign as a primary language in early childhood – and with little exception – establishes manual communication as a natural development in conditions comparable to those in which oral language naturally develops. That is not the problem. The problems of educating deaf children in bilingual manual and oral modes are practical – and many remain unsolved.

The most obvious concern pupil selection. Which children qualify for bilingual education and which children should be restricted to oral only? One approach would be to argue that any child deemed to require Special education because of deafness requires bilingual education. If this seems alarmist we might remind ourselves of the educational retardation of hard-of-hearing children. A suitable hearing aid will, in good listening conditions, bring the hearing of these children close to the normal range. Just the same it is evident that the linguistic input they have received is inadequate.

It would be difficult to determine whether this is simply due to practical problems of immediate environmental acoustics alone, or whether their retardation is compounded by continuous minor attrition of neurological function from their earliest years. The case for bilingual education is based on the possibility that, by school age, even hard-of-hearing children may have sustained enough neurological deficit to impair full utilization of linguistic information received exclusively through auditory pathways. Stated thus simplistically, once the need for Special education had been identified, it would not merely be technologically augmented normal education, but education adapted specifically to the linguistic handicap as well – at least in the earliest stages.

It is easier to see the criterion problem from the other end. Any child who reaches school age with no spoken vocabulary, whether receptive or expressive, requires a manual-language input. To some large extent this deficit itself will be determined by degree of hearing loss, but all of those well-known factors which distinguish between a privileged and a deprived home will play some part. From the available evidence it seems likely that even children with relatively small hearing-impairments will benefit. In fact it is probable that children with pure-tone losses greater than about 85 dB will without exception require and, if offered, develop a primary sign language. As with any kind of educational placement, a high degree of pragmatic compromise will necessarily occur. What does seem essential from all that we have said is that the deaf child from a hearing home should be offered rehabilitation as soon as is practicable – emphasizing the need for early audiological assessment as much as oral education does. On the evidence, what we foresee is that signing would be fluent within a few years, a situation we may contrast with the gross oral language impoverishment of the school-leavers we have reported on. We may assume that the neurological hazards of delaying a sign language input are as grave as delaying any other linguistic input, but with the compensation that, when sign is introduced, progress will be much less retarded as compared with an input dependent on a defective sensory system. Above all, since we see no circumstance which would justify excluding speech from the language environment, insofar as there is error when deciding the kind of intervention which is appropriate, it is of the fail-safe type.

The problem likely to be of greatest significance, and which clearly requires clarification of theoretical principles, concerns the nature of the specific sign language used. Here we need to be clear about the practical goals; to determine in the context of language usage what the language is for. Educationally this is a unique question which is not applicable to hearing children except those with very severe speech pathology. With deaf children we really do face the problem of what language to teach, knowing it will be the primary language. Even then, the question of what the primary language is for is far from straightforward. In the first place, every society has a native sign language – ASL in the USA, BSL in Britain. But it is mother-tongue only for those deaf children for whom deafness is already present in the home, and it is unlikely to be pure. We have seen that the grammar of true vernacular sign language bears little relationship to the grammar of societal languages, which all deaf children must be taught to read. But at the simpler interpersonal level of communication the key questions concern delineation of who is "talking" to whom, and for what purpose. Essentially, four kinds of discourse occur. Deaf children with each other; deaf children with teachers for whom special training in sign becomes mandatory; deaf children with other members of their family who may, but need not, learn a sign language; deaf children and all of the rest of their society.

Because of the grammatical and vocabulary differences we have referred to, neither ASL nor BSL translate verbatim into English; nor is there a written version. This absence of a written sign language, though not unusual amongst languages, creates unusual problems for educators willing to use sign language but wishing to teach their pupils to read English. This problem has led to the development of modified sign languages which use, in varying degree, vernacular signs where possible but with additional "markers". These indicate inflection such as tense which may not be required in the sign language. They also use "word" (i.e., sign) order reflecting the order of written English. These are languages of compromise – not used in a derogatory sense – and may well become a child's mother-tongue in conditions of relevance.

Bornstein (1973) has described a number of varieties of these contrived languages and the problems associated with their development. For example, note the fact that word order is not the same in English and BSL – though this is equally true of English and other spoken languages. Then a single English word, (e.g.) *train*, has two quite different meanings which are represented by two different signs in BSL. Both English and sign languages have developed compound words and compound signs independently; two signs cannot always be meaningfully put together to make one English compound – nor vice versa. Nevertheless, considerable strides have been made to represent the grammatical English of prose in nonvernacular sign languages.

Perhaps the most significant difference amongst these artificial sign languages is the extent to which they do use vernacular signs in their vocabulary. The first such formal system devised by Paget (1951), which has developed into the Paget–Gorman Sign System (Craig, 1976), and is in some use in Britain, virtually excludes any signs of BSL. But it has a basic vocabulary of some 3000 words together with markers to form plurals, possessives, etc. Bornstein describes 5 American systems in use, all of which do use some of the signs of ASL. Of the basic 2500 signs of Signed English (Bornstein, 1973), which is intended for the child aged one-six years, 1700 are drawn from ASL. All of these systems have the common features of being capable of direct translation into and from English. The same features mean that they can be used concurrently with spoken English. In practice, at least in Britain, it is unusual to see pure vernacular sign in use. Apart from personal deviations into unformalized signed English, finger spelling is in considerable use. There is some justification when educators criticize sign language on the grounds of its unsystematized usage. This is particularly relevant criticism for Britain. But the situation has developed directly from the hostility of educators to manual communication, forcing it into clandestine status, ignoring its classroom potential, and failing to train teachers to use it.

Any signed form of English will be learned more easily by people for whom English is already their mother-tongue, since the grammatical rules will be known. Because most languages have many of their own unique grammatical features, we would expect teachers, parents, and siblings of deaf children to be able to learn signed English far more easily than they would learn most other foreign languages or vernacular sign. It is also true that, in most schools, children already fluent in vernacular sign are influential in generating a linguistic culture based on that language. This is not a negative feature. The useful and more easily learned vocabulary will be naturally absorbed into the prevailing system of signed English, and the rules of finger spelling can be learned in minutes. However, the argument is not really evenly balanced. For the child with no language, there will probably be little difference in ease of learning vernacular or a form of signed English – though if it is taught by teachers who themselves have had to learn it as a second language, there is a strong likelihood of advantage for signed English. Here we have to consider the balance of users, the minority of children in signing homes against the majority who are not. In any case we would envisage that the signed English taught would be maximally based on vernacular sign with respect to vocabulary, so that children fluent in vernacular would in fact have a built-in advantage over those without language at all.

Of comparable importance is the fact that children will need to learn to read. There are self-evident advantages when coming to learn how to read, in already knowing the grammar in which the printed language is written. Vernacular sign will not provide this, and signed English will for English. This also applies, though to a lesser extent, with respect to lip reading; to a lesser extent because a good deal of the difficulty lies in decoding the stimulus as well as in knowing the language.

If vernacular sign is attempted concurrently with English speech, one or other will be paraphrase. While in many instances this may not matter, it is not easy to see when it might be beneficial. But, particularly for children who have some usable hearing, and are still at the stage of learning both sign and spoken language, noncongruent information could readily confuse. It is indeed easy to parody a classroom situation of linguistic confusion, with various forms of signing contemporaneously in use. Yet in fact it is likely, except in degree, to be little different from the language flexibility of inner-urban schools with ethnically and socially mixed populations, so familiar to socio-linguists – as well as to teachers and children. Finally, we see no justification for silent signing at infant level, and probably at no school level.

The question of the need for sign in education of deaf children is essentially theoretical. The question of specific sign systems is an independent one involving practical decisions requiring study and care, but not much fundamental research. In spite of the foothold in Britain enjoyed by the Paget-Gorman Sign System, the fact that its vocabulary has little relationship to vernacular BSL seems to carry nothing but disadvantage. Yet Britain has no other system of signed English in use. The system of Signed English (Bornstein, 1973) which is widely used in the USA, and amply supported by reading texts, has many attractive features. It is of course based on ASL for its vocabulary. In general, as Battison and Jordan (1976) pointed out, similarity between vernacular sign languages is largely restricted to iconic signs, and little might be lost at the infant level. The relevance of existing American reading material, consisting of coloured picture stories accompanied both by printed words and pictures of hand signs, would need to be determined and possibly heavily adapted. This will be greatly assisted by the publication of the first comprehensive dictionary of BSL (Hayhurst, in press).

The essential characteristic of a system of signed English is that it must be easy for children to learn. Whether or not it is also more or less expressive as a language than some other system is less important. In principle it could be as expressive as English – which suffices. One fortuitous factor in the ease with which deaf children – though not necessarily teachers or parents – will learn it is the extent to which it can use the vocabulary and phrases of BSL without violating English usage. There would be no advantage in adopting an American system if much of the benefit of the usage of BSL is thereby lost. The goal of an international sign language for the deaf has low priority in primary education.

Here we may briefly summarize the pedagogic aspects of the case for bilingualism. First, we should be clear that it will not improve the intelligibility of children's speech – though it will give them more to say. Because of this, it will not greatly increase the use of oral thinking except as spin-off from extended linguistic knowledge; that is, more words available, intelligible to the speaker, which can be used in a greater variety of linguistic contexts. What it will do is to provide valuable additional options for internal language representation which is not degraded by a sensory defect. When only oral language is actually taught, which will include phonic reading, deaf children with little fluency in sign may spontaneously discover the value of thinking in print. Their education will in no way foster this, since in most cases it will be an unfamiliar cognitive mode for most (hearing) teachers. The introduction of sign which is grammatically compatible with speech and print immediately brings the option of a third cognitive mode, which may have the advantage of being equally sequential in character. Children can choose to internalize the language which for them best meets the criteria for internalization we have discussed, perceptual discriminability and expressive consistency. Nor is there any reason why two or more should not coexist as they do with all bilingually fluent people. We assume that choice will be heavily dependent on degree of deafness. But there will be choice, where oralism provides none. The benefit of this need not be argued. A number of studies have shown that, when information is provided to deaf subjects in more than one mode concurrently, then more information passes (Evans, 1978; Johnson, 1976; Klopping, 1971; White and Stevenson, 1975). Whether the effect is based on a process of enhancement of cues or whether it merely provides greater freedom of choice is irrelevant in practical terms. This facility which has been proven for interpersonal communication can hardly be inoperable in the case of communication with one's self.

The case for educating deaf children bilingually in sign and speech can be argued on theoretical grounds, but not proved other than by post hoc evaluation. We have argued against oralism theoretically and have supported criticism equally by post hoc evaluation. Facts are events which have already occurred, and the outcomes of oral education cannot be evaded. Nor can they much change because there is no evident way that oralism can change the relationship between hearing loss, speech intelligibility, and oral thinking. We see no valid possibility that bilingual education could retard a deaf child's linguistic development; only specious arguments that it could have been advanced. Oralism has proved rigid in its applications, leaving handicapped children to devise devious ways of asserting their need to communicate. An unusual and wholly advantageous feature of bilingual instruction of deaf children, when signed English and speech are used, is that the two modes may be used concurrently. No question therefore arises of when to use one language and when the other. Bilingualism offers a child continuous choice. The freedom to hear what can be heard and the freedom to escape the crushing insistence on a phonetic system for which the child may have no audiological correlate.

It has become a cliché that the oral-manual controversy is now sterile and unimportant. Yet the oral method continues in Britain and elsewhere as established wisdom constantly discussed by enquiring teachers, supported by delusion, and supported by irresponsibly misled parents from whom the true social and vocational future of their deaf child is largely obscured. Oralists have protested that society has provided them with inadequate tools. We have suggested that they have inappropriate theory and that their achievements represent the theoretical limit of what is therefore possible. The speech production barrier remains insurmountable after one hundred years of intense assault of all kinds. We do not know what hope lies in what is perhaps still beyond the horizon, by way of surgical intervention. But enough is known about deafness to guarantee that surgery, even in the distant future, will leave many deaf children as deaf.

We greatly doubt, for the here and now, whether there can usefully be a unified set of principles suitable for educating all deaf children. In one critical variable, the population totally lacks the homogeneity required for a single simple panacea. But all children deemed to require Special education because of deafness have a right to choose to think, to learn, and to be taught in their biologically preferred mode. It might be thought that educators have a duty to present the options.

References

Ahlgren I. (1977). Early linguistic cognitive development in the deaf and severely hard of hearing. National Symposium on Sign Language Research and Teaching, Chicago.

Ahlström, K-G. (1971). On Evaluating the Effects of Schooling. Proceedings of the International Congress on Education of the Deaf. Stockholm, 1970.

Allen, D. V. (1969). Modality aspects of mediation in children with normal and with impaired hearing ability. Final report, Project No. 7-0837, Department of Health, Education and Welfare, Washington, D.C.

Allen, D. V. (1970). Acoustic interference in paired-associate learning as a function of hearing ability. *Psychonomic Science, 18,* 231-233.

Allen, D. V. (1971a). Modality of similarity and hearing ability. *Psychonomic Science, 24,* 69-71.

Allen, D. V. (1971b). Color-word interference in deaf and hearing children. *Psychonomic Science, 24,* 295-296.

Annett, M. (1970). A classification of hand preference by association analysis. *British Journal of Psychology, 61,* 303-321.

Arnold, P. (1978). The deaf child's written English – Can we measure its quality. *The Teacher of the Deaf, 2,* 196-200.

Babbini, B. E., and Quigley, S. P. (1970). A study of the growth patterns in language, communication, and educational achievements in six residential schools for deaf students. Illinois University, Urbana: Institute for Research on Exceptional Children.

Baddeley, A. D. (1964). Immediate memory and the "perception" of letter sequencies. *Quarterly Journal of Experimental Psychology, XVI,* 364-367.

Baddeley, A. D. (1976). *The Psychology of Memory.* London: Harper and Row.

Baddeley, A. D. (1978). On the importance of acoustic encoding in short-term memory: A reply to Morris. *Bulletin of the British Psychological Society, 31,* 120-121.

Bakker, D. J. (1973). Hemispheric specialization and stages in the learning-to-read process. *Bulletin of the Orton Society, 23,* 15–27.

Balow, I. H., and Brill, R. G. (1975). An evaluation of reading and academic achievement levels of 16 graduating classes of the California School for the Deaf, Riverside. *Volta Review, 77,* 255–266.

Batkin, S., Groth, H., Watson, J. R., and Ansperry, M. (1970). The effects of auditory deprivation in the development of auditory sensitivity in albino rats. *Electroencephalography and Clinical Neurophysiology, 28,* 351–359.

Battison, R., and Jordan, I. K. (1976). Cross-cultural communication with foreign signers: fact and fancy. *Sign Language Studies, 10,* 53–68.

Bay, E. (1975). Ontogeny of stable speech areas in the human brain. In E. H. Lenneberg and E. Lenneberg (eds.), *Foundations of Language Development: A Multi-disciplinary Approach, vol. II.* New York: Academic Press.

Beaumont, J. G. (1976). The cerebral laterality of "minimal brain damage" children. *Cortex, 12,* 373–382.

Bellugi, U., and Klima, E. S. (1972); The roots of language in the sign talk of the deaf. *Psychology Today,* 61–76.

Bellugi, U., and Klima, E. S. (1975). Aspects of sign language and its structure. In J. F. Kavanagh and J. E. Cutting (eds.), *The Role of Speech in Language.* Cambridge, Mass.: M.I.T. Press.

Bellugi, U., Klima, E. S., and Siple, P. (1974). Remembering in signs. *Cognition, 3,* 93–125.

Bench, R. J., and Murphy, K. (1977). Auditory rehabilitation with special reference to children. In R. Hinchcliffe and D. S. N. Harrison, *Scientific Foundations of Otolaryngology.* London: Heinemann.

Bench, R. J., Collyer, Y., and Mentz, L. (1976). Response cues in infant audiometry. In S. D. G. Stephens (ed.), *Disorders of Auditory Function II,* London: Academic Press.

Berger, K. W. (1972a). *Speech reading: Principles and Methods.* Baltimore: National Educational Press.

Berger, K. W. (1972b). Visemes and homophenous words. *The Teacher of the Deaf, 70,* 396–399.

Berger, K. W., and Popelka, G. R. (1971). Extra-facial gestures in relation to speechreading. *Journal of Communication Disorders, 3,* 302–308.

Berlin, C. I., Hughes, L. F., Lowe-Bell, S. S., and Berlin, H. L. (1973). Dichotic right ear advantage in children 5 to 13. *Cortex, 9,* 394–402.

Blair, F. X. (1957). A study of the visual memory of deaf and hearing children. *American Annals of the Deaf, 102,* 254–263.

Blank, M. (1965). Use of the deaf in language studies: a reply to Furth. *Psychological Bulletin, 63,* 442–444.

Blanton, R. L., Nunnally, J. C., and Odom, P. B. (1967). Graphemic, phonetic, and associative factors in the verbal behavior of deaf and hearing subjects. *Journal of Speech and Hearing Research, 10,* 225–231.

Blau, A. (1946). *The Master Hand.* American Orthopsychiatric Association, Research Monograph No. 5.

Bonvillian, J. D., Nelson, K. E., and Charrow, V. R. (1976). Languages and language-related skills in deaf and hearing children. *Sign Language Studies, 12,* 211–250.

Boothroyd, A. (1975). Technology and deafness. *Volta Review, 77,* 27–34.

Bornstein, H. (1973). A description of some current sign systems designed to represent English. *American Annals of the Deaf, 118,* 454–463.

Bornstein, H. (1978). Sign language in the education of the deaf. In I. M. Schlesinger and L. Namir (eds.), *Sign Language of the Deaf: Psychological, Linguistic, and Sociological Perspectives,* New York: Academic Press.

Bradley, L., and Bryant, P. E. (1978). Difficulties in auditory organisation as a possible cause of reading backwardness. *Nature, 271,* 746–747.

Brasel, K. E., and Quigley, S. P. (1977). Influence of certain language and communication environments in early childhood on the development of language in deaf individuals. *Journal of Speech and Hearing Research, 20,* 95–107.

Brennan, M. (1975). Can deaf children acquire language? An evaluation of linguistic principles in deaf education. *American Annals of the Deaf, 120,* 463–479.

Briggs, G. G., Nebes, R. D., and Kinsbourne, M. (1976). Intellectual differences in relation to personal and family handedness. *Quarterly Journal of Experimental Psychology, 28,* 591–601.

Brill, R. G. (1969). The superior I.Q.'s of deaf children of deaf parents. *The California Palms, 15,* 1–4.

Brimer, A. (1972). *Wide-span Reading Test.* London: Nelson.

Brindley, G. S. (1970). *Physiology of the retina and visual pathways.* London: Edward Arnold.

Brown, R. (1977). Why are signed languages easier to learn than spoken languages? National Symposium on Sign Language Research and Teaching, Chicago.

Bugelski, B. R. (1970). Words and things and images. *American Psychologist, 25,* 1002–1012.

Bullock, A. (1975). *A Language for Life.* London: H.M.S.O.

Burke, H. R. (1958). Raven's Progressive Matrices. *Journal of Genetic Psychology, 93,* 199–228.

Byers, V. W., and Lieberman, L. (1959). Lipreading performance and the rate of the speaker. *Journal of Speech and Hearing Research, 2,* 271–276.

Caccamise, F., Blasdell, R., and Meath-Lang, B. (1977). Hearing-impaired persons' simultaneous reception of information under live and two visual motion media conditions. *American Annals of the Deaf, 122,* 339–343.

Calvert, D. R. (1962). Speech sound duration and the surd-sonant error. *Volta Revew, 64,* 401–402.

Carmel, S. J. (1975). *International Hand Alphabet Charts,* Carmel, Rockville, Maryland.

Charrow, V. R. (1974). *Deaf English – An Investigation of the Written English Competence of Deaf Adolescents.* Institute for Mathematical Studies in the Social Sciences, Stanford University, Stanford, California.

Charrow, V. R., and Fletcher, J. D. (1974). English as the second language of deaf children. *Developmental Psychology, 10,* 463–470.

Chen, K. (1976). Acoustic image in visual detection for deaf and hearing college students. *Journal of General Psychology, 94,* 243–246.

Chovan, W. L., and McGettigan, J. F. (1971). The effects of vocal mediating responses on visual motor tasks with deaf and hearing children. *Exceptional Children, 38,* 435–440.

Cicourel, A. V., and Boese, R. J. (1972a). The acquisition of manual sign language and generative semantics. *Semiotica, V,* 225–256.

Cicourel, A. V., and Boese, R. J. (1972b). Sign language acquisition and the teaching of deaf children. In D. Hymes, C. B. Cazden, and V. P. Johns (eds.). *The Function of Language: an Anthropological and Psychological Approach.* New York: Teachers College Press.

Clarke, B. R., and Ling, D. (1976). The effects of using cued speech: a follow-up study. *Volta Review, 78,* 23–34.

Conrad, R. (1962). An association between memory errors and errors due to acoustic masking of speech. *Nature, 193,* 1314–1315.

Conrad, R. (1963). Acoustic confusions and memory span for words. *Nature, 197,* 1029–1030.

Conrad, R. (1964). Acoustic confusions in immediate memory. *British Journal of Psychology, 55,* 75–84.

Conrad, R. (1965). The role of the nature of the material in verbal learning. *Acta Psychologica, 24,* 244–252.

Conrad, R. (1970). Short-term memory processes in the deaf. *British Journal of Psychology, 61,* 179–195.

Conrad, R. (1971a). The chronology of the development of covert speech in children. *Developmental Psychology, 5,* 398–405.

Conrad, R. (1971b). The effect of vocalizing on comprehension in the profoundly deaf. *British Journal of Psychology, 62,* 147–150.

Conrad, R. (1972a). Short-term memory in the deaf: a test for speech coding. *British Journal of Psychology, 63,* 173–180.

Conrad, R. (1972b). Speech and Reading, In J. F. Kavanagh and I. G. Mattingley (eds.), *Language by Ear and by Eye: the Relationships between Speech and Reading.* Cambridge, Mass.: M.I.T. Press.

Conrad, R. (1977a) The reading ability of deaf school-leavers. *British Journal of Educational Psychology, 47,* 138–148.

Conrad, R. (1977b). Lip-reading by deaf and hearing children. *British Journal of Educational Psychology, 47,* 60–65.

Conrad, R., Freeman, P. R., and Hull, A. J. (1965). Acoustic factors versus language factors in short-term memory. *Psychonomic Science, 3,* 57–58.

Conrad, R., and Hull, A. J. (1964). Information, acoustic confusion and memory span. *British Journal of Psychology 55,* 429–432.

Conrad, R., and Rush, M. L. (1965). On the nature of short-term memory encoding by the deaf. *Journal of Speech and Hearing Disorders, 30,* 336–343.

Conrad, R., Baddeley, A. D., and Hull, A. J. (1966). Rate of presentation of the acoustic similarity effect in short-term memory. *Psychonomic Science, 5,* 233–234.

Conlin, D., and Paivio, A. (1975). The associative learning of the deaf: the effects of word imagery and signability. *Memory and Cognition, 3,* 335–340.

Corcoran, D. W. J. (1966). An acoustic factor in letter cancellation. *Nature, 210,* 658.

Cornett, R. O. (1967). Cued Speech. *American Annals of the Deaf, 112,* 3–13.

Cornog, D. Y., and Rose, F. C. (1967). *Legibility of Alphanumeric Characters and Other Symbols II. A Reference Handbook.* Washington D.C.: National Bureau of Standards.

Costello, M. R. (1957). A study of speech-reading as a developing language process in deaf and in hard of hearing children. Ph.D. dissertation. Northwestern University, Evanston, Illinois.

Court, J. H., and Kennedy, R. J. (1976). Sex as a variable in Raven's Standard Progressive Matrices. Proceedings of the XXI International Congress of Psychology, Paris.

Cowan, W. M. (1970). Anterograde and retrograde transneural degeneration in the central and peripheral nervous system. In W. J. H. Nauta and S. O. E. Ebbesson (eds.), *Contemporary Research Methods in Neuroanatomy.* Berlin: Springer.

Craig, E. (1976). A supplement to the spoken word – the Paget-Gorman Sign System. In P. Henderson (ed.), *Methods of Communication Currently Used in the Education of Deaf Children.* London: Royal National Institute for the Deaf.

Craig, W. N. (1964). Effects of preschool training on the development of reading and lipreading skills of deaf children. *American Annals of the Deaf, 109,* 280–296.

Craik, F. I. M., and Lockhart, R. S. (1972). Levels of processing: a framework for memory research. *Journal of Verbal Learning and Verbal Behavior, 11,* 671–684.

Critchley, M. (1938). Aphasia in a partial deaf-mute. *Brain, 61,* 163–169.

Dale, D. M. C. (1967). *Applied Audiology for Children.* Springfield, Illinois: Charles C. Thomas.

Daniels, J. C., and Diack, H. (1972). *The Standard Reading Tests.* London: Chatto and Windus.

Danish, J. M., Tillson, J. K., and Levitan, M. (1963). Multiple anomalies in congenitally deaf children. *Eugenics Quarterly, 10,* 12.

Davis, H. (1960). Military standards and medicolegal rules. In H. Davis and S. R. Silverman (eds.), *Hearing and Deafness.* New York: Holt, Rinehart and Winston.

Davis, H., and Silverman, S. R. (1960). (eds.), *Hearing and Deafness*. New York: Holt, Rinehart and Winston.

Delk, H. (1973). *A Comprehensive Dictionary of Audiology*. Sioux City, Iowa: The Hearing Aid Journal.

Department of Education and Science. (1964). *The Health of the School Child, 1962 and 1963*. London: H.M.S.O.

Department of Education and Science. (1967). *Units for Partially Hearing Children*. London: H.M.S.O.

Department of Education and Science. (1972). *The Health of the School Child, 1969–70*. London: H.M.S.O.

DiFrancesca, S. (1972). *Academic Achievement Test Results of a National Testing Program for Hearing Impaired Students – United States: Spring 1971*. Series D, Number 9. Washington, D.C.: Gallaudet College, Office of Demographic Studies.

Dodd, B. (1977). The role of vision in the perception of speech. *Perception, 6*, 31–40.

Dodd, B., and Hermelin, B. (1977). Phonological coding by the prelinguistically deaf. *Perception and Psychophysics, 21*, 413–417.

Dorman, M. F., and Geffner, D. S. (1974). Hemispheric specialization for speech perception in six-year-old black and white children from low and middle socioeconomic classes. *Cortex, X*, 171–176.

Douglass, E., and Richardson, J. C. (1959). Aphasia in a congenital deaf-mute. *Brain, 82*, 68–80.

Downs, M. P., and Sterritt, G. M. (1967). A guide to newborn and infant hearing screening programs. *Archives of Otolaryngology, 85*, 15–22.

Edfeldt, A. W. (1960). *Silent Speech and Silent Reading*. Chicago: Chicago University Press.

Elliott, L. L., and Niemoeller, A. F. (1970). The role of hearing in controlling voice fundamental frequency. *International Audiology, IX*, 47–52.

Erber, N. P. (1969). Interaction of audition and vision in the recognition of oral speech stimuli. *Journal of Speech and Hearing Research, 12*, 423–425.

Erber, N. P. (1971). Effects of distance on the visual reception of speech. *Journal of Speech and Hearing Research. 14*, 848–857.

Erber, N. P. (1972a). Speech-envelope cues as an acoustic aid to lipreading for profoundly deaf children. *Journal of the Acoustical Society of America, 51*, 1224–1227.

Erber, N. P. (1972b). Auditory, visual, and auditory-visual recognition of consonants by children with normal and impaired hearing. *Journal of Speech and Hearing Research, 15*, 413–422.

Erber, N. P. (1974a); Pure-tone thresholds and word-recognition abilities of hearing-impaired children. *Journal of Speech and Hearing Research, 17*, 194–202.

Erber, N. P. (1974b). Visual perception of speech by deaf children: recent developments and continuing needs. *Journal of Speech and Hearing Disorders, 39,* 178–185.

Erber, N. P. (1974c). Effects of angle, distance, and illumination on visual reception of speech by profoundly deaf children. *Journal of Speech and Hearing Research, 17,* 99–112.

Erber, N. P. (1975). Auditory-visual perception of speech. *Journal of Speech and Hearing Disorders, 40,* 481–492.

Espeseth, V. K. (1969). An investigation of visual-sequential memory in deaf children. *American Annals of the Deaf, 114,* 786–789.

Evans, L. (1960). Factors relating to listening and lip-reading. *The Teacher of the Deaf, 58,* 417–423.

Evans, L. (1965). Psychological factors related to lipreading. *The Teacher of the Deaf, 63,* 131–137.

Evans, L. (1966). A comparative study of the Wechsler Intelligence Scale for Children (Performance) and Raven's Progressive Matrices with deaf children. *The Teacher of the Deaf, 64,* 76–82.

Evans, L. (1978). *Visual Communication in the Deaf: Lipreading, Fingerspelling and Signing.* Ph.D. Dissertation, University of Newcastle upon Tyne.

Ewing, A. W. G. (1960). Deaf children in a new age. In A. W. G. Ewing (ed.), *The Modern Educational Treatment of Deafness.* Manchester: Manchester University Press.

Ewing, A. W. G., and Ewing, E. C. (1964). *Teaching Deaf Children to Talk.* Manchester: Manchester University Press.

Ewing, I. R. (1930). *Lip-reading.* Manchester: Manchester University Press.

Ewing, I. R. (1957). Screening tests and guidance clinics for babies and young children. In. A. W. G. Ewing (ed.), *Educational Guidance and the Deaf Child.* Manchester: Manchester University Press.

Farwell, R. M. (1976). Speech reading: a research review. *American Annals of the Deaf, 121,* 19–30.

Fenn, G., and Rowe, J. A. (1975). An experiment in manual communication. *British Journal of Disorders of Communication, 10,* 3–16.

Ferri, E. (1976). *Growing Up in a One Parent Family.* London: National Children's Bureau.

Fisch, L. (1964). (ed.). *Research in Deafness in Children.* Oxford: Blackwell Scientific Publications Ltd.

Fisch, L. (1976). Sex-ratio and congenital deafness. In S. D. G. Stephens (ed.), *Disorders of Auditory Function II.* London: Academic Press.

Fischer, S. D. (1971). *Two Processes of Reduplication in the American Sign Language.* San Diego: The Salk Institute.

Fisher, D. F., Monty, R. A., and Glucksberg, S. (1969). Visual confusion matrices: fact or artefact? *Journal of Psychology, 71,* 111–125.

Flavell, J. H., Beach, D. R., and Chinsky, J. M. (1966). Spontaneous verbal rehearsal in a memory task as a function of age. *Child Development, 37,* 283–299.

Fletcher, H. (1929). *Speech and Hearing in Communication.* New York: van Nostrand.

Fraser, G. R. (1964). Profound childhood deafness. *Journal of Medical Genetics, 1,* 118–151.

Fraser, G. R. (1976). *The Causes of Profound Deafness in Childhood.* London: Baillière Tindall.

Friedman, J. B., and Gillooley, W. B. (1977). Perceptual development in the profoundly deaf as related to early reading. *Journal of Special Education, 11,* 347–354.

Frisina, D. R. (1959). Some problems confronting children with deafness. *Exceptional Children, 26,* 94–97.

Frisina, D. R. (1963). Speechreading. Proceedings of the International Congress on Education of the Deaf. Washington, D.C. 191–207.

Fromkin, V., Krashen, S., Curtiss, S., Rigler, D., and Rigler, M. (1974). The development of language in Genie: a case of language acquisition beyond the "critical period". *Brain and Language, 1,* 81–107.

Frumkin, B., and Anisfeld, M. (1977). Semantic and surface codes in the memory of deaf children. *Cognitive Psychology, 9,* 475–493.

Fry, D. B. (1966). The development of the phonological system in the normal and the deaf child. In F. Smith and G. A. Miller (eds.), *The Genesis of Language.* London: M.I.T. Press.

Fry, D. B. (1975). Phonological aspects of language acquisition in the hearing and the deaf. In E. H. Lenneberg and E. Lenneberg (eds.), *Foundations of Language Development: a Multidisciplinary Approach, vol. II.* New York: Academic Press.

Fry, D. (1977). *Homo Loquens.* Cambridge: Cambridge University Press.

Furness, H. J. S. (1972). The linguistic potential of deaf children. *The Teacher of the Deaf, 70,* 107–122.

Furth, H. G. (1961). The influence of language on the development of concept formation in deaf children. *Journal of Abnormal and Social Psychology, 63,* 386–389.

Further, H. G. (1966a). *Thinking Without Language.* New York: Free Press.

Furth, H. G. (1966b). A comparison of reading test norms of deaf and hearing children. *American Annals of the Deaf, 111,* 461–462.

Furth, H. G. (1971). Linguistic deficiency and thinking: research with deaf subjects, 1964–1969. *Psychological Bulletin, 76,* 58–72.

Furth, H. G., and Milgram, N. A. (1965). The influence of language on classification: a theoretical model applied to normal, retarded, and deaf children. *Genetic Psychology Monographs, 72,* 317–351.

Furth, H. G., and Youniss, J. (1965). The influence of language and experience on discovery and use of logical symbols. *British Journal of Psychology, 56,* 381–390.

Furth, H., and Youniss, J. (1975). Congenital deafness and the development of thinking. In E. H. Lenneberg and E. Lenneberg (eds.), *Foundations of Language Development: a Multidisciplinary Approach, vol. II.* New York: Academic Press.

Garretson, M. D. (1976). Total Communication. In R. Frisina (ed.), *A Bicentennial Monograph on Hearing Impairment: Trends in the U.S.A.* Washington, D.C.: The Alexander Graham Bell Association for the Deaf, Inc.

Garrity, L. I. (1975). An electromyographical study of subvocal speech and recall in preschool children. *Developmental Psychology, 11,* 274–281.

Garrity, L. I. (1977). Electromyography: a review of the current status of subvocal speech research. *Memory and Cognition, 5,* 615–622.

Gates, R. R. (1971). The reception of verbal information by deaf students through a television medium – a comparison of speechreading, manual communication, and reading. Proceedings of the Convention of American Instructors of the Deaf, Little Rock, Arkansas, 513–522.

Geffner, D. S., and Hochberg, I. (1971). Ear laterality performance of children from low and middle socioeconomic levels on a verbal dichotic listening task. *Cortex, VII,* 193–203.

Gentile, A., and McCarthy, B. (1973). *Additional Handicapping Conditions Among Hearing Impaired Students – United States: 1971–72.* Series D, Number 14. Washington, D.C.: Gallaudet College, Office of Demographic Studies.

Gentile, A., and Rambin, J. B. (1973). *Reported Causes of Hearing Loss for Hearing Impaired Students – United States: 1970–71.* Series D, Number 12. Washington, D.C.: Gallaudet College, Office of Demographic Studies.

Geschwind, N. (1967). Brain mechanisms suggested by studies of hemispheric connection. In C. H. Millikan and F. L. Darley (eds.), *Brain Mechanisms Underlying Speech and Language.* New York: Grune and Stratton.

Gibson, E. J., Schurcliff, A., and Yonas, A. (1970). Utilization of spelling patterns by deaf and hearing subjects. In H. Levin and J. P. Williams (eds.), *Basic Studies on Reading.* New York: Basic Books.

Gilliland, J. (1972). *Readability.* London: University of London Press.

Goetzinger, C. P. (1962). Effects of small perceptive losses on language and on speech discrimination. *Volta Review, 64,* 408–414.

Goetzinger, C. P., Wills, R. C., and Dekker, L. C. (1967). Non-language IQ tests used with deaf pupils. *Volta Review, 69,* 500–506.

Goodglass, H., Denes, G., and Calderon, M. (1974). The absence of covert verbal mediation in aphasia. *Cortex, X,* 264–269.

Gray, W. S. (1956). *The Teaching of Reading and Writing.* UNESCO.

Hagen, J. W., and Kingsley, P. R. (1968). Labelling effects in short-term memory. *Child Development, 39,* 113–121.

Hammermeister, F. K. (1971). Reading achievements in deaf adults. *American Annals of the Deaf, 116,* 25–28.

Hamp, N. W. (1972). Reading attainment and some associated factors in deaf and partially hearing children. *The Teacher of the Deaf, 70,* 203–215.

Hardyck, C. D., and Petrinovich, L. F. (1970). Subvocal speech and comprehension level as a function of the difficulty level of reading material. *Journal of Verbal Learning and Verbal Behavior, 9,* 647–652.

Hardyck, C., Petrinovich, L. F., and Goldman, R. D. (1976). Left-handedness and cognitive deficit. *Cortex, XII,* 266–279.

Hardyck, C., Tzeng, O. J. L., and Wang, W. S-Y. (1978). Cerebral lateralization of function and bilingual decision processes: is thinking lateralized? *Brain and Language, 5,* 56–71.

Hartman, J. S., and Elliott, L. L. (1965). Performance of deaf and hearing children on a short term memory task. *Psychonomic Science, 3,* 573–574.

Hartung, J. E. (1970). Visual perceptual skill, reading ability and the young deaf child. *Exceptional Children, 36,* 603–608.

Hayhurst, A. B. (in press). *Sign-it.* Carlisle: British Deaf Association.

Healy, A. F. (1977). Pattern coding of spatial order information in short-term memory. *Journal of Verbal Learning and Verbal Behavior, 16,* 419–437.

Hebb, D. O. (1949). *The Organisation of Behaviour.* New York: Wiley.

Hécaen, H., and Ajuriaguerra, J. (1964). *Left-Handedness.* New York: Grune and Stratton.

Heim, A. W., Wallace, J. G., and Cane, V. (1950). The effects of repeatedly testing the same group on the same intelligence test. *Quarterly Journal of Experimental Psychology, II,* 182–197.

Hemmings, I. (1972). A survey of units for hearing-impaired children in schools for normally-hearing children. *The Teacher of the Deaf, 70,* 445–466.

Hermelin, B. M., and O'Connor, N. (1975a); Seeing, speaking and ordering. In N. O'Connor (ed.), *Language, Cognitive Deficits, and Retardation.* London: Butterworth.

Hermelin, B., and O'Connor, N. (1975b). The recall of digits by normal, deaf and autistic children. *British Journal of Psychology, 66,* 203–209.

Hicks, R. E., and Kinsbourne, M. (1976). Human-handedness: a partial cross-fostering study. *Science, 192,* 908–910.

Hine, W. D. (1970a). The abilities of partially hearing children. *British Journal of Educational Psychology, 40,* 171–178.

Hine, W. D. (1970b). The attainments of children with partial hearing. *The Teacher of the Deaf, 68,* 129–135.

Hine, W. D. (1973). How deaf are deaf children? *British Journal of Audiology, 7,* 41–44.

Hintzman, D. L. (1967). Articulatory coding in short-term memory. *Journal of Verbal Learning and Verbal Behavior, 6,* 312–316.

Hiskey, M. S. (1956). A study of the intelligence of deaf and hearing children. *American Annals of the Deaf, 101,* 329–339.

Hoemann, H. W. (1972). The development of communication skills in deaf and hearing children. *Child Development, 43,* 990–1003.

Hoemann, H. W. (1978). Categorical coding of Sign and English in short-term memory by deaf and hearing subjects. In P. Siple (ed.), *Understanding Language through Sign Language Research.* New York: Academic Press.

Hoemann, H. W., Andrews, C. E. and DeRosa, D. V. (1974). Categorical encoding in short-term memory by deaf and hearing children. *Journal of Speech and Hearing Research, 17,* 426–431.

Hood, J. D., and Poole, J. P. (1971). Speech audiometry in conductive and sensorineural hearing loss. *Sound, 5,* 30–38.

Hornby, P. A. (1977). Bilingualism: an introduction and overview. In P. A. Hornby (ed.), *Bilingualism: Psychological, Social and Educational Implications.* New York: Academic Press.

Ingram, D. (1975). Cerebral speech lateralization in young children. *Neuropsychologia, 13,* 103–105.

Jacobs, J. (1887). Experiments in "prehension". *Mind, 12,* 75–79.

James, W. (1901). *The Principles of Psychology, vol. 1.* London: Macmillan.

Jarvik, L. F., Salzberger, R. M. and Falek, A. (1963). Deaf persons of outstanding achievement. In J. D. Rainer, K. Z. Altshuler, and F. J. Kallmann (eds.), *Family and Mental Health Problems in a Deaf Population.* New York: Columbia University.

Jeffers, J., and Barley, M. (1971). *Speech reading (lipreading).* Springfield, Ill.: Charles C. Thomas.

Jensema, C. J. (1975). *The Relationship Between Academic Achievement and the Demographic Characteristics of Hearing Impaired Children and Youth.* Series R, Number 2. Washington, D.C.: Gallaudet College, Office of Demographic Studies.

Jensema, C. J., Karchmer, M. A., and Trybus, R. J. (1978). *The Rated Speech Intelligibility of Hearing Impaired Children: Basic Relationships and a Detailed Analysis.* Series R, Number 6. Washington, D.C.: Gallaudet College, Office of Demographic Studies.

Jensema, C. J., and Mullins, J. (1974). Onset, cause, and additional handicaps in hearing impaired children. *American Annals of the Deaf, 119,* 701–705.

John, J. E. J., and Howarth, J. N. (1965). The effect of time distortions on the intelligibility of deaf children's speech. *Language and Speech, 8,* 127–134.

John, J. E. J., and Howarth, J. N. (1973). An argument for oral communication. *The Teacher of the Deaf, 71,* 102–109.

John, J. E. J., Gemmill, J., Howarth, J. N., Kitzinger, M., and Sykes, M. (1976). Some factors affecting the intelligibility of deaf children's speech. In S. D. G. Stephens (ed.), *Disorders of Auditory Function II,* London: Academic Press.

Johnson, D. D. (1976). Communication characteristics of a young deaf adult population: techniques for evaluating their communication skills. *American Annals of the Deaf, 121,* 409–424.

Johnson, J. C. (1962). *Educating Hearing-Impaired Children in Ordinary Schools.* Manchester: Manchester University Press.

Jordan, T. E. (1961). Historical notes on early study of the deaf. *Journal of Speech and Hearing Disorders, 26,* 118–121.

Kates, S. L. (1972). *Language Development in Deaf and Hearing Adolescents.* Northampton, Mass.: The Clarke School for the Deaf.

Keller, H. (1956). *Teacher: Anne Sullivan Macy.* London: Gollancz.

Kendler, T. S. (1964). Verbalization and optional reversal shifts among kindergarten children. *Journal of Verbal Learning and Verbal Behavior, 3,* 428–436.

Kimura, D. (1963). Speech lateralization in young children as determined by an auditory test. *Journal of Comparative and Physiological Psychology, 56,* 899–902.

Kimura, D., Battison, R., and Lubert, B. (1976). Impairment of nonlinguistic hand movements in a deaf aphasic. *Brain and Language, 3,* 566–571.

Kirman, J. H. (1973). Tactile communication of speech: a review and an analysis. *Psychological Bulletin, 80,* 54–74.

Klare, G. (1963). *The Measurement of Readability.* Iowa State University Press.

Klima, E. S., and Bellugi, U. (1972). The signs of language in child and chimpanzee. In T. Alloway (ed.), *Communication and Affect.* New York: Academic Press.

Klopping, H. W. E. (1971). Language Understanding of Deaf Students under Three Auditory-Visual Stimulus Conditions. Ed. D. Dissertation. The University of Arizona.

Kodman, F. (1963). Educational status of hard-of-hearing children in the classroom. *Journal of Speech and Hearing Disorders, 28,* 297–299.

Koh, S. D., Vernon, M., and Bailey, W. (1971). Free-recall learning of word lists by prelingual deaf subjects. *Journal of Verbal Learning and Verbal Behavior, 10,* 542–547.

Konigsmark, B. W. (1971). Hereditary congenital severe deafness syndromes. *Annals of Otology, Rhinology and Laryngology, 80,* 269–287.

Krashen, S. (1973). Lateralization, language learning, and the critical period: some new evidence. *Language Learning, 23,* 63–74.

Kyle, J. G. (1977a). Audiometric analysis as a predictor of speech intelligibility. *British Journal of Audiology, 11,* 51–58.

Kyle, J. G. (1977b). Raven's Progressive Matrices – 30 years later. *Bulletin of the British Psychological Society, 30,* 406–407.

Kyle, J. G. (1978). The study of auditory deprivation from birth. *British Journal of Audiology, 12,* 37–39.

Lambert, W. E. (1977). The effects of bilingualism on the individual: cognitive and sociocultural consequences. In P. A. Hornby (ed.). *Bilingualism: Psychological, Social and Educational Implications.* New York: Academic Press.

Lane, H. (1977). *The Wild Boy of Aveyron.* London: George Allen and Unwin.

Lane, H., Boyes-Braem, P., and Bellugi, U. (1976). Preliminaries to a distinctive feature analysis of handshapes in American Sign Language. *Cognitive Psychology, 8,* 263–289.

Lantz, De L., and Lenneberg, E. H. (1966). Verbal communication and color memory in the deaf and hearing. *Child Development, 37,* 765–779.

Lenneberg, E. H. (1966). The natural history of language. In F. Smith and G. A. Miller (eds.), *The Genesis of Language: a Psycholinguistic Approach.* London: M.I.T. Press.

Lenneberg, E. H. (1967). *Biological Foundations of Language.* New York: Wiley.

Lenneberg, E. H. (1972). Prerequisites for language acquisition by the deaf. In T. J. O'Rourke (ed.), *Psycholinguistics and Total Communication: the State of the Art.* American Annals of the Deaf.

Lepley, W. M. (1952). The participation of implicit speech in acts of writing. *American Journal of Psychology 65,* 597–599.

Levine, B., and Iscoe, I. (1955). The Progressive Matrices (1938), the Chicago Non-Verbal and the Wechsler Bellevue on an Adolescent Deaf Population. *Journal of Clinical Psychology, 11,* 307–308.

Levine, D. M., Wachspress, S., McGuire, P., and Mayzner, M. S. (1973). Visual information processing of numerical inputs. *Bulletin of the Psychonomic Society, 1,* 404–406.

Levine, E. S. (1963). Historical review of special education and mental health services. In J. D. Rainer, K. Z. Altshuler, and F. J. Kallman (eds.), *Family and Mental Health Problems in a Deaf Population.* New York: Columbia University.

Levitt, H. (1973). Speech processing aids for the deaf: an overview. IEEE Transactions on Audio and Electroacoustics AU-21, 269–273.

Levitt, H. (1976). Language communication skills of deaf children, 1973/1975. Proceedings of Language Assessment for the Hearing Impaired – a Work Study Institute, New York State Education Department.

Lewis, M. M. (1968). *The Education of Deaf Children: the Possible Place of Finger Spelling and Signing.* London: H.M.S.O.

Liberman, I. Y., Shankweiler, D., Liberman, A. M., Fowler, C., and Fischer, F. W. (1977). Phonetic segmentation and recoding in the beginning reader. In A. S. Reber and D. Scarborough (eds.), *Towards a Psychology of Reading: the Proceedings of the CUNY Conferences.* Hillsdale, New Jersey: Laurence Erlbaum Associates.

Ling, A. H. (1976). Training of auditory memory in hearing-impaired children: some problems of generalization. *Journal of the American Audiology Society, 1,* 150–157.

Ling, D. (1959). The Education and General Background of Children with Defective Hearing in Reading. Cambridge, England: Institute of Education Library.

Ling, D. (1975). Recent developments affecting the education of hearing-impaired children. *Public Health Reviews, 4,* 117–152.

Ling, D. (1976). *Speech and the Hearing Impaired Child: Theory and Practice.* Washington, D.C.: A. G. Bell Association.

Ling, D., and Clarke, B. R. (1975). Cued speech: an evaluative study.

American Annals of the Deaf, 120, 480–488.

Locke, J. L. (1970). Short-term memory encoding strategies of the deaf. *Psychonomic Science, 18,* 233–234.

Locke, J. L. (1978a). Phonemic effects in the silent reading of hearing and deaf children. *Cognition, 6,* 175–187.

Locke, J. L. (1978b). Large auditory and small visual effects in the recall of consonant letters. *American Journal of Psychology, 91,* 89–92.

Locke, J. L., and Fehr, F. S. (1970). Subvocal rehearsal as a form of speech. *Journal of Verbal Learning and Verbal Behavior, 9,* 495–498.

Locke, J. L., and Kutz, K. J. (1975). Memory for speech and speech for memory. *Journal of Speech and Hearing Research, 18,* 176–191.

Locke, J. L., and Locke, V. L. (1971). Deaf children's phonetic, visual, and dactylic coding in a grapheme recall task. *Journal of Experimental Psychology, 89,* 142–146.

Lowell, E. L. (1959). Research in speechreading; some relationships to language development and implications for the classroom teacher. Proceedings of the 39th Convention of American Instructors of the Deaf. Lowell, E. L. (1976). Untitled. In P. Henderson (ed.), *Methods of Communication Currently Used in the Education of Deaf Children.* London: Royal National Institute for the Deaf.

Lumsden, J. (1953). Oralism: is there a need for an alternative? *The Teacher of the Deaf, 51,* 70–76.

Lynn, R. (1977). The intelligence of the Japanese. *Bulletin of the British Psychological Society, 30,* 69–72.

Magner, M. E. (1972). *A Speech Intelligibility Test for Deaf Children.* Clarke School for the Deaf, Northampton, Mass.

Manning, A. A., Goble, W., Markman, R., and LaBreche, T. (1977). Lateral cerebral differences in the deaf in response to linguistic and nonlinguistic stimuli. *Brain and Language, 4,* 309–321.

Mark, L. S., Shankweiler, D., Liberman, I. Y., and Fowler, C. A. (1977). Phonetic recoding and reading difficulty in beginning readers. *Memory and Cognition, 5,* 623–629.

Markides, A. (1970). The speech of deaf and partially-hearing children with special reference to factors affecting intelligibility. *British Journal of Disorders of Communication, 5,* 126–140.

Markides, A. (1976). Comparative linguistic proficiencies of deaf children taught by two different methods of instruction – manual versus oral. *The Teacher of the Deaf, 74,* 307–347.

Markides, A. (1977). Methods of assessing the speech intelligibility of hearing-impaired children. *The Teacher of the Deaf, 1,* 28–31.

Marshall, W. A. (1970). Contextual constraint on deaf and hearing children. *American Annals of the Deaf, 115,* 682–689.

Mavilya, M. (1971). Spontaneous vocalization and babbling in hearing impaired infants. Proceedings of the International Congress on Education of the Deaf, Stockholm, 1970.

Max, L. W. (1935). An experimental study of the motor theory of consciousness. III. Action-current responses in deaf-mutes during sleep, sensory stimulation and dreams. *Journal of Comparative Psychology, 19,* 469–486.

Mayberry, R. (1976). An assessment of some oral and manual-language skills of hearing children of deaf parents. *American Annals of the Deaf, 121,* 507–512.

McGuigan, F. J. (1966). *Thinking: Studies of Covert Language Processes.* New York: Appleton-Century.

McGuigan, F. J. (1967). Feedback of speech muscle activity during silent reading. Two comments. *Science, 157,* 579–580.

McGuigan, F. J. (1970). Covert oral behavior during the silent performance of language tests. *Psychological Bulletin, 74,* 309–326.

McIntire, M. L. (1977). The acquisition of American Sign Language hand configurations. *Sign Language Studies, 16,* 247–266.

McKeever, W. F., Hoemann, H. W., Florian, V. A., and VanDeventer, A. D. (1976). Evidence of minimal cerebral assymetries for the processing of English words and American Sign Language in the congenitally deaf. *Neuropsychologia, 14,* 413–423.

McNally, J. (1965). *The First Ladybird Key Words Picture Dictionary.* Loughborough: Wills and Hepworth.

Meadow, K. P. (1967). The Effect of Early Manual Communication and Family Climate on the Deaf Child's Development, Ph.D. Dissertation, University of California, Berkeley.

Meadow, K. P. (1968). Early manual communication in relation to the deaf child's intellectual, social, and communicative functioning. *American Annals of the Deaf, 113,* 29–41.

Menyuk, P. (1975). The language-impaired child: linguistic or cognitive impairment? *Annals of the New York Academy of Sciences, 263,* 59–69.

Mindel, E. D., and Vernon, M. (1971). *They Grow in Silence – the Deaf Child and his Family.* National Association of the Deaf, Maryland.

Ministry of Education. (1950). *Reading Ability.* London: H.M.S.O.

Montgomery, G. W. G. (1966a). The relationship of oral skills to manual communication in profoundly deaf adolescents. *American Annals of the Deaf, 111,* 557–565.

Montgomery, G. W. G. (1966b). Analysis of pure-tone audiometric responses in relation to speech development in the profoundly deaf. *Journal of the Acoustical Society of America, 41,* 53–59.

Montgomery, G. W. G. (1968). A factorial study of communication and ability in deaf school leavers. *British Journal of Educational Psychology, 38,* 27–37.

Montgomery, G. W. G. (1975). The efficiency of teachers' assessments of deaf pupils. *The Teacher of the Deaf, 73,* 21–29.

Moores, D. F. (1971). An Investigation of the Psycholinguistic Functioning of Deaf Adolescents. Research Report No. 18, Department of Health, Education and Welfare, U.S. Office of Education. Washington, D.C.

Moores, D. F. (1972). Neo-oralism and the education of the deaf in the Soviet Union. *Exceptional Children, 38,* 377–384.

Morkovin, B. V. (1960). Experiment in teaching deaf preschool children in the Soviet Union. *Volta Review, 62,* 260–268.

Morkovin, B. V. (1968). Language in the general development of the preschool deaf child: a review of research in the Soviet Union. *ASHA, May,* 195–199.

Morley, M. E. (1957). *The Development and Disorders of Speech in Childhood.* Edinburgh: Livingstone.

Moulton, R. D., and Beasley, D. S. (1975). Verbal coding strategies used by hearing-impaired individuals. *Journal of Speech and Hearing Research, 18,* 559–570.

Moyle, D. (1973). *Readability of Newspapers.* Edge Hill College of Education, Ormskirk, Lancs.

Murphy, K. P. (1956). A Survey of the Intelligence and Abilities of 12-year-old Deaf Children. Ph.D. Dissertation. The University of Manchester, Manchester.

Myklebust, H. R. (1964). *The Psychology of Deafness.* New York: Grune and Stratton.

Myklebust, H. R. (1966). The effect of early life deafness. Proceedings of the XVIII International Congress of Psychology, Moscow.

National College of Teachers of the Deaf. (1972). *Educational Provision for Children with Defective Hearing.* National College of Teachers of the Deaf.

Neisser, U. (1967). *Cognitive Psychology.* New York: Appleton-Century-Crofts.

Neyhus, A. I., and Myklebust, H. R. (1969). Speechreading failure in deaf children. Project No. 6–2582. Bureau of Education for the Handicapped, Department of Health, Education and Welfare, Washington, D.C.

Nicholas, S. M. (1976). Untitled. In P. Henderson (ed.), *Methods of Communication Currently Used in the Education of Deaf Children.* London: Royal National Institute for the Deaf.

Nickerson, R. S. (1975). Characterics of the speech of deaf persons. *Volta Review, 77,* 342–362.

Nickerson, R. S., Kalikow, D. N., and Stevens, K. N. (1976). Computer-aided speech training for the deaf. *Journal of Speech and Hearing Disorders, 41,* 120–132.

Nittrouer, S., Devan, M. A., and Boothroyd, A. (1976). It's never too late: an auditory approach with hearing impaired pre-teenagers. Clarke School for the Deaf, Northampton, Mass.

Nix, G. (1975). Total communication: a review of the studies offered in its support. *Volta Review, 77,* 470–494.

Nober, E. H. (1967). Articulation of the Deaf. *Exceptional Children, 33,* 611–621.

Nordén, K. (1975). *Psychological Studies of Deaf Adolescents.* Lund: CWK Gleerup.

Norman, D. A. (1970). *Models of Human Memory.* London: Academic Press.

Novikova, L. A. (1961). Electrophysiological investigation of speech. In

N. O'Connor (ed.), *Recent Soviet Psychology*. London: Pergamon Press.

Numbers, M. E. (1939). An experiment in lip reading. *Volta Review, 41,* 261–264.

O'Connor, N., and Hermelin, B. (1973a). Short-term memory for the order of pictures and syllables by deaf and hearing children. *Neuropsychologia, 11,* 437–442.

O'Connor, N., and Hermelin, B. M. (1973b). The spatial or temporal organization of short-term memory. *Quarterly Journal of Experimental Psychology, 25,* 335–343.

O'Connor, N., and Hermelin, B. (1976). Backward and forward recall by deaf and hearing children. *Quarterly Journal of Experimental Psychology, 28,* 83–92.

Odom, P. B., Blanton, R. L., and Nunnally, J. C. (1967). Some "cloze" technique studies of language capability in the deaf. *Journal of Speech and Hearing Research, 10,* 816–827.

Odom, P. B., Blanton, R. L., and McIntyre, C. K. (1970). Coding medium and word recall by deaf and hearing subjects. *Journal of Speech and Hearing Research, 13,* 54–58.

Oléron, P. (1950). A study of the intelligence of the deaf. *American Annals of the Deaf, 95,* 179–195.

Oléron, P. (1975). Deaf children's psychological evaluation. Proceedings of the International Congress on the Education of the Deaf. Tokyo.

Olsson, J. E., and Furth, H. G. (1966). Visual memory-span in the deaf. *American Journal of Psychology, 79,* 480–484.

O'Neill, J. J. (1954). Contributions of the visual components of oral symbols to speech comprehension. *Journal of Speech and Hearing Disorders, 19,* 429–439.

O'Neill, J. J., and Oyer, H. J. (1970). *Applied Audiometry*. New York: Dodd, Mead.

Owrid, H. L. (1970). Hearing impairment and verbal attainments in primary school children. *Educational Research, 12,* 209–214.

Owrid, H. L. (1971). Studies in manual communication with hearing impaired children. *The Teacher of the Deaf, 69,* 151–160.

Paget, R. (1951). *New Sign Language*. London: The Wellcome Foundation.

Paivio, A. (1971). *Imagery and Verbal Processes*. New York: Holt, Rinehart and Winston.

Paivio, A., and Csapo, K. (1969). Concrete image and verbal memory codes. *Journal of Experimental Psychology, 80,* 279–285.

Paivio, A., and Csapo, K. (1971). Short-term sequential memory for pictures and words. *Psychonomic Science. 24,* 50–51.

Peal, E., and Lambert, W. E. (1962). The relation of bilingualism to intelligence. *Psychological Monographs* No. 76.

Pettifor, J. L. (1968). The role of language in the development of abstract thinking: A comparison of hard-of-hearing and normal-hearing children on levels of conceptual thinking. *Canadian Journal of Psychology, 22,* 139–156.

Phippard, D. (1977). Hemifield differences in visual perception in deaf and hearing subjects. *Neuropsychologia, 15,* 555–561.

Pickett, J. M. (1968a). (ed.). Conference on Speech-Analysing Aids for the Deaf. *American Annals of the Deaf, 113,* 116–330.

Pickett, J. M. (1968b). Sound patterns of speech: an introductory sketch. In: Conference on Speech-Analysing Aids for the Deaf. *American Annals of the Deaf, 113,* 116–330.

Pickett, J. M., Gengel, R. W., and Quinn, R. (1974). Research with the Upton eyeglass speechreader. Speech Communication Seminar, Stockholm.

Pintner, R. (1929). Speech and speechreading tests for the deaf. *Journal of Applied Psychology, 13,* 220–225.

Pintner, R., and Paterson, D. G. (1917). A comparison of deaf and hearing children in visual memory for digits. *Journal of Experimental Psychology, 2,* 76–88.

Povel, D. J. L. (1974). Articulation Correction of the Deaf by means of Visually Displayed Acoustic Information. Doctoral Dissertation. Catholic University of Nijmegen.

Pugh, T. (1975). The Development of silent reading. In W. Latham (ed.), *The Road to Effective Reading.* London: Ward Lock.

Putnam, V., Iscoe, I., and Young, R. K. (1962). Verbal learning in the deaf. *Journal of Comparative and Physiological Psychology, 55,* 843–846.

Quigley, S. P. (1969). The Influence of Fingerspelling on the Development of Language, Communication, and Educational Achievement in Deaf Children. Urbana, Ill.: Institute for Research on Exceptional Children.

Quigley, S. P., and Frisina, D. R. (1961). Institutionalization and psycho-educational development of deaf children. Washington, D.C.: Council for Exceptional Children, Research Monograph, Series A, No. 3.

Quigley, S. P., and Thomore, R. E. (1968). Some effects of a hearing impairment on school performance. Urbana, Ill.: Institute for Research on Exceptional Children.

Quigley, S. P., Wilbur, R. B., Power, D. J., Montanelli, D. S., and Steinkamp, M. W. (1976). Syntactic Structures in the Language of Deaf Children. Urbana, Ill.: Institute for Child Behaviour and Development.

Raven, J. C. (1960). *Guide to the Standard Progressive Matrices.* London: H. K. Lewis & Co.

Rawlings, B. W. (1971). *Summary of Selected Characteristics of Hearing Impaired Students – United States: 1968–69.* Series D, Number 5.

Washington, D.C.: Gallaudet College, Office of Demographic Studies.

Rawlings, B. W., and Jensema, C. J. (1977). *Two Studies of the Families of Hearing Impaired Children*. Series R, Number 5, Washington, D.C.: Gallaudet College, Office of Demographic Studies.

Redgate, G. W. (1972). *The Teaching of Reading to Deaf Children*. Manchester: The University of Manchester.

Reeves, J. K. (1976). The whole personality approach to oralism in the education of the deaf. In P. Henderson (ed.), *Methods of Communication Currently Used in the Education of Deaf Children*. London: Royal National Institute for the Deaf.

Report of the Proceedings of the International Congress on the Education of the Deaf. Milan. (1880). London: W. H. Allen.

Reynolds, H. N. (1975). Development of Reading Ability in Relation to Deafness. Proceedings of the VIIth World Congress of the World Federation of the Deaf, Washington, D.C.

Ries, P. W., and Voneiff, P. (1974). Demographic profile of hearing impaired students. *PRWAD Deafness Annual, IV*, 17–42.

Riper, C. van, and Irwin, J. E. (1958). *Voice and Articulation*. London: Pitman.

Risberg, A., and Mártony, J. (1972). A Method for the Classification of Audiograms. In G. Fant (ed.), *International Symposium on Speech Communication Ability and Profound Deafness, Stockholm, 1970*. Washington: Alexander Graham Bell Association.

Rodda, M., Godsave, B., and Stevens, J. (1974). Some aspects of the development of young hearing-impaired children. *American Annals of the Deaf, 119*, 729–735.

Ross, B. M. (1969). Sequential visual memory and the limited magic of the number seven. *Journal of Experimental Psychology, 80*, 339–347.

Rozanova, T. V. (1971). Verbal memory. In I. Solovjev, R. H. Shif, T. Rozanova, and N. Yashkova (eds.) *The Psychology of Deaf Children*. Moscow: Pedagogica.

Rozin, P., and Gleitman, L. R. (1977). The structure and acquisition of reading II: the reading process and the acquisition of the alphabetic principle. In A. S. Reber, and D. L. Scarborough (eds.), *The Proceedings of the CUNY Conferences*. Hillsdale, N. J.: Laurence Erlbaum Associates.

Sadick, T. L., and Ginsberg, B. E. (1978). The development of the lateral function and reading ability. *Cortex, XIV*, 3–11.

Sarno, J. E., Swisher, L. P., and Sarno, M. T. (1969). Aphasia in a congenitally deaf man. *Cortex, V*, 398–414.

Satz, P. (1972). Pathological left-handedness: an explanatory model. *Cortex, VIII*, 121–135.

Saxman, J. H., and Miller, J. F. (1973). Short-term memory and language skills in articulation-deficient children. *Journal of Speech and Hearing Research, 16*, 721–730.

Schiesser, H. F., and Coleman, R. O. (1968). Effectiveness of certain procedures for alteration of auditory and oral tactile sensation for speech. *Perceptual and Motor Skills, 26,* 275–281.

Schildroth, A. M. (Personal communication). The relationship *of nonverbal intelligence test scores to selected characteristics of hearing impaired students.* Office of Demographic Studies, Gallaudet College, Washington, D.C.

Schlesinger, H. S., and Meadow, K. P. (1972). *Sound and Sign.* London: University of California Press.

Sheavyn, E. M. (1976). Untitled. In P. Henderson (ed.), *Methods of Communication Currently Used in the Education of Deaf Children.* London: Royal National Institute for the Deaf.

Silverman-Dresner, T., and Guilfoyle, G. R. (1972). *Vocabulary Norms for Deaf Children.* Washington, D.C.: Alexander Graham Bell Association for the the Deaf.

Simmons, A. A. (1959). Factors related to lipreading. *Journal of Speech and Hearing Research, 2,* 340–352.

Siple, P. (1978). Linguistic and psychological properties of American Sign Language: an overview. In P. Siple (ed.), *Understanding Language through Sign Language Research.* New York: Academic Press.

Siple, P., Fischer, S. D., and Bellugi, U. (1977). Memory for nonsemantic attributes of American Sign Language signs and English words. *Journal of Verbal Learning and Verbal Behavior, 16,* 561–574.

Smith, C. R. (1973). Residual Hearing and Speech Production in Deaf Children. Communication Sciences Laboratory Report No. 4. CUNY Graduate Center, New York.

Smith, C. R. (1975). Residual hearing and speech production in deaf children. *Journal of Speech and Hearing Research, 18,* 795–811.

Sokolov, A. N. (1972). *Inner Speech and Thought.* New York: Plenum Press.

Sperling, G. (1960). The information available in brief visual presentations. *Psychological Monographs, 74,* whole No. 498.

Sperling, G. (1963). A model for visual memory tasks. *Human Factors, 5,* 19–31.

Stark, R. E. (1974). (ed.) *Sensory Capabilities of Hearing-Impaired Children.* Baltimore: University Park Press.

Stein, B. E., and Schuckman, H. (1973). Effects of sensory restriction upon the responses to cortical stimulation in rats. *Journal of Comparative and Physiological Psychology, 82,* 182–187.

Stokoe, W. C. (1960). Sign language structure: an outline of the visual communication system of the American deaf. In: *Studies in Linguistics, Occasional Papers: No. 8.* Buffalo, New York: University of Buffalo Press.

Stokoe, W. C. (1971). *The Study of Sign Language.* Silver Spring, Maryland: National Association of the Deaf.

Stokoe, W. C. (1978). Sign language versus spoken language. *Sign Language Studies, 18,* 69–90.

Stockwell, E. (1952). Visual difficulties in deaf children. *Archives of Opthalmology, 48,* 428–432.

Strong, W. J. (1975). Articulation of the deaf. *Exceptional Children, 33,* 611–621.

Stroop, J. R. (1935). Studies of interference in serial verbal reactions. *Journal of Experimental Psychology, 18,* 643–662.

Stuckless, E. R. (1976). An interpretive review of research on manual communication in the education of deaf children: language development and information transmission. In P. Henderson (ed.), *Methods of Communication Currently Used in the Education of Deaf Children.* London: Royal National Institute for the Deaf.

Stuckless, E. R., and Birch, J. W. (1966a). The influence of early manual communication on the linguistic development of deaf children. *American Annals of the Deaf, 111,* 452–460.

Stuckless, E. R., and Birch, J. W. (1966b). The influence of early manual communication on the linguistic development of deaf children. *American Annals of the Deaf, 111,* 499–504.

Suchman, R. G. (1968). Visual impairment among deaf children – frequency and educational consequences. *Volta Review, 70,* 31–38.

Sudman, J. A., and Berger, K. W. (1971). Two-dimension vs. three-dimension viewing in speechreading. *Journal of Communication Disorders, 4,* 195–198.

Sumby, W. H., and Pollack, I. (1954). Visual contribution to speech intelligibility in noise. *Journal of the Acoustical Society of America, 26,* 212–215.

Taylor, W. (1956). "Cloze Procedure": a new tool for measuring readability. *Journalism Quarterly, 33,* 42–48.

Thomassen, A. J. W. M. (1970). *On the representation of verbal items in short-term memory.* Nijmegen: Druk: Drukkerij Schippers.

Tinker, M. A. (1928). The relative intelligibility of the letters, digits, and of certain mathematical signs. *Journal of General Psychology, 1,* 472–496.

Tucker, I. G. (1978). The incidence of hearing-impairment and trends in the hearing-impaired school population. *The Teacher of the Deaf, 2,* 43–47.

Tulving, E., and Donaldson, W. (1972). *Organization of Memory.* (eds.). New York: Academic Press.

Tureen, L. L., Smolik, E. A., and Tritt, J. H. (1951). Aphasia in a deaf-mute. *Neurology, 1,* 237–249.

Underwood, B. J., and Schulz, R. W. (1960). *Meaningfulness and Verbal Learning.* New York: Lippincott.

Upton, H. W. (1968). Wearable eyeglass speechreading aid. *American Annals of the Deaf, 113,* 222–229.

Utley, J. (1946). Factors involved in the teaching and testing of lip reading ability through the use of motion pictures. *Volta Review, 38,* 657–659.

VandenBerg, D. M. (1971a). *The Written Language of Deaf Children, a Comparative Study*. Wellington, New Zealand: The New Zealand Council for Educational Research.

VandenBerg, D. M. (1971b). *Children with Hearing Aids in Classes for the Normally Hearing: Report to Schools*. Department of Social Administration and Sociology, Victoria University of Wellington, New Zealand.

van Dijk, J., and van Uden, A. (1976). Problems of communication in deaf children. *The Teacher of the Deaf, 74*, 70–90.

van Uden, A. (1970). *A World of Language for Deaf Children, Part I, Basic Principles*. Rotterdam: University of Rotterdam Press.

Vernon, M. (1967). Relationship of language to the thinking process. *Archives of General Psychiatry, 16*, 325–333.

Vernon, M. (1972). Language development's relationship to cognition, affectivity and intelligence. *The Canadian Psychologist, 13*, 360–374.

Vernon, M. (1976). Communication and the education of deaf and hard of hearing children. In P. Henderson (ed.), *Methods of Communication Currently Used in the Education of Deaf Children*. London: Royal National Institute for the Deaf.

Vernon, M., and Billingslea, H. (1973). Hard-of-hearing children in a public school setting. *The Maryland Teacher, Spring*, 16–28.

Vernon, M., and Koh, S. D. (1970). Early manual communication and deaf children's achievement. *American Annals of the Deaf, 115*, 527–536.

Vernon, M., and Koh, S. D. (1971). Effects of oral preschool compared to early manual communication on education and communication in deaf children. *American Annals of the Deaf, 116*, 569–574.

Vestberg Rasmussen, P. (1973). Evaluation of reading achievements of deaf children. In E. Kampp (ed.), *Evaluation of Hearing Handicapped Children*. Fifth Danavox Symposium, Denmark: Abeltoft.

Vincent, K. R., and Cox, J. A. (1974). A Re-evaluation of Raven's Standard Progressive Matrices. *Journal of Psychology, 88*, 299–303.

Vygotsky, L. S. (1962). *Thought and Language*. Cambridge, Mass.: M.I.T. Press.

Wada, J. (1969). Interhemispheric sharing and shift of cerebral speech function. Paper presented at the IXth International Congress of Neurology, New York.

Wallace, G., and Corballis, M. C. (1973). Short-term memory and coding strategies in the deaf. *Journal of Experimental Psychology, 99*, 334–348.

Watson, T. J. (1976). Untitled. In P. Henderson (ed.), *Methods of Communication Currently Used in the Education of Deaf Children*. London: Royal National Institute for the Deaf.

Weir, R. H. (1966). Some questions on the child's learning of phonology. In F. Smith and G. A. Miller (eds.), *The Genesis of Language*. London: M.I.T. Press.

Whetnall, E., and Fry, D. B. (1964). *The Deaf Child*. London: Heinemann Medical.

White, A. H., and Stevenson, V. M. (1975). The effects of total communication, manual communication, oral communication and reading on the learning of factual information in residential school deaf children. *American Annals of the Deaf, 120*, 48–57.

Wickelgren, W. A. (1965). Distinctive features and errors in short-term memory for English vowels. *Journal of the Acoustical Society of America, 38*, 583–588.

Wickens, D. D., Born, D. G., and Allen, C. K. (1963). Proactive inhibition and item similarity in short-term memory. *Journal of Verbal Learning and Verbal Behavior, 2*, 440–445.

Wilson, J. J., Rapin, I., Wilson, B. C., and van Denburg, F. V. (1975). Neuropsychologic function of children with severe hearing impairment. *Journal of Speech and Hearing Research, 18*, 634–652.

Winkelaar, R. G., Arnold, J., and Johnson, E. (1976). A comparison of speechreading abilities using live and recorded presentation. *Human Communication: a Journal of the Canadian Speech and Hearing Association, 1*, 43–48.

Withrow, F. B. (1968). Immediate memory span of deaf and normally hearing children. *Exceptional Children, 35*, 33–41.

Witelson, S. F., and Pallie, W. (1973). Left hemisphere specialization for language in the newborn: neuro-anatomical evidence of asymmetry. *Brain, 96*, 641–646.

Wollman, D. C. (1964). The attainments in English and arithmetic of secondary school pupils with impaired hearing. *British Journal of Educational Psychology, 34*, 268–274.

Woodward, J., and Erting, C. (1975). Synchronic variation and historical change in ASL. *Language Sciences, 37*, 9–12.

Woodworth, R. S. (1938). *Experimental Psychology*. New York: Holt.

Wrightstone, J. W., Aronow, M. S., and Moskowitz, S. (1963). Developing reading test norms for deaf children. *American Annals of the Deaf, 108*, 311–316.

Yik, W. F. (1978). The effect of visual and acoustic similarity on short-term memory for Chinese words. *Quarterly Journal of Experimental Psychology, 30*, 487–494.

Youniss, J., and Furth, H. G. (1967). The role of language and experience on the use of logical symbols. *British Journal of Psychology, 58*, 435–443.

Youniss, J., Feil, R. N., and Furth, H. G. (1965). Discrimination of verbal material as a function of intrapair similarity in deaf and hearing subjects. *Journal of Educational Psychology, 56*, 184–190.

Youniss, J., Furth, H. G., and Ross, B. M. (1971). Logical symbol use in deaf and hearing children and adolescents. *Developmental Psychology, 5*, 511–517.

Zangwill, O. L. (1975). The relation of nonverbal cognitive functions to aphasia. In E. H. Lenneberg and E. Lenneberg (eds.), *Foundations of Language Development: a Multidisciplinary Approach, vol, II*. New York: Academic Press.

Appendix 1

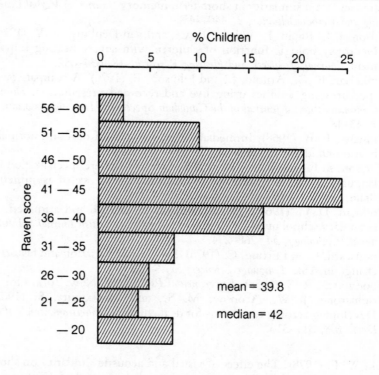

Appendix 2

Test for internal speech: Part I test items

1	blue	11	who	16	blue	21	home
			through		zoo		farm
2	door		true		true		bare
			few		do		furs
3	who				through		lane
	true	12	bare				
			farm	17	bare	22	zoo
4	lane		home		have		screw
	have		furs		home		blue
			have		farm		through
5	through				bean		do
	do	13	have				
			lane	18	who	23	furs
6	farm		bean		few		bean
	bare		door		zoo		door
			home		true		bare
7	zoo				blue		farm
	screw	14	do				
	few		true	19	lane	24	through
			who		bare		who
8	furs		screw		furs		screw
	home		zoo		have		blue
	bean				door		few
		15	farm				
9	do		home	20	screw		
	zoo		lane		do		
	blue		bean		through		
			furs		few		
10	have				true		
	door						
	bean						
	lane						

Appendix 3

Test for internal speech: Part II test items

1		5		9		13	
	have		farm		furs		bean
	door		home		bean		bare
	bare		lane		home		furs
	farm		bean		have		home
	furs		bare		farm		lane
	bean		have		lane		door

2		6		10		14	
	true		do		zoo		through
	who		through		screw		few
	zoo		blue		true		who
	screw		who		few		do
	do		few		blue		zoo
	through		true		who		blue

3		7		11		15	
	lane		door		bare		home
	furs		lane		have		farm
	farm		have		door		bean
	door		bare		lane		furs
	have		bean		home		door
	home		furs		farm		bare

4		8		12		16	
	who		blue		few		screw
	blue		do		true		zoo
	through		few		screw		do
	zoo		through		blue		true
	true		screw		through		who
	screw		zoo		do		few

17	door	21	lane
	bare		home
	farm		door
	home		furs
	lane		have
	furs		bean

18	true	22	through
	do		who
	screw		true
	blue		few
	zoo		screw
	few		do

19	farm	23	have
	bean		furs
	have		lane
	bare		bean
	door		farm
	home		bare

20	screw	24	zoo
	few		blue
	zoo		through
	who		do
	through		true
	blue		who

Note: if three-word trials are required, use the first three words shown.
Similarly for four-, five- and six-word trials.

Appendix 4

Wide-span Reading Test conversion of nominal scale score to reading age
(by permission of Dr. A. Brimer)

Yr.	Mth.	N.S.S.	Yr.	Mth.	N.S.S.
7	0	0–2	12	0	41
	2	3		2	42
	4	4		4	43–44
	6	5		6	45
	8	6		8	46
	10	7–8		10	47–48
8	0	9	13	0	49
	2	10		2	50
	4	11–12		4	51–52
	6	13		6	53
	8	14		8	55
	10	15		10	56
9	0	16–17	14	0	57
	2	18		2	58–59
	4	19–20		4	60
	6	21		6	61
	8	22		8	62–63
	10	23–24		10	64
10	0	25	15	0	65
	2	26		2	66–67
	4	27–28		4	68
	6	29		6	69
	8	30–31		8	70–71
	10	32		10	72
11	0	33	16	0	73–74
	2	34			
	4	35–36			
	6	37			
	8	38–39			
	10	40			

Appendix 5

Examples of items from the speech intelligibility test

Jane had a <u>toffee</u> to bring with her but <u>sold</u> it.
The <u>pear</u> trees were <u>twenty</u> seven feet high.
The <u>pretty</u> girl ran down the narrow <u>stairs</u>.
Here is the <u>gift</u> that Mother wants you to <u>post</u>.
Five hundred <u>sailors</u> wanted to join the <u>race</u> but it was far too late.
<u>Painting</u> the bridge, he saw a big <u>box</u> in the middle of the river.
They <u>marched</u> to the edge of the <u>lake</u> to look for the enemy.
The bedroom was very <u>cool</u> and the windows were <u>tall</u>.

Words underlined are omitted from listeners' answer sheets, where their location is indicated by a space.

Subject Index

Author Index